SWEET SUFFERING: Woman as Victim

Pointing no finger of blame, Dr. Natalie Shainess explains why no woman in our culture escapes masochism altogether. Dr. Shainess clarifies the primary symptoms of masochistic behavior: desire for approval, fear of offending, self-doubt, fear of authority, fear of abandonment, feelings of humiliation and guilt, self-punishment, and a sense of being the center of critical attention.
Ask yourself:

- Do you shrug off compliments instead of accepting them graciously?
- Do you find yourself saying "thank you" unnecessarily?
- Are you afraid to send back a dish in a restaurant that has something wrong with it or is cold?

SWEET SUFFERING: Woman as Victim belongs in the hands of every woman who has ever felt that she is being stepped on by others, put down, ignored, or abused. Dr. Shainess shows you how to "dig out," as she puts it, how to assert yourself—and become a truly confident, self-possessed woman.

"[An] intelligent, accessible, very informative book . . ."
—*Philadelphia Inquirer*

"Written with clarity in a crisp, no-nonsense style . . . for those who really wish to change their perception of self-worth . . . A TIMELY CONTRIBUTION TO PSYCHOLOGY."

—*San Francisco Chronicle*

SWEET SUFFERING

WOMAN AS VICTIM

NATALIE SHAINESS, M.D.

A WALLABY BOOK
PUBLISHED BY POCKET BOOKS NEW YORK

For permission to quote from *Mrs. Warren's Profession, Candida,* and *Saint Joan,* acknowledgment is made to The Society of Authors on behalf of the Bernard Shaw Estate.

"Scarlet Ribbons," copyright 1949 by Mills Music, Inc. Copyright renewed. Used with permission. All Rights Reserved.

Patient names and identities have been disguised in the case histories presented in this book.

A Wallaby Book published by
POCKET BOOKS, a division of Simon & Schuster, Inc.
1230 Avenue of the Americas, New York, N.Y. 10020

Published by arrangement with The Bobbs-Merrill Company, Inc.
Library of Congress Catalog Card Number: 83-18762

ISBN: 0-671-54635-X

First Wallaby Books printing May, 1985

10 9 8 7 6 5 4 3 2 1

WALLABY and colophon are registered trademarks
of Simon & Schuster, Inc.

Printed in the U.S.A.

This book is dedicated to two of my teachers—outstanding psychiatrists and psychoanalysts—who shaped my life's efforts. Though I did not appreciate their legacy to me immediately, as time went on I came to realize their great value and skill.

To Frieda Fromm-Reichmann, I am indebted for her relentless search for truth, wherever it might be found. Known for her work with schizophrenics, she also understood family dynamics and the nuances of interaction between husband and wife. Her sensitivity was profound.

I am particularly indebted to Harry Stack Sullivan for his recognition of hypocrisy at the social level. He was ever on the alert for expressions of anxiety in communication, believing, in contrast to standard psychoanalytic approach, that they must be answered not by "interpretations" but with an appropriate response from another person, albeit a professional person.

I want also to acknowledge the contribution of my analyst, Clara Thompson, whose refusal to totally accept Freud's metapsychology of women helped me follow her in exploring the role of culture in shaping the lives of women.

Another Clara was indeed important to me—my mother. A self-educated artist, gifted with a broad understanding of social issues, she exemplified for me the tradition of Henri Matisse, who said, "The artist must be at pains to retain his radical freedom of perception, which is at odds with custom and convention." Daily, in both my office and home, my life is enhanced by her art work.

Finally, I am indebted to my patients, who helped me grow in the experience of our interactions—both professionally and personally.

Contents

1

Setting Up the System of Self-Punishment

Some years ago a patient of mine, during her first analytic session, recounted a fairy tale she had carried with her since childhood, one that seemed to have special significance for her. The tale she told me was this.

Once upon a time there was a handsome prince whose ship was wrecked at sea. Everyone aboard perished except the prince, who was rescued by a little mermaid and taken to safety on an island. When a second ship appeared and carried the prince off to his homeland, the mermaid, who had fallen desperately in love with him, vowed that she would follow and claim him. Seeking advice on how to accomplish this, she traveled through treacherous seas to the lair of the sea witch. "You will come to grief if you attempt this," the witch warned, but seeing that the mermaid would not be deterred, she agreed to grant her her wish. She gave the mermaid a potion to drink that caused her tail to wither and be replaced by legs. The mermaid was now as beautiful as any mortal on earth, but every step she took was agonizingly painful. The mermaid was glad to bear this suffering, however, and set out for the land of her prince. Alas, as she arrived, the prince's marriage to another was already in progress, and the little mermaid, witnessing this, fell into a fatal swoon. Upon her death, the other mermaids lamented that she had not even gained an immortal soul. She could only have possessed that had she won the love of a human.

This story is a nearly perfect parable of masochism, for it expresses the self-punishment, the submission to another, and the sense of suffering as a way of life that lie at the heart of masochistic behavior. The young woman who told it to me identified strongly with the little mermaid for reasons that soon became obvious. Her mother had been pressured into marriage with a man she did not love; the daughter was conceived on a wedding night that her mother experienced as nightmarish. The mother and child's relationship developed into a difficult one: It did not involve any physical cruelty, but the child was very fearful of her mother's power over her. She told me how she had once been punished by being put under the kitchen table—her mother commanding her to remain there until she returned. The mother then went off and did not return for three hours. When she finally came back into the kitchen, apologetic and chagrined by her forgetfulness, the child was still crouched beneath the table. It had not occurred to her, the young woman told me, to come out from under the table as the hours went by. Her absolute submission told me how greatly she feared her mother.

This same mother began too early to try to make a ballet dancer of her daughter. The little girl's still-soft bones responded poorly to the strain, and she was left with a legacy of terrible foot trouble. Certainly this very specific parallel with the little mermaid was one reason the young woman had been so drawn to the fairy tale. But she also responded to it on a metaphorical level. Largely because of the troubled relationship with her mother, every psychological step she took was difficult for her as well.

By telling me the fairy tale, this patient presented her own problem in an imaginative and succinct fashion. But she could have been speaking for countless other women as well, women who, like the mermaid, believe that life and love are hinged on suffering. Descartes' declaration, "I think, therefore I am," made the act of thinking the definitive characteristic of human existence. The masochist, who might say, "I suffer, therefore I am," puts pain in the pivotal position. And it is the masochist herself who perpetuates the pattern of suffering in her life, primarily by processes of communication that alert other people to her submissiveness and her fear of their power over her.

Observing this, many people (including Freud) mistakenly conclude that masochists take pleasure in their suffering. But this is not so. They simply do not know any other way to live. They have not considered and then set aside alternative methods of coping. They do not, as a rule, even realize that there *are* any alternatives. They have developed an all-pervasive defensive style that is based on suffering, and it has become the only way they know how to experience life. They are like the princess in another fairy tale who could feel the pea that lay beneath twenty mattresses: exquisitely sensitive, they are easily wounded. And because they follow the same destructive patterns over and over again, we make the mistake of thinking their pain is pleasurable.

While men also suffer from the masochistic syndrome, it is much more common among women, for reasons I will develop at greater length in Chapter 3. But, briefly, it is because women in our society bear such liabilities as inferior social and economic status, lesser biological strength, and reproductive handicaps that masochism is a special problem for them. In nearly four decades of practice as a psychiatrist and psychoanalyst, I have all too frequently encountered masochism in women and only occasionally in men. Both women and men may have early experiences that dispose them to masochistic behavior, but the cultural elements that continually reinforce masochistic behavior in women are largely absent for men. Women, in this sense, experience a real double whammy. Many emerge from their childhoods with a damaged sense of self. Then the culture in which they live ratifies that distorted image rather than helping them to repair the damage. And the odds are longer for women in the struggle to overcome masochism. To eradicate something as stubborn, compulsive, and destructive as masochism, people need all the help they can get. Our society, in its attitudes and judgments, gives women precious little of that.

One would think, in the wake of the women's movement and its attendant societal changes, that this might not be so today. Certainly women have gained greater freedom to control their reproductive destinies and greater opportunities for more varied kinds of fulfillment. Progress *has* been made. Yet in my practice and in my observations at large, I have noted no corresponding drop in the number of masochistic people I encounter. In fact, in today's atmosphere of greater promise and higher expectation, masochism may be a more destructive problem than ever. For as many women find doors opening, they also find their own masochism pulling the rug out from under them, rendering their new chances useless. And that can make experience bitter indeed.

The emphasis today on assertiveness training is very telling, I think. Why do all these liberated women need to be trained to stand up for themselves? Assertiveness, which is the ability to express honest feelings comfortably, the ability to be direct and straightforward, the ability to exercise personal rights without denying the rights of others and without experiencing undue anxiety and guilt, ought to come naturally. Why is it women must be *taught* these simple human prerogatives?

The reason is that masochism undermines women by eroding their capacity to stand up for themselves. But the assertiveness trainers do not acknowledge, or perhaps even realize, that masochism is what they are dealing with. They have stayed on the surface, teaching women strategies to be employed primarily in their professional lives. They have not addressed the underlying problem that all the tactical expertise in the world will not eliminate (although tactics are very helpful once the underlying problem is understood). Masochistic women suffer from anxieties that make it difficult, if not impossible, for them to translate assertiveness strategies into effective behavior in their personal lives.

Assertiveness and autonomy go together. But someone who has learned her assertiveness in a course is not necessarily autonomous. She is still basing her actions on those of someone else. She may have no comprehensive understanding of the psychological sources of her behavior. But someone who has addressed her central problem and overcome her masochistic tendencies can achieve true autonomy—operating under her own steam, making her own decisions, feeling a sense of confidence in her own actions as she moves through life essentially unafraid of criticism or attack. Because she is able to stand up for herself appropriately, she no longer feels hate or contempt for herself.

My concept of masochism has two facets: one is the set of feelings the masochist possesses; the other is the process by which she communicates these feelings to others, her masochistic style, if you will, a style that makes life perpetually difficult for her. The masochistic person's feelings, like the rest of her emotional framework, have their roots in early childhood. In Chapter 3 I discuss this in detail, but it is important to note here the common denominator in these experiences: All of them involve abuses of power in the relationship between parent and child, abuses that leave the masochistic person fearful of others, filled with self-doubt, and utterly unable to resist, refuse, offend, or insist on limits. The masochist's feeling of guilt is all-pervasive, her stream of apologies constant, her capacity for self-punishment and self-denial seemingly endless. She does not dare to question, too quickly takes things at face value, too readily accepts someone else's premise. She is dependent upon the wishes, whims, and judgments of any authority figure. If you were to ask a masochist to define her own best interests, she would not know where to begin.

Lucille, a patient of mine, works in a public relations firm and was part of a group assigned to develop a publicity campaign for an important new client. Her proposals were marked by the brilliance characteristic of her work, and they became the focal point of the campaign. In a meeting between the group and the client, Lucille was asked to justify the tactics her firm was proposing, and she did so competently and smoothly until suddenly the client asked a rather technical question about some radio spots that were planned.

"I don't know," Lucille recalled saying. "I'm sorry, but it just never occurred to me that this was important. I guess I wasn't as thorough as I should have been. I'm sorry . . ."

Another member of the group jumped in to take over, and the difficult moment passed. But a few weeks later, when an executive was named for this account, Lucille was passed over and another woman, whose contribution to the project had been far less substantial, was designated. Lucille's response to this was to tell me that while she was unhappy, she was also relieved. "I don't think I have the drive or the personality for an executive position," she said.

Anne is married to a well-known writer and has two teenaged children. She had been a junior editor in a large publishing house, a job she gave up at the time of her marriage, a union marked from the beginning by her husband's short-lived affairs with other women. After each affair, he always returned to Anne, contrite, loving, and passionate in his promises to reform. On a number of other occasions, however, he slapped Anne, once punching her so hard that she had to have a dentist repair the damage to her teeth.

Early in the marriage, Anne had gone to her mother to complain of her husband's infidelities. Her mother had been sympathetic, but she also reminded Anne of her marriage contract— for better or worse—and she cautioned her about separating as that would throw Anne into a world where she had little status and only a limited ability to support herself. Today, Anne herself says, "When the kids were small it didn't seem fair to them to leave and bring them up by myself. Now that so much time has passed, I don't think I'd have a very good chance of making a living or much of a life for myself. Being George's wife does put me in contact with lots of interesting people, and I guess I have to accept the fact that a creative person like him is under tremendous pressure. He has to vent his frustration somewhere. Part of my job as a wife is to help him through difficult times."

Daniel, a big, strong young man who had been an athlete in college, told me of finally getting his own apartment. He bought an old upright piano and arranged to have it moved into his apartment on the third floor. The piano proved to be too large for the elevator and had to be brought up the stairs, which took a turn partway up. The piano movers, two burly men, were being paid well for their work. But as they negotiated the stairs, they began to curse—at the piano, at the steps, and at Daniel himself for living on the third floor—and made plain their expectations of a good tip at the end of the job. Listening to them, Daniel grew anxious, and guilty. When, sweating heavily and still cursing, they finally got the piano into the apartment, he offered them beer and, because they were angry and he was frightened, gave them double the tip he had planned on.

Alice's husband asked her for a divorce after two years of marriage, complaining that he found life with her stifling. Alice, who felt the marriage had been a reasonably happy one, protested, but her husband went ahead with the divorce. Although she felt her contemporaries were shunning her as a divorced woman, Alice forced herself to attend any social occasion she could. Telling me about a large cocktail party, she reported that she stood alone for a long time, apart from the rest of the crowd, unable to initiate an exchange with anyone. Eventually, a young man approached her and stood nearby, apparently trying to think of a way to capture her attention. Alice turned to him and said, "It's difficult when you don't know people at a party like this. I don't know why I bothered to come." The man frowned and walked away, his original interest erased by her sour remark.

Myra is a middle-aged woman, separated from her husband, who one evening accepted a fellow student's offer to drive her home after class at a local college. When they pulled up at her apartment building, Myra said, "I'd ask you in for coffee, but I'm tired and I have to be at work early tomorrow." Her classmate said he would like to come in and would not stay long, but Myra demurred. He then asked if he could come in just to use the bathroom before heading home. Myra hesitated but decided she was obliged at least to extend him that courtesy. After using the bathroom, he demanded a kiss from her and, when she resisted, threw her down and raped her. She called me in the middle of the night, crying hysterically, and, although terribly upset, she refused to call the police or visit a hospital, as I urged her to do. As a matter of fact, she had already bathed and removed the evidence of the assault. The man, she said, had told her that since she was separated from her husband, the police would never believe her—and he would deny that it had been rape.

As these examples indicate, masochism can provoke a relatively minor social gaffe or lead to a life-threatening situation. It can erupt in any setting, any time anxiety triggers the masochistic person to respond to a perceived, or inner, threat that has no basis in outer reality.

Anxiety is based on experiences in childhood with significant adults, figures who are now phantoms that insinuate themselves into people we encounter in our adult lives. Masochists constantly respond to the present as if it were happening in the past, participating in a kind of shadow play in which people are not who they seem to be. What was an appropriate response for a child vis-à-vis a threatening parent is inappropriate when it occurs, for instance, between employee and boss, doctor and patient, husband and wife. What may have been necessary, and useful, adaptive behavior for a child can become a terrible liability when it continues in the adult.

The masochist is quick to apologize because she assumes she is always in the wrong. A patient of mine put it this way: "I know I haven't done anything bad, but I am constantly expecting an accusation." Another said: "If anything goes wrong, I immediately think it has to do with me." The masochist chooses self-punishment in the belief that it will ward off a worse fate. She is unable to say no because she desires other people's approval, indeed desperately needs it, and cannot risk offending them. She is fearful of authority, a quality with which she is likely to endow just about anyone: a waiter in a restaurant or a clerk in a store. She has no sense of her own rights, or her own worth, nor any ability to develop her own point of view. For all of these, she is dependent on other people. And in her acceptance of the pain that is generated by these deficits, she is completely passive. She accepts the suffering as her due.

The communication process, the use of self-damaging words, is the key to this system of self-punishment, the mechanism by which the masochist signals her feelings to other people and thus sets in motion a kind of cybernetic feedback that guarantees that the pain will continue. At its simplest level, the masochistic communication, or message, is very often simply saying the wrong thing: "I'm sorry but it just never occurred to me that this was important. I guess I wasn't as thorough as I should have been. I'm sorry." Or, "It's difficult when you don't know people at a party like this. I don't know why I bothered to come."

Several summers ago when I was in Salzburg, Austria, to attend meetings of the World Federation for Mental Health, the organizers of the conference arranged for all of us to attend a Mozart concert in the contemporary Festival Concert Hall. During the intermission, as I walked around the auditorium, admiring the hall's design, I found myself standing next to a young woman who was by herself.

"I'm holding up the wall," she said, looking at me.

"I beg your pardon?" I replied, uncertain that I had heard her correctly.

"I'm holding up the wall," she repeated.

"Oh?" I noted that her manner was as strained as her statement was peculiar. Then I excused myself and moved on.

This was a quintessential masochistic communication. It contained an open declaration of vulnerability and helplessness and a plea for pity: I'm holding up the wall . . . I'm a wallflower . . . I'm embarrassed . . . I'm alone . . . who would want to talk to me? It indicated the young woman's feelings of inverted grandiosity: She felt herself to be the center of negative attention; she felt all eyes were on her, critically witnessing her humiliating aloneness. It was strictly defensive: She advised me of her weakness and sought pity in order to ward off the criticism and contempt she expected. And it was unproductive: Her remark did not engage me; it caused me to walk away and leave her alone again. I did not want to make this a busman's holiday by responding therapeutically, and she had made me certain that I would not enjoy talking with her.

This woman, preoccupied as she was with her inner defenses, had no clear sense of outer reality. If she had, she could have spoken to me about the music, the concert hall, the conference, Salzburg itself, or even Viennese pastries—any number of things that might have drawn me into conversation with her. Instead, she was doomed to act out a self-fulfilling prophecy. She was alone and felt guilty for being so, perceiving her aloneness as a reflection of her low worth. She believed that other people would see it that way also. Out of that belief, and the anticipation of criticism, she rushed to defend herself by offering a statement of her aloneness—I'm holding up the wall—which only served to make it more apparent. Her defense, because of its inappropriateness, made real the very thing she feared. And what if I had been a predatory man with a sixth sense about masochistic women? I might have picked up her self-consciousness about being alone and invited her out after the concert with less than benign motives. The potential damage could have been much worse than simply being alone once more, holding up the wall.

When wolves fight and one recognizes that it is nearing defeat, it signals its submission by baring its throat to the opponent. Often, this gesture of capitulation is victory enough for the winner, and the loser is permitted to slink away. In human exchanges, bowing the head, symbolically offering the jugular for the kill, often does not get one off the hook so easily. The masochist thinks that a declaration of weakness will divert punishment but, in reality, it usually has the opposite effect. The declaration tends to promote victimization rather than prevent it. The more someone communicates fear, guilt, weakness, and helplessness, the worse her situation becomes.

This is how the masochist perpetuates her pain, and that is why I see the communication process as such a critical part of masochism. It is the fuel that feeds behavioral fires. In exchanges with other people, the masochist does not express herself; she tries, rather, to anticipate what will please or placate them. She never asks herself, What do I want to say? She always asks, What do they want to hear? She never asks someone else, What do you have in mind? Instead, she supplies her own answer in advance because she is afraid of what the other person will say. She readily articulates her impotent position: I'm weak . . . I'm not worth much . . . please don't hurt me. But this announcement, the linchpin of her anticipatory defense system, does not protect her. It leads her into further trouble, whether a social slight, a lost promotion, or, the ultimate danger, a lost life. Advertising one's vulnerability is *not* a good defense strategy.

Masochism is kept alive by a process of feedback. A woman who is acting masochistically collects wounds. The more wounds she collects, the lower her self-esteem falls. As her image of herself worsens, and her regard for herself decreases, she behaves more masochistically—and collects more wounds.

All of this I saw in the young woman "holding up the wall" in Salzburg. Perhaps it seems that I have read a great deal into her five simple words. You may think I have asked one remark to bear a great deal of weight. I am reminded, however, of something Ray Birdwhistle, the anthropologist and communications theorist, once said to me, referring to a tribe he had studied. "If you know the Kwakiutl people," he said, "you only have to see one funeral to know it's a Kwakiutl funeral." So it is with the masochistic communication. One short sentence can truly speak volumes to the expert. Just as a naturalist can identify a tree by its bark or by seeing only one of its leaves, so I was able to identify the young woman at the concert.

That experience in Salzburg provided an illuminating moment for me, a moment in which much of my professional thinking of the preceding years crystallized, a moment in which I decided to write this book. I hope that it may provide a similar kind of illumination for its readers. I did not set out to write a self-help book. Masochism is too complex and obstinate to lend itself to easy panaceas and glib general formulas. I wanted, rather, to raise the reader's consciousness about masochism, to make this widespread and devastating phenomenon understood.

You may recognize yourself in the pages that follow. You may, as you read, identify a problem of your own because no woman in our culture can be completely free of masochism. The conditioning that helps to produce it is almost in the air we breathe, and none of us escapes it entirely. But masochism *can* be overcome. In some ways an analogy can be drawn between masochism and color blindness. Just as someone who has grown up color-blind cannot recognize what is red and what is blue and what is green because she has never been able to distinguish and perceive those colors, so the masochist cannot identify nonpainful alternatives to her behavior because she has never experienced them. Early in life she was programmed, in effect, to have access to only a certain portion of the behavior spectrum, that part that would cause her suffering. The rest of the spectrum, the other choices, were effectively blocked from her. But while color blindness is an inherent defect, masochism is not. It is learned behavior that can be altered and, in some instances, eliminated altogether.

2

Are You
Masochistic?

Many of us have no trouble analyzing other people's behavior. Someone else's self-destructive tendencies are easy to spot. Reading the first chapter, you may already have identified friends or acquaintances who appear to fit the masochistic mold. But when it comes to self-examination, our clarity often deserts us. As I've said, however, no woman in our culture escapes masochism altogether; societal attitudes guarantee this. Intelligence, education, career standing, social position—none of these can immunize us. And it is vital for us to sharpen our awareness of our own masochism, for certainly awareness is the first step toward freedom from this grave handicap.

The questionnaire that follows is not a test that you will pass or fail. It is designed as an aid to awareness, a means of provoking new perceptions, new knowledge about yourself. Your answers may afford you clues to anxieties and dependencies you have not recognized before. It is never productive to close your eyes to things. Freud noted that people suffer from repression, that they expel from their consciousness those feelings, ideas, memories that are painful or disagreeable to them. The goal of psychoanalysis, of course, is to undo that repression, to make conscious that which is unconscious. "Know thyself" is a dictum that goes hand in hand with any sort of growth or enlightenment.

QUESTIONNAIRE

1. If someone bumps into you on the street, do you find yourself apologizing?

2. If you drop something, do you find yourself saying "I'm sorry" even though there is no one to hear you?

3. Do you find yourself saying "thank you" frequently, even unnecessarily?

4. Do you go into lengthy explanations for being as little as five minutes late?

5. When playing tennis, do you say "I'm sorry" after every flubbed ball?

6. In an important discussion or argument, do you back down readily?

7. Do you tend to postpone asking for things that are important to you until it is too late?

8. At school or work, do you usually let others go through the door first?

9. In a restaurant, are you afraid to ask for a glass of water because it might annoy or trouble the waiter?

10. Do you usually choose the cheapest dish on a menu rather than the one you would like to have even though you can afford the latter?

11. Are you afraid to send back a dish that has something wrong with it or is cold?

12. Do you overtip, not to impress other people but for fear of offending the waiter?

13. Are you meticulous about sending out birthday cards and gifts?

14. Do you spend an inordinate amount of time buying presents for others and worry that they will not be "right" or good enough?

15. Are you always lending people money?

16. Do you shrug off compliments instead of accepting them graciously?

17. In group endeavors, either at work or socially, do you tend to follow someone else's lead?

18. At a large social gathering, do you try to remain inconspicuous?

19. Do people tend to ignore you when you talk?

20. On a date, are you afraid to express your preference about the evening's entertainment or choice of restaurant even though you may be going Dutch?

21. If you want to ask the boss for a raise, are you afraid you will not approach him or her properly or that, when the moment comes, you will not know what to say?

22. Are you afraid to offer an idea you have at work for fear it will be considered foolish?

23. Are you afraid to call someone you don't know on the phone—making a business call, for example, or in applying for a job?

24. Are you afraid to say no when you are asked to perform an unpleasant job that it is inappropriate for you to do?

25. Do you have difficulty talking to the landlord, or insisting that the doctor tell you what is wrong so that you understand it, or reporting an accident to the police?

26. If you have an argument with your boyfriend or husband, do you prefer to let it go instead of later discussing the cause and trying to reach some understanding or agreement?

27. If your husband or lover wants sex and you don't, do you give in rather than "make a fuss" over it?

28. Are you afraid to initiate sex with your husband or lover?

29. Do you fantasize being tied up, raped, or in some way overwhelmed in order to be more sexually responsive?

30. During sex, have you ever felt more aroused when you have accidentally been hurt, or have you ever arranged to be hurt, even in a small way?

31. Are you afraid to end an unhappy, destructive relationship because you can't face being alone or fear you will never have anyone else?

32. When your children have been naughty, do you tell them to wait until their father comes home rather than mete out punishment or correction yourself?

33. Do you feel your children are not respectful of you?

34. Are you very sensitive to pain?

35. Have you had more than your share of accidents or broken bones for someone your age?

36. Do you anticipate situations in which you will be hurt, emotionally or physically?

37. Do you imagine or daydream about situations in which you gain something by being injured?

38. Do you tend to have "accidents" when you're upset or angry—breaking dishes or dropping things, tripping or falling?

39. Do you enjoy "a good cry" at tear-jerking movies?

40. Do things always seem to go wrong for you?

41. If you were on a dark, deserted street, would you feel obliged to stop and answer a man who (a) asked for directions, (b) asked for a match, (c) asked for a quarter?

42. In your dreams do you find yourself (a) falling into black holes, (b) paralyzed and unable to walk, (c) unable to scream for help, (d) pursued by cops or robbers, (e) nude?

43. As a child were you very much afraid of one or both your parents?

44. Do you think you're excessively apologetic?

If you answered yes to fifteen of the preceding questions, it is likely that you are somewhat masochistic. If you gave affirmative answers to substantially more than fifteen questions, you are likely to be seriously masochistic. Later in the book I will discuss the sort of help you might seek.

The questionnaire makes obvious the primary symptoms of masochistic behavior: desire for approval, fear of offending, self-doubt, fear of authority, fear of abandonment, feelings of humiliation and guilt, self-punishment, nightmares of helpless-

ness and flight, and a sense of being the center of critical attention. These are the forces that manifest themselves in the
masochistic woman and shape the way she communicates with
the world.

The questionnaire also, I think, prompts in women another
set of questions: Why am I always apologizing? Why am I impelled to do things that hurt me? Why do I feel guilty about little
nothings? Why is the boss always right, especially when the boss is
a man? Why do I defer so often to my husband or lover? Why
must I go into lengthy explanations for even minor matters? Why
do I follow orders abjectly? Why can't I say no?

Answers to these questions can only be found by exploring the
roots of masochism—in the pysche, in history, and in our
present-day culture.

3

The Roots of Masochism

At one time masochism was considered a purely sexual phenomenon. Richard von Krafft-Ebing coined the word to describe a syndrome he found in the work of Leopold von Sacher-Masoch, a nineteenth-century German writer whose tales, based upon his own life, were replete with men desiring to be sexually punished. Masochism, wrote Krafft-Ebing, was a state in which "the sexual instinct is directed to ideas of subjugation and abuse by the opposite sex." Today masochism is recognized as a much more complex constellation of tendencies than that narrow definition implies. At this point it might be helpful to review some of the psychiatric thinking about it from Freud onward.

Some of Freud's basic observations about masochism were sound. He recognized that it was not a purely sexual disorder and called it "moral masochism" since it related to problems of the superego and to guilt. He also correctly concluded that maintenance of suffering was of crucial importance. "The true masochist," he wrote, "always holds out his cheek wherever he sees a chance of receiving a blow." But the rest of Freud's interpretation was skewed by his theories about instinctual behavior and the pleasure principle, by the society in which he lived, and by his general notions about the psychology of women.

Freud believed that since a woman lacked a penis she was born defective, and, when she noted this lack, she conceived of herself as wounded. This feeling of castration was not only physical but psychological. Women were born innately passive, narcis-

sistic, more prone to jealousy than men, and with weaker consciences. To assuage women's "penis envy" and to compensate
them for this exceedingly negative view of their sex, Freud
equated the production of a child with the acquisition of a penis.
In other words, a woman could be restored to psychological balance by motherhood, most especially if she gave birth to male
children. Feminine development, in Freud's view, was a pitiable
affair. And because all psychoanalytic theory was based on the
maturation of libidinal stages, all of which were instinctual, he
never took into account the cultural influences that strongly affected women in late Victorian, patriarchal Vienna.

"Anatomy is destiny," Freud said, and in his view masochism
was a key part of female destiny. The female suffers first from a
sense of being defective. Then she suffers guilt because of her
Oedipal wishes in regard to her father. Finally, she suffers pain in
the course of fulfilling her reproductive destiny. There could be
male masochists, Freud allowed, but he noted that their fantasies
invariably placed them in characteristically feminine situations.
The pleasure principle—Freud's notion that the avoidance of
pain is the overriding aim of human behavior—led him to conclude that the masochist must enjoy the suffering that is her lot

There are inevitable points of pain in a woman's reproductive
life. Defloration can be painful; childbirth inevitably produces
pain. But to assume, as Freud did, that because women suffer
these pains they must also want or need to suffer psychologically,
and to enjoy their suffering, is a sad and dangerous inaccuracy.
The notion of pleasure-in-pain is one, unfortunately, that still
enjoys life, both in the analytic community and outside of it.
"She must enjoy it or she wouldn't keep doing it." We have all
heard that sort of comment about someone whose behavior is
patently self-destructive.

Karen Horney rejected Freud's idea that certain personality
traits in women are the result of bio-instinctual substrata.
"Psychoanalysis is the creation of a male genius," Horney wrote,
"and almost all those who have developed his ideas are men. It is
only right and reasonable that they should evolve more easily a
masculine psychology and understand more of the development

of men than women." Then Horney went on to emphasize the role that cultural conditioning plays in female masochism, an idea that Freud's view of humankind prevented him from seeing. Society views women as weak and helpless, Horney pointed out. It encourages them to be emotionally and economically dependent; it restricts their functioning to the sphere of family life; it blocks their outlets for expansiveness and sexuality. A personality influenced by these factors, Horney noted, will most likely suffer from low self-esteem and feelings of powerlessness, and such a personality may tend to provoke further punishment and suffering, viewing these as her due.

Clara Thompson, Horney's contemporary, was the first to abandon completely the pleasure-in-pain hypothesis and to argue strongly that penis envy is a culturally determined trait not a bio-instinctual one. It is not the penis itself that a girl envies, Thompson pointed out, but the rights and privileges conferred by the culture upon those who have a penis.

Irving Bieber, my contemporary, places problems of power at the center of masochistic behavior. A child's first acquaintance with power occurs in the family, and it is there that a child, who is initially weak and helpless, develops the fear of power in others. There are many ways, aside from physical aggression, that parental power may be abused, Bieber asserts. Parents can exploit children in order to further their own goals, or compete with them or constrict them, and any such behavior can make a child fearful of authority. That fear, says Bieber, is the trigger in any masochistic exchange. He sees masochism as a defense mechanism that seeks to prevent or extinguish hostile aggression in others; its operating principle is that self-inflicted injury can ward off even more dangerous threats.

Psychoanalyst Ruth Jean Eisenbud has summarized the masochistic process in a dramatic outline she calls "The Drama of Masochism (a continuous performance)." First she sets The Scene: The protagonist has an "unsatisfied basic need," thwarted in childhood with a resulting, and traumatic, loss of efficacy. The ego depends for that need's satisfaction on an external and denying force, as in childhood. "There is the atmosphere of a charade," Eisenbud says. Next she outlines The Struggle: The ego strives to win over the denying force, focusing on winning rather than satisfying the need, clinging to the unrealistic hope that its antagonist will agree to lose. Then there is The Defeat: The ego suffers pain at frustration of the need, shame at having lost after trying so hard. It gives up the struggle and lapses into despair. Finally, there is The Outcome: Despair is reduced by secondary gains; a protest of persecution and pain to outside judges of morality supports the unrealistic hope; denial of reality and restoration of unrealistic hope allow the resumption of the struggle. Eisenbud's perceptions should in no way be diminished by the humor with which she presents them, for she catches vividly the debilitating, self-perpetuating nature of masochism.

The psychological origins of masochism, most would agree, are established in the first days of life, and these early roots go very deep. By the end of the child's first year, the groundwork of personality is firmly laid. Other phases of life certainly make contributions to personality, but the early infant experience is particularly significant. A child's first experience of the inequity of power comes in its relationship with its mother, or the primary mothering person. An infant is small and helpless, a mother large and powerful. The way a mother exercises her power through the care of the child will, in large measure, determine her child's psychological health or lack of it. If the mother uses her power for the infant's good, anticipating its need, subordinating her own, the child will probably emerge from its first six to eight months of life with what Erik Erikson called "basic trust," a view of the world and its inhabitants as benevolent and nonthreatening. If the mother, on the other hand, is inattentive or exhibits overconcern or cruelty of any sort, the child can suffer all kinds of personality warp or deflection from what she or he might have been. Masochism is one form of personality warp.

The importance of the early infant experience has been underscored by the work of several professionals. The great American psychiatrist Harry Stack Sullivan recognized what he called a kind of empathy between mother and child, a sort of emotional contagion that is transmitted in large measure during the feeding experience, whether that is breast or bottle. If a mother is feeling happy and satisfied or irritable, anxious, dissatisfied, or angry, the infant will by affected by those states, Sullivan said. A satisfied, nurturing mother will produce an infant who grows up trustful of other human beings and not unduly fearful of the powers of others.

The work of Harry Harlow, familiar perhaps to many readers, made important additions to our ideas about early infancy. Harlow did research with baby monkeys, rigging three different kinds of frames for them to respond to: a hard wire frame that held a bottle; a frame covered with soft material but without a bottle; and a frame that offered both softness and food. He found that the hard frame made the monkeys anxious; even though there was a bottle present, they did not like to feed there. The monkeys placed on the soft frame exhibited greater ease, even though there was no food present. The monkeys placed on the frame that was soft and also held a bottle did best of all. This experiment established that the comfort of holding and softness matter as much to the infant as feeding.

Harlow's findings were reinforced by the work René Spitz did with infants in orphanages. Spitz found that these infants, who were fed but had no human contact, not only lacked emotional responses but actually did not grow properly, were greatly underweight, were much more vulnerable to disease than infants in normal surroundings, and occasionally died of neglect.

Englishman John Bowlby studied children with tuberculosis who were removed from their home settings to a hospital at the discovery of their disease. He found that the rupture of their ties to significant adults caused them to fall into severe depressions.

All of these studies and experiments give us valuable information about the genesis of psychological problems. If the ability to trust is impaired, the sense of powerlessness and vulnerability is exacerbated, and some of the seeds of masochism are sown.

Another Harlow experiment has particular relevance for the mothering experience in our culture today. He found that when he raised female monkeys in isolation, they refused to mate with males. When they were forcibly mated, became pregnant, and eventually became mothers, they were child-abusers. Harlow recorded their reactions on film, and I found watching these films an extremely disturbing experience. The mothers ignore their infants, refuse to carry or nurse them, and fling their pathetic little offspring across the cage, slamming them against the cage walls, sometimes even killing them. Harlow had to step in and rescue the babies or they might all have been killed. The results of this experiment, it seems to me, contain a warning: The more technical our society becomes, the less natural we become as mothers, the greater the potential harm there is for our children to suffer.

Our society, because it places such a low value on mothering, has done little to help women caught in the conflict between motherhood and work. Ideally, a woman should be able to stay home for the first year of her child's life. Attending to her child's welfare should be her first priority. At the end of that time, having given her child a solid foundation of love and attention, she ought to be able to return to a job that has been guaranteed to be available to her. But that sort of arrangement is rare; it is common for mothers today to turn to alternative caretakers very early in their children's lives. It is not that these mothers do not love their children; it is that they feel, rightly, entitled to other satisfactions as well.

Women in our culture are led to understand that mothering is a natural, ongoing, and rewarding process. In nature that is so, but in civilized society the experience is more complex. A woman may not always understand that a conflict exists between her needs and those of her infant's. She often doesn't realize that she may be irritated each time those two sets of needs come into conflict. And she may not recognize that, because she resents the infant's demands, she begins, one way or another, to punish the child. This punishment can take many forms: She may delay attending to the infant's cries, thus putting its needs second to her own; she may get angry; she may scream at or even slap the child. Any of these punishments, from the mildest to the most severe, because they are repetitive, continuing actions, prepares the ground for masochism.

Toward the end of the first year of life, the child, now beginning to be a person, starts to assert her own will. This capacity involves choice: Should the infant please herself or should she please her mother? For example, when being toilet trained, should she wait to have a bowel movement on the potty or give in to the sensation and have a movement at once? Clashes between mother and child now become common as the child becomes increasingly self-assertive or submissive, depending to a great degree on how the mother deals with the imposition of *her* will as she expresses it through discipline.

As a child acquires language, two other developments involving the abuse of power can occur—and both help to produce masochism. The first of these is the so-called double-bind communication between parent and child. In this situation the child, because she is the less powerful, the weaker of the two, feels obligated to listen to and understand the message being given by the parent. The parent, however (usually without realizing it), is giving out a message that is impossible to understand clearly because it contains two contradictory parts: its overt content and its latent, or covert, content. The child knows that if she makes any attempt to question the message, she can get in trouble.

"Come here, dear," a mother says to her child with an edge of hostility in her voice. The appellation "dear" indicates that this is a loving mother who might wish to do something for her child. That is the overt content of the message. The latent content, however, is conveyed by tone of voice— and perhaps even clenched teeth—which suggest that the mother is not loving at the moment; she is angry. If the child does not come immediately but asks, "Why are you angry, Mommy?" the damage may be compounded by a reply like: "You're imagining things. I'm not angry. You know how much I love you." Confusion, hurt, and self-doubt are generated in the child by this sort of exchange. The erosion of a child's ability to trust her own perceptions is one more factor that leads directly to masochism.

The second of the damaging mechanisms that occurs as a child learns to understand language is hypnotic suggestion, a parent's repeated designation of the child as bad or wrong: "You are bad." "You are naughty." "You are stupid." "Why are you such a pest?" "Why can't you be a good girl?" These assertions, heard often enough, become part of the child's image of herself as surely as if they had been hypnotically implanted. This is a child who will grow up with a belief in her own badness, her own wrongness, always feeling guilty about something despite the absence of a realistic reason for guilt.

In addition to establishing specific pieces of the child's self-image, this hypnotic process also intensifies the child's pattern of submission to someone else's will. Just as a wolf attempts to escape death by baring its throat to a conqueror, the masochist offers a gesture of subservience by attempting to anticipate what an authority figure wants and rushing to comply. But this is not effective in the adult human world because the masochist is attempting to second-guess what authority figures will do on the basis of her childhood learning. What was appropriate as a child's response is inappropriate to an adult out in the world.

Another psychological factor important to the development of masochism is an unresolved symbiotic attachment to the mother. It is necessary for a kind of symbiosis to exist between mother and child at the beginning of a child's life. They are not completely separate emotionally, and this furthers attention to the child. But if this attachment continues too long it fosters extreme dependency in the child. An overprotective mother binds her child to her by refusing to allow the child to move away from her. Unable to recognize the separateness of her daughter, unable to acknowledge the boundaries between them, such a mother refuses to let the child develop her own thoughts and perceptions. This symbiotic relationship breeds passivity and a sense of inadequacy in the child, two prime requisites for the development of masochism.

As the child becomes more competent with language, the parents begin to mediate cultural attitudes; they introduce the child to gender roles and gender-role stereotypes. Gender roles, of course, encompass the customary functions each sex is expected to perform, and gender-role stereotypes consist of the narrowest, most rigid interpretations of those roles, of what is "fitting" behavior for a man or a woman. Stereotypes play a large part in making women feel inferior, helpless, and guilty.

A mother may encourage a boy to go out and play while she keeps a girl at home close to her side. She may give her son a toy that involves the use of a hammer and pegs, her daughter a doll. But why shouldn't a girl have fun hammering? Why shouldn't a boy fantasize being a father with a doll? A mother may emphasize how her little girl *looks*, what her little boy *accomplishes*. Fathers do this even more frequently. And so gender lines begin to be drawn. As the child grows and moves into the culture on her own, she will, of course, encounter more and more insistence on gender differences. But her first acquaintance with them comes through her mother and her mother's own feelings about herself as a woman.

There are subtle psychological differences between men and women, and it would be foolish to insist otherwise. Women possess a quality I would call receptivity, which should not be confused with passivity. Passivity implies inaction caused by a feeling of helplessness. Receptivity signals action. It relates to reproduction, and in strictly biological terms it is reflected in a woman's being receptive to a man and in taking in the penis during sexual intercourse. It is also expressed by the uterus taking in the fertilized egg, by the womb surrounding the fetus, and by the provision of support and nurture for the infant. Metaphorically, women's receptivity is represented by a kind of openness in intellectual and work endeavors. Men, on the other hand, possess a penetrating quality. This is, in obvious fashion, reflected in sexual intercourse but also perhaps in such undertakings as the exploration of the world and outer space. But these differences cover only one facet of personality and do not exclude men from being receptive and women from being penetrating. That acknowledgment is a far cry from the rigid notions of sex-appropriate behavior that are perpetuated through gender-role stereotyping.

One last factor must be emphasized when one is considering the early roots of masochism: the favoritism toward boys that still exists in families. This bias immediately puts girls on notice that they are second-class, that they are not worth quite as much as their brothers. I saw a marked expression of this some years ago when I was house-hunting and looked through the home of a couple about to have a child. The mother-to-be was ready to leave for the hospital, her suitcase packed and near the front door. The father-to-be had made his preparations also: On a bench in the entryway lay a tiny baseball glove, a small bat, and a tiny football. The equipment this man had gathered said only one thing: It *had* to be a boy!

Dr. Shirley Press, a pediatrician connected with the University of Miami School of Medicine, reported in an article in the *Journal of the American Medical Association* that she noticed disappointment in the faces of fathers, and even mothers, when they learned their child was a girl. And once she encountered a patient who said that she and her husband wanted a boy, and she did not feel that she could love a girl. When Dr. Press said that if they felt that way, *she* would adopt and love the baby, the patient subsided, probably out of a sense of shame rather than any change in point of view. People often profess that all they want is a healthy baby, but Dr. Press has found that what they really hope for is a healthy *boy*.

There is a story about Freud himself that illustrates the preferential treatment he received as a boy. Freud's sister loved music and began to play the piano, studying and practicing diligently. Unfortunately for her, little Sigi wasn't a music lover and didn't like hearing his sister play. One day his sister arrived home to find that the piano had been removed in her absence. Mrs. Freud, deferring to her son's wishes, had had it taken away.

My treatment of the historical context of masochism must necessarily be rather simplified. But the first point to be made should be that masochism in women has its historical roots in two biological facts: Women bear children and are physically weaker than men. As a result, women have been vulnerable and men have been dominant. The reproductive function dictated from the outset of civilization that women would be tied to the home, that men would serve as the providers. And until very recently, when women gained control of their reproductive function, this was a great handicap for women, keeping them in a position of dependence that fed their powerlessness. This must have been as true for a female member of a nomadic tribe, whose mate foraged and hunted for food, as it is for a contemporary woman with no independent income, whose husband keeps her on an allowance.

Throughout much of history, women have lived as a devalued subgroup. One of the forces that has institutionalized this devaluation, sadly enough, is religion. I have no desire to attack any faith or to advocate that anyone relinquish it. Religion can serve as a great comfort, and if it helps anyone to travel more satisfactorily through this difficult life, I think that is fine. However, it is necessary to recognize that religion has been male-dominated and has promulgated views of women as decidedly inferior to men. The Bible itself, whether one regards it as the law of God or as an important collection of myths about humankind, was written essentially by men and reflects a skewed view of women. In the Bible, women appear in only three roles: as the wifely need-satisfier for a man, as the sufferer, or as the prostitute. That is a fairly narrow range of options. The Scriptures define God as "He," and that single pronoun perpetually reinforces the notion of male dominance. The appellation God the Father makes the male position of father important, while the female role of mother has no deistic significance. One could ask why God is seen as having any sexual attribute at all since He is One, above all living things.

Chapter 3 of the First Epistle of Peter outlines the respective duties of husbands and wives and accurately capsulizes the absolutely discriminating view of the sexes that holds sway throughout the Bible: "Likewise ye wives, *be* in subjection to your own husbands; . . . Likewise, ye husbands, dwell with *them* according to knowledge, giving honor unto the wife, as unto a weaker vessel." "Knowledge," as used here, has a sexual meaning. So wives are commanded to submit to their husbands, while husbands are directed to use their wives sexually at their pleasure and, at the same time, to honor them for their submission and weakness. What a crumb thrown to a trapped bird!

Then there is the covert content of many of the Bible's stories, content often at odds with the tale as stated. The story of Adam and Eve is a perfect example of this. We all know how it goes: Eve seduces Adam by causing him to eat of the fruit of the Tree of Knowledge and, as a result, they are banished forever from Eden, the paradise of innocence. But looking beneath the surface of this tale—just as one would look to decipher the latent meaning of a dream, it is interesting to note that coiled in the Tree of Knowledge, which stands for sexual knowledge, is the serpent who first tempts Eve with the apple before she succumbs and tempts Adam. Could there be a more perfect phallic symbol than the snake? Sexual excitement in the male cannot be concealed, and an erect phallus is a powerful sexual stimulus to the female. Is it possible, therefore, that the true story of the Temptation is Adam's seduction of Eve, even though it is Eve who is punished forever for this alleged sin?

St. Thomas Aquinas fixed women firmly in their inferior position in his *Articles on the Production of Women*. A female, he stated, was a misbegotten male who must, by virtue of her sin, be under man's power. Subjugation was also dictated by the fact that reason predominates in men. Woman had been created only because man needed a sexual helper to carry out the task of generation. Man could perform other work efficiently on his own, Aquinas said. Then he pounds the last nail in woman's coffin by declaring that God's image exists in every man but in no woman, because woman was made in the image of man, not God.

In his book *Eve's New Rib* Robert Francoeur makes a wonderfully sly, satirical statement about the view of women that has grown out of Christian doctrine. The first human mother was Adam, he suggests because "From Adam's rib came the first baby and men kept her a social infant even when they left their father's house. . . . The child bride remained the emotional, half-human, imperfectly formed, miscarried male whose world would revolve around the men to whom she was meant to cater."

Christianity, of course, is not the only religion to give women exceedingly short shrift. Orthodox Judaism's morning prayer begins with a man giving thanks to God that he is not a woman. A *minyan*, ten male Jews, must be present for services to be conducted properly. Orthodox women are required to bathe in the *mikvah*, a special pool, to cleanse themselves after a menstrual period, before a marriage ceremony, and after bearing a child. Surely many Orthodox Jewish women experience this requirement as a humiliating punishment that makes clear their lack of worth—one that is hardly compensated for by the women's role of lighting candles for the Sabbath.

A patient of mine some years ago recounted the fight that erupted in her Orthodox Jewish family over whether or not she, who had her first menstrual period, should be allowed to go to the cemetery for the burial of her beloved grandfather. A menstruating woman was forbidden by Orthodox law to set foot on hallowed ground. She was finally allowed to go after her grandmother intervened and advocated bending the rules—she believed it would do no harm to the holy ground since there was no chance the blood would touch it.

The Muslim faith consigns women to an even lowlier place. Not only are they, as in Roman Catholicism and Orthodox Judaism, denied high religious office, but their legal and social rights are severely restricted. Their bodies must be covered by the all-encompassing *chador*, and a veil leaves only the eyes exposed. Thus men are shielded from their sexual attractions. A Muslim man can marry as many women as he wishes provided he can support them—and the degree of support is not spelled out. Further, he can divorce a wife simply by saying "I divorce you."

Nor did secular societies do much better by women. Roman law ordered women "to conform themselves entirely to the temper of their husbands, the husbands to rule their wives as necessary and inseparable possessions." To preserve their "property," Roman men were extended the right to beat their wives, to punish them for drinking and/or adultery. The insistence on premarital virginity in women—the only way to maintain certainty about paternity—was another way men sought to protect their property by insuring the pedigree of male children.

In ancient Greece, Sophocles asserted that "a woman's glory is in not departing from her woman's nature, which is to have no fame in the world of men whether for praise or blame." Socrates, at the same time, proposed that women be given equality in intellectual, political, and sexual activities. Is it surprising that

Sophocles lived to an old age, revered for his wisdom, while Socrates killed himself by drinking hemlock after being condemned to death as a corrupting influence?

Custom and code bolstered the tradition of female subjugation in succeeding centuries, too. French men were accustomed to beating their wives for contradicting them or for refusing reasonable commands. And it was men, I am certain, who decided what was reasonable and what was not. Laws governing the chastisement of wives and women began to be codified in the Middle Ages. As the English jurist Sir William Blackstone put it in the eighteenth century, looking back: "The husband also, by the old law might give his wife moderate correction. For as he is to answer for his misbehaviours, the law thought it reasonable to entrust him with this power of restraining her by domestic chastisement." Another Englishman, William Winter, eager that his countrymen be seen in the most favorable light, explained it this way: "It is not that the gentlemen of England are tyrannical and cruel in their treatment of women; but the predominance of John Bull in any question between him and Mrs. Bull is a cardinal doctrine of British law."

The whipping of female vagrants was permitted in England until 1791. Ducking stools, used to douse a "scolding woman" repeatedly in a pond or river, were in use as late as 1809. The brank—a particularly cruel sort of gagging device—was commonly used to punish "a certain sort of woman" during this same period. Not until the middle of the nineteenth century did the English, traditionally so noted for protecting animals against cruelty, begin a campaign against wife-beating. Until then it was an established principle of English common law that a man could beat his wife provided that the stick he used was no thicker than his thumb.

No one saw more clearly or wrote more cogently about the inequities in the treatment of women than the nineteenth-century philosopher John Stuart Mill. "At the present in the more improved countries," Mill pointed out in *On the Subjection of Women*, "the disabilities of women are the only case save one in which laws and institutions take persons at their birth and ordain that they shall never in all their lives be allowed to compete for certain things." This is considered part of the natural order of things, Mill wrote, because "the subjection of women to men being a universal custom, any departure from it quite naturally feels unnatural."

Mill's description of relations between the sexes reads like a blueprint for the development of masochism. "The position of looking up to another," he said, "is unpropitious to sincerity and openness with him. The fear of losing ground in his opinion or in his feeling is so strong that even in an upright character there is an unconscious tendency to show only the best side. How much more true then when one is not only under the authority of the other but has it inculcated on her as a duty to reckon everything else subordinate to his comfort and pleasure and to let him neither see nor feel anything coming from her except what is agreeable to him."

Addressing the question of marriage, Mill wrote that the husband was literally regarded as his wife's sovereign, while the wife was as much her husband's bondservant as a common slave. "She vows a lifelong obedience to him at the altar and is held to it all through her life by law. She can do no act whatever but by his permission." Then Mill noted that "a female slave has in Christian countries an admitted right and is considered under a moral obligation to refuse to her master the last familiarity. Not so the wife. However brutal a tyrant she may be chained to, though she may know that he hates her, though it may be his daily pleasure to torture her, and though she may feel it impossible not to loathe him, he can claim from her and enforce the lowest degradation of the human being, that of being made the instrument of an animal function contrary to her inclination. While she is held in this worst description of slavery as to her own person, what is her position in regard to the children in whom she and her master have a joint interest? They are by law his children. He alone has any legal right over them."

Acceptance of a heritage of brutality to women and wives has played a major formative part in shaping our modern societies. And women, traditionally, have responded to their subjection by accepting it and attempting to fit into the expected passive mold in order to avoid trouble. They have turned their anger inward and adopted a "suffering style"—the essence of masochism.

Originally handicapped by biology, women have been caught in a vicious historical circle that has been extremely difficult to break. In an industrialized world, skill, dexterity, and intelligence were the qualities needed for the production and distribution of goods. Women who shared those attributes equally with men were not given equal opportunities to gain economic or professional power, however, and their reproductive function was used as an excuse. To this day, we still hear women being judged unfit for certain jobs because of the supposed instability engendered by their menstrual cycle. When women did begin to gain a toehold in the professional world, the possibility of pregnancy was used to justify their low pay and to deny them promotions. It was not deemed necessary for women to be as well educated as men because they were considered unsuitable for the higher echelons of work endeavors. And so, because of their inferior education they were judged less qualified than men to hold certain positions. Thus the relentless circular diminution went on, keeping women unequal, keeping them dependent.

I recently came across a splendid example of how such erroneous conclusions have been drawn to women's detriment in Margaret Rossiter's book *Women Scientists in America: Struggles and Strategies Up to 1940*. Rossiter, writing about a book on men of science published in 1910 by James McKean Cattell, notes that Cattell was struck by the low performance of women in the sciences, giving the statistic that only 1.8 percent of scientists ranked in the top thousand were women. Rossiter says, however, that rather than concluding that something in the cultural environment favored the exclusion of women from scientific endeavor, Cattell suggested that women's poor showing indicated that they were genetically inferior. "There does not appear to be any social prejudice against women engaging in scientific work," Cattell wrote, "and it is difficult to avoid the conclusion that there is an innate sexual disqualification."

The greatest liberating force for women in our time has been the development of contraceptive means that free them from excessive and unwelcome childbearing. Today anatomy is *not* destiny. But attitudes that are centuries old don't just wither and die in a generation or two. History teaches that those who hold power do not surrender it without a struggle, and it seems unlikely that men will willingly relinquish or share the power they have enjoyed for so long. Women will have to wrest it from them, and women, unused to handling power, are fearful of doing that. In our present culture male dominance–female subordination is still maintained in a number of ways, and all of them contribute to masochism.

I noted earlier that gender constriction, which is what we might call the limitations that continue to be placed upon women and their capacity to exercise power, often begins in the home when the mother, and somewhat later the father, starts to transmit cultural attitudes and expectations to the children. This is the starting point of the gender stereotyping that will later be experienced more directly in the culture at large. The focus of a little girl's upbringing is still, more often than not, on being nice and being pretty rather than on being successful at accomplishing something, the focus for little boys. In this most competitive society, girls are still acculturated to be timid, docile, and self-effacing, attributes that are poor weapons in competition of any sort. Teachers still tell girls they can be nurses, not doctors. Boys are encouraged to go out and play; girls learn that it is dangerous for them to go very far afield. A girl may get less allowance than her brother, the implication being that it is more appropriate for him to handle larger sums of money, that his need for his own money is greater.

And girls have only to look around them—at television, the movies, very possibly at the relationship between their own parents—to see where the power lies in our society. It is evident that men are the important sex, the ones running things, whether it be the country, the broadcasting station, or the home. Of course there have been some changes in recent years, but still, when one observes a legislative body, a courtroom, a corporate board meeting, the floor of the stock exchange, one sees a sea of male faces. The gender stereotype that emerges from this sort of conditioning is this: A nice girl is one who does what her parents tell her, acquiesces to the needs and wishes of the males around her, and does not compete against men but tries to win them over.

Women who refuse to conform to this stereotype are subjected to certain, almost institutionalized, attacks. A woman who works hard at her career is labeled "aggressive." A man making a similar effort is complimented on his ambition. A woman who doesn't knuckle under to men is called a "ballbreaker" or a "castrating female." A man exhibiting the same behavior is described as admirably tough. A woman with exacting work standards is called a "bitch," while her male equivalent is praised for being meticulous.

When women, despite the odds against them and the resistance they meet every step of the way, do manage to succeed in a traditionally male-dominated area, the praise they receive will probably be couched in male terms. How often have we heard it said of a successful woman that she thinks like a man. I am reminded of the remark a friend of mine heard from an Israeli who was complimenting the Israeli prime minister at the time, Golda Meir. "She's all right," the man said. "She's got balls!" The implication is that only someone endowed with masculine characteristics could achieve such success.

Perhaps nothing does more to keep women in their traditional place, that second-class sphere of lower expectations and lower self-worth, than the image in advertising to which we are constantly exposed. Much has been written and said about this, particularly about those ads that show women as very marginal characters indeed, whose biggest challenge in life may be to get the ring off the collar, the hair out of the drain, or to turn up (in Maidenform bras and bikinis) where the men are. Medical journals, whose drug ads appeal mainly to male doctors and contain extremely distorted and misleading images of women, are culprits as well. But worst of all, I think, particularly in the wake of the women's movement and its struggle to free women of old notions of femininity, are the fashion ads that focus relentlessly on female sexuality.

Clothing has many functions, one of which is to convey impressiveness and power. When part of a person is revealed that would ordinarily be concealed by clothing, that person becomes less impressive. I was struck by this quite forcibly one night at the opera *Alceste* when I realized that the king, though magnificently garbed, suffered a slight loss of grandeur because he was bare-legged. Ads in which women are partly nude make women less impressive. It also seems to me that one is hard pressed these days to find a fashion ad in which a woman's legs are not spread. The message here is a masculine one, to be sure. Another damaging aspect of these ads is that they put women into competition with each other by focusing on sexual desirability as the primary characteristic that women project. This is made to seem women's stock in trade, with intelligence, ambition, talent, and competence nowhere in the picture. As long as the sexual self is stressed, it is difficult for the intellectual self to come forward and receive notice. Women's chances for success in business and the professions are severely undermined when they are assigned to sex-object status.

Then there is the sort of ad typified by the Saks Fifth Avenue fashion slogan: "We are all the things you are." The implication is that a woman is nothing but an assemblage of things, items from her wardrobe. And the further implication is that should she not have these things, she would be nothing.

An ad for the Lebenthal investment firm features Myrna Loy, looking as glamorous as ever, wrapped in a fur, saying: "I'm afraid I'm a novice at this. Please be patient with me." The sexual innuendo in these lines is unmistakable. Then she inquires: "May I ask a stupid question?" The notion this ad promotes is that it is all right for women to be inadequate, suffering, and stupid as long as they look nice.

Another cultural phenomenon that devalues women by making them sex objects is pornography. It is on the rise today, and it often takes an exceedingly violent turn. Women who are viewed as mechanistic entities whose primary purpose is to serve men sexually cannot be considered very worthwhile creatures. The tolerance exhibited today for pornographic films, publications, and bookstores underlines that sense of worthlessness.

The primary fact of female economic life—that women are paid less for what·they do—produces a deadly feeling of inconsequence. The message cannot be clearer: You are not worth as much as a man.

Defeat of the Equal Rights Amendment was extremely damaging to the image of women in our society. A simple statement guaranteeing the opportunity to be equal, the amendment's defeat suggests that women are *not* equal and are not entitled to be treated equally. The defeat also suggests that women do not have what it takes to get this sort of law passed. They are neither skillful nor powerful enough. And one way that women's power is, in fact, abridged is by their fighting each other. Women have always been divided and conquered, and the ERA experience was a vivid illustration of that. Women who were afraid to risk losing what they had, women who were afraid to rock the boat, fought the amendment's passage. If women had stuck together and spoken with one voice, the ERA would never have been defeated. The fact is that the defeat harmed not only the image of its supporters but the image of those who worked against it as well.

Two less tangible influences that strike me as pushing our culture in a masochistic direction are the notion of "stonewalling," which Richard Nixon refined to an art in his last few years as president, and the emphasis on team-playing. One used to assume certain minimal standards of decency and conscience on the part of the public and of public officials. One expected appropriate behavior, and when that expectation was not met, one anticipated, and generally received, an acknowledgment of wrongdoing. Today, however, there seems to be a growing tendency to deny culpability—to stonewall. We have seen this repeatedly in scandals involving government officials: Faced with evidence of misconduct, impropriety, and even crime, the accused simply refuse to acknowledge that there is anything wrong with what they have done. I see this as well, and more and more frequently, in passing encounters I have with clerks in stores, for instance, or tellers in the bank. The motto today would seem to be "The customer is always wrong." The masochist, who always believes she is in the wrong anyway, has a harder time than ever in this sort of atmosphere.

People do not speak up today as much as they used to, and I fear that the time of the individual, the maverick, is rapidly disappearing. Today it seems almost dangerous not to be a member of one team or another. Deviation from a group brings on ostracism, which in turn promotes masochism. The masochist always fears speaking up, always tries to avoid offending the powers that be. In a society that stresses conformity, going along, and team-playing, the masochist will find it especially difficult to overcome her fear-ridden behavior.

Obviously, the roots of masochism are deeply planted. The last few decades have brought some changes and, unquestionably, women today feel freer to demand their rights. But even as laws, policies, and codes of behavior begin slowly to change through political action, masochism remains firmly, obstinately, entrenched. A woman who rushes eagerly to the barricades in the fight for women's rights may conduct herself in a self-destructive way when she confronts her landlord, her boss, her husband. As resistant as society is to change, it still yields more readily than does the individual personality. It is in their own psyches that women must struggle against their masochistic heritage. To do that it is vital that they understand the process of communication that lies at the heart of the problem; it is vital that they learn to recognize what I call the messages of masochism.

4

Sending Out the Signals

"I'm probably way off base on this one."
"How stupid of me!"
"I don't mind if it's cold. I'll eat it anyway."
"I'm sorry. It must be my fault."
"I hope you won't be angry with me."
"I've just never been able to understand these things."
"It's nothing really. I was just lucky."
"Whatever you say."
"Just wait until your father comes home."

Masochistic communication has a distinctive style; its messages are the means by which the masochist exhibits and perpetuates her suffering. A masochist's aim is to appease or second-guess another person, someone she perceives as having power over her. Since the masochistic person perceives nearly everyone as more powerful than she, this strategy colors virtually all of her speech. The messages the masochist transmits, either through words or actions, are attempts to ward off the harm she fears and expects. Unfortunately, she is rarely a successful appeaser. In fact, her efforts to placate, to buy off, usually lead to further self-damage. Real communication between people involves give and take, a true exchange. The masochist, fearful as she is of the power of others, concentrates solely on keeping harm at bay. Her modus operandi is based on a system of anticipatory defense.

Masochistic communication is in many ways like a tennis match between an accomplished player and a duffer. The accomplished player serves, let's say, at high speed into the duffer's court. The duffer, unable to handle the powerful serve and afraid of it, may be hit by the ball, miss it altogether, or dink it into the net. Lost point! In the same way, the masochist, when a statement perceived as threatening comes at her, is paralyzed by terror, unable to position herself to reply properly. She may stand helplessly and just watch the ball (the statement) go by. She may allow it to plow right into her, causing a wound. Or she may make an ineffectual effort to return it that never clears the net. What she does not *dare* to do is to hit out strongly at the ball and return it forcefully to the server. She seems not to know how. The masochist is too fear-ridden for strategy of that sort. She always feels helpless and small; the server always looms large and powerful. When she muffs a shot, the best she can do is to murmur, "I'm sorry."

I will focus here primarily on verbal, rather than behavioral, messages of masochism since they are more easily conveyed. But, actions can impart messages just as definitively and forcefully as words do. Again, I emphasize that *all* masochistic messages, verbal or behavioral, are marked by an inability to express true feelings and by submission to another's power. And all of them are generated by the desire to appease. But beyond these general characteristics, there are some specific mechanisms one must examine to understand thoroughly the nature of masochistic messages.

The Use and Power of Apology

The masochist is an inveterate apologizer. "I'm sorry" is a phrase that comes to her lips all too readily, reflecting her low self-esteem and her sense that she is always in the wrong. She is the woman who, when someone bumps into her on the street, murmurs that *she* is sorry.

The apologetic message also demonstrates the masochist's more than ordinary belief in the power of apology. She uses it like a talisman that can turn away anticipated harm. If she says "I'm sorry" quickly enough, perhaps the damage and hurt she expects can be deflected. Most small children have a belief in the magic of words. After all, their initial experience of speech is that when a sound is uttered, all sorts of activity ensue. For the masochist, the phrase "I'm sorry" retains a kind of magical aura. More than likely as a child she was often found naughty, punished for her misdeeds, and made to apologize before being dismissed by her punishers. Saying "I'm sorry," or "I apologize," never helped her to understand why what she had done was wrong; it never helped her to learn anything. But it was the ritual expression that had the power to bring a painful episode to a close. She believes that "I'm sorry" is the statement that makes everything all right, in the same way that attending confession is supposed to wipe the slate clean. The phrase has great potency for the masochistic person, and she often utters it almost without thinking.

I was riding in the elevator with another woman and, having just picked up my mail, I was reading a postcard. It slipped out of my hand and I stooped to pick it up.

"I'm sorry," the woman said. "I should have gotten that for you."

"There was no reason for *you* to pick it up," I replied, "and besides, bending is good for me."

"I'm sorry," she repeated.

Her insistence on being wrong, her need to apologize was a defensive ritual: there was no realistic reason for her to attempt to placate me. She simply could not help doing it. And the result? I felt annoyed with her, a common reaction to this sort of self-abasement. People get tired of hearing the masochistic person's apologies; they weary of her rush to assume guilt and blame.

The husband of a patient of mine is extremely critical and demanding. One of the things he insists on is that his shirts be taken to the Chinese laundry every Monday. Usually his wife succeeds in meeting this demand; sometimes she does not. Her husband often asks her on Monday night whether she took the shirts to the laundry. If she has not, she immediately begins to apologize: "I'm sorry. I'll do it first thing tomorrow. But I'm really sorry that I didn't get to it today." She hopes her apology will appease her husband whom she knows will be angry. In fact, it makes him angrier and he becomes even more critical of her. What if, instead, she said to him: "Look, I run a big house and I have a lot to do and I'm not perfect, so the shirts don't always get to the laundry on Monday." Her husband might not be pleased, but this sort of statement would not provoke him to further invective the way her apologies do.

Accepting the Premise of the Other

The masochistic person, confronted with a powerful other, often experiences a state of what I call hypno-suggestibility. Related to hypnosis, but limited to the exchange at hand, hypno-suggestibility causes the masochist to accept whatever the other person says as correct just as surely as if she had been hypnotized into believing it. Totally paralyzed by the power and the idea of the other person, she loses any ability to think for herself and allows the other's viewpoint to be imposed on her immediately and totally. Having accepted the premise of the other, the masochist will then rationalize why it is so as a means of justifying her acceptance.

Hypno-suggestibility, as I noted in a previous chapter, begins in childhood vis-à-vis significant adults, and it is there that the masochist begins to accept the premise of the other as a defensive maneuver. Eric, for example, had a mother who frequently forced food down him. One item she always pushed was her chicken soup, which he abhorred because of the layer of fat that floated on top. "I'll eat the soup," he would say, "but can't you take the fat off?" "There's no fat on the soup," his mother would insist. "But," he would protest, "when the pot was in the refrigerator I saw the hard layer on top." "I took it off," his mother would answer even though Eric, looking into the pot, could see that the fat was now floating in liquid form on the top of the soup. Then she would force Eric to drink the soup. Eventually, he reported years later to me, he came to believe that, despite the evidence of his eyes, he must be wrong, that there was no fat on top of the soup. And he also believed that he must be very peculiar to believe that he saw fat when his mother didn't. Her constant, repetitive denials ultimately led him to doubt what he saw, to reject the proof he possessed. She implanted the hypno-suggestion that the fat did not exist and, as he yielded to her, he came to accept her premise.

A young woman who worked in an industrial firm ordered a twelve-dollar subscription to a trade magazine. When her boss got wind of this he was very annoyed. Despite the fact that the firm commonly made large outlays of money with little thought or scrutiny, the boss made a big fuss over the money spent on the magazine. Confronted by him, the young woman immediately accepted his assertion that ordering the subscription was wasteful. Panicky in the face of his annoyance, she apologized. Talking to me about it later, she said: "You know, this magazine is very useful. It's necessary to keep in touch with what's going on in the field. It's really not wasteful at all." When I observed that that would have been the perfect reply to her boss, she said she felt much too threatened by him to have thought of such a rejoinder; it only came out with me because she felt safe.

The masochistic person always feels in the wrong. When someone powerful comes along and says you *are* wrong and this is right, she has no capacity to fight that thesis. She succumbs instantly, as if she had been given a hypnotic command.

I ask patients of mine to keep a pad and pencil by their bedsides to write down dreams when they awaken and the dreams are still fresh. A male patient has been doing this for some time. One night when he got up and wrote down a dream, his wife said to him: "Listen, you're fifty-one years old. You shouldn't still be writing down your dreams." During his next session he reported this to me and revealed that he had accepted his wife's premise. "You asked me to write down my dreams," he said, "but my wife says I shouldn't have to. Why should I keep on doing this?"

There are many elements expressed in the wife's remark: her resentment that he still continues in treatment, her interference, her contempt for him. But the important thing here is that when this man's wife made an assertion, he immediately, unquestioningly, accepted it. Why did he not say to her: "Who the hell do you think you are to tell me what to do about this?" He did not say that because of fear, the same fear that caused him to accept his wife's premise with such alacrity.

Hypno-suggestibility is a striking element in man-womn relations. That should not be surprising in light of the cultural inequities that I outlined in the preceding chapter. And yet I am amazed at the degree to which women still continue to accept men's premises. Despite some social changes in man-woman relations, time has stood still for the masochistic woman, it seems. A friend of mine, a beautiful woman in her late forties whose body still looks almost the way it did twenty years ago, called me in a panic recently. "Natalie," she said, breathless with consternation, "I'm losing my figure. I'm going to start exercise and dance classes and go on a strict diet." Since I had seen her only a week before, and her figure had been as lovely as ever, I knew there was no basis in fact for her alarm. "Who said something to you?" I asked. She admitted that the man with whom she was involved had said something rather unpleasant about her figure—and she had taken it to heart with hypnotic effect.

Anna met Roger when he was in New York doing some buying for his firm in the Midwest. When his work was over and he was preparing to drive back home, he said to Anna, "Why don't you drive out with me and then fly back to New York? It'll be fun. We'll have a good time." Despite the fact that this meant giving up her own work at a time when she was quite busy, Anna accepted Roger's premise that this would be a great thing to do and, of course, she also counted on his implication that the trip would further their relationship with each other. She made the trip with him and they had an enjoyable time.

Over the next few months Roger called from time to time. Then Anna received a letter saying he was coming to New York to do some buying, he would be in town for two weeks, and he would like to stay with her. Thrilled, she took this as a sign that he was serious about their relationship. She made elaborate preparations for his arrival, getting her apartment in order, buying tickets to some Broadway shows, stocking her refrigerator with a lavish assortment of food. And when he arrived, she took considerable time off from work in order to drive him to some out-of-the-way places where he was doing his buying. When she did not drive him, she gave him her car to use and sometimes put gas in it for him. So solicitous was she that when Roger ran out of his favorite shaving lotion, she immediately noticed and replenished it, a gesture he acknowledged with pleasure but without thanks.

The night before Roger was to leave, Anna felt that his behavior was somewhat stiff, but she brushed aside her perception. The following morning, after some very satisfying sex, he told her that he would not be back in New York for quite a while. He had a vacation coming up soon and was planning to go rafting out west. When he was gone Anna found in her car a parking ticket he had received and never bothered to tell her about. Recounting this to me, Anna was plaintive about Roger's vacation plans. "He never even asked me to come with him," she said. And she was reluctant to write to him about the parking ticket because she did not want to seem petty.

The moment Anna accepted Roger's premise that it would be a fine idea for her to make the drive out to the Midwest with him, she sent him the message of absolute submission. Her unquestioning acceptance showed that she was willing to drop everything, that she did not consider her own affairs very important, that he was free to call the tune between them. And Roger obviously read that message clearly. When he returned to New York, he had no serious intentions about Anna; his raft vacation, probably with someone else, was already planned. But he did need a place to stay, a car to drive, meals, entertainment—and Anna furnished them all. Even as this gradually became evident to her, the thing she continued to worry about was whether she would appear petty to him if she asked him to pay for the parking ticket. At the outset of their relationship, Anna signaled Roger that she was vulnerable and submissive. Did signaling this serve her in any way? Did it cause him to treat her better, to respect her more? Quite the contrary. Anna's masochism alerted Roger to the fact that he need not regard her feelings at all. She did not, after all; why should he?

Avoidance of Questioning

Closely related to accepting another's premise is the masochist's fear of asking a question of the other person. Asking a question is the equivalent of returning the serve in a tennis game, putting the ball into the opponent's court, and forcing him to respond. Response, of course, is what the masochist fears. Hence, avoidance of the question. She also has no confidence in herself and her own views. Asking a question, returning a serve, feels dangerous and she avoids it.

I think of the junior executive I knew whose boss directed her to collaborate with a male colleague on a rather complicated project. After some deliberations, the male associate suggested they hire an outside firm to coordinate the operation. The woman felt she could have handled the matter herself, but her colleague persuaded her that to do so might be penny-wise and pound-foolish, so they engaged the outside firm.

When her employer learned of this he sent for this woman. "How could you spend all that extra money to hire another company?" he asked. "What do you think I pay you for?" The best she could do was to stammer that it was not her idea even though she had gone along with it. But this response did not appease her boss and his rebuke continued. The incident also jeopardized the woman's career.

How differently this encounter might have gone if she had been able, after her employer's initial accusation, to ask: "Why do you think this is a waste of money?" The question would have interrupted his attack on her and forced him to justify it. It would have, at the outset, erased the automatic assumption that she was at fault. And it would have allowed her then to focus on the real issue: why she and her colleague made the decision. Her avoidance of questioning her boss was an attempt to placate him, but it just encouraged further reproach and did nothing to support the notion that she had done what she considered best for the firm.

Equivocation

A masochist's uncertainty about herself and her opinion, her fear of taking responsibility for her own decisions, and her desperate desire to appease are on full display in a cartoon I saw some time ago. A woman sits in a restaurant, looking at the menu, and the caption reads: "Well, to be honest, maybe I'm way out of line on this one, but I'm pretty positive that I probably don't want the sole, I almost think." Of course this is caricature but, as with all good caricature, it is based on truth.

This kind of language is known in psychiatric parlance as tangential or circumstantial speech. In the former, the speaker constantly moves away from the center, away from the issue at hand; in the latter, she focuses on any circumstance that arises and talks about *it* rather than the primary issue. In either case, she is like a traveler who never reaches her destination. She starts down one avenue, then detours onto a side road, from there finds another path, and then another, each byway taking her farther and farther afield. These delaying tactics, she believes, buy her more time in which to attempt to second-guess the other person. They also keep her from being pinned down, from being stuck with any clear-cut position.

Repeating obsessively is another form of equivocation. Masochists find numerous ways of saying exactly the same thing, often prefacing each repetitious statement with a phrase like "I want to be sure you understand this," or "Let me just clarify what I mean," or "In other words, this is what I'm saying."

Language marked by ambiguity and lack of concision can only produce impatience. Will she ever get to the point? the listener wonders.

Polonius in *Hamlet* could well be called the Great Equivocator. When he is in the presence of royalty, his anxiety pushes him into tangential and circumstantial speech. He splits off first in this direction, then that, always avoiding any point that feels dangerous to him, ducking down any avenue that will keep him from having to make a direct, clear statement. Queen Gertrude, impatient with his indirection, chides him by saying,

"More matter, less art." Today she might simply say, "Get on with it," a phrase people often feel like directing at a masochist.

Circumstantial or tangential speech often has an underlying aim that goes deeper than concern with defensive maneuvering. This aim is to stave off abandonment. Masochistic people, by never getting to the point, hold on to their listeners and their listeners' attention. They don't recognize that the quality of the attention has been severely marred by the irritation and impatience the listener feels. They are simply interested in hanging on for dear life, and they try to do so by spinning out an endless stream of speech.

I'm reminded of a particular sort of stalling operation in an extremely masochistic patient of mine. She prefaced everything she was going to say with qualifying remarks that not only took up time but were also efforts to make me see her upcoming statements in a certain light. She never simply entered a session, sat down, and began to talk about what was on her mind. First she characterized what she was going to talk about. These are some of the phrases she used: "I have a lot to tell you today." "Today I'm going to deal with such-and-such." "I have something funny to tell you." "I have to say something very unpleasant." "I have something very complicated to discuss with you." "What I'm going to tell you about is a very difficult and terrible situation." "I'm going to change the subject now." These preliminary remarks allowed her to delay substantive discussion, and they reminded me of the remark of the mathematician/semanticist Alfred Korzybski: "The map is not the territory." This woman constantly handed me maps, delaying out of fear her entry into the territory.

Capitulation

The submission to authority that underlies all masochistic communication is perhaps most evident in the messages that turn on the mechanism of capitulation. Here the masochist exhibits her inability to hold her own, her tendency to collapse in the face of opposition, her failure to counterattack when such a maneuver is called for. The abandonment of autonomy is displayed with a painful clarity.

Evelyn had started her own business, which quickly became quite successful. In need of additional capital, she took in some partners, one of whom immediately began acting like her boss, questioning the hours she kept, referring to *his* business and *his* success. Part of his responsibility was to place an ad in which Evelyn had requested that she be mentioned as founder of the business. He had already "forgotten" once to include her name, so she raised the matter with him at a board meeting.

"Did you remember to put my name in the ad?" she asked.

"Oh, I forgot," he replied. "Remind me to call tomorrow morning at ten."

"I'm not sure I'll be able to call you then," Evelyn said.

"Well, I hope I'll remember," he said, adding, "Wait a minute. I think I did call . . . yes, I think I did."

"All right," she said, "case closed."

Evelyn's submission began when she accepted her partner's order that she be responsible for reminding him rather than pointing out that it was his obligation to remember. After all, she was not his secretary. By saying "I'm not sure I'll be able to," she revealed the degree to which she accepted his premise that it was her task. It deepened when she didn't question his obviously false last-minute recollection. And her final statement, "case closed," indicated total surrender. By saying that, she told him she would not cause trouble; she was a nice girl who just wanted to be liked; she would not fight. Appeasement—and where did it get Evelyn? Could she realistically have had any expectation that her partner would deal with her differently in the future? Of course not. She had just dug herself in deeper.

On her birthday, a patient of mine named Joyce was given a large camellia plant by her lover with whom she lived. The plant came from the florist shop of a friend of theirs. When, a day after she received it, the buds dropped off, Joyce picked up the heavy, rather unwieldy plant and returned it to the florist. "Keep it for a week," he said. "If it doesn't have some blooms by then, I'll give you something else in its place." So Joyce lugged the heavy pot home again.

A week later, when no blossoms had appeared, Joyce carried the large pot back to the florist again. He was not in the shop, but his assistant agreed to an exchange, and she picked a plant she liked and took it home. An hour later she received an angry phone call from the florist, who accused her of failing to water the camellia. He could tell this, he said, because the soil was dry. She had not watered it that day because she had not wanted to make it heavier than necessary for the trip to the shop, but she did not dare say so. The florist ordered her to return the new plant.

Joyce asked her lover if he would tote the new plant back and try to get a refund, but he refused. So once again she set out for the shop. When she arrived, the florist greeted her with annoyance and insisted that she take back her original camellia. Joyce acquiesced and hauled the moribund plant back to her apartment, where it failed to flourish and was eventually pronounced dead.

One last time, now carrying an obvious camellia corpse, Joyce returned to the shop and requested a refund. The florist refused, and Joyce left empty-handed.

Here and in the preceding example, there is evidence of submission to what can be called symbolic rape. Each of Joyce's heavily laden trips to the florist shop was a violation of her rights. And she submitted to these repeated violations without protest. Because she knew the florist socially, her fear was that it might be embarrassing to run into him if she was too demanding about an exchange or a refund. It never occurred to her that *he* should be embarrassed about giving her a flawed plant in the first place or by not telling her that camellias are temperamental. It never occurred to her that it might be more embarrassing to see him socially after she had let herself be exploited. And it never occurred to her that if she had been politely firm from the beginning, insisting that her unhealthy plant be replaced the day after she received it, the whole pathetic and outrageous incident could have been avoided. She felt she had no choice but to submit, to go along, to attempt to appease the florist by accommodation. And she ended up with nothing. Notice, also, that she capitulated to her boyfriend. After all, he bought the plant for her. Why was he

unwilling to help return it? Why did she accept his refusal un-
complainingly?

Jennifer, a married woman with a five-year-old child, occasionally did some free-lance writing in a special field but she
began to feel that she wanted to take on something more substantial. After mailing out resumes, she was offered an assign-
ment that involved several months of work. She decided to take
on the project and to work at home four days a week, a decision
that curtailed the time she had to devote to her family. But she
was delighted to be working and her husband seemed pleased
also. When a bedroom lamp broke, she asked her husband if he
would take it to the repair shop on a Saturday when he was free.
He refused; he did not feel it was his job. She did not force the
issue but took the lamp herself. In order to conserve time she
began preparing simpler meals. Her husband complained. As a
series of these clashes grew between them, Jennifer's anxiety
mounted and she began to question whether she should continue
with the work she was doing.

"Wasn't your husband pleased when you took on the job?" I
asked.

"Oh, yes," she replied, "he's already decided how he'd like to
spend the money."

Jennifer was capable of taking steps in her own behalf as long
as she had her husband's approval. But the moment she
encountered resistance from him, she capitulated. She suggested
that he take a greater part in household tasks but when he refused
she never asked again. When he complained about their less
elaborate meals, she questioned whether she should be working
rather than questioning his unwillingness to make an accommodation to their new circumstances. She tried to effect changes in
the basic framework of their marriage that would make more
room for her self-fulfillment but when he insisted that things remain the same she could not stand up to him. Her capitulation to
his wishes was fear-driven: she was afraid to make waves, to rock
the boat; her husband would be angry if she asserted herself; she
must appease him or he would not think of her as a good girl, a
nice wife. All of these are typical masochistic fears and, in this

instance, they kept Jennifer from pointing out to her husband that if he wanted to share in the benefits of her work he should be prepared to share in the difficulties as well.

Spilling

This is manifested in the tendency to say too much, to overexplain, to be too self-revealing. Insecure about her own power, the masochist feels she has no right to keep her own counsel, no right to maintain a self-contained position. So she believes she can ward off harm by a stream of words, the way a fire hose directed at an attacking dog can keep him at bay.

A patient of mine afforded me a textbook illustration of this phenomenon when she told me of an exchange she had had with a man who was selling textiles to her company. She was the buyer for her firm and the seller quoted a price to her. "That's about what we can pay," she responded, "but I'd like you to do better." Already she had said too much. By indicating that her firm could pay this price, she handed him a solid reason to hold the line and not bargain with her. She then went ahead and gave him a lengthy explanation of why her firm could pay the price, a completely unnecessary contribution for her to make. She was not obligated to give him any explanation whatsoever.

At the outset of their encounter, she held the advantage: He wanted to sell to her. But she quickly squandered it by divulging things she should have kept to herself. Her tendency to spill cost her dearly. In the figurative sense, she gave away little pieces of herself by being unable to stand up to the seller and deal with him effectively. In the literal sense, the price was also high—$70,000 more than she needed to have paid, she told me.

Another patient was at an art gallery opening when an attractive man approached her and struck up a conversation. After they had talked for a time, he asked if he might see her the following Friday night. "Well," she answered him, "I'm going through a very difficult time in my life right now. I have a lot of things on my mind, a lot going on, and I'm in the midst of a divorce and that's hard. I don't know whether it would be a good idea for me to see you or not." And on and on. Why, I asked her when she reported the incident, could she not simply have said no thank you, if she did not wish to see this man again? She thought she might want to see him sometime in the future, she said. In that case, I pointed out, she could have said no to Friday night but asked him to call another time. Or she might have asked for his phone number and said she would call him when she had some free time.

She did none of those things, however, because she was afraid to say no, even to a man she barely knew. She was afraid to be definite, afraid to take the responsibility for making a choice. She did not owe him an explanation, but she gave one. She was not obligated to reveal anything about herself, but she chose to. Her litany of woes probably made the man sorry he had issued the invitation in the first place.

One of the functions of spilling is that the words that pour out of the masochist fill up pauses that feel threatening to her. She is fearful of silence because during such an interval an attack might come. She may associate silence with the times her mother picked on her during childhood. I think of a patient who recalled her mother's behavior when she would come upon her daughter sitting quietly and reading. "Why are you just sitting?" her mother would ask in an accusing manner. "Why aren't you doing something, like cleaning your room or putting away your laundry or straightening up the mess you made in the basement?" Eventually, quiet moments came to feel dangerous to this child; she learned that if she wanted to sit still and read she would have to leave the house and take her book elsewhere. This was her way of avoiding her mother's attacks. Masochistic spilling seeks that same end by filling every moment with words. If words take up all the space, the masochist believes, there will not be room for the attack she is always expecting. But in the course of spilling, she almost always lets the other person know something that does not serve her at all. The content of what she reveals may, in fact, precipitate a negative reaction, the very thing she was trying to avoid by her outpouring of words.

Acquiescence and Accommodation

Masochistic people are invariably compliant, willing to let other people call the tune, reluctant to put their own stamp on anything. They concentrate on not making waves, not rocking the boat. The messages they transmit that are marked by acquiescence and accommodation almost seem to be efforts to be invisible. Their own feelings play virtually no part in their exchanges with other people; they are utterly agreeable.

A woman began seeing a male gynecologist shortly after her marriage and from the time of her first appointment found his internal examinations rough and painful. Nevertheless, she continued under his care, and he delivered her three children. His hurtful, inconsiderate methods never varied over the years, and he was given as well to delivering condescending lectures on diet and nutrition though he was himself obese. When she told me of these experiences, I said it seemed that it might be time for a change of physicians. "How could I do that?" she answered me. "I'd be too embarrassed to tell him I was leaving him."

This woman submitted for years to a situation that caused her pain, acquiescing in the doctor's authority over her (appropriate if he had been considerate and capable), making endless allowances for him, none for herself. Once in the situation, she felt powerless to change it. To do so would have been to risk the doctor's disapproval, a risk she was unwilling to take.

Suzanne reported to me a phone call she had received from a young man who wanted to arrange a blind date. She said it had been a very long conversation, and it had interfered with some tasks she had intended to do and made her extremely uncomfortable as her need to go to the bathroom became increasingly urgent throughout the call. Despite this, she had been unable to cut it short, waiting instead for the young man to end it. That fact alone was a masochistic message.

One of his first comments to her was that she did not seem as aggressive as many women in her line of work. "I don't think of myself as aggressive," she answered him, "but I suppose I must be in order to survive." They talked further, and then he suggested that they go out. "I don't suppose there's anything much on the West Side where you live," he said. "Oh, there are places," she responded, "but I'd just as soon go elsewhere, if you like." "Do you like to get dressed up, or would you prefer to be more informal?" he asked. Although she had a new dress she was longing to wear, she said that informality would be fine. They decided to meet at eight o'clock at her apartment, but then, uncertain whether he would have enough time to go home from his office and change into jeans, he said he would call her just as he was leaving his apartment. At the end of the conversation he said, "Sorry to have kept you so long." "Oh, that's all right," she replied.

This entire conversation was a series of maneuvers in which the young man moved aggressively and Suzanne countered with a masochistic defense, acquiescing and accommodating, which is really no defense at all. Her responses constituted a reenactment of the way she had as a child responded to her tyrannical father.

Letting Others off the Hook

With this device, the masochistic person rushes to hand other people excuses, to justify their attacks on her, and to rationalize away her own feelings in deference to theirs. Returning to the analogy of the tennis game, it is as though she hits a good, firm shot, but when her opponent misses it, she says it was not really good, it must have taken a bad bounce, the sun must have been in his eyes, he must have been slowed up by a rough spot on the court, and so on. She will not just keep quiet, content with the knowledge that she has made an effective stroke. She fritters away her advantage, fearful of the response of this authority figure across the net from her.

A patient of mine who is beautiful, intelligent, and a success in her job had just begun a new relationship with a young man she liked very much. After they spent a lovely weekend together, he asked when they might see each other again. "How about Wednesday?" she replied but then added, "But maybe you won't enjoy it because it's so soon." She, too, was attempting to ward off disappointment by offering the young man an out. And the out she offered him was to suggest that she was not really enjoyable and that perhaps too much of her was not good. This blatant display of low self-esteem could have done little to enhance her in the young man's eyes. She handed him an excuse for not seeing her and did so in a manner that could very well make him think twice about continuing the relationship. A nonmasochistic woman would have said simply, "How about Wednesday?"

When another woman patient of mine was promoted, her employers offered her a car along with an increase in salary. She could pick any car she liked as long as it fell within a certain price range. She chose a sports car and, excited and proud, drove immediately to a neighboring state to show it to her mother. Her mother's response to her daughter's good news was: "Don't you think it's selfish of you to get a two-seater?"

My patient should have recognized this gratuitous insult as part of a lifelong pattern of exchange between the two of them. She always persisted in seeking her mother's endorsement, and when she received an attack instead, she justified the attack by responding defensively. A small car uses less gas, she now told her mother; it is also easier to park in the city, she pointed out. Inherent in her response was the tacit admission that her choice needed defending. This let the mother off the hook and shifted blame to the daughter. What a different tone the exchange would have had if she had been able to say: "The car suits me fine since I live alone in the city." That would have placed the ball firmly in her mother's court, where it belonged.

Avoidance/Evasion

In some human encounters, avoidance can be an effective, and healthy, device to employ. It can be good strategy. But the masochist, who evades out of fear rather than tactical maneuvering, uses avoidance in a neurotic way.

A woman attending a party was greeted by her host who said, "You have nice legs and you can afford to uncover them. This is the first time I've seen you in a dress rather than slacks." His remark was upsetting to her, revealing as it did the unflattering assumptions he had been making about her, divulging as well his presumption that he had the right to make such a comment to her. But fearful of offending, eager to appease, she said nothing to her host, and her lack of response constituted a masochistic message. There were any number of replies she might have made that would have prevented her upset over the encounter, but she did not dare to respond at all.

This same woman told me a story about her parents. Her father was a very demanding, authoritarian man, her mother the archetypal "good little housewife" who cleaned, cooked, sewed, and always agreed with her husband. During a recent visit, her mother had told her about a trip she and her husband had taken to Philadelphia, focusing on an unsatisfactory dinner they had had. As she and her mother talked, the woman discovered that this dinner had taken place in a "topless" restaurant her father had insisted on going to. When she asked her mother what her complaint was, the mother said, "The food was no good." Repeating this to me, my patient was able to see the blatant avoidance in her mother's remark. "Of course," she said, bursting out laughing, "my mother wouldn't dare say she hated being forced to go to a topless restaurant. She often evades when she doesn't like what my father does . . . and so do I."

Inability to Change Direction of an Encounter

An obese woman ran into a friend she had not seen for some time. "Oh, dear," the friend said, "it looks to me as if you've put on some weight." This remark caused the woman to launch into a lengthy explanation of how difficult things had been for her lately, of how her troubles had caused her to overeat, and of how she had indeed put on weight. Undoubtedly, she believed that explaining away the weight was in her own best interests, that the explanation would lead her friend to be less critical and accusatory. In point of fact, she made matters worse by emphasizing the negatives about herself and left her friend with the image of someone who had no willpower, was preoccupied with her weight, and felt ugly and helpless. But what if she had been able instead to give her friend's remark a cursory reply and then move on to something else? The direction and nature of their encounter would have changed; the stigma of her weight problem would not have colored the entire meeting.

Masochistic people don't recognize that they need not be stuck with the topic raised by the other person. They don't dare to ignore it or give it brief lip service and then inject something new. Instead they focus on the topic like a fish drawn toward bait and then they hang on, hooked, unable to get free. Lawyers sometimes attempt to "change the venue" because they feel their clients will receive a fairer trial in another area. Masochistic people might receive a more favorable hearing if they were able to change the venue in a conversation.

Underscoring Mistakes

This characteristic is closely allied to spilling and to the use of apology. Fearful, guilty, certain that she will be caught out in her misdeeds, even if they are only imagined ones, the masochistic person rushes to point out her shortcomings. She hopes by doing this to disarm what she sees as her opposition. She will beat others to the punch, so to speak, underlining her errors before they can and, by doing so, deflect the negative judgments she anticipates. The woman in Salzburg who was "holding up the wall" certainly falls into this category.

At a dinner party I attended recently, the hostess sat with her guests and her quite critical husband in the living room for a while, and then got to her feet and said, "I'm terribly sorry but I have to go into the kitchen for a bit. I know I should have had everything absolutely ready so we wouldn't have any delays, but you do have drinks and hors d'oeuvres to tide you over, and I'll be as quick as I can getting dinner on the table."

What party does not require some last-minute attention? Our hostess could have excused herself simply and quietly. But she insisted on seeing her last-minute tasks as errors that could have been avoided; with apology and self-recrimination, she succeeded only in calling the attention of the guests to something we most likely would not have noticed at all.

I knew that this woman repeatedly acted out this same pattern with her husband. When she did something she construed as a mistake, she launched into profuse apologies that threw the spotlight onto her shortcomings. Many of the things she was at such defensive pains to point out might have passed unnoticed without her relentless underscoring—and the more she underlined her weaknesses to her husband, the more critical he became.

Rigidity of Language

The masochistic person is not free, to use again the tennis metaphor, to take a good swing at the ball and then wait to see what kind of a return she receives. Frozen in her defensive posture, she structures everything around that; her thought processes are carefully organized to effect defensive maneuvers. This necessarily produces a kind of rigidity of thought that is reflected in her language. She tends to see things in extremes and to express herself accordingly. Her speech is riddled with dualistic couplings like right and wrong, good and bad, weak and strong, and there is seldom much middle ground.

"Nothing I ever did was right—everything was bad or wrong. My outstanding work at school was ignored, except when I got less than a 95, and then I was punished. The punishment was so unyielding. I was confined to my room for a whole week for being a half hour late one afternoon when I was in high school. Now, when anything goes wrong, no matter how small, I blow it up out of proportion. I realize what I am doing, I know it's wrong, but I can't help it."

The language of this patient, a young woman who grew up in a harsh and punishing environment that left her always feeling "bad" and "wrong," was characterized by black and white extremes. Note the number of times she uses "right" and "wrong" in this one short speech.

The linguistic style of masochism often has an extreme tone

that comes from the liberal use of such words as "totally," "completely," "absolutely." While the masochistic persons uses these words freely, it is important to note that they generally go far beyond what the situation calls for.

Meta Messages

Words are not the only means by which human beings transmit messages. Often the tone or inflection of the voice, the body posture, or the gestures or actions accompanying the words say something as well. These communications, counterpoints to speech, are meta messages, and often they are even more important than the verbal message. Let me give a rather crude but clear illustration. A man says to a woman "I love you," but at the same time he kicks her. "I love you," the verbal message, conflicts with the kick, the meta message. In this instance, because the kick is more powerful, it is the true communication.

Meta messages can be conveyed by body language. Intimidated people, people with bad feelings about themselves, often fear looking another person in the eye. A direct look might be construed as a challenge or it might increase the possibility that one will be seen through. Masochistic people may reveal how they feel about themselves by their posture, which is often slouching, indicating their sense of servility and fear. They generally don't carry themselves with the air of erect self-assurance common to people who feel comfortable with themselves. Head-nodding is another bodily communication masochistic people frequently use. The moment someone else starts to speak they begin nodding affirmatively, eager to show just how agreeable they are.

Crying is another meta message the masochistic person transmits. Because masochists do not dare to be angry, they convert their anger into hurt. And when they are hurt, they frequently call upon tears as a way of getting themselves off the hook and warding off further harm. This is not a *conscious* choice, of course. Their crying is an unconscious mechanism that says: I'm pitiful, look at me cry, you must feel sorry for me, and if you feel sorry for me you won't hurt me anymore. The masochist's tears are no more effective a method of appeasement than any of the others I've mentioned. By evoking pity, the masochistic person seeks to evade harm. What her tears produce in reality are just more pain and suffering.

A physician told me of an experience of hers some years ago that illustrates the masochistic tendency to cry. She was an intern at the time and served as anesthesiologist, using the open-drop ether method, for another intern who was doing a tonsillectomy. During the operation he ran into some difficulty with bleeding, and the operation ended up taking longer than it should have. The next day the other intern approached her in the hall of the hospital and, in front of other people gathered there, said to her: "Goddammit, if you ever tell me what to do again during surgery, I'll get you." Stunned, she immediately began to cry. She tried to think back and remember if she had said anything to him during the operation and could not recall that she had. "I didn't say anything to you," she said, her assertion undercut by her continuing tears. "I was having enough trouble trying to keep the child anesthetized." "The hell you didn't," he said and stormed off.

The stand the young woman doctor took in this exchange—that she had said nothing—was rendered meaningless by the meta message of her tears. It signaled her weakness to him but did not deflect his attack. If she had delivered her challenge without crying, the outcome of the encounter might have been different. Also, she told me, she went over and over this incident, wondering what she had done wrong, accepting his premise that she had been at fault. Only years later did she realize that the attack on her had been a defensive projection on the other intern's part. He was embarrassed by the botched job he had done, and she had witnessed his inadequacy, which enraged him.

A patient reported to me that she had had a terrible week. She had slammed her hand in the apartment door, bruising it badly; she had burned her arm on the stove; and during a dinner party she had broken an old china dish she loved. Completing this recitation of damages incurred, she said, "I can't imagine why all this happened." "What are you angry about?" I asked her. She denied that she was angry, but as we talked further her denial began to diminish. She was in the process of getting a divorce, her husband had constantly delayed signing an agreement, and she had not pushed for a settlement even though she was desperately short of money in the meantime. This situation filled her with rage, but because she didn't dare to talk to her husband and urge him to move ahead on the agreement, she turned the rage on herself. The bruised hand, the burned arm, and the shattered dish were meta messages that said: "I'm angry at you, but I don't dare say so. I'm angry at you, but I'd rather damage myself than express it."

Misinterpretation of Visual Cues and Tone of Voice

Watching and listening for trouble, a masochistic person pays particular attention to the looks on other people's faces and their tones of voice. Unfortunately, many of these "signals" the masochist believes she is picking up exist only in her own fantasy. She may, for instance, look at someone who is expressionless and interpret the impassivity as anger. Or she may hear an inflection in someone's voice and read anger into it when, in fact, the person may have an abrupt style or a head cold or just have come from an unpleasant encounter with someone else.

This extreme attention to visual and vocal cues is rooted in the infancy of the masochistic person and based on what Harry Stack Sullivan called "forbidding gestures." These gestures, which include angry looks and angry tones of voice, come from a parent and indicate displeasure with the child. In order to appease and ward off harm from the parent, the child learns early on to try to interpet these gestures, and that predilection becomes imprinted on the child's psyche. These interpretations may have been correct in childhood and perhaps necessary adaptational solutions for the child trying to deal with an abusive and powerful parent. But carrying the mechanism into adulthood is extremely destructive. The masochistic person misinterprets a look or a sound, expresses that misinterpretation and, by so doing, creates trouble for herself.

Martin and Jack were brothers who ran a business together.

When Martin learned Jack was planning a trip to Massachusetts, he went into Jack's office, where Jack was studying some material spread out on his desk.

"What's the purpose of the trip to Massachusetts?" Martin asked.

Raising his head, staring at his brother, Jack said, "What?"

"Why are you looking at me like that?" Martin said.

Martin's response expressed his fear of some fantasied criticism by his brother. While he had asked a perfectly legitimate question, his fear made him feel he was somehow in the wrong and deserving of an attack. So he took his brother's "what?" coupled with his stare, as an accusation.

Jack's reaction to Martin's original question could have meant several things, and if Martin had not been masochistic he might have forced Jack to clarify it by saying, "What do you mean 'what?'" Or, "Didn't you hear me?" If he had hit the ball back into Jack's court, Jack would have had to explain himself. Perhaps he was reluctant to discuss the purpose of his trip. Perhaps he was bothered by being questioned. Or perhaps he was simply engrossed in his work and missed the sense of Martin's query. Martin never had the chance to find out, because he immediately focused on his own assumption that he was wrong to have asked Jack the queston, and that led him rather far afield from his original purpose. All he succeeded in doing was putting the spotlight on his own liabilities.

Rejection of Praise and Attention

Often when she is singled out for commendation, the masochistic person transmits a self-damaging message, snatching defeat from the jaws of victory, as it were. Unable to accept a compliment, she rushes to undercut it with a dismissive remark.

A thirteen-year-old girl was at a summer camp, and one weekend a dance was held with boys from a nearby camp. Slightly chubby and awkward and, like most adolescents, uncomfortable with herself, she sat with a group of other "wallflowers," watching the dancing and feeling wretched about the entire affair. Noticing one especially handsome boy, she thought how she would give anything to dance with him, and, to her astonishment, he approached and asked her to dance. As they moved out onto the floor, she said to him, "Are you a Boy Scout doing his good deed by dancing with me?" The boy gave her a searching look and soon excused himself. She never saw him again. One might dismiss this as just the behavior of a typical teenager who had not yet learned to deal with the opposite sex, but as the girl's later history confirmed, she had definite masochistic problems. And they were already showing themselves in an active fashion at the camp dance. Obviously she was not as homely or clumsy as she thought; the handsome boy did go out of his way to choose her. But because she felt she was worthless and unappealing, she was unable to believe that the boy's interest in her was genuine. Reacting defensively, she transmitted a message that drove him away, thus giving herself more ammunition to reinforce a distorted image of herself.

A common exchange one hears between women goes something like this: First Woman: "What a pretty dress." Second Woman: "Oh, I don't think I really like it. It's too frilly" (or tailored or drab or bright). The masochistic woman is unable to accept praise or attention; in fact, she seems to have an overriding need to push it aside. She is incapable of just thanking her friend for the compliment, whether she agrees with it or not, and then moving on to something else.

Unresolved Symbiosis and Poor Maintenance of Boundaries

As soon as Jane returned from her honeymoon, her mother began to nag her. "When are you going to write your thank-you notes?" she asked. "Don't you think it's about time you showed some gratitude for the nice gifts you received?" Exasperated, Jane snapped, "Are you going to keep annoying me?"

Because of their symbiotic relationship, the mother still regards Jane as a part of herself, as someone she can control. Even though Jane is now married, the mother's nagging is an assertion that her daughter has not achieved independence. She doesn't accept the fact that Jane is no longer part of her sphere of influence. Jane, because of her masochism, acquiesces in her mother's assertion of authority. Her response—"Are you going to keep annoying me?"—is an improvement over her past behavior, when she silently absorbed all her mother's reproaches. But it falls short of confronting the issue head on. It still includes a tacit acknowledgment of her mother's right to power over her. If Jane had been able to say something like, "Mother, you attend to your affairs, and I'll attend to mine," that would have been a direct, clear-cut statement of boundaries, putting the mother on notice that she was no longer the commanding authority in her daughter's life.

Symbiosis, especially in relation to a son, and usually an only son, has been called the "silver cord" syndrome, this standing for the umbilical cord that, symbolically, has never been severed. This is most common when the mother is widowed and wealthy and has the means to coerce her son into doing her bidding and dancing attendance on her. Clear boundaries have never developed between mother and son. But this cord attachment applies to daughters as well.

Occasional Negativism and Defiance

Masochistic messages exhibiting this characteristic are much less common than most of the preceding examples I have cited. However, they do occur. Continual self-abasement certainly breeds anger and resentment, and while the masochistic person guards vigilantly against any display of these feelings, occasionally they erupt. The docile, yielding accommodator can, every so often, lash out in a hostile fashion. At a glance, this may seem an improvement over her ordinarily immutable submissiveness. In fact, it is no improvement at all, for her anger is usually expressed inappropriately and ends up causing her just as much trouble as her subservience.

A physician had a difficult relationship with one of her male colleagues. She found his obsessive nature extremely irritating, and the two of them had had a number of unpleasant confrontations. One day, looking over a patient's chart, she saw his diagnosis and wrote next to it: "No. I do not agree with you." When the male doctor saw her statement he asked that she erase it. She refused, and the incident erupted into a heated argument. He was right in believing that her dissenting comment could support a malpractice suit if the patient or family were so inclined.

The female physician's remark was provocative, unnecessary, and inappropriate. When her primary concern should have been for the patient, she was focusing on her own need to pick a fight with her antagonist. Instead, she ought to have taken a positive approach to the medical problem by stating her impressions and substantiating the reasons for them. This would have allowed her to register her disagreement but in a constructive way. It could have been helpful to the patient, and it might not have triggered further difficulties for her.

The defensive communication style of masochism is a mosaic of all the different types of messages just described.

Often a single communication can contain several messages, and the characteristics I have delineated are present in masochistic speech all the time. They are like themes in a piece of music that recur over and over, sometimes stated plainly, sometimes phrased with elaboration, but always recognizable no matter how many instruments or notes have been added or taken away. The masochistic message, whatever its form, is always an expression of powerlessness and a plea for leniency. Unfortunately, the signal of weakness does not discourage injury. More often than not, it promotes it. The masochistic person, fearful though she is of the power of others, is truly her own worst enemy, the victim of a system of suffering that is self-fulfilling and self-propelled.

5

Active or Passive Voice

Chance plays a part in all human affairs. A hand of cards is dealt each of us in life; while we have no say in what those cards will be, the way in which we play the cards is very much within our control. And in life, as in a card game, there seem to be people who win consistently and people who lose with equal regularity. Masochists play the cards they have been dealt with a notable lack of skill, signaling their vulnerability at every turn, invariably saying or doing the self-damaging thing.

The messages a masochist transmits signal vulnerability at every turn. These messages are, of course, just the tip of the iceberg, that portion of the personality that is visible, the outward manifestations of the masochist's inner sense of fear and powerlessness. But it is important to recognize the messages if one is to explore and understand what lies beneath the surface. And equally important to understand is the difference between active and passive masochism, a somewhat artificial distinction, perhaps, but a crucial one nevertheless.

Active masochism exists when a person *initiates* something that is self-punitive; passive masochism exists when an outside event triggers a masochistic response. Hard though it may be to believe, if the masochistic person could just learn to keep her mouth shut, she would eliminate half her problems, the active half, the half she brings upon herself. But keeping still, refraining from using her anticipatory defense system, is one of the most difficult things for the masochist to do. Impaled upon the notion that things are made better by assuaging power, deferring to power, and apologizing to power, the masochistic person finds it almost impossible to believe that her best interests may be served by saying or doing nothing.

Genevieve was in the midst of a divorce and involved with a younger man in an enjoyable, though not serious, romance. He had made it clear he was not interested in a deep commitment for a number of reasons, but they did spend most weekends together. During one stay at his apartment, Genevieve saw tickets to the ballet on his phone table, but he did not mention them to her and she knew better than to press him. A few weeks later, however, he invited her to accompany him to the ballet. "Oh, I noticed those tickets," Genevieve said, "but you didn't ask me and I wondered if you were planning to take someone else."

This is active masochism. Genevieve could simply have said, "Thank you, I'd love to go." But her masochism pushed her to spill out self-revealing information that would do her no good whatsoever. She divulged to the young man that she was jealous, worried about her relationship with him, and desirous of greater commitment. By conveying to him her relief that the tickets were for her she, the powerless one in the relationship, put herself even further in his power. If she had been able to accept his invitation with thanks but without masochistic embroidery, she would have done herself a favor.

Some time later, when Genevieve had occasion to be in the man's office, she noticed that he still had on his desk a picture of his former girlfriend. She said nothing in the office, but when they came downstairs and got into his car, she could no longer contain herself. "I see you still have Elizabeth's picture on your desk," she said, a remark that enraged the man and constituted another example of active masochism. It may have been wise of her to note the picture for future reference, but it did her no good to spill it out to him.

Ralph and Sam are business partners who arranged with their burglar alarm company that Sam was to be called first if the alarm went off, since he lived twenty minutes closer to their business location. One night the company called Ralph to say the alarm had rung; he was annoyed they had not called Sam and told them to do so even though he was now awake and alerted to the situation. The next morning, Ralph asked Sam what had happened the night before. "How do you know about it?" Sam asked angrily. "They called me," said Ralph, "and I told them to call you." At this, Sam flew into a rage. Why would Ralph do such a thing, Sam asked, if he was already awake? Why would he be so inconsiderate? And, while Sam was at it, he might as well mention that Ralph had not been pulling his weight lately in a lot of ways. Sam claimed he was doing the lion's share of the work while Ralph just coasted along.

Again, this is active masochism. Ralph, who knew what his partner's personality was like and who also knew that it had been unreasonable of him to have Sam called, could easily have called the alarm company the next day to find out what had happened. But, instead, he volunteered information to his partner that was bound to boomerang and deal a blow to him. You will recognize both spilling and underscoring mistakes in the active masochistic message that Ralph transmitted. If he had just stayed quiet, there would have been no trouble with Sam. But he could not help saying more than was necessary.

When masochistic people feel defensive about something, which is most of the time, they invariably attempt to correct it, to fix it up. Just as invariably, that attempt makes things worse. They feed the flames rather than putting them out. Learning not to do that involves learning to say no to themselves: No, I will not rush to explain, to rectify, to mollify, to disarm . . . I will keep still. Few human beings find ambiguity comfortable, but for the masochistic person it is nearly unbearable. She would rather translate her inner discomfort into a sure loss than to remain in a limbo of uncertainty. She experiences a release upon ending the suspense. But what a high price she pays for temporary relief.

A patient of mine was invited to a party several weeks ahead of time. As the date approached, she called the friend who was giving the party and said, "I'm calling to ask if I should come to the party." "Well, of course," said her friend, "I'm expecting you." My patient's remark revealed unmistakably her sense that she did not belong, her belief that she did not deserve to be invited to the party, her pervasive self-doubt. If she had called to check on the day and time of the party, that would have been one thing. But to call and ask if she should come, when she had been invited and had accepted the invitation was another matter.

In this instance, her friend responded warmly, but that is not the customary response to masochistic behavior. In fact, people who are repeatedly on the receiving end of a masochist's messages come to expect certain behavior from her and may even treat her unfairly before she hands them the opening. In this way, over the long haul, masochistic messages encourage further aggression. Cumulatively, they create a climate where attack is more likely.

Susan has a friend who lives out of town, and each time the friend visits, the first thing she says to Susan is, "How *are* you?" The question, with its telling inflection, makes it obvious that the friend expects Susan to be perfectly awful. The friend's asking the question is an implicit put-down of Susan, something she has come to resent as she has grown healthier. In the past, the same question, asked in a conventional, polite way, was always the trigger for a recital of woes, and now, in a certain sense, the damage has been done. Even though Susan no longer jumps at any opening to catalogue her wounds, her friend continues to respond as though that were happening. She has been conditioned by her exposure to Susan's masochism to expect it, and her attack, subtle though it may be, occurs without Susan's doing anything. Now, of course, it is up to Susan to reverse the pattern, to change the direction of the encounters with her friend. The next few times her friend asks, "How *are* you?" Susan should say, "Things are great. What's going on with you?" or, "Just fine, thanks," and then move on to something else. Her friend will be puzzled because she has heard nothing but complaints for so long, but eventually she will catch on.

Active masochism also reveals itself in the masochistic person's propensity toward physical damage of the self or of possessions. Masochists do not dare to express their anger directly, but often that anger makes an appearance in the guise of destructive events that appear to happen by accident. Ludwig Eidelberg, a noted psychoanalyst, has observed that some masochistic people bring about their own discomfiture by a roundabout process in which they manipulate the reverses they suffer. It is a kind of self-mortification.

Karen had three very special Japanese cups and saucers that she treasured. A couple with whom she was somewhat friendly, even though she did not like them all that well, arrived from out of town and asked Karen to have dinner with them. She felt it would be incumbent upon her to take them to dinner, but since she couldn't really afford that, she invited them to come to her apartment for coffee and dessert, even though she preferred not seeing them at all. She had to rush that evening to get home in time to get things ready. As she was taking her irreplaceable cups from the closet, one fell to the floor and smashed, an expression, I think, of her annoyance at finding herself in an unwelcome position.

I will never forget the first sight I had of a patient who came to me very specifically seeking help for what she knew was her masochism. She was having a difficult time in her marriage, and the therapist she had seen previously had attempted to establish a sexual liaison with her. When I opened the door for her, I saw that she had an arm in a cast, a large purple bruise on her hand and her hair had obviously been singed by fire. She was a masochistic disaster area! We all know people who tend to be accident-prone; the blows that fall on them seem to be dealt by fate. But it is just as likely that their preoccupation with unexpressed anger causes them to be careless.

Very often, in the background of people who express their masochism in this fashion, there is an overprotective mother who constantly issued warnings: watch out, don't trip, don't fall, be careful, look out. Through repetition of these admonitions, the mother implants hypno-suggestions in the child. What she is really saying is that the child is clumsy, careless, worthless, and inept, and the child, out of defiant, masochistic rage, begins to act this out: All right, Mom, you expect me to break the plate? I'll show you. I'll break the plate. You think I'm going to fall? Okay, I'll fall. And so on. It is a kind of self-fulfilling prophecy and can be triggered by unconscious fear as well as by more overt defiance.

In passive masochism, the triggering event is unavoidable because it comes from outside. The masochistic person is not responsible for initiating the interchange. She is, however, responsible for her reaction. Apologizing when someone bumps into you is a perfect example of passive masochism. You may recall the young woman in the last chapter whose boss took her to task for ordering a twelve-dollar magazine subscription. The attack on her came from the outside, something she could not control, but she responded masochistically by becoming panicky and apologizing. That is passive masochism.

Passive masochism often consists of silent submission to a difficult or painful situation, an unwillingness to speak up, to make one's wishes or feelings known. A young woman was studying for her exams in her New York apartment when her upstairs neighbor began to play his stereo loudly. The noise interfered with the student's ability to concentrate, as did her anger, which grew as the noise continued. But she made no effort to change the situation; she just accepted it. Her fear of confronting the neighbor prevented her from acting in her own best interests.

Marcia went to the bank during her lunch hour to take care of a matter that needed the attention of a bank officer. Soon after she sat down, the woman officer took a phone call that was obviously personal and went on talking while Marcia waited in silence. There were other officers available to whom she could have taken her business, but Marcia stayed where she was, awaiting the end of the seemingly endless phone call. When the officer finally hung·up, Marcia did venture timidly that she didn't have much time and hoped they could take care of the business as quickly as possible. The officer, obviously annoyed, said, "My mother is sick in the hospital," a statement that caused Marcia to abandon even her paltry effort at assertion and lapse into an orgy of apology. "Oh, I'm so sorry," she said. "I feel just terrible. I didn't mean to be impatient. I didn't realize you were talking about your mother. I hope she'll be all right."

The provocation of this instance came from outside of Marcia in the form of the phone call. She made a half-hearted effort to protest the treatment she was given, but the moment the officer presented her with what appeared to be an excuse, Marcia capitulated and began to backpedal furiously to let the woman off the hook. In fact, the excuse was no excuse at all. Marcia could have replied, "I'm sorry that your mother's ill, but that doesn't mean you needed to stay on the phone for fifteen minutes. You could have said what was necessary and ended the call, or you could have called back after we'd finished our business." Instead, *she* ended up apologizing and feeling in the wrong.

Almost anyone is fair game for unprovoked abuse or rudeness, particularly in today's climate of ever-diminishing civility. However, the masochistic person reacts to these slings and arrows in a particular way. She absorbs the punishment, rather than deflecting it. Because of her fear, her feelings of guilt, and her persistent sense of being in the wrong, she doesn't put up effective resistance to the assaults she encounters. The neurotic defensive responses of passive masochism are in large measure due to the masochistic person's lack of a sense of her own limits and boundaries, the legacy of her still unresolved symbiotic attachment to her mother. She has great difficulty perceiving when she has been infringed upon. So meager is her sense of herself as a separate, autonomous person that she often does not even realize that an offense against her has been committed.

It is, of course, self-defeating to respond heatedly and pointedly every time someone shoves ahead of you in a line or keeps you waiting for an appointment or jostles you on the street. It is especially true that people who live in large cities could use up all their energy simply reacting to incidents of that sort. Obviously, one must bring a sense of proportion and judgment to exchanges with other people, a sense of what is appropriate and what is not. A minor brush with someone during the day may not rate much concern; its consequences may be insignificant. On the other hand, some slights or attacks absolutely merit a response; the failure to respond may, in fact, provoke further aggression. But making these kinds of distinctions is very hard for the masochist. Her perceptions are not grounded in present reality. She lives in a world peopled by the harsh phantoms of the significant adults of her childhood, and it is to these shadows that she is perpetually responding. Her anxiety-driven defensive behavior is a fantasy expression of something no longer real—not real, that is, until she recreates it over and over again by employing her system of anticipatory defense. In a situation that has the potential for passive masochism, it is necessary to determine whether true injury has been done, whether the failure to defend oneself may encourage further aggression, and whether one is in a position to defend oneself adequately. Masochistic people, bound to the past, indeed haunted by it, have not developed the autonomy that would allow them to ask these questions and then answer them objectively.

As I said at the outset of this chapter, the reason for making the distinction between active and passive masochism is that someone attempting to overcome her masochism must understand as precisely as possible the part she plays in the masochistic process: When is she the initiator, when the respondent? Both active and passive masochism exist in the same person, side by side, and both are equally destructive. But active masochism is perhaps more easily conquered. Here the masochistic person has her fate in her own hands. It is up to her whether or not she will hand someone the rope with which to hang her. If she can learn to keep quiet, to be self-contained, to refrain from volunteering information that will be damaging, she will have taken a major step toward eliminating her own suffering.

6

Masochism and
the Maiden

. peeked in to say goodnight
And then I heard my child in pray'r,
"And for me some scarlet ribbons,
Scarlet ribbons for my hair."

All the stores were closed and shuttered,
All the streets were dark and bare,
In our town no scarlet ribbons,
Not one ribbon for her hair.

Through the night my heart was aching,
Just before the dawn was breaking,
I peeked in and on her bed
In gay profusion lying there,
Lovely ribbons, scarlet ribbons,
Scarlet ribbons for her hair.

If I live to be a hundred,
I will never know from where,
Came those lovely scarlet ribbons,
Scarlet ribbons for her hair.

The first time I heard "Scarlet Ribbons," which sounded like a
folk song, was in the early 1960s as my daughter was playing the
guitar and singing. I had just begun to do research on the
menarche, the onset of menstruation, and the song struck me as
a powerful metaphoric expression of that most significant event.

It had a dreamlike quality, moving fluidly between the symbolic and literal levels, and I felt almost as though it had been written for me.

The mother-daughter relationship reflected in the song is a positive one. The mother is loving and caring; she hears her daughter's prayer and yearns to be able to answer it. Metaphorically, I thought, what the daughter prays for are the scarlet ribbons of menstruation, the flow of blood that will signal her physical maturity. It is a request the mother would do anything she could to grant, but it is beyond her power to do so. Then, the ribbons do appear ("I will never know from where"), and the mother is delighted that her daughter's longing has been fulfilled. The song captures the anxiety and eagerness a young girl may feel awaiting her passage past this milestone, the mother's empathetic heartache as she feels her child's yearning, and the beauty and sense of reassurance of menstruation when it does arrive.

The girl in the song was fortunate to have a mother who really loved her and wanted to see her wishes fulfilled. At this crucial time in the girl's life, her mother wanted to give maturity to her, to support her development, rather than deprive her or hold her back. And it is likely that such a girl would not grow up masochistic, even though cultural forces could evoke masochistic tendencies. Certainly the mother's caring attitude would mitigate against the negative effects of the cultural input. Quite the opposite is true when a mother is uncaring and unloving; her insensitive, indifferent, or even hostile behavior will only serve to reinforce the cultural and social inclination toward masochism.

Adolescence, which generally begins with the menarche, is the last period of intensive interaction between mother and daughter, the time when a girl either receives an assist from her mother that enhances her chance of becoming an emotionally healthy young woman or suffers at her mother's hands the kind of ego damage that makes a healthy womanhood unlikely. The menarche itself, that first nodal point in the reproductive process that ends with menopause, serves as a focus for all the attitudes of mother and daughter relating to feminine sexuality and also con-

tains a summation of all the feminine feelings and attitudes that
have been established up to that point.

Contrary to much psychoanalytic thought, the menarche is
not a time of *capitulation* to femininity, a time when girls are
forced to give up their inherent desire to be boys and to succumb
to their incipient womanhood. It is a positive first step on the path
toward womanhood and reproduction and ought as such to be
viewed as an auspicious and joyous occasion. Mothers who behave destructively at this time give their daughters a substantial
push toward masochism.

Consider the damaging treatment afforded a patient of mine
on the occasion of her first menstrual period. She was eleven
years old and had been given no preparation whatsoever. One
morning she awoke early, feeling wet. Throwing off the bedclothes, she saw that she was covered with blood and ran in panic
to her mother's room. Her mother greeted her with a show of
irritation and slapped her face. She then told her daughter that
the flow of blood was a natural occurrence but added that it really
should not have appeared for another year or two. This left the
girl feeling that something was wrong with her. The mother instructed her daughter how to care for herself hygienically, advised
her to take to her bed for the day but gave her no other information. This was not an isolated experience, of course, although it
was a most significant one. The context of the mother-daughter
relationship was a series of experiences that resulted in the daughter's feeling devalued as a woman, viewing her menstruation as
something undesirable and carrying into adulthood a masochistic
heritage that was extremely difficult to overcome.

The slap on the cheek, by the way, is apparently a legacy of
the Jewish-Russian culture. It is said that the slap brings a blush
to the cheek, thus guaranteeing good color as an adult. Psycho-
analytically, one is hard pressed not to consider the slap a castrating gesture, suggestive of the mother's anger at her daughter's
newfound maturity and the potential threat it may indirectly pose
to the mother.

As a mother watches her daughter approach puberty, all the
anxieties and fears she felt at that time in her own life are fre-

quently evoked. The mother may also find her daughter's emerging sexuality threatening. She, after all, is heading toward menopause, the end of one part of her life as woman, while her daughter is poised at the very beginning of her sexual life. The sense of threat and the recapitulated fears and anxieties may cause great difficulty between mother and daughter, and often they struggle fiercely at this time.

A parable by the Lebanese writer Kahlil Gibran called "The Sleep Walkers" catches the ebb and flow of the currents and undercurrents that can exist between a mother and daughter at this time of life. It involves a mother and daughter who walked in their sleep. One night they meet in a mist-veiled garden. The mother speaks first, calling her daughter "my enemy," declaring that the girl has "built [her] life upon the ruins of mine." The daughter in turn calls the older woman selfish and accuses her of hatefulness in standing "between my freer self and me," and wanting "my life an echo of your own faded life!" When both women awake they revert to their polite and loving daytime selves.

Gibran's mother and daughter reveal their true feelings about each other when they appear in the mist-veiled garden. This is similar to a dream in which, under the conditions of sleep, the truth comes out. Each sees the other as her enemy, the mother resenting her daughter because she has sapped her youth and fed off her life in an almost parasitic way, the daughter bitter about her mother's desire to prevent her from becoming an independent sexual being. They wish each other dead. Yet when they awaken they slip automatically into a stereotyped sort of behavior, their deepest feelings obscured by a routine and superficial affability.

The emotions that are articulated in the garden, however, frequently come into play between mother and daughter at the time of the menarche. The fairy tale of Snow White and Rose Red, in which the old woman asks the mirror who is fairest of them all, also speaks of the sense of competition that can exist between an older and younger woman, between mother and daughter.

A masochistic patient who did not have many dates as a young woman recalled how she felt when a date *did* come to pick her up and her mother engaged him in conversation, going on and on, not letting go until it was too late to go anywhere. The young woman stood by helplessly, unable to intervene. Part of the mother's success at this was due to the fact that she was an attractive and charming woman. She had never taken second place herself and perhaps did not realize what she was doing to her daughter. But the daughter did and felt murderous rage.

The fact is that a mother may find it difficult to witness her daughter being launched sexually while she feels her own sexual powers waning. This is especially true when the mother's life has not been a particularly satisfactory or fulfilling one. The mother wants to continue being declared the fairest of them all, but it is usually evident that the daughter has, in fact, become the fairest. The mother feels usurped. Very often at this time the mother is also compulsively reenacting with her daughter the pubescent experience she had with her own mother.

Feeling threatened, beset by old fears, the mother may perceive her daughter as being out of control and make a last-ditch effort to assert her dominance over her child. Her attempts to rein in her daughter may be cruel and unduly suppressive. When this occurs, the daughter generally responds by becoming more defiant. Mother and daughter are then locked in a battle marked by escalating cruelty on the mother's part, deepening defiance on the daughter's. The other response an anxious mother may evidence is avoidance of the problem altogether, refusing to discuss menstruation with her daughter, denying that it is happening. Either response is clearly harmful to the girl's sense of her self-worth.

The father may also play a part in this preadolescent drama. To protect himself against any incestuous desires he may have for his daughter, a father may accuse her of being seductive, of being promiscuous. The daughter's behavior may be completely innocent, but the father projects his own fears onto her and then makes accusations against her that are deeply hurtful. The father of a patient of mine, as the girl approached adolescence, required her to come directly home after school every day. He knew exactly how long it should take her to make the trip, and if she was even slightly late, he would march her to the basement and beat her with his belt. Occasionally varying the punishment and making it even more cruel, he would require her to wait in the basement while he ate his dinner, and then he would come down and beat her afterwards.

It has become increasingly clear recently (Freud's interpretations of such reports as fantasy to the contrary) that sexual molestation and sometimes rape by a father or stepfather are far from rare. Sexual child abuse is often an ongoing phenomenon that occurs over a period of years. This does *not* make a young girl feel desirable. She recognizes the exploitative and damaging nature of such behavior even though she may be given rewards for enduring it. And the net effect of such exploitation is to make her feel contaminated and debased. Often such girls turn in desperation to their mothers to report what has happened, and often they are met by anger and denial on the mother's part, especially if the mother is totally dependent on the father who is being accused.

When a patient of mine reported sexual abuse to her mother, the mother's reaction was to begin accusing the girl of being a tramp if she put on lipstick or asked for high-heeled shoes, hardly suspect behavior in an adolescent girl eager to grow up. The mother was attempting to support her denial of the father's behavior by projecting blame onto her daughter for anything connected with sexual interest or sexual maturity.

A young woman who arrives at this time in her life having already developed masochistic tendencies will probably view the onset of menstruation with fear, the same way she views nearly everything. If, on top of this, her parents treat her cruelly or make accusations that further diminish her self-esteem, she will commence her life as a mature female with additional burdens of fear and a greatly increased inclination toward masochism.

The menarchal research I mentioned earlier was a study of premenstrual tension and the mother-daughter relationship. It is generally acknowledged that a large number of women suffer premenstrual tension, some estimating the proportion at 70 percent, my own study indicating it to be as high as 85 percent. By premenstrual tension I mean that wide variety of symptoms that includes feelings of tension, irritability, and quarrelsomeness; swelling of body parts (this is physiological, not psychological); headache (which may be either physiological or psychological), nausea, and vomiting; depression; hunger; desire for sweets; extreme lassitude; a tendency to cry easily; and a wish to call mother.

Because I found there was a virtual absence of any of these symptoms the first time the women in my study menstruated, I inferred that the behavior of significant persons, especially the mother, must account for the symptoms. Today the psychological connotations of PMS are being denied, and it is being ascribed almost exclusively to physiological causes. Contrary to this, I found that the mother's role in the daughter's menarchal experience was the crucial determining factor in whether or not she developed premenstrual symptoms. The following were the important elements: how the mother prepared her daughter for menstruation, her emotional and behavioral response to its occurrence in the daughter, and her other more subtly expressed attitudes toward womanhood that came to the fore at this key point in her daughter's life. A woman's menstrual periods throughout her life seem to represent a constantly recurring recapitulation of the circumstances of the first menstruation, a kind of hypnotic recreation reflecting a compulsive obedience to the demands and expectations, conscious or unconscious, of the mother. As the bodily climate is reproduced each month, so are the emotions.

Only 15 percent of the more than 100 mothers in my study reacted with joy to this sign of maturation in their daughters. An additional 25 percent responded in a generally positive, helpful way. The remainder, 60 percent, exhibited responses that were negative and damaging, and ten mothers had responses I would classify as extremely destructive. They failed to give any explanation of the meaning of menstruation, and/or they exhibited signs of annoyance, and/or they implied the girl was now in some sexual danger, and/or they failed to give help with the hygienic aspects of menstruation.

In those instances where the mothers responded joyfully to news of their daughters' first menstruation, and had adequately prepared their daughters for its onset, thirteen out of fifteen were free of any symptoms of premenstrual tension. In all those instances where women suffered seriously disturbing signs of premenstrual distress, there was either no preparation by the mother for the onset of menstruation or harmful action by the mother on being informed of it. Women in the former group made these remarks: "My mother was thrilled at having a grown daughter. She had prepared me with the necessary equipment and now showed me how to use it." "Mother said joyfully I had become a woman. She brought me flowers." Women in the latter group volunteered the following: "I had great difficulty telling my mother—I left the house to feel comfortable." "My mother told me if a man came near me I could get pregnant. I felt enormous fear." "My mother slapped me and called it the curse. I got no help from her. Somehow I adjusted." It is easy to see that the women in these two groups might grow up to be very different kinds of people, the former assured and unafraid, the latter fearful and vulnerable.

Women whose mothers responded negatively described their reactions to menstruation with the following words: fear, panic, embarrassment, bewilderment, resentment, alarm, terror. These reactions were occasioned not by the appearance of the blood itself but by the mother's response to its appearance. Negative terms, such as "the curse," reflect how damaging such negative responses can be.

Psychiatric News reported in its June 1983 issue that Dr. Uriel Halbreich of the Albert Einstein College of Medicine compared some forms of premenstrual problems to mild depressive disorders, especially the dysphoric changes, such as anxiety, the tendency to overeat, and so on. I believe this confirms my research findings because at the heart of depressive problems is object loss, the loss of the love of a significant person, leaving a feeling of bereavement that is characteristic of many premenstrual responses.

The symptoms of premenstrual tension have specific meanings that can be divided into two main categories. The first includes symptoms like hunger, need for love, craving for sweets, wish to call mother, depression, and weepiness. These suggest feelings of helplessness and vulnerability, emotional hunger, and a yearning for love. The second category, including such symptoms as irritability, tension, headache, anger, quarrelsomeness, nausea, and vomiting, suggests the need to defend against anticipated attack. Nausea and vomiting are also sometimes expressions of anger that say symbolically "I cannot contain it." Both categories suggest the cornerstones of the masochistic personality: helplessness, vulnerability, defensiveness, hidden rage, passivity.

It is natural for a certain amount of anxiety to accompany the menarche. It is a first experience of something unknown. It heralds the possibility of motherhood and, like all creative experiences, is linked with a kind of vulnerability. But the degree of anxiety, the extent of its perpetuation, and the sense of self with which a young woman emerges from this period depend to a great extent on the nature of the mother-daughter relationship. The onset of menstruation is a time at which there is great potential for enhancement or impairment of a girl's ego, especially in relation to her femininity, her approaching womanhood. A mother like the one in "Scarlet Ribbons," who is loving, accepting, reassuring, will surely give her daughter the gift of enhancement.

7

Sexual
Masochism

The term *sexual masochism* conjures up for many people visions
of whips and chains, bondage and flagellation, de Sade and
Krafft-Ebing. They think of cruelty connected with sexual activity, the need to have pain inflicted by a sexual partner. And this
form of extreme sexual masochism exists, of course. But it is a
small part of the picture. Of greater interest to me, and far more
prevalent—if less spectacular—is the everyday variety of sexual
masochism, the reflection in the sexual sphere of the passive,
power-fearing, suffering personality.

Sexual expression and experience are a distillate of the total
person. A woman's essence is articulated in the sexual aspect of
her life, just as it is in her family life, her working life, and her
social relationships. In the sexual area, it may even express itself
in its purest form because the intimacy of the sexual connection
tends to highlight behavior and make it particularly intense. A
woman who in general behaves masochistically and who operates
from the defensive stance of the masochistic communication style
will surely suffer from masochism in her sexual life. It is part and
parcel of the same damaging conduct that pervades every other
area of her life.

When considering this subject, I always think of the song by
Carly Simon called "I Haven't Got Time for the Pain." The song
reveals a lifetime of suffering and pain and a desire to overcome it
through a relationship with a new sexual partner. In the lyrics,
the line, "*Suffering* was the only thing that made me feel alive" is

a clear statement of someone beset by masochistic tendencies. And, "That's just how much it cost to survive in this world" implies recognition of the high price that masochism exacts. The singer, declaring that she hasn't got time or room or need for the pain, wishes to leave her masochism behind. The only catch in this song, the only fallacy, is that she thinks this transformation will occur through a liaison with another man. To be literal about the song lyrics, that's highly unlikely. What is more probable is that her destructive patterns will come into play in the new relationship and, sooner or later, she will find herself crying herself to sleep over *him*.

Theoretically, when a man and woman meet they are equal. But if one of them is masochistic, as they begin to express their personalities, as they begin to interact with one another, the power situation quickly becomes loaded in favor of the non-masochist. One person (and, as we have seen, this is nearly always the woman) begins to surrender power, the other to acquire it. As the relationship progresses, this disparity becomes more and more extreme; the equation between the two becomes like a scale that is imbalanced: heavily weighted with power on one side, light with weakness and fear of power on the other. In other words, the relationship does not alter the basic personality patterns of the participants; it reflects, and sometimes accentuates, those patterns.

The slide into inequality can be set in motion the moment a man and woman first come into contact with each other. A beautiful, capable young woman who ran her own business received a phone call from a man she'd met on vacation months earlier and liked very much. When he suggested they get together, she immediately invited him to come to dinner although she was exhausted from a long day's work. Already she was responding masochistically and beginning to tip the power scales in his favor. Why didn't she wait to see what he had in mind? Why did she immediately volunteer to make a special effort? Since she was tired, it might have been nicer for them to go out. When he asked her at the end of the evening if he might spend the night, she said, "Well, I've been waiting since July for you to kiss me," a piece of information she might better have kept to herself. The sex that occurred that night was not particularly satisfying to her.

Fearful that she might not hear from him (worrying perhaps that since she had not enjoyed the sex, neither had he), she called the next weekend to say that she was having some friends over and asked if he would join them for dinner. He did and again he spent the night. The next day he suggested that when they went the following weekend to their summer places, which were near each other, they might go riding, a thought that delighted her. But a few days later he called to say he had studying and other things to do and would not be able to make it. She volunteered to come to his place instead so he would not have to interrupt his studying—yet another offer to put herself out. He agreed and said that if she would shop for dinner, he would reimburse her and cook dinner. Instead of graciously accepting his offer to share in the work, she said she had some leftovers and she would bring them along so that he would not have to cook. The next morning he told her that he did not want to get seriously involved with her. She was devastated.

Even in today's relatively free atmosphere, this woman was *too* eager, *too* willing, *too* compliant, *too* giving, and all of this *too* soon. Her eagerness to subordinate herself signaled how little self-worth she had. She went out of her way to let this man know that she considered herself a leftover, just like the food she provided. And I would imagine he found her behavior absolutely engulfing from the very beginning as she almost literally poured herself over him, revealing her lack of a sense of limits. Had this relationship continued, it is easy to see what the power alignment would have been.

In the following instance, the inequities in power were also established early on. At the end of their first date, which had been delightful, the young man escorted the young woman home in a taxi. As they rode along, he took her hand in his and held it on his lap. This was some years ago, before the "sexual revolution," and she was extremely uncomfortable when she recognized that she was touching an erect penis. But, despite her embarrassment, she did not dare to pull her hand away. "What if I'm wrong?" she thought. "What will he think of me?" This couple married quite quickly, and the marriage was a lengthy one marked by a decidedly sado-masochistic style and an eventual ending in wife-battering, marital rape, and, finally, none too soon for her sake, divorce. Looking back, it is clear to see that the power lines were drawn on that first date when she conveyed the message: I'll go along; I won't rock the boat; I'll do whatever you like; you're the one in charge here.

I have noted how women's history and acculturation have conditioned them for a masochistic role, and nowhere is this clearer than in the sexual area. Until quite recently, women were supposed to be virginal at the time of their marriage, and this lack of experience led them to suffer from sexual ignorance. They simply were not knowledgeable about sexual matters. This, in turn, caused them to feel that they had no rights in the sexual encounter. Both women and men operated on the assumption that it would be men who called all the sexual shots. Women felt it incumbent upon them to capitulate in this area, as in so many others; they were instructed to defer to their husbands.

Until the last several decades, marriages were often based on economic necessity, the desire to get ahead in the world rather than on any attraction that existed between two people; and women were often in the position of bartering themselves sexually for the sake of financial or social advantage. It was important for a woman to try to please or win over—certainly not to challenge—any man who seemed a good potential husband. This sort of pragmatic arrangement did nothing to allay their sexual fears. The severe inequities of power from which women suffered were made even worse in the sexual area by the addition of fear and ignorance.

These circumstances have affected female sexual responses in many ways, the most important among them being that they have deflected women's attention away from their own needs and feelings and directed it toward the pleasing of men. (This accounted for the large numbers of "frigid" women in the past, an unfair and entirely erroneous description that reflects the male viewpoint. More accurate terms might have been "impotent" or "unresponsive.") Women have obscured their own responses to such a degree that it is often difficult for them to determine what is an authentic sexual response and what is not. This uncertainty has not been helped by all the "experts" who have weighed in publicly and volubly with their notions of what women *should* want, prefer, and expect.

Pornography is a growing cultural force that continues to reinforce women's belief that the sexually masochistic role is rightly and properly theirs. Pornographic films and photographs generally show the woman serving the man, by definition a display of unequal power: The woman follows the man's dictates, does things that please him. Pornography also increasingly shows men hurting women in the course of sexual activity, tying them up, hitting them, attacking them in some violent way. And this is extremely destructive to women, lending support to the idea that they are inferior, that they have no right to say what they would like in a sexual relationship.

The extent to which women can be made to subscribe to such injurious views was evident in a recent "Letter to the Editor" column in *Ms.* magazine. Several letters responded to an earlier letter from a woman who said she enjoyed being spanked by her husband. More than one of the letters echoed this excerpt: "Unmarried, I have shared this desire [to be paddled] with only one boyfriend, and the results have been consistently terrific. When we tried role reversal of this particular activity, it turned neither of us on."

Sexual impotence in a woman is the ultimate expression of sexual masochism. When this condition exists, a woman has in effect castrated herself; she has rendered herself incapable of sexual response out of fear: a general all-pervasive fear of the other person, fear of his sexual desires, fear of asserting herself and refusing him what he wants, fear of asserting herself and requesting what would give her pleasure. These fears are a part of all expressions of sexual masochism in women, although they don't always lead to such a devastating result. Present in a less virulent form, these same fears make women feel that they must go along with whatever men want sexually, that they must put their own preferences aside. Whenever a woman does that, she is behaving masochistically. Sexual impotence may also reflect the fact that a woman has (for nonsexual reasons) chosen a man who does not appeal to her or who does not try to win her over in the sexual realm but is only concerned with himself.

Also at the extreme end of the continuum of sexually masochistic behavior was a patient of mine who was very hypnotizable and had gone to see a hypnotist for help with an obesity problem. She ended up working for him without salary and also became his compliant sexual partner. Therapy rescued her from this relationship, but she soon took up another man who had an especially disturbing sexual style: As orgasm was impending, he liked to put his hands around her throat and squeeze. Fortunately, in treatment with me, she was able to extricate herself from this relationship before anything seriously harmful occurred. But obviously the potential for violence was present throughout her association with this man, and she submitted to living with that threat.

Another patient of mine who exhibited very masochistic sexual behavior had actually been taught to be masochistic by the sadistic actions of her parents. They abused her mightily as a child and sometimes had kept her chained to her bed for as long as a week at a time. As an adolescent, she met men in the streets and went home with anyone who asked her. Sometimes she would have a brief sexual encounter with her pickup and leave. On a few occasions she was held prisoner for several days, being used and abused sexually before managing to escape. From none of these experiences did this young woman, who was a very isolated, alienated human being, derive any sexual pleasure. Her sexual involvements were a form of punishment, something her parents had taught her she deserved. The involvements obviously suggested that she felt herself to be utterly worthless, a piece of refuse. I think it is also possible, sad to say, that she gleaned some meager feelings of companionship from these encounters and that she paid for the momentary, fragmentary sense of relationship with sex. In any case, the punishment she absorbed was a high price indeed.

Masochistic women are wound-gatherers; they accumulate hurts, injuries, sorrow. In the sexual area, these are women who often manage to contract one venereal disease after another (a patient of mine once described herself as having "crotch rot"); they are women who need to have repeated abortions. They collect sexual wounds. The "crotch-rot" woman, by the way, was married to a very authoritarian man who constantly issued orders to her (which she willingly followed). When she left him she became involved with a succession of minor gangsters.

Caroline was a brilliant, attractive young lawyer who came to me in an extremely depressed state shortly after having an abortion. Her pregnancy had resulted from a sexual relationship with a married man who had been a law school classmate and had ended up in the same firm as she. This man had always been given to making sardonic and disparaging remarks at Caroline's expense, and she had felt he did not like her. Nevertheless, when they one day found themselves alone in a conference room, he locked the door and they had sex on the long table in the center of the room. Caroline did not experience any real pleasure from this, but the occurrence turned out to be the start of an ongoing arrangement. They never saw each other anywhere else; he still never had a kind word for her; they just met every so often in the conference room and had sex. Caroline submitted to this perfectly extraordinary behavior even though she found it humiliating. When she discovered she was pregnant, she did not tell him, for she knew he would either ridicule her and/or deny that the child was his.

Those people who need to have pain inflicted in order to participate sexually are seriously neurotic. My feeling is that they must have had a connection established during childhood between pain and erotic sensation. A woman reported, for example, that she liked to be shaken and slapped as a way of initiating sexual foreplay, which then soothed, comforted, and ultimately aroused her. When the rough handling was absent, she didn't enjoy the foreplay and became aroused very slowly. This is another example of how problems that occur in the sexual area are rarely purely sexual. This woman was reenacting, in transferential fashion, a prevailing condition of her early relationship with her mother whose style was to alternate punishment and beating with remorseful embracing and seductive forgiveness. I would also venture to say that women who exhibit this pattern, and it is not an uncommon one, seldom experience true sexual excitement. It is more likely that they make a trade-off: acceptance of pain in return for physical closeness and a semblance of attention that they might not receive any other way.

More minor expressions of sexual masochism occur when, for instance, a woman avoids initiating sex because she fears the man will think ill of her or, perhaps, ridicule her. To wait always for the man to initiate sex is self-punishing. If a woman feels she can never refuse sex, regardless of how she feels, this is self-punishing in a different way and constitutes another example of fear-ridden, masochistic behavior.

During sexual contact, if a woman would like to be kissed and held first but fears to request physical affection and foreplay, knowing that the man is eager to get directly to the sexual point, this is sexual masochism. If she prefers a particular position during sexual intercourse but does not dare ask for it, that is another manifestation of the same destructive syndrome. It is masochistic when a woman is afraid to discuss contraception with a man or to question someone she does not know well about venereal disease. In short, when a woman would like some change in the sexual encounter but does not dare request it, or when she would like some information but fears to demand it, then she is exhibiting sexually masochistic behavior. Clearly I do not mean that a woman should *always* have her way. But she is certainly entitled to it some of the time.

One would think that sexual masochism might be less prevalent in nonmarital relationships than it is within marriage, which carries with it certain obligations and demands, foremost among them the consent to a sexual relationship. Women engaging in sex outside of marriage should in a sense be freer, more able to exert their free will. Yet I have been interested and distressed to observe over and over again that once a sexual relationship is established, unmarried women adopt the most negative aspects of the behavior of married women: They become afraid to assert themselves sexually, they assign their own sexual interests a low priority, and they capitulate to the expectations of their male partner, even though they are under no obligation to do so. They are as quick to negate themselves sexually as are women bound by marriage.

Eileen came to New York to be near her lover, who was a medical student in the city. She, like so many of the young women I have described, was a bright, attractive person with a good job. When I first began seeing her, she was eager to hide the destructive nature of her relationship with the young man, and only gradually did its extreme inequity become clear. Because the boy was studying hard, it was understood that he would not come to Eileen's apartment to pick her up when they went out, nor would he call ahead and state a time when they might see each other. She was simply to be available, sexually and in every other way, whenever he was free. He would call, for example, half an hour before show time and say, "I want to see such-and-such a movie. Can you come?"

There was never any caring involved in their sexual contact. They had intercourse when they were together because that was when he had time. The sex was all right, she said, when I questioned her about it. I took this to mean that he probably did what he wanted to do sexually, and since it did not really offend or irritate her, and she got a little affection from it, she considered it "all right." She certainly did not experience much pleasure, however, and my guess would be that she was not orgastic, although she would never say so directly. Despite the paucity of regard, tenderness, or satisfying sex involved in this relationship, Eileen hung onto it tenaciously.

In an article called "Masochism in Love and Sex" in the *American Journal of Psychoanalysis*, Dominick A. Barbara questions why masochistic women let themselves be used sexually in relationships with men who treat them badly. His explanation, a correct one, I believe, emphasizes the masochistic longing for surrender and notes that in sex, of course, one merges with another person. The relationship between this yearning and the unresolved symbiosis to mother, or another significant adult, is obvious. The masochistic person seeks to return to the symbiotic state via sex, fantasizing that if she submerges herself in another, if she becomes part of him, she will feel safe and he will love her.

Something that I have long considered almost a diagnostic sign of masochism is the almost involuntary need to cry immediately after orgasm.

In an earlier chapter, I described crying as a masochistic message and mythology offers ample evidence that this has existed in women for a very long time. Niobe was a mother in Greek mythology who was punished for maternal pride—she declared her children to be like gods—by having her children slain. When this occurred she wept so copiously that her tears turned her to stone. She reminds us, of course, of Lot's wife, an obviously dependent, masochistic woman who was unfairly accused of looking back at Sodom and Gomorrah for salacious reasons. A poet I know has tried to set the record straight.

Women

Like Lot's wife
nameless
and forced
to leave her homeland
I know now
she looked back
having no way to look ahead.

Too long has the world
insisted
a willful curiosity
turned her head—
not even suspecting
unconquerable
ties to home.

But even this was
half truth:
the rest—that
no road opened.

She and I
sisters
could not move on
nor has history
recorded
it was torrents of tears
transformed us
to
pillars of salt.

Involuntary tearfulness speaks of a woman's lack of identity, her sense of worthlessness, her feeling that she is nameless, faceless, that she must follow her partner's dictates, accepting whatever he does or says. Her orgastic release leaves her feeling even more helpless and vulnerable than usual, and her tears are a plea that she not be attacked in her defenseless state and that he extend some sympathy and understanding to her at this moment when things between them ought to be tender.

Fantasy can play an important role in the sexual life of the masochistic woman. Coital fantasy, it should be noted, generally serves a diametrically opposed purpose in men and in women. Men usually employ fantasy in order to *engage* in sex despite problems; women use it to help themselves to *submit* to sex where it seems unavoidable. Harry Stack Sullivan used the term "long-circuiting" to describe the process of taking a complicated series of steps, like a lengthy detour, to achieve an end one is incapable of attaining directly and simply. And that describes very well the way many masochistic women use sexual fantasies. They need the assistance of an often elaborately constructed story to enable them either to tolerate something that is intolerable or to perform something that without the fantasy would be impossible. Such a story, encompassing many complicated steps toward a simple end, might be that the woman imagines herself a princess who has been brought into the grand hall of a majestic palace in order to be initiated into the rites of love. The initiation begins with many men in a variety of splendid costumes playing with the woman, teasing and exciting her, and ends with the men having intercourse with her.

The notion of being a passive, almost lifeless performer in the sexual act is at the heart of most masochistic sexual fantasies. Women fantasize themselves being bound or restrained in some way so that they have no ability to assert themselves sexually or to refuse the sexual involvement in the first place. Sometimes these fantasies extend to being raped or, in the most extreme cases, being raped and tortured. The latter, of course, indicates severe pathology. But the former, and more common, fantasy is simply another part of the masochistic stance I have been exploring. It grows out of that same sense of guilt and fear that the masochistic woman feels about virtually everything in her life. In this instance, she is guilty about her sexual desires and fearful of acknowledging them. After all, mother or father or both parents, those forbidding authority figures, would not approve. So the masochistic woman long-circuits that disapproval by concocting a fantasy that robs her of her own volition. When she is bound or restrained, when she is forced to submit to rape, there is no question of free will; she cannot be held responsible for her sexual involvement; she is, in effect, the man's victim—helpless, passive, compliant. In this way, via the extraordinary human capacity for rationalization, she can have her cake and eat it too.

The sexual fantasies of masochistic women sometimes become highly elaborated, reflecting the grandiose aspect of masochism that makes the masochistic person think all eyes are focused on her, that she is the center of the universe. They also frequently include the princess figure: The woman fantasizes herself a royal personage and thus special; she imagines that many people are serving her, that her clothing and her appearance are beautiful. If she feels extremely special, that balances the sense of defective ego and worthlessness from which she suffers. Rape occurs in many sexually masochistic fantasies not only because it allows the victim a completely passive role but also because it permits sex under violent, cruel, and painful circumstances. The masochistic person's need to receive punitive treatment expresses itself in this way during sexual relations. Not surprisingly, rape fantasies may frequently occur in women who have been the victims of sexually violent behavior within their own families. Their first sexual experiences were violent and abusive ones, and these elements are incorporated in their fantasies.

The sexual fantasies of masochistic women have another curious and, unfortunately, predictable element. They almost always focus on the woman imagining how she can make herself more desirable, more appealing, to the man. She turns herself into a princess; she glorifies her appearance. Virtually never does she envisage what she would find desirable in a male partner. In her fantasies she attempts to idealize herself, but she tends to include the man pretty much as he is. Of course there are exceptions, such as the woman who imagined herself a princess being sexually aroused by princes. But even in that instance the emphasis was on the woman's passive submission to the things that were being done to her. The princes were incidental, nothing very much more than the instruments of her initiation. This stress on being desirable so as to appeal to a man has interfered with women's true expression of their sexuality and taken the focus off what it is *they* find arousing, what it is *they* desire sexually. I am not denying that a woman must arouse desire in a man for true consummation of the sexual act. But the emphasis on physical appearance as an avenue to arousal has been exaggerated. Other factors are involved as well.

Most women in our culture probably suffer from some sort of sexual masochism because women generally have been led away from their own notions of authentic sexual response and had imposed on them, by the media as well as by professionals, a set of sexual standards to which they are told they should aspire. It is as though they have been handed sexual thermometers, told what temperature they should run, and instructed to check frequently to see how they are doing. Of course this is fallacious, and the result is to put more and more distance between women and their true sexual selves.

The only real indicator of authentic sexual expression is what is going on in the person, and being in touch with that requires introspection and self-awareness. It cannot be dictated from out-side. All living creatures are in a sense worlds unto themselves, containing within them knowledge of their behavioral and physiological functions and a sense of when these functions are operating properly. If a dog breaks a leg, you don't have to tell it not to walk; it knows that it can't. It gets along fine without the benefit of expert opinion, operating instead from instinct that lets it know when something unhealthy has happened. Human beings have higher perceptive and cognitive levels, but they also contain within themselves the maximum amount of information about their own proper functioning. Women have been led to abandon this in the sexual area. They are singular beings trying to accom-modate themselves to general standards, with disastrous results.

In the past there was a greater belief in selectivity, a greater premium put on individual tastes. All women were not thought to find beefy, muscular men (the "hunks," as they are currently billed) attractive; all men were not expected to respond uniformly to a certain shape and size of breast (every woman did not have to be a "10" to be deemed worthy of attention). But gradually our own individual cues about what is sexually appealing are being eradicated. A woman used to know whether or not she wanted to kiss a particular man. Today, if he looks a certain way, if they are in a certain situation, she *presumes* that she wants to kiss him and she acts on that presumption.

This absence of sexual autonomy is reflected, for example, in a play like Neil Simon's *The Last of the Red-Hot Lovers*, in which an attractive woman involves herself in a sexual escapade with a dull, uninviting fish store owner who perpetually smells of fish and is married besides. I see it reflected also in what used to be called the May/December romance but might now more aptly be called the *April*/December syndrome because older men are get-ting involved with ever-younger women. Of course there is a trade-off involved in such a liaison, and the woman gets some-thing from it as well as the man. However, I believe it is masochistic on the woman's part, because a sexual relationship with such age disparity goes against natural human inclinations.

Adam and Eve were roughly the same age, whatever it was. And until quite recently relationships with a large age gap were exceptional.

The belief that it is all right not to have sex with a man if you don't feel like it has been chipped away at. The dilution of this belief and of individual cues certainly prepares the ground for sowing the seeds of sexual masochism. Women increasingly, I think, are doing things sexually that they do not want to do, submitting themselves to the power of their sexual partner, or partners, and their sexual autonomy is the casualty. They hew to external guidelines, ignoring their own feelings, moving further and further away from them until these authentic indicators vanish altogether. Holding out for what one wants, feeling powerful enough to be assertive about what one wants, constitutes true autonomy. But there is precious little of this being practiced by women today.

The great orgasm debate of a few years ago certainly highlighted the conflict between individual cues and "expert" opinion and illustrated as well the idea of the sexual thermometer, that gauge women were told they should regularly and rigorously consult. (Few people realize that Masters of Masters and Johnson, the "gods" of the sexual response arena, began his work studying the masturbatory habits of prostitutes. Perhaps this showed something about sexual physiology, but it had little to do with intercourse in which involvement with another person and feelings and responses to him are present.) Women's sexual responses were being debated, and out of the argument came more of those general standards: Women *should* feel this, they *should not* feel that, if they felt this it was real, if they felt that it was false, and so on. I could not help thinking as the discussion raged how unnecessary it would all be if women had not suffered such estrangement from their own feelings. For a woman who experiences authentic orgastic response needs no outside reassurance that what she felt was real or superior or legitimate. She knows what is genuine and what is not. But when a woman deserts this knowledge of herself, when she abandons her own preferences in favor of those espoused by a book on sexual techniques or a film or an "expert," when she relinquishes her sexual autonomy, in other words, then she is behaving in a sexually masochistic fashion.

8

Sado-Masochistic
Partnership

On a recent warm day, as I walked in a New York City park, I watched some people playing tennis, and I was reminded of the tennis analogy I had used to describe certain masochistic communications. One of the mixed-doubles players was a man who was built like a tank. Extremely compact, with virtually no protrusions destroying the solid line of his body (his nose did not even seem to break the plane of his face), he looked as though he could resist any assault upon him. His form was quite poor: He played aggressively, pushing the ball over the net with a vicious, slashing motion, rather than swinging easily and stroking it. But there was obviously something in his behavior that rattled the other players, even though they were superior, and he repeatedly came out on top. Somewhat later in a singles match with a man who was also a better player, his aggressive tactics became even more pronounced. He charged each ball as if hitting it were a matter of life and death, pounding it into the corners of the court, making no pretense whatever at playing a friendly game that might be made enjoyable by volleying a bit. And gradually the other, better player became demoralized and began to lose. This, I thought, is exactly what happens between a masochistic person and a sadistic one, most especially in a marriage. The masochist may be better equipped in all sorts of ways, but as the sadist exercises his abusive skills, those advantages are nullified. The masochist, as she succumbs over and over again to the power of the other, becomes more and more inept and self-destructive.

Nowhere are the effects of the historical and cultural forces that predispose women toward masochism more keenly realized than in marriage. St. Paul's epistle to the Ephesians, echoing the passage I cited earlier from St. Peter, lays the groundwork for the inequities that often exist between husbands and wives. "Wives," Paul writes, "*submit* [italics added] yourselves unto your husbands, as unto the Lord." The submission Paul speaks of is primarily sexual, but lest there be any doubt that it also includes all other areas of marital life, he adds: "For the husband is the head of the wife, even as Christ is head of the church." "Head," in this context, has more than one symbolic meaning: The husband is the ruler of the wife, the one who possesses power over her; he is also the thinker, the one with brains enough for both of them. Although Paul softens his admonition somewhat by directing husbands to "love your wives, even as Christ also loved the church, and gave himself for it," he exhorts wives to *revere* their husbands in addition to loving them, another indication of the higher level on which the man is placed. I cannot help but feel that Paul gave a substantial push to the sado-masochistic marriage with the arrangement he outlined (and, of course, he had plenty of help from others). For bestowing the gift of power on one partner and withholding it from the other virtually guarantees that a great inequity will exist between them. The fact that husbands are often sadistic and wives masochistic stems from the unequal power balance in marriage. The sado-masochistic marriage is characterized by an ongoing battle between the two parties as they engage in a kind of primitive struggle for power.

I once overheard a group of single men talking about women and one of them said, "Women tend to gravitate toward men who treat them badly. I have a great deal of trouble understanding this." Probably he could not understand simply because he was a man. The early, heavy weight of acculturation toward submissiveness that women receive would be incomprehensible to him. But what may have eluded him as well was the notion of the repetition compulsion, that tendency to engage in relationships with people in the present who bear a psychic resemblance to significant and powerful figures of the past.

It is a common psychoanalytic mistake to believe that people marry someone reminiscent of the parent of the opposite sex. My view is that people generally marry a surrogate for the more powerful parent, the parent whose behavior has had the greatest impact on them. The sex of that parent is irrelevant. Masochists tend to marry surrogates for the more dangerous, hurtful parent. Meeting a man who evokes the repetition compulsion, the masochistic woman deludes herself into thinking he is strong. She knows herself to be weak, she admires strength, and she believes she has found it in him. What she sees as strength is most likely the same kind of coldness or cruelty that existed in her damaging parent.

A patient gave the following description of how she perceived her husband when she first met him. "He was quite noncommunicative, but I thought that indicated he was self-contained, self-sufficient. I admired this. I thought it meant he was strong." In fact, her husband turned out to be an extremely brutal man who was incapable of true, intimate interaction. And in many ways he resembled the patient's mother—who had held her daughter captive for years.

Psychoanalyst Reuben Fine said that a sado-masochistic marriage does not begin as a love affair, but as a *hate* affair. It generally is of long duration, often lasting a lifetime, and becomes the center of the psychic lives of both partners, with each seeing the other as the enemy. Fine noted that both people involved in a hate affair are extremely dependent. Neither has resolved the symbiotic attachment to mother; neither has firm boundaries. They become part of each other, clinging to the attachment, unable to give it up despite its destructiveness. This suggests that what they fear most is not being attached to another person. Men may function well sexually in such a relationship because the sexual activity is allied to rape in its hostility. A man in a hate affair may have the fantasy of destroying the woman, and that fantasy will give him potency, Fine said. One woman cited had the fantasy of the man's penis breaking off inside her. Obviously her goal was destruction of the man. Interestingly, the superegos of both partners involved in such a relationship are similar. They have harsh, punitive consciences and tend to project all blame for wrongdoing onto the other person. The relationship involved in sado-masochistic marriage is that of slave-master, Fine observed, the master being the sadist who possesses the power, the slave being the masochist who is subservient to that power and victimized by it.

This, of course, relates directly to early experience and, again, conjures up the repetition compulsion. The parent is always the powerful figure, the source of supply of all things; the child possesses little on its own and is dependent upon the parent's desire and ability to give. In a sense, this earliest relationship in life is a form of the master-slave relationship. If love is present, the power between parent and child gradually evens out, and the master-slave framework disappears. If it is not, the child suffers from the parent's coercion and may become either submissive and passive, or assaultive and destructive. The sadistic husband in a sado-masochistic marriage attempts—through cruelty, blame-projecting onto the wife, humiliating her, inciting guilt in her and sometimes even through raping her—to gain the control he did not have as a child subject to powerful, abusive parents and to destroy those early, hurtful figures. The masochistic wife— through capitulation, submissiveness, and acceptance of the premises of the husband—attempts to appease, to placate, the stern authorities who governed her early life. Both are immature, anxiety-ridden people displaying transference reactions and irrational distortions, deeply dependent on each other as partners in what one therapist has called the "choreography of unconscious dissociated tendencies."

The absorbing, all-encompassing nature of the sado-masochistic connection was illustrated in Ingmar Bergman's film *Wild Strawberries*. A doctor picks up a couple as he is driving along a road. Once in the car, the couple ignores the fact that anyone else is present, continuing the horrendous argument they were in the midst of when the doctor stopped for them. All social amenities are displaced, all notions of proper social conduct obliterated by the couple's obsessive need to continue their struggle.

One thing that keeps the partners in a sado-masochistic marriage locked together is that each one's sense of self depends upon the responses of the other. The sadistic husband develops his self-esteem by denigrating, humiliating, and criticizing his wife. The masochistic wife gleans her meager self-worth from the occasional kind, or at least nonabusive, word from her husband. Masochistic women, it has been said, pay the price of suffering in a sado-masochistic relationship in order to receive what they believe is love. I would add that a woman who has been driven by the repetition compulsion to marry a sadistic person finds it very difficult to understand the ruling negativisms of her husband's behavior. She continues to labor under the delusion that the marriage began as a love affair, not a hate affair.

The sadistic partner in such a marriage is just as wretched as his wife, although that may not be evident, since he is the one who appears to be inflicting all the wounds. His victim, the masochistic wife, is sacrificed to his need to have a companion in misery. The sadist may also show little overt evidence of the guilty feelings so prominently displayed by the masochist. But he, too, suffers from a deep sense of guilt, although it is most often unconscious, and from a need for punishment.

The sado-masochistic marriage and its detrimental effects on both partners was eloquently depicted in Federico Fellini's film *La Strada*. As a daughter reaches puberty, her mother sells her to the strongman in a traveling circus, a man neither of them knows. This relationship automatically has a masochistic inception for the daughter because she enters it filled with feelings of abandonment. Her mother's action has told her in effect that she is unloved and that her mother is willing to exploit her in order to fight against her own crushing poverty. The girl, who plays the horn, is a sensitive, tender sort, and when she and the strongman first have sex together it awakens love in her and the expectation that they will establish a close, caring union. He does not share her feelings, however, and when she learns that he has had another woman, her hurt and despair are overwhelming. She then learns that he has killed a man, and she suffers terribly from this knowledge; she attempts once to escape but finally capitulates and rejoins him; she develops a hiccough, a psychosomatic expression of her inability to contain her distress completely; she grows sicker and sicker, and he becomes correspondingly taciturn and attempts to care for her; and finally he puts her out by the side of the road and leaves her behind. When he returns to this spot some time later and inquires about her, he is told that she has died. Hearing the news, he is obviously disturbed. Most perceptively, Fellini shows that the sadistic partner in a sado-masochistic marriage is just as pitiful as the masochist and, even though he is the one doing the punishing, he is being damaged, too. The relationship ultimately destroys both people.

As the power struggle continues between partners in such a marriage, they may at times seem to reverse roles, sadistic elements expressing themselves in the woman, masochistic elements in the man. A woman who has been repeatedly degraded by her husband may decide to fight back, and when she does her attack will be fueled by rage.

A patient of mine was a sensitive woman who was subjected by her husband to constant criticism. Every so often, her anger at this would reach a certain pitch and she would erupt. Once this occurred as they were getting into bed at night. He began his litany of criticism about how she ran the house, handled money, disciplined the children, and behaved sexually. Infuriated, my patient put her feet against her husband's body and gave a shove, pushing him onto the floor. This retaliation was mild, of course, compared with some we have read about in the newspapers: Wives no longer able to suppress their rage at being abused have turned on their husbands and killed them.

Behavior of this sort is what has led to the theory that each person has both sadistic and masochistic tendencies. But I do not subscribe to this. The masochistic wife's retaliation, or eruption of rage, is more likely due to the fact that even the worm turns when it has absorbed all it can tolerate. Then the anger is such that life is no longer meaningful and any risk is acceptable. Desperation is the name of the game, not sadism.

I came across a particularly blatant example of sado-masochistic interaction in a newspaper article recounting a divorce proceeding in which the wife maintained that the main problem in the marriage was her husband's "authoritarian dominance." To say the least, I thought as I read on. The husband, a physician, disciplined his wife with a demerit system, forty demerits, for example, each time she left the patio door open. For each demerit he required that his wife give him an hour's pay. To avoid demerits he also required that she cut her hair to his specifications, lose weight, lower the pitch of her voice, become a movie buff, and take dancing lessons. As if this was not enough, the wife, during the time her husband was in medical school, had to type his papers, clean the house and cook the meals, maintain the family cars, and work to support both of them. She and her parents, the wife said, had also contributed $32,800 toward her husband's medical school expenses.

This case not only illustrates the sado-masochistic marriage in full bloom but spotlights an unhappily typical attitude of the courts as well. In granting the divorce, the judge awarded the wife $24,600 and noted that this was a "very clear case of a woman putting a guy through medical school and wanting some good back from all those years." The judge never even addressed the obvious suffering this woman had endured, or the curious system of control her husband had employed. And the monetary award was $8,000 less than she and her family had spent and did not take into account in any way all the extra work this woman had done (in and out of the home) during the time her husband was in school. Judges are all too commonly unsympathetic and unfair toward women.

Witness the recent case in Colorado in which a judge sentenced a man to two years in jail for *killing* his wife, a case that caused an enormous outpouring of protest. The man maintained that his wife provoked him into killing her by leaving their home without any warning (we have reached a sorry state indeed if every woman attempting to get away from an abusive man is required to warn him of her intentions). Obviously, the defendant's reasoning fell on sympathetic ears, despite the prosecution's evidence that there had been a history of abuse in the marriage. The furor triggered by the two-year sentence (protesters included the governor of Colorado and his wife) eventually caused the judge to reconsider—and the sentence was changed to *four* years, still making the life of the dead woman rather cheap.

Judges have also been reluctant to validate the idea of marital rape, although it certainly exists. For some time, ironically, Israel was the only country whose courts had convicted a husband of rape. Recently, a marital rape conviction was handed down in a New York state court.

Relatively minor, but deeply wounding nevertheless, was the behavior of the husband who arrived at a party separately from his wife, went around the room greeting every woman with a kiss on the lips, but when he reached his wife he turned away and did not kiss her at all. This common tactic of a sadistic husband not only evoked jealousy in her, it publicly humiliated her in a sexual way, an especially vulnerable area. This same husband refused to stop when his wife had to go to the bathroom while they were driving. When they finally arrived home and she asked him please to open the door in hurry, he refused to put the key in the lock, instead hopping about from foot to foot and taunting her about her discomfort.

Another woman reported to me that her husband's way of tearing her down was never to compliment her, no matter what she did. This woman, who was "just a housewife," said, "I work so hard to please him. I keep the house nice and I try to have a good dinner ready for him when he comes home at night, and I take good care of the children, and I try to look attractive. After all, I get no other rewards. But he refuses to comment. He never says I look nice when we're going out. The most he might ever say is that it's not a bad dinner. That's the height of his praise."

Allied to this is the "silent treatment" that some sadistic husbands give their wives. In general, women tend to be loquacious; they are meant to be the entertainers and carry the burden of social involvement. Men, on the other hand, are often more taciturn, not as likely to feel obliged to speak, knowing they maintain more control when they keep their mouths shut. But the sadistic husband may punish his wife by refusing to speak at all, for hours, days, or even weeks. Some psychoanalysts maintain in regard to the parent-child relationship that indifference, not hatred, is the opposite of love. I think that applies here as well.

Silence is one of the most painful punishments the sadist can mete out. Hatred at least contains some emotion, some passion. Indifference, conveyed by the refusal to speak, the refusal of a husband even to acknowledge his wife, says: You do not matter, you are not really there, you do not exist.

That was communicated by the behavior of Sylvia's husband on their return flight from a European vacation. A film was being shown that she had seen several times and did not want to see again. An hour or so into the flight, the husband disappeared and was gone for two hours. When he returned he told her he had been watching a different film in another part of the plane. "Why did you just disappear?" she asked, quite upset. "Why didn't you come and get me and see if I was interested in watching it too?" He just shrugged and said he hadn't thought it was important.

With this as background, Sylvia then told me of her husband's shopping habit on Sunday nights when they returned from their weekend house in the country. He never asked her what she wanted from the store, and he never bought anything extra to stock the refrigerator after their being away. He only purchased those things he liked and wanted to eat on Sunday night, and the two of them had quite different tastes.

She also recalled the time her husband had plans to meet a friend for dinner and said she was welcome to come along. She pointed out that she would have to be a little late because of her work schedule but suggested that the others have a drink first and wait for her. When she arrived she found that they had not waited for her. They had, in fact, arranged to meet even earlier and were already through with their dinner.

Her husband, Sylvia said, displayed no real warmth toward her, even during sex. He didn't kiss her, there was no foreplay, and his only communication was to ask her afterwards if it had felt good, a query she felt was a demand for her to give a report on his performance, something she resented. When she told him this, he said that she took things too personally. I wish Sylvia had been able to reply that perhaps he took things too *impersonally* and perhaps their sexual life was not gratifying because it was devoid of feeling.

Sylvia's husband also displayed his indifference toward her by disappearing on weekends to play tennis for hours at a stretch, always without consulting her about their plans, often leaving her with a completely empty weekend. His behavior transmitted the message that Sylvia's existence did not matter to him. Any one of the incidents I've mentioned might seem minor standing alone, but when this sort of behavior is woven into the fabric of a marriage, it is undeniably sadistic.

Despite elaborate exhibitions of indifference, however, husbands in these partnerships do not generally want to see the marriage break up. And to this end they develop a kind of sixth sense that tells them just how far their masochistic wives can be pushed. When a sadistic man senses that his wife's tolerance for abuse has reached its limit, he will often pull back and sometimes even do something nice to disarm her and make her feel that perhaps her reactions were exaggerated, that he was not really as mean as she thinks. This is how, with her husband's collusion, the masochistic wife manages to keep fooling herself that she loves him. She mistakes dependence for love.

The issue of money is often the focus of sado-masochistic exchanges within a marriage. This was even more common no doubt when women worked less and a husband's cruelty took the form of squeezing his wife where money was concerned. I think of a patient whose husband was a doctor with a substantial income. The allowance he gave her for years and years was fifty dollars a week, even though during that period the cost of living escalated steeply. Out of that she was supposed to feed the family, buy clothes for herself and the children, pay any entertainment costs for the family, give the children their allowances, and so on. When she objected that she could no longer manage on that amount, he told her that she was not handling the money correctly. If she were, he said flatly, fifty dollars would still be sufficient to cover her expenses.

Another battleground for the sado-masochistic power struggle is the children. The woman whose husband gave her fifty dollars a week was frequently humiliated in front of her children by her husband's countermanding her instructions to them. This conveyed the message to the children that their mother's ideas were insignificant and her discipline worthless. It bred disrespect in the children and made them potential adversaries as well—two more people who would regard her as ineffectual and helpless.

The practice of wife-swapping we heard so much about during the so-called sexual revolution is something that could only occur in a sado-masochistic marriage. The term alone makes it clear that it is something generated by the husband, something the wife would probably feel powerless to resist. When a husband insists that switching partners is acceptable and suggests it to his wife, she is faced with a choice that is really no choice at all: She can refuse and risk ending her marriage, or she can go along, knowing her husband will do it anyway, and at least she will not be left out. I believe men are aware of their wives' position when they make the suggestion. Another common occurrence when the swapping actually takes place is that the husband questions the wife afterward, simultaneously robbing her of any privacy and claiming her back, while withholding from her any information about his own experience.

I mentioned earlier the projective blaming of the mate that occurs in sado-masochistic marriages, most especially by the sadistic partner. This can cover an extremely broad spectrum of offenses, the husband holding his wife responsible for everything from his performance at work to the cut he incurred shaving in the morning. The masochistic wife, no matter how hard she works to avoid giving offense, is fighting a losing battle—for her husband's complaints frequently have little basis in reality.

A woman invited her family to Thanksgiving dinner. When the time came for the meal, she set on the table a beautifully prepared turkey on a large platter. As her husband began to carve, a piece of turkey slipped onto the table. Then he unwittingly tipped the platter slightly, so that some juice spilled from it. The moment he made these mistakes, he began loudly blaming his wife for not having used a big enough platter. His harangue ruined the dinner. He attempted, of course, to hide his own inadequacy by accusing his wife of incompetence—and perhaps he took special pleasure in doing this in front of her family.

The sadistic husband may also use physical assault and rape in his ongoing offensive against his wife. When he attacks his wife physically, however, the assault is likely to be different from that of the run-of-the-mill wife-batterer. These latter men tend to be either passive-aggressive males, who feel helpless and vulnerable themselves and react with rage and anger in interactions with their mates, or obsessive-compulsives, who explode and attack when their defenses are threatened; or men, usually paranoid, who live with congealed rage and will assault anyone close to them.

Usually, a trivial event triggers the batterer, and his actions are never warranted by the triggering occurrence. For instance, his wife's breaking a yolk while cooking his breakfast eggs, or the first piece of birthday cake's being offered to a guest instead of him may send him into a battering fury. Wives have reported that wearing a ponytail or saying they did not like the pattern of the wallpaper resulted in beatings. Or the wife herself may not do anything, as in a case I know of in which a man beat his wife because his driver's license had been suspended. These triggering actions are simply pegs on which to hang the hat of rage.

The sadistic husband, on the other hand, uses a beating as just one of many weapons he wields against his wife in his campaign to destroy her. His attacks are not heated but calculated. On the surface, while administering this punishment, he will seem neither irrational nor out of control and unbalanced. His manner is more likely to be marked by icy calm. Any resort to brute force, of course, signals that the husband's resources are taxed to the limit. It also indicates that he is insistent on employing power as a means of resolving differences: His wife *must* defer—he *must not* compromise.

Certain special problems, most especially addictions, also add to the probability of a husband's becoming assaultive. If the husband is alcoholic, for example, he is particularly dangerous, because rage is a component of his personality and, while he may drink to anesthetize the rage, the effect is to increase it, making assault more likely. The narcotics addict, on the other hand, is not likely to be a threat when he is high, but when he begins to withdraw and needs a fix, he is given to explosive rages and can become very dangerous.

Marital rape, which exists whenever a wife is coerced into having sexual relations against her wishes, can also be an element in the sado-masochistic power struggle. In some marriages it may constitute the basic sexual style and occur quite frequently; in others it may happen rarely and perhaps serve as an indication of a severe crisis in the relationship. In a marriage illustrative of the former condition, the husband was crude, impulse-driven, and cruel, the wife sensitive and friendly. She chose a man who was a replica of the father who had belittled and ridiculed her; he behaved like his domineering, threatening, aggressive mother. His sexual behavior was always sadistic, forcing relations without his wife's consent. He had long ago identified with the aggressor and now behaved as one himself. Another patient whose marriage has been decidedly sado-masochistic but free of assault and rape found that those elements entered in as the deterioration escalated. She and her husband were at a party and when he did not introduce her to some people he knew and she asked why not, he got angry and walked away from her. At home later that evening, he beat her up for the first time in their lengthy marriage. The next day she went to a lawyer. He said she still seemed to love her husband and suggested that perhaps she was not really ready to leave him. She returned home although she was extremely fearful. But when, a few months later, her husband raped her, she visited the lawyer again and ended the marriage.

This same woman, looking back on her marriage, expressed puzzlement that the sexual area had not been troubled by difficulties until the end. "The sex was pretty good," she said, "and that's hard to understand in light of the problems between us." What she did not realize, until she uncovered it in treatment, was that it was the potency of rape, not a positive, loving orientation based on mutuality, that fueled her husband's sexual performance throughout the marriage. She began to recall that her husband had refused to kiss her during lovemaking; she remembered that there was virtually no foreplay. She also told me of his habit of issuing commands at the beginning of the day. "I expect sex tonight," he would say to her as he was leaving for work. This unromantic, uninviting approach to sex also reflected his hostility to her, as did his habitual comment after they had had intercourse. "That was a good one, wasn't it?" he would say, referring to his prowess rather than to anything mutually gratifying that had happened between them. Even if the sex had been satisfying for her, this was his way of obliterating any pleasure she might have felt. That he was also frequently involved with other women was something she managed to deny to herself until she left him.

Sometimes the sadistic husband may literally become murderous. One thinks of Claus von Bülow, sentenced to twenty years in prison for the attempted murder of his wealthy wife, appealing his conviction but still living free in society. A patient of mine, whose husband did not precisely fit the profile of the murderous exploiter but who was a bona fide sadist nevertheless, recounted to me how her husband took out double indemnity insurance on her life before they were to take a trip to Europe. On two separate occasions he attempted to maneuver her close to the edge of a cliff so that he could push her over. Once her own instincts saved her; the second time the fortuitous arrival of other tourists caused him to back off.

As I have said, the repetition compulsion is the basis for these marriages. But how do they evolve into such extreme situations? What is the process that takes place? Even when a woman makes a poor choice and picks a sadistic man, things can't be all that bad, all that unequal, at the outset. How do they get that way? When I say that the masochistic wife bears a major share of the responsibility for the negative direction the marriage takes, I want to be clear that I am not *blaming* her. I am simply attempting to describe what occurs in a sado-masochistic partnership. Because the wife is fearful of standing up to her husband, fearful of asserting herself and making her own wishes, needs, and opinions clear, she adopts a submissive stance, capitulating to her husband at every turn. As she succumbs and exhibits her fear and uncertainty, the husband's sadistic tendencies rise increasingly to the fore. The more he witnesses her fear, the more he pressures her with his cruelty. She, in response, exhibits greater and greater weakness. He, in turn, steps up his brutality. She has demonstrated to him that she will not take a stand and stick to it, that her protests, should they arise, will be hollow, that she will always, ultimately, give up and give in. Faced with such a willing and pliant victim, he cannot resist attack. And one must remember that such a woman, especially if she has children, may have no place to go if she decides to leave her sadistic husband. Until very recently, there has been little help and support from society for women in this position.

Let me cite what may seem like a minor example of the submissive, acquiescent behavior that can become so destructive when established as a pattern in a marriage. This comes from a story by Mary Kay Blakeley in the *New York Times*. Shortly after marrying, she was out shopping with her husband and saw a pint of ice cream she wanted to buy. It was a special flavor she liked and more expensive than many other brands. Her husband objected. There was no way, he said, that he would pay $1.95 for a pint of ice cream just because the box said "hand packed by Agnes." They did not get the ice cream that day and Ms. Blakeley recognized that this had something to do with the marriage vows she had taken, although she did not recall saying at the time of her marriage "I defer all ice cream judgments to you." She recognized, happily for her, that capitulating on the ice cream decision would also mean forfeiting her opinions in the areas of vacuuming, children, entertainment, sex, and so on. Ultimately, she got herself the ice cream, later recognizing that moment as the beginning of the end of her marriage. "We did not fully understand," she writes of women of her generation, "how much a husband's sense of *entitlement* and a wife's sense of *duty* reflected their decisions."

The struggle over a $1.95 pint of ice cream may seem trivial, but it is not. A woman's acquiescence on such a matter is symptomatic of much more than whether or not there will be butter pecan in the family freezer that night. Giving in on the ice cream would indicate that she has already made a crucial choice in terms of the equity of power in the marriage. It would mean that she accepted her husband's premise without questioning it, capitulating to him, letting him off the hook without objection or discussion. She would have abandoned her own rights, set aside her own desires in deference to his. By her total surrender she would have played a key part in her own victimization. Could she not say to him that she loved the ice cream, so why not indulge her now and then as she would him? After all, $1.95 was involved, not a million.

A woman need not always have her own way, of course, but the point here is to recognize when she has succumbed because she didn't dare defy her husband or assert herself. Once the balance of power begins to swing toward her husband (and it is through the accumulation of just such "trivial" incidents that this takes place) the masochistic woman becomes less and less able to stand up for her own views, the inequity between husband and wife grows progressively greater, and the marriage moves increasingly in a sado-masochistic direction.

9

Long-Suffering Wife and Mother

"Sorrow-Acre," a poignant and moving story by Isak Dinesen, describes the return to his ancestral home of Adam Rosenkrantz. Since the death of his father, the home has been owned by Adam's uncle. When Adam meets his uncle, he reports that someone has set fire to his barn, and it is believed that Goshe, a widow's son, is guilty, although he swears his innocence. Goshe is locked up. His mother, Anne-Marie, comes to the lord of the manor, Adam's uncle, to plead for her son's release. In a voice cracked from days of weeping, she maintains Goshe's innocence and begs the lord to save him. Staring out at his wheat field, the lord replies that if between sunrise and sunset she can mow the entire field, her son will go free. Anne-Marie kisses his hand in gratitude. But Adam is appalled when his uncle tells him that mowing the field is a three-day job.

The next day, as Anne-Marie begins her work in the rising heat of the day, Adam asks his uncle if he believes Anne-Marie can fulfill her bargain. She might, the uncle says, because her work is extraordinary, and he orders the bailiff to bring Goshe to the fields to see his mother struggling for his sake. As Anne-Marie advances through the fields hunched over, stumbling, hair plastered against her head with sweat, moving like a tired swimmer, people stand by watching. At one point when a young boy tries to help her, the lord calls out for him to desist. Adam finally can stand it no longer and pleads with his uncle not to force her to continue. "Do you not see she is dying?" Adam asks. He has given his word, the uncle replies. It is obvious that she is prepared to die for her son, Adam points out; is that not enough? If he were to nullify the terms now, the uncle says, Anne-Marie might feel he was making light of her feat. Adam, although he tells his uncle he can no longer sleep under his roof, is swept by a series of realizations: that his uncle has had much suffering in his own life and even watched his own son die; that all living creatures suffer; that his uncle is old and dreads death; and that to die for the one you love is an idea too sweet for words.

As sunset approaches, the old lord dresses in his brocaded court suit and goes to the fields. Anne-Marie completes her mowing, and when she sees there is nothing left, she seems confused and drops to her knees; her son drops to the ground beside her. Then the lord steps forward. "Your son is free," he declares. "You have done a good day's work, which will long be remembered." When it is obvious that Anne-Marie cannot hear him, the lord tells her sobbing son to relay the message. Collecting himself, Goshe repeats the lord's words. His mother raises her eyes to him, reaches out to touch his cheek, then slumps against his shoulder and dies. Some time later, the lord raises on the spot a stone to Anne-Marie's memory, and the peasants ever after call the field Sorrow-Acre.

This Dinesen story reflects a concept of mother love that held sway in an earlier day. At its core was the dictate that a mother would make any sacrifice for her child. And in life, as in the story, it used to be assumed that the love between mother and child was reciprocal, that the child understood and appreciated the mother's sacrifice, that the child loved the mother for her generous gift of herself.

How radically times have changed! Now it seems that perhaps there is some reason to question whether or not love begets love between mother and child, to question whether or not children generally appreciate the sacrifices made for them, even when they are freely given. Perhaps the loaded question is: How often is maternal self-sacrifice really only masochistic martyrdom, destructive to the mother and destructive to the child as well?

The poem that follows was written by a patient of mine, a

bright but quite disturbed young woman whose mother had refused to let the symbiotic tie dissolve and allow her daughter to grow up and become an independent person. It conveys, however amateurishly, the punishing consequences to the child of a mother's masochism.

> She stuffed her ears with cotton
> and violently shook her head—
> the masochistic mother with
> the blue eyes said:
>
> "I don't believe you love me
> and I'm better off dead."
>
> "Mother I love you,
> you're not better dead—
> how must I convince you?"
> I sincerely said.
>
> WELL (she said)
>
> "You must do everything I say,
> for mother's always right—
> just to tell me that you love me
> is not very bright.
>
> "You must come to me with problems,
> you must come for advice,
> and if you really love me
> you will also come at night."
>
> "I love you, mother—
> that's all I have to say,
> but I've a mind of my own—
> don't turn me away."
>
> She turned to the door,
> and dropped on the floor—
> and the masochistic mother
> with the blue eyes said:
>
> "I don't believe you love me,
> and I'm better off dead."

The mother in the poem uses her own negative feelings about herself to incite guilt in her child, an extremely damaging course to pursue and one that will more than likely cause the child herself to be masochistic.

Many masochistic mothers either imply the following or state it directly to a child: If you don't do what I ask, it will kill me. Coercing behavior in this way makes the child, who can take such a statement literally, feel responsible for hurting the parent and, as a consequence, guilty. Constant repetition of this sort of threat makes guilt all-pervasive.

The masochistic wife and mother often experiences a sense of conflict between her need to appease her husband and her obligation to her children. Whom should she strive to please? If she does not maintain control over the children and meet her sadistic husband's disciplinary standards, she risks angering him. If she hews to his standards, it may be at the expense of the children. Often her efforts to be good to her children cause her husband to become envious and angry. Infantile himself, he feels in competition with his children rather than fatherly toward them. He resents the attention she pays to them and attacks both them *and* her. Conflicted and fearful, a mother may simply abandon her authority and resort to an old dodge vis-à-vis her children: "Wait until your father comes home," she says, rather than disciplining them herself. This is a disastrous step: She yields still more of her dwindling reserves of power to her husband, loses important ground with her children, and digs herself even deeper into her masochism.

Even today, women's dependence on men increases their vulnerability. As homemakers, they are largely cut off from social contact and, in the absence of other resources, they may focus an unhealthy attention on their children, endowing them with inappropriate power. Imagine what it is like—I'm sure some of you readers know—to live in fear of your children because you cannot discipline them and in fear of your husband because he will find fault with everything you have done in the course of the day, especially in relation to the children. The more he criticizes you in front of the children, the less will they respect you and follow your orders, no matter how much you have done for them. It is truly a no-win situation. And very often, of course, the sadistic husband will play the children off against their mother, countermanding her directives, ridiculing her in front of them, doing whatever he can to erode their respect for her. As the children fall into line behind him and disregard her orders, the husband sees even more shortcomings to chastise her for.

Sociologist Judith Wallerstein, in her study of divorce, verifies that children often feel greater respect for their father and notes that this imbalance can become even more pronounced when a family splits up. Children often fantasize about and idealize the absent parent, who is usually the father, and resent the caretaker parent, more frequently the mother. Even when she has abdicated her authority before the divorce, afterward she is a single parent and must serve as disciplinarian. She may find, as she attempts to take on this role, that her children simply will not respond to her as an authority figure.

A woman with two adolescent sons was having great difficulty with her husband who was extremely critical of her. Her response to his assaults was to apologize constantly, thus inviting him to believe even more deeply that she was always wrong about everything. When it was discovered that their younger son was ill with leukemia, and advanced treatment was unavailable in the town where they lived, she arranged for a housekeeper to look after her son and her husband and traveled with her sick son to a distant medical center where chemotherapy and radiation therapy took about three months. This experience turned out to be a kind of Sorrow-Acre for her. She went through it alone, living in uprooted fashion in a hotel room, trying to keep up her son's spirits and hold herself together psychologically. Her husband called occasionally to see how their son was progressing and to complain about how things were running at home, and he visited her and their son a few times, generally seeming annoyed by everything he encountered, including the fact that she wasn't very interested in sex (he chose this period, she later learned, to become involved with another woman). During this extremely difficult time, his criticism of his wife increased, and when he was not criticizing her, he gave her the "silent treatment." She ended the marriage soon afterward, a positive step for her and one that is extremely difficult for the masochistic wife and mother to take.

A woman who was referred to me by a neurologist for a consultation was married and the mother of three daughters. She was suffering from the following symptoms: migraine headaches of increasing severity, dizziness, blackouts, blurred vision, difficulty hearing on occasion, buzzing in her ears, occasional difficulty seeing food on her plate, loss of taste sensations, weak feelings in her thighs and arms, and, on one occasion, an inability to raise herself out of a chair. The neurologist wanted to know whether I thought she was suffering from multiple sclerosis or whether her symptoms were psychological in origin. Laboratory tests had been inconclusive in regard to any neurological or brain damage.

Although uneducated, she was a bright woman who had married young (her husband was only the second man she ever dated) and immediately been subjected to explosive expressions of anger from her husband when she was reluctant to submit to his sometimes bizarre sexual behavior. He began to criticize her constantly, accusing her of being incompetent, although she worked as a bookkeeper and cared for their home and three children. He especially delighted in putting her down in front of the children, undermining her disciplinary efforts.

What were her parents like? I inquired. As a small child she had been scared to death of her father, she said. Most of the time he was punishingly silent, but he also beat her occasionally. Her mother was a timid, submissive woman. Her own marriage, it was clear, mirrored her parents'. How was she feeling right now? I asked at one point. "I've been away from the noxious source of my difficulties for the last few weeks, so I'm feeling better," she replied. This was a direct, and surprisingly incisive, acknowledgment that her problem lay in her relationship with her husband, not in any physical illness. She had chosen, however, to retreat into sickness rather than to consider leaving her husband, a common masochistic solution to a difficult problem.

This woman's experience was characteristic of the masochistic wife/mother in many ways. Her marriage represented a shift from one dependency to another, the transference of the symbiotic tie from one person to another. She never had the opportunity to develop social interpersonal ties that might have served to strengthen her enough to leave her husband or to acquire the skills she would have needed to survive on her own. Because of her tenuous sense of her own boundaries, she did not feel herself to be a separate, independent person. In addition, she suffered extensive feelings of guilt that caused her to doubt herself even further and underscored her hesitation to consider divorce: What about the children? Would she not be hurting them? How could she deprive them of their father? The consideration of whether or not he was a good father played no part in her thinking. Nor did the idea that the children might possibly be better off in a more peaceful home. She clung to her marriage, turning her anger in upon herself instead of expressing it outwardly, making herself sick and thus providing yet another rationalization for staying put: Now I'm sick . . . I can't possibly leave under these circumstances. Her masochistic anxieties and fear of the unknown outweighed the familiar misery of her current situation.

I am happy to report that this woman, however, as she began to receive support from treatment and from her own mother, who had grown more independent since the death of her husband, was able to begin confronting her situation in realistic terms. Her recognition of her husband as a damaging, "noxious" influence was not just a fleeting insight that occurred in a conversation with me. She no longer needed to deny this at such a high price to herself. And I think it is likely that she will eventually dare to leave her husband and attempt to build a new life for herself.

A seeming contrast to the brutality this woman experienced occurred in the marriage of another patient of mine. But the results were equally destructive. She had hypertension, a mild cardiac problem, and was somewhat obese. Despite these problems, she was far from being an invalid. Her husband, however, had a great need to promote her dependence on him, and he constantly stressed that she was sick and helpless; he cast himself in the role of benevolent caretaker. In social situations, he discussed her illnesses so that whenever she ran into people they always inquired, "How *are* you, Georgia?" When they traveled, he insisted that she ride in a wheelchair to the airport gate although she had no difficulty walking. "I wonder what's wrong with that poor woman?" she recalls hearing people say. He issued daily reminders to the children not to upset their mother. The result was that the children turned to him for everything, and their mother became virtually invisible to them.

Finally, feeling quite desperate, she came to me for help. In treatment, she grew increasingly strong, began to assert herself and to challenge him, and the children once again became aware of her as a mothering figure. She did not consider divorce, as she was getting on in years and could not contemplate spending the rest of her life alone. But because she was able to recognize that her husband was not always right and to hold her ground without feeling threatened, their relationship underwent substantial changes. His earlier treatment of her, which had the veneer of loving care, was an expression of hostility and anger just as surely as are physical abuse and the silent treatment. It damaged and undermined her just as effectively as if he had beaten her regularly. And the end was the same; only the means differed. He had been killing her with kindness.

"To Room Nineteen" is a Doris Lessing story that speaks to the subject of the masochistic wife/mother in an especially affecting way. It tells of two bright, handsome, successful young people who fall in love, marry, and seem to have everything. Whatever they do is right and appropriate and graceful, and for a time their life together is charmed. When the young woman becomes pregnant, she quits her job, as seems fitting, and they have the first of four delightful children. They live in a beautiful home. They have a housekeeper to make life easier still. Then, in the midst of all this perfection, the husband confesses that he has had a sexual involvement with another woman, a one-time thing, not an ongoing arrangement. The wife says nothing—what is there to say after the fact?—and life goes on as it was. But beneath the unruffled facade of their existence, the wife thinks about this constantly. How could he experience with someone else the pleasure he has shared with her whom he loves? There is nothing she can do, she knows. She has no other resources. All the joy has gone out of life for her, and she feels a kind of deadness in her heart.

At one point the wife announces that she must have a room in the house where no one will bother her. It will bring her some kind of peace, she thinks, if she has a place of her own. Once she has the room, however, she finds it is not satisfying because now she is aware that the children can get along without her and that the housekeeper does not really need her to help run the house. She feels superfluous. Rather than adding to her life, the room seems to have diminished it further. She decides she needs to get a room outside of the house.

She has very little money, and the room she settles on is in a small hotel. The hotelkeeper is suspicious, believing she probably wants the room to bring men to, but she gives it to her grudgingly, and the wife sits for a day looking out the window at the Thames. When the hotelkeeper will not give her the room again, she tells her husband that she needs to have enough money to take a hotel room once a week. He gives her the money, and she asks him if he suspects that she is meeting a man. It is just as well you told me, the husband replies, because I have become involved with another woman.

The wife goes to a poor neighborhood, where she finds a room in a dingy hotel with a manager who keeps intrusively offering her things for the room when all she wants is to be left alone to sit quietly within the four walls. After a day of this, she returns home and feels even more acutely how unnecessary she is. No one has missed her. One day she goes to her hotel room and sits for a number of hours. Then she gets up and pushes a rug under the door, puts money in the gas meter and turns it on, and lies on the bed and waits to die.

This story focuses on a phenomenon I have encountered often in my practice but one that is never really addressed by psychiatry and psychoanalysis. This woman, like so many others, has had certain expectations imposed on her by her sociocultural surroundings. Society has, in effect, promised her that certain things will come to pass if she is a good, loyal, caring wife and mother. If she cares for her husband, depends on him, lets him call the shots, nurtures him and their children, and maintains a nice home, she will be rewarded with certain satisfactions. The corollary, of course, is that she must sacrifice her own needs and desires along the way. But the woman keeps her part of the bargain and gives in to the masochistic tendencies that are a part of it. When she is betrayed in this bargain, the results are catastrophic. Life never again has the same meaning for her. When the means of betrayal is infidelity on the husband's part, as is so often the case (male infidelity being socially acceptable, after all), it literally kills something in the woman, something that can never be restored. Because she makes her trade-off for this man, his faithlessness is especially devastating.

The masochistic wife/mother is in a situation where she may have *several* people aligned against her. No matter how good and caring a mother she is, she loses status by her husband's constantly criticizing her in front of the children. The powerlessness she feels becomes an increasing, and debilitating, reality. Like it or not, power is what children learn to respect, and someone who is without it sinks very rapidly in their estimation. Deprived of respect and caring from either husband or children, the masochistic wife/mother suffers from feelings of isolation and abandonment that make her existence sometimes seem unbearable. She is often unable to contend with this and begins to withdraw more and more in a variety of ways. Depression is one form of withdrawal. Suicide, as in the Lessing story, is another.

10

Vulnerability to Violence

In our increasingly violent society, violent crimes against women are on the rise. Certainly there is greater recognition of their incidence. Awareness of rape, wife-battering, and marital rape has increased sharply in the last few decades. And at long last, professionals are studying and attempting to understand these disturbing crimes. But there is great disagreement among those conducting the studies as to what factors produce such violence, disagreement about the personality traits and situational elements vis-à-vis the victimizer and the victim as well. Some victimologists have concluded that victims *do* contribute to their own victimization in some ways; others maintain that victim-blaming is a cruel and unwarranted stance that ignores the random nature of most personal crime.

I would certainly agree that victim-blaming is neither helpful to the victim nor productive of understanding. *She asked for it. It was her fault.* These are common responses to violent crime against women that are almost always inaccurate as well as being investigatory dead-ends. However, I do believe that the victims of violent crime may sometimes play a part either in triggering or exacerbating those crimes. That this is especially true of masochistic women there can be no doubt.

Let me stress that to say a victim has in some way contributed to her own victimization is not to say that she is to blame for it, that she is responsible for it, or that she in any way desired such an assault or deserves it. The lack of compassion for the victim

that exists in our society today dismays and saddens me. Bizarre
though it is, people seem more inclined to rally around and identify with the victimizer than with the person who has suffered an
attack. Eager to distance themselves from the victim position,
influenced unconsciously, I suspect, by the pervasive taste for violence that infects our national life, people all too often direct
their interest and even sympathy to the perpetrator of a violent
crime rather than to the victim. I want to make it clear that when
I examine those ways in which a victim may contribute to her
own victimization, I am not judging her to be blameworthy. I am,
rather, suggesting that she may not have taken all the preventive
steps available to her.

All violent crime constitutes a drama of power and danger that
is played out between the victim and the victimizer. All violent
crime turns on the issues of fear and control, these underlying
the more easily discernible issue of gain, be it for money or sex.
The raison d'être of the victimizer is to seek power and control,
those elements of which he was deprived in his early life when he
was himself a victim. In the moment of committing a violent
crime, he possesses both. The victim of a violent crime, on the
other hand, is riddled with fear and overwhelmed by a sense of
powerlessness and lack of control.

The latter description fits the masochistic person in general,
not just at the moment of crisis. This very fact puts the masochist
at greater risk when it comes to violent crime. Because of her
tendency to provoke self-destructive events and to submit abjectly
to a perceived powerful other, she is in greater danger than, say, a
woman who is comfortable exercising her own autonomy and
unafraid to assert herself. That is why this issue, sensitive though
it is, bears thinking about. How can someone with masochistic
tendencies keep her masochism from igniting a potentially
dangerous situation?

Psychologist Lenore Walker and others have recently disputed
that female masochism plays any role in the violence that erupts
in wife-battering. They have, in fact, thrown out the term
"masochism" altogether—feeling it too readily recalls Freud's
notion that women seek suffering instinctually and enjoy it—and

have replaced it with the concept of "learned helplessness." I, too, disagree with the idea that masochists derive satisfaction from their suffering. And, of course, I subscribe to the idea that women's sense of powerlessness is culturally and developmentally—not biologically—determined, an idea implicit in the phrase "learned helplessness." However, it is not a phrase or a concept I find particularly useful. Its essence is a kind of amorphous and overwhelming sense of impotence. It seems almost to imply that there is very little women can do to combat this deficiency that has been imposed on them by conditioning.

On the other hand, my concept of masochism and the communication style that reflects it allows one to focus on specific aspects of behavior that may be harmful and to learn to do something about them. Masochistic women *do* do things that make them more vulnerable than they need to be. They *do* send out messages signaling inadequacy, helplessness, and fear, which in a dangerous situation may make them more powerless than they need be. No one does women a favor by denying this. The term "masochism" has been in use for so long, both generally and professionally, that I think it is useless to try to eliminate it. It is better to reinterpret it, to use it appropriately.

Of course chance plays a large role in violent crime. There are times, no matter what precautions one has taken, when there is no way to escape a dangerous confrontation. We must recognize that there are situations in which there is absolutely nothing a woman can do to help herself: The cards are totally stacked against her. If I make suggestions of how a woman might best handle herself in dangerous situations, I am not implying that those suggestions will necessarily make the difference between life and death. But I *am* talking about raising the odds in her favor. As I said earlier, there are people who consistently win at cards because of the skill with which they play. By the same token, there may be times when, facing potential danger, a woman can override her masochistic tendencies, play her cards right, and make a difference in the situation that does result in saving her life.

Listening to the news one evening, I heard Alexander D.

Lehrer, prosecutor of Monmouth County, New Jersey, offer what I consider a gem of advice. "Conduct your life with care," he said, "and you won't be a victim." That may seem simplistic at first, but it actually says a great deal.

Treating herself and her life with care is one of the most difficult things for a masochistic person to do. Preoccupied with her own narrow field of vision, suffering from the perpetual anxiety that keeps her thinking confused, she is ill-equipped to respond properly to the world around her, prone to overlook real danger signs in favor of perceived threats that are based on her projections from childhood. So busy is she warding off these phantom dangers that she often fails to see or respond to real peril. She tends to be care-less in the way she conducts her life.

For example, a woman is standing alone in a loft building waiting for an elevator. A man arrives and stands waiting with her. Although something about him makes her uneasy and she is nervous about the prospect of boarding the elevator with him, she stays because she is concerned that if she walks away he will be offended and will assume she is thinking unpleasant things about him. This woman is not taking care with her own life. In fact, she puts an absolute stranger's opinion of her ahead of her own safety. She risks endangering herself just so that a man she doesn't know and will never see again will think she is a "nice person." This is the masochistic victim psychology in a nutshell.

Or, to give another example, a woman is walking alone on a deserted street at night and a man approaches her, asking for directions or a match or a quarter toward subway fare. She feels uncomfortable but stops to assist him anyway. Otherwise, she reasons, he will think she is unkind, ungenerous. This woman, too, is setting herself up to be victimized.

It is distressing that we live in a world where it is necessary to be so wary of our fellow creatures. I dislike advocating that people not help one another and, of course, where it is responsible—and safe—to do so I think we should offer assistance freely. I dislike promoting what appears to be selfishness. But I am not talking about selfishness; I am talking about self-preservation—and self-preservation is not something that comes naturally to the masochist. It is, in fact, at the bottom of her list of priorities, far below concern with another's opinion of her (another who is automatically powerful in her eyes) and acceptance of his premise (that he needs a match or dime or whatever).

Psychologist J. Selkin, who conducted a study of rape resisters, reported that the first act of resistance is a refusal to stop and talk to a strange man, a refusal to agree to help or to be helped by him. He also noted that those women who resisted were far more flexible than those who did not. Flexibility accompanies an autonomous personality, whereas rigidity—narrow options, the inability to think for herself or to trust her own perceptions, compulsive defensive reactions to any threatening situation— prevents the masochist from being careful with her own life. She gets herself into trouble by not daring to seem unkind or disagreeable, by being unable to assert herself, and by being unwilling to use her own premises as the basis for the encounter, rather than the premises of her victimizer.

Laura was a patient whom I invited to hear a lecture I was giving on a subject of particular interest to her. She sat next to a pleasant-looking, attractively dressed man who told her, at the conclusion of my talk, that he had been a student of mine some years earlier and that I had also invited him to attend the lecture. She had no way of verifying this but accepted it as true. It was a cold winter night and quite late when the lecture ended.

"Let me give you a ride home," the man said to Laura. "We'll stop and get a cup of coffee on the way."

"It's late but I do need to get right home," she said hesitantly. "I can easily get a cab."

"No, no," he insisted, "I'll drop you off. Besides, it's very cold and we can stop for coffee or a drink."

At this point, his insistence was showing, and a cup of coffee had begun to metamorphose into a drink. Laura could have given him a definitive no and headed for the cab. But she did not. Fearful of offending him, she continued to equivocate and finally let herself be persuaded to get into his car.

Once in the car, she continued to protest that she didn't want to stop, but her protests, like her initial demurral, were weak and ineffective.

"It really is late," she said. "I really ought to get home."

"Oh, come on," he said, "let's just have a quick drink and then I'll take you right home."

Each time he insisted, she yielded.

Once in the restaurant, he ordered a drink and she had a cup of coffee. As he drank, he talked and talked, and she grew increasingly concerned about the time.

"Look," she said finally, "I appreciate your bringing me this far, and it will be easy for me to get a cab from here. So why don't you stay and finish your drink and I'll just go on home?"

He wouldn't hear of it, he said. He had offered to take her home and he would. He finished his drink and they got back in the car. By this time Laura was quite aware that she was involved in a situation in which her voice carried no weight whatsoever, and she found her companion's persistence alarming.

As they approached her building he said, "I'll walk you to the door to make sure you're safe."

"That's not necessary," she replied pointedly. "There's an elevator man in the building and I'll be fine."

She put her hand on the door handle and when the car pulled up to the curb in front of her building, she said, "Thank you very much, I have to go," as she pushed open the door and ran inside.

As it turned out, I did know the man with whom Laura had this encounter, and I doubt that he would have harmed her. But certainly his insistence had ominous undercurrents in it and suggested his intention of a sexual encounter. Perhaps one has to say that there is always a potential for danger when someone is so tenacious. There can be no doubt, however, that Laura's behavior was masochistic.

First of all, she accepted the premise that he knew me, though she had only his word for this. He was a complete stranger to whom she owed nothing, but she was concerned that he think well of her, so she let him accompany her. There were so many points during the enounter when she could have extricated herself, but she capitulated to his wishes rather than defend her own. Her responses, until the final one, were always dilatory, never definitive. It took her a long time to register how completely he was disregarding her wishes. If the man had been truly dangerous, Laura could have been in deep trouble.

R. J. Gelles in *The Violent Home* gives a detailed accounting of factors that conspire to create violence within the family. First among these is the *offender's identity*, characterized by a vulnerable self-concept and low self-esteem. The *family of orientation* and *socialization* (including violence to which the offender has been exposed, violent role models, and self-devaluating experiences) are among the factors that shape the *offender's identity*; I will deal with these in some detail in my chapter on the victimizer. Gelles also enumerates other violence-producing factors such as *family structure, social isolation, structural stresses* (unemployment, financial problems, health problems) and *situational factors* (such as gambling, drinking, and so on). But there is one crucial factor he omits from his construct: the *victim's* personality and identity. This can play a part in evoking violent responses, in society at large as well as within the family.

The masochistic person cannot read power relationships accurately. She sees virtually everyone as more powerful than she, and she is automatically fearful of them. Any potential victim, facing a dangerous situation, is likely to be overcome by fear and a sense of powerlessness. But how much worse is such a confrontation for the masochistic person, whose daily life is pervaded by those feelings. To make the best of a bad situation, it is necessary to exert autonomy, to be self-assertive. This is extremely difficult for the masochist. But it is *not* impossible; the masochistic person can learn to be more powerful in a potentially dangerous situation.

I have already mentioned taking care ("prevention is nine-tenths the cure") as one inportant part of lessening one's vulnerability to violence. Do *not* put yourself on a dark street alone at night. Do *not* stop to answer the requests of strange men. Do *not* get onto an elevator alone with a man who makes you feel uneasy. Do *not* place yourself in positions of potential jeopardy.

If a volcano began to spill lava and you were in its path, you would move swiftly to get out of the way. If you find yourself actually confronting a potential assailant, run if you can. If screaming for attention will help, scream. Don't consider what the other person will think of your behavior. Don't wonder if you might be making a mistake about his intentions. If you are, so what? It truly is better to be safe than sorry. If there is any chance of escape, take advantage of it quickly and resolutely. Vacillation will keep you frozen in place as well as advertise that you are an easy mark. Decisive action will make you a less appealing target. Just as a thief might be discouraged from breaking and entering if he saw that the only means of entrance was the noisy smashing of windows, so an assailant might be less likely to tangle with someone who does not readily submit.

Let me make a point here about something that is never mentioned in discussions of this subject. Fear and excitement often affect's one's bodily functions, causing some people to feel like urinating; others feel the urge of a bowel movement. We are socially conditioned to think that to lose control in an inappropriate setting is among the worst things that could possibly happen to us. But it is well to remember that it is not worse than being killed. So if you are in a dangerous situation, don't let your concern with propriety get in the way of your thinking clearly. Don't be distracted. Simply let go if you must. Leave your brain free to address the exigencies of the crisis confronting you rather than take up precious thinking time with worry about your body's needs.

If escape is impossible and you are truly embroiled in a violent encounter, you still need not accept the idea that all is lost. In fact, if you do accept that, chances are all *will* be lost. You still have an opportunity to raise the odds in your favor. Maybe you will only increase your chances from one in a hundred to ten in a hundred, but that margin could make a difference. It may buy you an extra few moments of time during which, for instance, someone might appear to assist you. It may deflect your assailant temporarily and offer you a new possibility of escape. Of course, much of your behavior in such a confrontation will be determined by whether or not your assailant is armed and by what you construe his motives to be. If someone is holding a gun to your head, your method of resistance will be different from what it would be if he were unarmed. If it is clear that he wants only your money and intends no physical harm, your behavior will be governed by those circumstances. Flexibility and a belief in your own perceptions will serve you well.

The question of physical self-defense arises here. My own view is that women are not well served by studying karate or other self-defense methods and, in fact, may even be saddling themselves with dangerous illusions by doing so. Mastering these tactics in class is a far cry from being able to employ them effectively in a moment of attack. In a class, a student is performing a known ritual. In a moment of violent confrontation, everything is unknown. The victim is taken by surprise. She has no way of knowing what effect such a situation will have on her. Studies have shown, in fact, that people trained in self-defense skills (both men and women) have sometimes had these skills desert them in a moment of crisis. The belief that you are equipped to defend yourself physically may lead you to stand and fight, with disastrous results. It may prevent you from seizing an opportunity to escape.

If you cannot escape from your victimizer, how can you raise the odds in your favor? First, try to keep from transmitting any of the masochistic messages outlined in Chapter 4. These will be just as provocative to your attacker as they are to your boss, your lover, or your husband. If you signal that you are vulnerable and fearful, your fear will in fact excite fear and anxiety in your attacker and perhaps make him even more violent.

But remember never to threaten a potentially dangerous person. Never indicate that you don't believe in his capacity for violence. Appeal to his power but never question it. Enhance his ego, don't try to diminish it. The victimizer is full of hate and rage that mask an underlying sense of utter worthlessness. Anything you do that strikes that chord of worthlessness brings you closer to a death sentence. Anything you do to inflate his self-image gives you a better chance of escaping alive. When you challenge or degrade the victimizer, he is likely to feel even more threatened. Your challenge is equivalent to an accusation that he is not potent enough to carry out his threat. Questioning his power undermines still further whatever pitifully fragile sense of self-esteem he already has, and that is what makes questioning it so dangerous. Now he *must* prove his potency by fully unleashing his rage. let me repeat: I am not saying that if you do this or that you will get off the hook entirely. I am simply talking about increasing your chances, buying time.

A few years ago there was a homicide in New York City that seemed a particularly brutal, senseless, wasteful crime. A gifted and attractive young violinist with an orchestra playing in Manhattan was sexually assaulted and murdered by a stagehand in the Metropolitan Opera House. It is sad beyond expression to think of such a life being eradicated in this way, and in my speculation about what may have happened between this victim and her murderer, I'm not implying that she was in any way to blame for what befell her. Fate dealt this young woman a truly horrible blow. Once engaged with her assailant, perhaps nothing could have interrupted his brutal crime. I use this case simply as a framework to illustrate those elements that are present in violent confrontations, to show the common responses that occur in such situations, and to suggest alternatives responses that *might* be lifesaving. Let me stress that the following account is purely speculative.

During the intermission of that evening's performance, the young woman found herself standing at an elevator with the stagehand in the labyrinthine backstage area of the Metropolitan. It seemed legitimate for him to be there, and when the elevator came they got on together. By definition, given the act he committed, this young man was disturbed, alienated, and very dangerous. Also, it was reported that he had been drinking heavily that night. None of this may have been apparent to the young woman. My hunch is that once they were on the elevator, he made an obscene remark to her and she responded as many women would have, with outrage. Whatever her words, the tone would probably carry an assumption of superiority. And that note may have been what triggered the consequences. Why? Because this was a vicious young man whose self-esteem was abysmally low and whose fear of women was great; a scornful response only pushed him further in the direction of fear and rage. It emphasized the disparity between him and the young woman. "I'm a lady, you're a brute" was probably the essence of her remark. Registering that, he responded out of the great accumulation of disturbance within him and struck her.

Is there anything that young woman might have done to alter the outcome of this confrontation? Perhaps not. Perhaps the odds against her were insurmountable. But let me speculate about responses that *might* have prevented this situation from deteriorating into a vicious murder. He makes an obscene remark. She, instead of deflating his already frail ego, says something that will support it. "You're such a nice-looking young man," she might have said, "I can't believe you meant to say that. Perhaps it was a mistake. Or maybe I didn't even hear it right." If there was anything she could have said to make him feel better, rather than worse, about himself *maybe* she could have bought those few seconds in which luck or new opportunity could come into play. Perhaps she could have pushed the elevator button on the next floor and then gotten out and run. Perhaps the elevator would have come to a stop and opened of its own accord. With any gain of time, there is the possibility that something or someone might intervene.

Another tack might have been to change the premise of the encounter and move it into more neutral territory. "I wonder," she might have said, "since you work here, do you like music?" She might have gone on to ask what kind of music he liked or if he played an instrument. This would have enhanced rather than diminished his ego. She would have moved the two of them onto an equal footing, placing him on a par with herself. She also would have changed the venue from the inflammatory province of sexual interaction to the relatively bland terrain of musical taste. By doing so, she might have gained time for possible intervention, time in which fate might have offered her a way out.

Perhaps even if he had made a physical pass at her, rather than just uttered an obscene remark, she might have been able to delay and deflect him for a precious few extra seconds. "Oh, please don't," she might have said, thus making a direct appeal to his power. She admits her own helplessness and speaks to whatever is benign in him, asking that he be merciful to her. Ordinarily, of course, one would not want to exhibit abject helplessness. But what you might do trapped in an elevator with an assailant is very different from what you would do confronting an attacker in the street where you might be able to get away.

I realize that these possibilities of escape are extremely flimsy. I also realize that none of the responses I have suggested would be easy to effect. They call for keeping a cool head, refusing to panic, exercising a flexibility that allows one to put aside conditioned reflexes, and responding autonomously and assertively to the situation. That is a tall order when one unexpectedly finds oneself in a dangerous situation, particularly so for the masochistic person. But just because these are long shots does not mean they are not worth thinking about. At least they offer a chance of raising the odds in your favor, whereas contempt or hauteur, I am convinced, remove absolutely any possibility of escape.

Let me recount a series of incidents in the life of a patient of mine whom I'll call Estelle. Each of these contained the potential for her to become a victim of violence, but she emerged from each safely, due in large part to her own behavior. The first incident occurred when she was twelve and walking home from school with a friend. They had decided to take a shortcut through a somewhat empty, rundown neighborhood, certainly an unwise choice. When they were about halfway home, Estelle became aware of a group of a dozen or so boys massed on the stoop of a building ahead of them. She could see that they were leering, and she approached them with an ominous feeling. Surely the best thing would have been for Estelle and her friend to have turned and run back in the direction of the school, but they did not and quite suddenly the boys surrounded them, shouting obscenities, grabbing at their breasts and genitals. Estelle's friend somehow managed to escape, but she herself was still surrounded. Feeling a surge of adrenaline from her rage at being assaulted, she shouted "Get away," swinging her heavy school bag around her in a circle, scattering her tormentors enough to allow her to run off toward a busy thoroughfare.

Estelle made one mistake in taking a shortcut and another in not turning back the moment she saw the boys. But once she was in a dangerous situation, she played her cards right. She did not consider, when surrounded, that all was lost. She did not yield to her attackers. Nor did she provoke them further by talking back or taunting them in any way. She said two brief, decisive words ("get away"), took a definitive action (swinging her bag), and made her escape. All her actions were assertive.

Some years later, when Estelle was in her early twenties, she again had occasion to pass through a rather rough area of New York City, and it seemed that the earlier incident was about to repeat itself. Looking ahead, she saw a tunnel that served as a subway underpass and, in the block before it, a building stoop with a group of leering boys sitting on it. The sight, kindling memories of the earlier episode, terrified her. Her first thought was to turn and run; but she knew that if they chased her she couldn't run fast enough to elude them. So she went ahead and, as she approached the stoop, one boy separated himself from the group and came toward her. "She's my girlfriend and you're not going to hurt her," he told his cronies. Then he held out his hand to Estelle. In a split second she assessed her options: ignoring his offer and running forward, rebuffing him verbally, accepting him as an escort through this dangerous territory. She decided to gamble on trusting the young man. She took his hand and he led her away from the other boys and through the tunnel. Safely on the other side, she thanked him. "You're a nice lady," he said to her.

Once again, Estelle did not vacillate but took decisive action. She said nothing nasty, nothing provocative, to her would-be attackers. And she trusted her own perceptions: She sensed something decent in the young man's offer of assistance and chose to gamble that it was genuine.

The third incident occurred when Estelle was on an outing with her two young children, one of them still in a stroller. They were in a park near home, picking blueberries. The bushes were heavy with fruit, and Estelle and the children eagerly moved along, filling their baskets with berries. Absorbed in the task, Estelle didn't realize that they were no longer on a path and had moved deep into an area of thick shrubbery. Suddenly, just ahead of them, a man darted out of the bramble, uttering obscenities. Estelle turned and said quietly and firmly, "Children, come." With them in tow, she moved swiftly away from the man—and fortunately, he did not follow.

The last incident occurred years later when Estelle attended a meeting in the Columbia University area of New York. Heading home afterwards she boarded the wrong subway and ended up in a completely unfamiliar neighborhood, one that appeared quite rough. It was late afternoon, and the few people on the nearly deserted streets were, as Estelle described them to me, "the most horrendous characters" she had ever seen. She was concerned and frightened. Looking around, she saw a bus stop with a police car parked at it and she went over to the police. She told them she was lost and asked if they could possibly escort her to safer, more familiar territory. No, she should take the bus, they told her; they could not leave their post. Immediately thereafter, however, they drove off, and Estelle was left standing at a deserted bus stop. After a few moments she looked up to see a fierce-looking man with a decidedly menacing air coming out of a building and heading straight for her. She knew she could not outrun him. All she saw to do was to move farther into the street where she would be more visible; perhaps a car or bus would come along. She did that, hanging on tightly to her purse and briefcase. Suddenly, just before reaching her, the man veered away, turned sharply back in the direction from which he had come and reentered the building. Looking around for an explanation of this seemingly miraculous reversal, to her surprise Estelle saw, standing on an opposite corner, the largest policeman she had ever seen, easily six feet six, sturdily built, complete with luxuriant handlebar mustache. It seemed he had appeared out of nowhere—or perhaps from Gilbert and Sullivan's *Yeoman of the Guard*. He watched over her silently until the bus came a few minutes later.

One could say that Estelle was blessed with extraordinary good luck in each of these instances, that fate was on her side. And indeed fate, luck, chance—whatever one chooses to call it— probably did play a part in these events. But I think it is also important to note the part that Estelle's behavior played. Although she was afraid in each of these dangerous situations, she didn't panic. She stayed cool, thought clearly, examined her choices rapidly and took definitive action. Hesitation could have been deadly in any of these instances, but Estelle didn't temporize. She decided quickly what was the safest thing for her to do in an unsafe situation, and then she acted decisively. She didn't send out any masochistic signals that might have served to invite further attack. Quite the opposite. Her autonomous behavior acted as a deterrent. This was particularly interesting because Estelle *was* a masochistic woman and was not always capable of bringing this autonomy to bear in other areas of her life. But she had the rare quality of being good in emergencies. They caused her to tap into assertive reserves ordinarily she did not have access to.

It is important to recognize that there *is* a connection between masochism and victimhood, even though every victim of violence is certainly not masochistic. Denying that connection is a disservice to women, eager though some of them are to sweep it aside as part of the patriarchal baggage that must be shed if women are to claim, and fully exercise, their independence. An example of this was the remark a woman made to me after recounting how she had been harassed by a man at the beach. She had gone alone to one of the many beaches surrounding New York City and found it deserted. Because it was empty, she decided to take off her shirt and bra and lie topless on the sand. Soon a man appeared and struck up a conversation with her. Even though she made it clear she wished to be left alone, he refused to leave. Then he began making suggestive remarks to her. While she did finally manage to get her clothes on and get away without being harmed, she found the incident upsetting and frightening. "But I'm not going to start thinking I had any responsibility for this," she said to me, "because that will just lead into 'she asked for it,' and we've all had enough of that."

This woman believed it was constructive and self-protective to deny that she played any part in the incident. She believed that her denial represented a sloughing off of old, negative conditioning. In fact, her denial just reinforced her ignorance about her own behavior, and that ignorance most likely doomed her to repeat her behavior. How much better it might have been to recognize that it was careless in the first place to put herself in the position of being a woman alone on a completely empty beach. Certainly, the situation—lying on the sand topless, without her shirt at the ready, oblivious to a stranger approaching— comprised a masochistic act, one that left her completely vulnerable. Recognizing one's own masochism and becoming willing to examine it is not the same as saying "she asked for it."

The she-asked-for-it syndrome is delineated with great clarity in "The Murderer and His Victim," an article by David Abrahamsen, a brilliant forensic psychiatrist with whom I differ strongly on this point, although often agreeing with him on other matters. He cites the case of a woman who went to bars to pick up men and who eventually found her own Mr. Goodbar and was murdered. Abrahamsen says that neurosis impelled this woman to frequent bars, that she wanted to be killed, and was searching for a means to that end. In other words, he says that "she asked for it." On the contrary, I believe that this woman placed herself in the position she did in an effort to live, although the effort was a somewhat pathetic and misguided one. She was an older woman, suffering from loneliness, from the dearth of possibilities that exist for older women to meet men, and from the lack of interest that men today have in older women. She was rather desperate, as many victims are, and her desperation drove her to take risks and put herself in potentially dangerous situations. But none of this came from a desire to die. I would say that her behavior was generated by a desire to live.

The she-asked-for-it syndrome blames the victim. My notion that women may contribute to their own victimization by feeling powerless and conveying a message of vulnerability does not. Self-blame just adds to the accumulated suffering that is caused by the masochistic system of self-punishment and does no good whatsoever. Examining one's own actions, however, attempting to see where anxiety, helplessness, and carelessness may have led one into trouble, is worthwhile for the simple reason that it may help prevent it from happening again.

Dr. F. Pepitone Rockwell of the University of California Davis Medical School asked convicted rapists how they selected their victims, and he contrasted these characteristics with the characteristics of women whom the rapists were not successful in assaulting. The data he compiled are valuable aids in counseling women how to be less vulnerable to rape or any violent crime.

The rapists chose victims who seemed innocent or uncertain. They avoided women they described as "rude," an appellation I would interpret to mean definite or resolute. The rape victims were likely to be polite, friendly, and obliging, the nonvictims suspicious. Women who avoided rape thought of resistance methods and recalled advice about rape prevention when confronted with an attacker; actual rape victims focused on survival and death. They were so rattled by anxiety and confusion that they were unable to think of anything but whether or not they would be killed. Women who avoided rape used more verbal and physical resistance at the onset of the attack than did actual rape victims.

It is important for women to believe that they can resist violent attack. It is important for them to counter the socialization that causes them to behave politely and submissively, i.e., masochistically. Confronted by an attacker, they must not believe they are automatically helpless and have no choice but to give in. It is this attitude that leaves women feeling depressed in the aftermath of a rape. They translate their failure to defend themselves into a belief that they must have done something to invite the attack in the first place.

In *The Assertive Woman*, S. Phelps and N. A. Austin, writing about battered wives, observe that these women are not the domineering shrews that male psychiatrists, unfortunately, have long portrayed them to be. According to those who operate shelters for battered women, they are generally inhibited, passive, and helpless. "In anxiety-arousing situations, they are unable to act," Phelps and Austin report. "They are at a loss to come up with an effective response—in fact, any response at all." Debra Dalton and James Kantner support this in their article "Aggression in Battered and Non-Battered Women as Reflected in the Hand Test." Non-battered women, they note, show a higher activity score, while battered women show a lessened capacity to manipulate their environment constructively and a more passive, yet hostile, dependence and helplessness. This, of course, is a description of the masochistic woman. She exhibits these characteristics in all her life situations, including potentially dangerous ones, and these masochistic qualities increase her vulnerability to violence.

What tendencies do you possess that get you into trouble and might make you more vulnerable than someone else in a dangerous confrontation? Might your masochism get in the way and make things even worse than they are? How can you prepare yourself to deal more adequately with a situation that possesses the potential for physical harm? How can you learn to raise the odds in your favor?

The responses I have suggested are not guaranteed to get one off the hook. Being able to respond effectively may not make the difference between life and death. But it will raise your chances of escape as opposed to lowering them. Anything that can do that is worth studying, and thinking about and trying. Being willing to do that can be the beginning of learning to conduct your life with care.

11

The Victimizer

Victimizers come in many different shapes and sizes. Some are easily recognizable, others much less conspicuous. They exist at all levels of society. The degree to which they injure their victims varies widely. And, of course, every instance of victimization is shaped not just by the victimizer but by his victim as well. The personalities and characters of both people color and govern any interchange. There are, however, three broad categories into which most victimizers fall.

The first type is certainly the most innocuous, and the injuries he inflicts are of a nonviolent, almost prosaic nature. He is the person who perpetrates the garden-variety slights the masochist encounters in the course of the day. He may be someone who has no relationship at all with his victim, someone who encounters her in a transient exchange: the clerk who ignores her in the store, the bank teller who treats her with contempt, the insurance company representative who patronizes her. Or he may be someone who maintains ongoing contact with the victim, her gynecologist, for example, or her accountant or perhaps a casual acquaintance. When any of these people are abrupt, impatient, intolerant, they are inflicting a small injury upon the victim. This category includes those everyday instances where the masochistic person, feeling powerless, places herself in the power of the other person who then attacks her in some way. Many of these victimizers, I should add, may be perfectly decent people. But when the masochist extends her jugular to them, so to speak, they can't resist slashing at it because she has been so gallingly submissive.

The second type of victimizer is someone who has an established relationship with the victim, a relationship that could be called sado-masochistic. The masochistic person, as I have indicated, often forms an alliance with someone who has sadistic tendencies. He tends to be cruel, to sense that he has power over his partner, and to be decidedly egocentric, his needs taking precedence over anyone else's. His victim is useful to him, usually providing him with an operating household, perhaps extra income, and a sexual outlet. She thinks that he loves her, but, in fact, he is just exploiting her. The paradoxical nature of his tie to her is that he wants both to possess her and to eliminate her. At the heart of sadism is devotion to the complete defeat of the other person. In pursuit of that end, the sadistic person can become increasingly brutal. Many acts of suicide, in fact, are due to this progressive cruelty, although psychiatry generally tends to blame the suicide. In my years in practice I have seen things that lead me to think it is often the victimizer who drives the masochistic person to suicide by his continuing cruel destructiveness.

I have already discussed these first two types of victimizers at some length in preceding chapters. The third category is the one we read about in the headlines of our newspapers all too frequently, the one to which television news broadcasts devote an inordinate amount of time. He is the killer, the rapist, the man who commits both those atrocities, the mass murderer, the terrorist, the man who holds innocent people hostage in pursuit of his own pathological goals. These victimizers suffer from a grandiosity that is not so prevalent in the other two categories, a grandiosity built upon ever increasing isolation from society and other people. These victimizers are vicious; their rage increases as their isolation deepens. Whereas anxiety makes one feel helpless and vulnerable, rage imbues one with a sense of power and invincibility. These victimizers come to feel above it all, larger than life. They don't believe they are subject to the same laws, the same forces that govern ordinary people. Without any ballast of connective social ties to hold them down, they exist in a stratosphere created by their own madness. Many of these victimizers are sociopaths or psychopaths, men without conscience who feel no remorse or shame for their acts. Generally held social beliefs and values are absent in them. They live at odds with society, not as part of it. Like sharks, they navigate the societal waters searching for fodder to satisfy their needs, utterly unconcerned with how they get it. These are the victimizers I will focus on now.

Psychological traits are learned at mother's and father's knee. Children are formed by the treatment they receive from their parents or other caretakers, by the examples set for them, by the values they see espoused. And inevitably, I would say, those people who are given to violent behavior surely suffered from violence themselves early in their lives. The victimizer has himself been in the victim position; that more than anything is responsible for the genesis of the rage he takes out on others when he is grown.

The stereotyped image of the cruel child is the little boy methodically pulling the wings off a fly. Occasionally, this is rationalized away as the first signs of scientific curiosity, a young mind exploring the outside world. I would wager that budding inquisitiveness never takes that form. The little boy who pulls the wings from a fly is a child who has himself been abused. He knows that what he is doing is painful and destructive to the fly. He knows because he has been on the receiving end of such harsh treatment. His cruelty to the fly says one thing loud and clear: I am doing to the fly what has been done to me—I want to have power over someone or something, too.

A patient once wrote me a letter of apology that included a very explicit expression of this element of the victimizer's personality. "I have been an abusive person," the letter said, "compulsively abusive to people I care about and to people who care for me or begin to like me or want to help, doing what has been done to me by others, as if my hurts give me the right, as if the hurt would be less if I hurt others. . . . When I look at the messy state I got myself into, as I do now, I ask how much of this struggle is because I have not forgiven the hurts caused me."

Psychologist Stanley Rosenman, discussing anti-Semitism, points to crucial elements of the victimizer psychology. Individuals, like nations, help build self-esteem and insure the ego's coherence by participating, either directly or vicariously, in the decimation of others, Rosenman says. The violent victimizer regains a lost sense of omnipotence by his violent behavior. Frequently dependent and ineffectual, the victimizer helps to conquer his fear of debility or death by killing his victim. When he kills or rapes, he is the godlike creator. By destroying, usually symbolically, the powerful person whom he blames for his weakness, he hopes once again to regain control of his own destiny.

The victimizer and the masochist both grow up in great fear, as both are the victims of abuse during childhood. But in the victimizer, who has generally suffered more flagrant abuse and abuse that is more often physical than verbal, rage at the mistreatment takes over and supplants the fear. The masochist, on the other hand, remains mired in the fear. But these two types, who often come together in a terrible conflagration, share a common wellspring in childhood.

The ill-treatment a victimizer receives from his caretakers may be physical or psychological, intentional or not. Unintentional psychological harm may be done to a child by a mother, for example, who is trapped in a role she never wanted and angry because of it. Her anger, unfortunately, will be turned on her child. A reluctant mother inevitably damages her child no matter how hard she tries to be caring (a powerful argument for abortion, I believe).

Basically, there are three fundamental stances or attitudes toward motherhood that recur continually throughout a child's development. They are based on the reproductive experience itself, the motivation for the pregnancy, and, finally, the basic acceptance or rejection of the child. Two of these stances can be very damaging to the child. Two of them could produce a potential victimizer.

The first stance involves denial: You have not really been born, you are still a part of me and cannot grow without my constant care. M. J. Zemlick and Robert I. Watson conducted a study that demonstrated a relationship between maternal rejection and the development of overprotective behavior as a defense serving to deny the mother's true feelings about her child. The mother, seeing the child as part of herself, demands that he grow and develop as she wishes. To this exploitative end, she uses a variety of manipulative, coercive, and seductive techniques that can be extremely damaging to the child.

David Levy, writing about the development of the criminal, addresses the question of maternal overprotectiveness. When this is combined with an absentee or cruel father, Levy found, it is a factor in creating a criminal personality. This mothering stance produces a vulnerability to seduction, as well as a rage at it, and it also fosters the charm-boy aspect that so many victimizers seem to possess. They learn early how to get around their mothers, how to charm them to achieve their own ends. They practice this charm on their mothers even as they are filled with hatred of them for their tenacious, clinging, or seductive behavior.

The second maternal stance can be expressed like this: You have been born, but I cannot abide it. Here there is less denial and more overt rage on the mother's part. She participates as little as possible in taking care of her child, exhibiting inattention, distraction, isolation, and a variety of other distance-creating techniques. In extreme instances, this woman may become an attacking mother and treat her child with cruelty and murderous rage. The potential for damage to the child is obvious here as well.

The third, and ideal, stance says to the child: I will help you grow up in the way that is best for you. This generally produces a psychologically and emotionally healthy child.

When a child receives ill treatment, he comes to believe that his parents do not love him. That translates into his believing that he is not lovable. Since he is not lovable, he must be worthless and bad. Otherwise, he would not be abused. To compensate for feelings of worthlessness, he begins to formulate a sense of his own power in a negative, dangerous way and to develop the grandiosity I mentioned earlier. "I'm better than all the rest of you," this young man begins to think. "I'm stronger, more important, more potent." This grandiosity, present in almost all violent victimizers, is most easily detected perhaps in the presidential assassin: "If I kill the president, I'm more important than he is."

The rage that grows in a child who is seriously ill-treated leads him to see first his abusers, then all other people, as the enemy. And he is never concerned with what the enemy feels. He is concerned only with himself, his own needs, his desire to avoid being hurt, to avoid being a victim himself. The enemy has hurt him; therefore it doesn't matter what he does to retaliate. He sets himself up against society, and as his isolation and antagonism grow, he fails to see the part he himself plays in this process. Now he is the victimizer, preying upon other people as he was once preyed upon. In a perversion of the golden rule, he is now the dispenser of violence, doing unto others what was done unto him.

Unquestionably, the victimizer suffers grave wounds in his early life. But I want to repeat that that does not seem to me sufficient reason to extend sympathy to him. It is tragic that his has been a blighted life. But more tragic is the harm he inflicts on innocent lives. His victims are the truly deserving recipients of our compassion.

All violent victimizers are filled with hate and rage. In rapists, the hatred is for women; the rage is with mother. Rapists are not oversexed demons. They are men in whom impotence is common in ordinary sexual situations and in whom there is a strong link between sex and violence, sex and force. Their only sexual satisfaction may come in relation to violence. It has been said recently that rape is not a sexual act but an act of aggression. It would be more accurate to say that rape is a sexual act in which the violent degradation of the other person is the primary goal.

Freud provided the first important insight into this. In a paper titled "A Child Is Being Beaten," he noted that some patients connected feelings of pleasure with expressed fantasies of being beaten and that these feelings excited considerable shame and guilt. He also observed that being beaten on the bare behind was a common element in these fantasies and that sometimes the fantasies reflected genuine childhood experience. Inevitably, a spanking on the bare bottom carries with it penile stimulation, especially if the child is either across the knee or lying down on something. These fantasies illustrate the link between pain and erotic stimulation. It is not a very big leap from this to see how hatred and sexual stimulation come together. Violence and cruelty in childhood can impart a legacy of resentment and hate and erotic arousal linked with pain. The rapist in effect says: I was the beaten, powerless, sexually stimulated child; now I am the powerful, sexual, punitive parent.

This kind of turnaround is evident in the styles of many criminals. The form their violence takes is not arbitrary. They enact upon their victims what they feel has been done to them. Strangling is a quite common example of this. Men who strangle their victims most likely had mothers who were extremely controlling and who tried to shove things (food, concepts, points of view) down their throats. This made them feel they were choking to death. These men grew up with tremendous rage against women, and they carry out on their victims the feeling they had of being strangled by their mothers.

I mentioned that the victimizer often develops considerable charm. This results from his looking for a way to get by, looking for a mode of behavior that will allow him to deflect the harshness he expects and to disguise his true feelings of hate. He may stumble upon this quite by accident, usually in relation to his mother, when one day something he does gains him approval rather than punishment. He notes what seems to be winning behavior; he sees that it gets him what he wants. And he begins to develop his charm the way someone else would set out to learn how to use a new set of tools. He knows it is a skill that will stand him in good stead.

Charm is something the victimizer studies and learns, though not necessarily consciously, to carry him over the hurdles he faces; it is something that allows him to "pass." This charm, though highly developed, is only skin deep, of course. Someone with a discerning eye, someone autonomous, might be able to see through the superficial charm and note those signs of underlying hate and rage that are bound at some point to show through the victimizer's efforts to hide them. The masochistic person is less likely to penetrate the disguise, more likely to be taken in by the charm, leaving her more vulnerable to victimization. Chaplin's film *Monsieur Verdoux* provided an excellent portrait of the victimizer as charmer. Verdoux is a man who utterly captivates and wins over older women before he strangles them.

There are three other types of victimizer who also belong in the third category: the voyeur, the exhibitionist, and the obscene phone caller. These men are allied with the rapist in that their hostile feelings find sexual expression. They possess the same psychic ingredients as the rapist, but the ingredients take a different form in them. The voyeur hates women, as does the rapist; he can't experience genuine sexual involvement but must keep his distance. The exhibitionist certainly suffers from the same kind of rage toward women and he has the same desire to humiliate them as the rapist does. The obscene phone caller stays more remote from his victim but his act is nevertheless an attack, a form of symbolic rape.

The professional view has been that these types are essentially harmless, that they would never commit actual sexual assault. But I am not so sure. I think it is entirely possible that any one of them might be capable of genuine rape; given the right circumstance, he could move easily from the symbolic to the actual realm of attack. In fact, I know of more than one instance in which rape eventuated from a background of exhibitionism.

The necrophiliac should also be mentioned here. In *The Anatomy of Human Destructiveness*, Erich Fromm makes the point that the necrophiliac is death-preoccupied, that his drive is to create death out of life. This comes through graphically in the French film *Le Bonheur*, which tells the story of a seamstress who is married to a sadistic charmer. One day while they are on a picnic, the husband, completely indifferent to his wife's feelings, goes off and seduces another woman. The wife drowns herself, and when the husband returns and sees her body, which has been pulled from the water, lying on the ground, he throws his own body across it and begins miming intercourse. Her death gives birth to potency in him. In death he can love her, in a sense, because now there is no person there to deal with, only a corpse.

I think it would be instructive at this point to take a detailed look at someone established as a violent victimizer. Surely there is no better example of the species than Ted Bundy, currently on death row in Florida State Prison for the murders of two women and suspected of having killed perhaps dozens more. It was Bundy who, in 1978, entered the Chi Omega sorority house at Florida State University in Tallahassee and, in a matter of just minutes, killed two women with the club he was carrying and battered two others into unconsciousness. One of the dead women suffered such a powerful blow to her forehead that her brain was exposed. The other was sodomized with a can of hair spray, and one of her nipples nearly torn off by a bite, and had another deep wound in her buttock, where she had also been bitten. Directly after leaving the scene of this slaughter, Bundy attacked another sleeping coed in a nearby apartment; she survived only because the thumping noise of Bundy's club as he dealt blows to his victim awakened her neighbors, and he was frightened away. When he was arrested a month later, he was also indicted for the kidnapping and murder of a twelve-year-old girl six days before his arrest. He had begun killing several years earlier, when he was a law student. His young women victims numbered at least sixteen and came from four different states: Washington, Oregon, Utah, and Colorado.

After Bundy was convicted in Florida and revealed as the likely perpetrator of the baffling murder spree in the Pacific Northwest, a number of books and articles were written about him. The emphasis in all of them was how unlikely a candidate Ted Bundy was for a mass murderer, how in fact he was the antithesis of everything that role conjures up. Nothing about Bundy, apparently, appeared monstrous. He was handsome and well educated; people described him as intelligent, caring, and compassionate, the devoted son of an adoring mother, charismatic, politically adept and, some even said, a possible future governor of the state of Washington. He had even come close to being appointed director of Seattle's Crime Prevention Advisory Commission, a notion almost unbearable in its degree of irony. These accounts presented him as a terrific, talented, marvelously likable fellow whose life, inexplicably and horrendously, suddenly went bad. I submit that the picture can be neither so simple nor so rosy.

While I have no firsthand knowledge of Bundy, and the information I possess about his background is limited, what I do know tells me that the seeds of his psychopathy were sown early, as they always are. He is, first of all, often described as his mother's darling, and that in itself can be a dangerous position for a child. It usually indicates that the mother is getting vicarious satisfactions from an offspring that she ought to be getting from another adult, from a mate. In the case of Bundy's mother, no such figure existed. She and her out-of-wedlock child lived with her parents, his illegitimacy obscured by the fiction that Ted was the child of her parents, that he and his mother were brother and sister. One can imagine the conflicts, tensions, and anxieties that existed in that household. The parents must have resented and been deeply ashamed of their daughter, who had defied them and their religious code; the daughter must have resented their judgments and the child with whom she was saddled, denying these latter feelings by adopting a doting attitude toward her son.

Currents of hate, anger, guilt, and resentment must have continually washed over the adults and the child, and, presumably, they became unbearable because when Ted was four he and his mother moved to Tacoma, Washington, to live with other relatives. Even after they made this move, the fiction was maintained that Ted and his mother were siblings. Knowing no more than this, I can say that this is a child with an extremely disturbed family background. Add to it that when his mother finally married a man named Bundy, Ted took the man's name but refused any fathering from him; that Ted in elementary school was the butt of humiliating teasing from his classmates (teasing is very commonly directed at disturbed children); and that growing up he was never seen to date or to be involved with girls—and the picture changes considerably from the one of relentless normality that is usually presented.

That Bundy was charming I have no doubt. As I said, the development of charm is a commonplace among psychopathic people. It is their stock-in-trade, their means of passage, and as such it becomes a single, overdetermined trait that can be almost overwhelming. This accounts, I think, for the descriptions of

Bundy as charismatic, prepossessing, "Kennedyesque." But despite his considerable charm, there must have been signs of his underlying disturbance that would have been visible to the discerning eye. Unfortunately, none of his victims, nor any of the people who knew him in his "normal" life, had such a capacity, apparently.

Bundy has always maintained that he is innocent of any murders, those with which he has been charged, those he is suspected of committing. In the course of doing a book about him, with his supposed cooperation but frustrated by Bundy's constant refusal to address the issue of his guilt, journalists Stephen G. Michaud and Hugh Aynesworth devised a format they thought might appeal to Bundy's ego and penetrate his denial. As the suspect in these cases he had amassed a great deal of knowledge, they pointed out. He also had been a psychology student. And obviously he had a keen intelligence. Why, they suggested, didn't he *speculate* about the sort of person who would commit such crimes and about his motives for doing so? Bundy was willing, even eager. Psychiatrists who have listened to the tapes made by Michaud and Aynesworth say there is no doubt that Bundy is talking about himself.

Bundy describes the progressive growth within "the killer" of an "entity," a "distorted self," a "malignant being." And most interesting to me was the part that pornography played in this growth. Pornography, Bundy says, pushed him along the road of increasing violence. His thoughts about sex had begun to center on ideas of sexual violence. Pornography gave him permission to pursue these thoughts, to consider acting on them. Essentially violent toward women, pornography, which is tolerated by society and even by many professionals, set the societal seal of approval on Bundy's vicious tendencies. It lifted such limits as he possessed; it removed the restraints.

The late Alexander Bickel, who was professor of constitutional law at Yale University, was one of the few courageous voices in the legal profession willing to declare unreservedly that pornography is a menace. In his book *Morality of Consent*, he asserted that it is not always possible to carry out the intent of our laws, but he argued that nevertheless our laws represent a consensus of how we feel; they express society's general beliefs of what is right and what is wrong. Removing antipornography laws from the books, he said, was to declare that pornography is acceptable to us as a society.

In *Understanding Sexual Attacks* by Drs. West, Roy, and Nichol, the authors point out that group therapy among imprisoned rapists revealed how unhappy and conflict-driven rapists are. Their compulsive behavior is aggressive and violent in all its aspects; a preoccupation they all shared was with pornographic materials and fantasies. Of course, this preoccupation can be seen as a defensive response to their alienation and lack of relatedness. But it also sets off still further alienation through violence. Bundy certainly picked up in pornography the message that violence toward women is acceptable and, with that message, his sickness escalated.

Diana Scully and Joseph Marolla, professors at Virginia Commonwealth University, believe that rapists are in many ways no different from most men, that they are products of a culture that teaches that sexually aggressive behavior is all right and that rape is just the extreme example of that learned attitude. Not only do these men learn sexual violence from the culture, Scully and Marolla maintain, they also learn to master a vocabulary that can be used to explain violence against women in socially acceptable terms.

Bundy recounts how violence against women and sexual activity merged in "the killer's" mind, how he stalked his victims, and how he began to kill. He makes clear that the killer's exhilaration came from the capture and degradation of women. Describing one killing in some detail, he tells of how he picked up a young woman hitchhiker, invited her to come to a party at his place, flattered and entertained her on the drive there ("for the purpose of making the whole encounter seem legitimate and to keep her at her ease"), once there, giving her more alcohol on top of the drinks she had already had that evening, drinking a great deal himself, and eventually strangling her after having sex. What a perfect example this is of a woman's contributing to her own victimization. She put herself in a dangerous position by hitchhiking, particularly after she had had a few drinks. She agreed to accompany Bundy—an unknown person—to his house, accepting his premise that a party was in progress there. She failed to hear any discordant notes in his conversation in the car, although they were bound to be present. When they arrived at his house and she saw there was no party, she failed to leave immediately, if that was still possible. She continued to drink heavily. She submitted to "more or less voluntary" sex with him.

A second incident Bundy describes quite fully contains another cautionary message. Disturbed by the murders, suffering remorse in the aftermath of each, the killer decided on a compromise of sorts: He would rape his victim instead of murdering her, making sure there would be no possibility of detection so that he would not be forced into killing. To this end he set out one evening, cruising through the suburbs of the city in which he lived. Spotting a young woman walking alone on a dark street, he parked his car some distance behind her, made his approach brandishing a knife, and pushed her off the sidewalk into a wooded area. He told her to submit and do what he wanted. She began to argue with him, saying she did not believe he would do anything to her. He tried very hard to focus on his intention of not harming her; she continued arguing and began screaming as well. He began to panic, fearing someone would hear, and he put his hands around her throat and squeezed, "just to throttle her into unconsciousness so that she wouldn't scream anymore." Then he raped her, not realizing until afterward that she was dead. My hunch is that this was a real act of necrophilia, that Bundy knew she was dead and enjoyed it because she was dead and he had killed her.

When this young woman challenged Bundy by saying she did not believe he would hurt her, she signed her own death warrant. A rapist or murderer reassures himself about his own inadequacy through his violent act. Any challenge to his veracity is extremely dangerous, constituting as it does an accusation that he is not powerful enough to carry out what he has threatened. Accused of impotence, he is bound to prove that he means what he says, and the chances increase of his viciousness escalating. As I've said, when one is locked into an encounter with a violent assailant, it is important not to do anything that threatens his fragile self-esteem. One should concentrate instead on doing everything possible to bolster it. It is also well to remember, as Bundy indicates, that the victimizer is frightened, too, struggling to maintain a delicate balance between his fear of getting caught and his need to act out his savage compulsion.

Near the end of his "speculative" session with Michaud and Aynesworth, Bundy remarked on how vulnerable society is to the depredations of people like himself. "The really scary thing," he told them, "is that there are a lot of people who are not in prison, a *lot* of people who were far more successful than I." And therein lies the point of spending time thinking about a mass murderer like Bundy. These people exist. Their primary emotions are rage and hate, and their self-preoccupation is enormous. Other people serve only as fodder for their needs. Isolated, alienated, they are separate from other people but constantly studying them. And they become, in some ways, quite acute in their judgments of people. They develop a large fund of knowledge about their prey. Just as a fisherman learns about the movements of fish, the currents in which they swim, the times and seasons at which they run, the bait they rise to, so a victimizer learns where to find his victims, how to spot who is a likely prospect, who is not, and how to hook them. Bundy more than once used the ploy of putting his arm in a cast, traveling to a resort area, launching a small sailboat, and then requesting help of a young woman when the time came to take the boat out of the water and secure it atop his car. More than one responded to his plea, rode along with him to help unload it, and ended up a murder victim because of her willingness to assist the handsome stranger.

Recently at a legal conference, I heard a judge describe a particular victimizer's modus operandi. This mugger/rapist carefully chose a set of conditions that would be advantageous to him. He frequented suburban areas that had large supermarkets but also a fair number of apartment buildings, and he watched for a woman entering her building with packages in both arms. Going into the building after her, when the elevator came he would ask if he could press her floor. After doing that, he would press the floor below hers, making it seem he belonged in the building and also indicating to her that he would be getting off before her, just in case she had fears that needed to be allayed. Once the elevator closed, he would attack her and grab her bag. If he was not done with the robbery when the elevator door opened, he would put his foot in the door so that the elevator wouldn't operate. If he saw that there was no one around, he would rape her. Here the odds were entirely in favor of the victimizer. He has picked his own situation and environment. He knows he is operating from a position of strength because he has waited for someone who is alone, whose arms are full, and who will be inclined to be trustful because he has offered to help her. He knows, in other words, where the fish are running and the lure to which they will respond.

In this connection, I think of a patient of mine, a professional man who had the clean-cut good looks of a grown-up choirboy. His habit was to go to a singles bar and pick up a young woman, invite her to his apartment, have sex with her, and, as soon as it was over, kick her out of his bed and his house. "Get your clothes on and get the hell out of here fast or you'll regret it," he would say. As soon as she left, he would take a shower so that he could feel "clean" again. This man was potentially very dangerous, and the young women who accompanied him were taking a great risk, but he seemed to have no trouble finding willing partners. Women went home with him knowing nothing about him and without anyone else knowing where they were.

While superficially this man must have seemed like God's gift to women, I am certain he exhibited clues to his true nature during his approach to a prospective conquest. A self-contained woman would pick up on these clues, whereas his victims (and indeed he victimized women in his utterly selfish use of them), masochists all, I'm afraid, did not. His behavior was undoubtedly arrogant and grandiose, focusing exclusively on himself, showing little or no interest in the woman. He would have no natural curiosity about her because he would not really see her as a person in her own right. She would be simply the catch he was going to hook. And why should he bother feigning interest in her when it was not necessary? After all, he would know it was going to be just a one-night stand.

I am sure he also displayed a persistence in pursuit of his own ends that might have been a clue to someone perceptive. And no doubt he flattered the women profusely. The compliments he bestowed were, I feel sure, obvious attempts to get the woman to respond to him and had probably very little to do with her. But a person with masochistic tendencies would not understand or detect this; her focus would be on how nice it feels to be flattered. If she felt any disbelief, she would ignore it. Succumbing to flattery that has no depth is a masochistic trait.

The one thing a victimizer must have in order to commit an assault is opportunity. And he will seize it whenever and wherever it presents itself. He is always looking for a chance to strike. That is why the notions of self-protection and moving away from the masochistic tendencies that undermine it are so important. Any potential victim can play a definite part in her own destiny, denying the victimizer opportunity by her own prudent behavior.

12

Dream Worlds, Fantasy Lives

The daydreams, or fantasies, of masochistic people are fueled by a pervasive sense of ineffectuality; predictably, they exhibit a distinct split along gender lines, since boys and girls receive such different parental and cultural conditioning. The masochistic man who feels himself to be helpless and passive will tend to have fantasies of the Walter Mitty variety: He will imagine himself *transformed into another person*, someone of great appeal and accomplishment—a pilot, a politician, a mathematical genius, a movie star. He will tend to be like the Woody Allen character in *Play It Again, Sam* who has Humphrey Bogart alongside him at all times, coaching him in how to assume a tough-guy stance.

Masochistic women, on the other hand, daydream of overcoming their helplessness and passivity by meeting and attaching themselves to someone who possesses power. It is borrowed power they fantasize. They will *fall in love with* the pilot, the politician, the genius, the movie star. And they often arrange to establish this liaison with a minimum of initiative or forcefulness on their part: They will bump into someone electrifying on the street, and he will evince a sudden interest in them, and one thing will lead to another, and soon romance will blossom. A masochistic patient of mine would visualize herself walking down Fifth Avenue, being hit lightly by a car or twisting an ankle and falling. A gorgeous man would come along and either transport her to the hospital or, if she was not badly hurt, suggest they have a cup of coffee, and out of this a love affair begins.

This fantasy of rescue is very common. Chance and accident are prominently featured as the means by which the masochist overcomes her sense of inadequacy and incompetence. It is, of course, the Prince Charming or Cinderella story. The transformation that occurs for the masochistic woman is almost invariably through the agency of someone else. It is a sad commentary that even in their fantasies women do not often imagine themselves as powerful people; they imagine themselves *attached* to powerful people.

The same woman who fantasized the Fifth Avenue accident recalled to me a childhood daydream of hers that contained some of the same elements. She and her family lived in New York, and her mother forbade her to have a pet in their city apartment. When they went on vacations to a beautiful wooded area of New Jersey, the girl was particularly taken with the bushy-tailed squirrels, and she wished she could have one of them as a pet. She fantasized that a squirrel would go out on the limb of a tree, the limb would break, the squirrel would fall to the ground, hurting itself, and she would then nurse it back to health, care for it, and keep it as a pet. Her masochism is evident in the helplessness she felt in obtaining a pet in any way except through a disaster. Though the accident happens to the squirrel, not to her, the feeling behind the fantasy is the same.

Erich Fromm observed that the quality of daydreams, due to their being largely wish-fulfillment, is often slightly cheap. They seem rather simplistic and unelaborated, almost adolescent in their emphasis on easy gratification, revealing of the fact that the masochistic person is not quite grown-up.

Suicide is a frequent masochistic fantasy and one that also occurs fairly often in adolescents, another indicator of the common denominator of powerlessness in these two groups. The adolescent, while beginning to be free, is still dependent upon parents who may be mean or unkind or involved in an ongoing negative relationship with her. The masochist has been mired in a prolonged sense of dependence and tends to see nearly everyone as a stern authority figure who has the capacity to mistreat her. The purpose of the suicidal fantasy for both groups is to say to their adversaries: You will be sorry you treated me this way; when I am dead and gone you will regret that you treated me badly. The suicidal fantasy of the masochist is nearly always directed toward someone, and thus there is a coercive element in relation to the significant other person on whom the fantasy is focused.

Dreams express things in a much more complex way than do daydreams or fantasies. Many people view the world of dreams as a phantasmagoric one, filled with enigmatic images that share more of a kinship with the theater of the absurd than they do with the dreamer's daily life. Dream content seems arcane, fractured, and destined to stay clouded by mists of unintelligibility. We have all heard people say, "I had the craziest dream. There's no way any one could figure this out." Or, "You won't believe the dream I had last night! It made no sense at all." But despite the dreamer's assessment, you can rest assured that it *did* make sense, for the dream world is neither as cryptic nor as inaccessible as it appears to be. Montague Ullman, a psychoanalyst who has done a great deal of work on dreams, puts it this way: Dreaming is nothing more than thinking under the conditions of sleep.

Dreams may serve as a time for the mind to relieve and clear itself, offer a theater for the enactment of wish-fulfillment, or constitute an arena for working on the problems of our waking lives. But whatever their purpose, dreams are bound up with those things of the preceding day. However obscure they may seem at first glance, dreams are not arbitrary visitations from another realm. They come from us and belong to us. They are reports from the unconscious about what matters most to us.

"Why does the mind see more clearly in sleep than the imagination of the day?" Leonardo da Vinci asked, his question accurately reflecting the fundamental quality of the dream, that distillation of essence that occurs during sleep when all the day's distractions are set aside. Dream time is not interrupted by diversion of eye or ear. It is solitary, silent time in which the dreamer focuses intensely on the issues arising in the dreams.

The language of dreams is different from the language we use when awake. Dream statements are expressed in metaphoric or symbolic terms, a fact that accounts for their seemingly elusive nature. But one can come to understand dream language in the same way one masters any foreign tongue, by study and exposure. This was recognized in the Old Testament, in which Joseph was shown rising from captive to right-hand man to the pharaoh on the strength of his accurate interpretations of dreams and his predictions based on them. All dreams are predictive in the sense that they are expressions of the present illuminated by the past and pointing to the future.

Very often, dream language can be highly individualistic. I am sure, for instance, that if I were shown accounts of dreams from my patients, I would know which dreams belonged to which patient. Each dreamer has his or her own language or style. And it is important to note that to be understood a dream need not be examined in minute detail, each small facet traced and explicated like the clues in a detective story (though there are times when this might be necessary). Dreams can be understood through a kind of synthesis. If one fathoms the metaphor, one grasps the dream. "A skillful man reads his dreams for self-knowledge," said Emerson, "yet not the detail but the quality."

A wonderful example of the metaphoric nature of dreams came from a woman patient of mine who was both masochistic and menopausal. Her dream consisted of a single image: a suitcase that had belonged to her husband sitting on the shelf in her closet. She dreamed she saw this and she awoke very upset. Dreams are made comprehensible, of course, by the associations of the dreamer to the material of the dream, and she said of the suitcase that it was very expensive and all leather, and when her husband first bought it he absolutely loved it and used it all the time. Then it began to get scratched and worn and battered, and a point came at which he did not want to use it anymore and he bought a new one. He threw the old one out, but she could not bear its loss, so she rescued it. The single image of the suitcase contained a recapitulation of this woman's entire marriage: She was the suitcase, originally cherished and valued, gradually showing signs of wear, and eventually tossed out and replaced by the much younger woman for whom her husband had left her; despite this, however, she rescued herself, she went on with her life, although she still felt that she was "on the shelf."

Dreams are the metaphoric expressions of the concerns of our daily lives, highlighted and distilled. As Alexander Pope put it: "You eat in dreams the custard of the day." And the dreams of a masochistic person are filled with images of pursuit and paralysis. She is often being chased, hunted, hounded; people are out to get her. In the face of this threat, she exhibits total impotence; she is unable to move, unable to hear, unable to scream or speak, sometimes unable to see.

For example, a young woman is being abducted by robbers in a car that tears along a road at high speed; they reach an intersection with a red light; the car stops and the young woman feels the excitement of victory as she manages to get out of the car; but the moment she is out, she finds that her legs are paralyzed and she is unable to move; she wakes up in a sweat. Potency, or lack of it, is a key problem for the masochistic person. And virtually all the imagery of her dreams has to do with recognition of this. She is someone who is attempting in her dreams to solve the problem of helplessness: How can I scream? How can I walk? How can I run? How can I escape? How can I handle my life more successfully?

In the following discussion of masochistic dreams, or perhaps, more properly, nightmares, it may seem that the interpretations I present are rather arbitrary. But that is due to the limitations of space. Obviously, I can't give the complete background material on each patient that would serve to clarify each interpretation. So I will focus on the central metaphors of the dreams, those metaphors that illuminate masochistic tendencies, and not attempt to deal with all the complexities of the dreams. Often, as a problem becomes clearer, the dreams that reflect and address that problem become less complex. And often they state in one simple metaphor some complicated things the patient has come to understand. That was true of the suitcase dream as it is of the dreams that follow.

A man dreamed that he entered his place of business and saw three men who appeared to be joined together, frozen into a block. He felt this was dangerous and that they might attack him. He also saw, before awakening frightened, that his daughter was observing the three men. This dream states clearly the problem of a very masochistic man. In business with two brothers who criticize and ridicule him and refuse to let him make his own decisions, he feels locked into them, frozen between them in a powerless position yet open to attack by them. His daughter's observing only intensifies the situation as she is also contemptuous of him and often "fresh" and abusive to him.

The next dream suggests in a single image both the patient's problem and her struggle to cope with it. She dreamed that she stood at the Dutch doors of a stable. The top half of the doors was open, and on the other side she could see a lion. She was terrified. In her hand she held a bowl of Jell-O, which she attempted to offer to the lion. As it raised its head above the door, she woke up feeling extremely anxious. Reporting this dream to me, she said, "You certainly can't mollify a lion by offering him Jell-O. Lions are out to devour meat; lions are out to make a kill." She was talking about her husband, who liked to ride horseback and was symbolized in this instance by the lion behind the stable door. The woman experienced her husband as a frightening figure; she had never been able to deal with him adequately. The best she could do was to offer him Jell-O when obviously something more substantial was called for. Talking further about her associations, the woman said, "Lions are dangerous. I felt this one was, too. But male lions are so regal and beautiful that it's always been hard for me to believe how dangerous they are. Still, I wouldn't like to find out." These associations illuminate the conflict at the heart of the sado-masochistic marriage in which the husband is brutal and the wife attempts to go along in conciliatory style: The wife believes her husband is dangerous, but she also finds him compelling, even magnificent in some ways, and she finds it hard to believe how cruel he really is.

A typical masochistic dream metaphor is a woman finding herself nude before a group of people. A patient of mine who was a concert artist dreamed that she had all sorts of difficulties getting to the hall on the night of a concert. She finally arrived, came out on stage, and realized she had no clothes on. This terrified her and she woke up in a sweat. Her nudity expressed several things: the fear that she would be revealed at her worst, her feelings of being seen through, her doubts about herself as an artist, and a general feeling of humiliation that was an ongoing aspect of her life.

Common also, as I said earlier, are images of paralysis or some other sort of impairment that keep the dreamer from being able to function or to assist herself in a threatening situation. One of the starkest of these was a dream of a masochistic patient in which she saw a woman standing alone in an empty room. The woman was paralyzed and could not move. The bleak metaphor speaks powerfully of the absolute sense of incapacity and inadequacy that engulfed this woman and of the feeling of alienation that was a consequence of her masochistic style.

Another masochistic woman dreamed that as she and her husband were entering a restaurant to have dinner, a gang of thieves burst in, robbed the patrons, and took the woman and her husband along with them, demanding to go to their home. Once there, the thieves began looting the house, and when she threatened to call the police, they just laughed at her and said they had cut the lines. Finally, however, she managed to get outside and planned to find a phone and call the police but found that she was paralyzed and could not move. Here the paralysis theme is accompanied by two others that frequently turn up in the dreams of masochistic people: being menaced or pursued by evil people and calling on the authorities for help. The woman in this dream never completes a call to the police, but the idea of doing so looms large. Authority figures, good and bad, appear prominently in masochistic dreams. Also notice that the dream started with the woman seeking sustenance—going to a restaurant for food. This speaks of her emotional hunger that was not satisfied in her marriage.

Another common masochistic dream, related directly to low self-esteem, focuses on making a connection with an important public personalty and deriving strength from the association. Some years ago, a patient of mine dreamed repeatedly of establishing relationships with one or another member of the Kennedy family, an expression of the wish to share in some of the luster and power that attaches to the Kennedy name. This same patient dreamed she was ingesting the flesh of a renowned opera star, a metaphoric statement of her desire to become (literally, and cannibalistically in this instance, by incorporating the diva's body within her own) someone with stature, creative gifts, and power.

A male patient dreamed he was standing in line, waiting to talk to the mayor of New York City, Ed Koch. All the others taking their turn seemed to be at ease and to have no problem talking with the mayor. But this man realized he would have nothing to say, and so he stepped out of line, feeling very disappointed with himself. In the dream he thought, "What is this? Everybody else can talk to this guy. Why can't I?" That he was unable to approach even the seemingly very accessible mayor is indicative of how completely helpless he feels to express himself, as well as how inadequate and worthless.

The dreams of masochistic people, even when they don't center on easily recognizable metaphors such as pursuit, paralysis, nudity in a crowd, or connecting with someone famous, certainly exhibit those aspects of the masochistic personality that have by now become familiar to the reader: fear of other people, a sense of being misused by them, self-destructiveness, a perception of the world as a dangerous place, an inability to stand up for oneself.

A sense of fear of the power of others comes through strongly in the dream of a male patient who saw himself being driven by a chauffeur in a limousine to an exclusive house outside of the city. He was in the car with "other children," he said. When they arrived at their destination, he got out of the car but then realized that he had left behind his coat and some other things he had brought with him. When he finally had those items in hand, he looked toward the front door of the house and realized that the man standing there was waiting for him to give the name of the person he had come to see. He couldn't remember the name. Throughout the dream, this man feels and behaves like one of the children he feels himself to be. When he gets out of the car, he forgets to take his things with him. Confronted with the authority in the doorway, he forgets the name of the person he has come to see. His sense of helplessness paralyzes his brain and he is unable to conduct himself as an adult.

A woman who experienced other people as dangerous reported a dream that resembled an adventure movie. She and some other people were being held prisoner by a group of Nazis in an encampment alongside a river containing a large and frightening alligator. She wondered how she would escape but took no steps to effect that end. Finally, she and her brother were rescued by helicopter. The feeling throughout the dream was that she was surrounded by danger but completely unable to contend with it. Her only hope was to get away, which she did, but through no effort of her own. Another time this same woman dreamed she was in a vacation spot in the Caribbean, waiting at the airport to go home. Suddenly, a military coup occurred and she was detained, held for a long time in one place and questioned by someone who said he came from the police and who she feared might torture her. Ultimately, she was allowed to go, but here again she found herself in the hands of dangerous authority figures.

Another quite masochistic woman dreamed that she and a man were swimming just off a deserted beach when she saw a shark in the water nearby. They quickly swam to a rock, but before the man could pull her up on the rock, the shark bit off her leg below the knee. The man decided it would be best if they stayed on the rock until morning, although she wondered if she might bleed to death. The shark symbolizes this woman's fear of other people, her sense that they are dangerous and can do terrible damage. Even so, she submits to the man's judgment although she believes it may put her life in jeopardy. (Of course, his judgment, whomever he stood for, may have been right, since swimming with a bleeding stump would hardly be safe in shark-infested waters).

This woman also had frequent chase dreams in which she was pursued by either cops or robbers—both authorities, both dangerous—or she dreamed of terrible car accidents with mutilated bodies sprawled all over the scene of the accident. In these dreams, her sense of danger and of being vulnerable to damage and her anger at her own helplessness in the face of others' power come through over and over again.

Then there was a young woman who dreamed she was engaged to a young man who sent her a ring through the mail. At first the ring seemed pretty, but then she began to find it ugly. Just as she was going to meet him for lunch, a friend of hers commented on what a weird person he was, and when they met, she suddenly saw him as sloppy and disheveled, with obviously dirty hair and fingernails. She felt embarrassed to be seen with him, but she did not have the nerve to tell him that she didn't want to marry him, and she awoke feeling very anxious. The central point of this dream is that she saw this unappealing, distasteful man as the sort she would marry because that fit her image of herself as being unattractive and without value.

A young professional woman who is a patient of mine dreamed that she was to attend a conference in her field. When she arrived at the entrance to the room where the conference was being held, she was told she could not be admitted. She didn't ask why but simply walked away and decided to go to the ladies' room. There she waited in line, but when her turn came a woman appeared and said it was not her turn, that she (the woman) had been there first. She accepted the woman's assertion and continued to wait. Aside from her obvious and masochistic inability to stand up for herself, you will recognize that two types of masochistic communication are reflected in her dream: fear to question and the closely related acceptance of the other's premise. This woman was a legitimate participant in the conference, but when she was turned away, she didn't question why, she simply capitulated. Once again in the ladies' room, though she knew it to be her turn, she accepted the other woman's premise that she should go first rather than questioning it or taking an opposite stand.

The masochistic message of spilling is revealed in the dream of a woman who saw herself undergoing surgery for the removal of part of her body. She did not know why this surgery was being performed, but while she was under the anesthetic, she talked volubly. When she awakened in her dream, she found many people standing around who had been listening to her, and she was embarrassed because she felt they were laughing at her and critical of her. The most important feature of this dream is that the woman felt her talking was out of her control and that it left her vulnerable to damage from others. Feelings of helplessness also come through in the metaphor of anesthesia and in the sense of being acted upon by others, carved up by others, without even knowing why.

Helplessness before others was also revealed by a woman who dreamed she was getting dressed to go on a date. Her closet was filled with clothes, but she felt she looked awful in each outfit she tried on. Finally, she settled on something as her date was about to arrive, but he never appeared. This dream reflects the woman's general anxiety, symbolized by the repeated changing of clothes, and her sense that she is vulnerable to being hurt by others and must try to ward off criticism by wearing "the perfect outfit."

Yet another dream displaying feelings of helplessness and being ill-treated by others came from a woman who dreamed she was taking a holiday with three other women, sharing a cabin. The women began to fight with her and told her to leave. When she refused, they tried to push her out. Then they insisted she ought to pay for the entire vacation. They asked to borrow money from her. She said she would not lend it to them but handed over the money nevertheless. This woman made small attempts to stand up for herself, token efforts, but she was powerless to stop the attacks of the others, and ultimately she capitulated to them.

Masochism, ignored or untreated, tends to get worse as the defensive style continues to reinforce itself and the sum of suffering grows. One woman's dream reflected this sense of progressive difficulty. She and a friend attended a tennis class, and the gymnasium was filled with hundreds of people, making her fearful that the pro would not be able to pick her out of the crowd. Members of the class lined up to serve, but just before it was her turn, the pro blew the whistle and said they should all go outdoors. Everyone began to run from the gym, but she couldn't find her way out. When she finally did, she found herself running in a tunnel that gradually inclined uphill, making the going increasingly tough. When she reached the end of the tunnel, she found it was blocked and she could not get out. She awakened in an anxious state.

Many things come through in this dream: the woman's fear

that she is invisible, that there is nothing distinctive about her to make her stand out in a crowd; her sense that she doesn't get her fair share of things, that she never gets to take her turn; feelings of powerlessness and inadequacy, of being unable to do what other people do easily. But the overall atmosphere of the dream is most important, the atmosphere of unending struggle, constantly confronting obstacles, stymied at every turn, and traveling an increasingly arduous and dangerous path that leads nowhere.

This same woman had grave doubts not only about herself but about me as well, as was revealed in a dream in which we had decided she would spend the day with me and go wherever I went. She looked forward to this as a comforting prospect, but then, quite suddenly, I appeared to her as a ten-year-old with pigtails, and *I* was following *her* around. This woman was questioning whether help was available to her. Obviously, I was of no use if I was a child. Her need to be totally dependent in order to survive and her fear that perhaps I wasn't the omniscient figure she fantasized I was, but a child like herself, was very threatening.

In the following dream of a masochistic woman, she was both killer and victim. She was on her way to a shopping center where she had heard there was a sale. Arriving at the parking lot, she saw it was strewn with dead bodies and flowing with blood. Although she was frightened, she pressed on with her shopping, entering the supermarket and grabbing hold of as much as she could carry. Suddenly, she realized her children were home alone and in possible danger, so she rushed home and was relieved to find them alive. This woman saw herself surrounded by death and destruction, an expression of her raging anger about her life predicament. She felt in a sense that she was dead. But, nevertheless, she went on with her life, by rote, as it were, trying to grab what satisfactions she could. Only her children were capable of penetrating the negative, destructive wall around her and exciting in her genuine love and concern. Her dream indicates this woman's awareness of her own destructiveness and its effect on her life, but it also indicates a kind of resignation about it, except insofar as her children are concerned.

A patient of mine is an extremely bright young woman, only a few years out of college but already in a good job with a very decent salary. Extremely attractive as well, she nevertheless has had few relationships with men, as she finds it difficult to reach out to other people and make herself accessible in any way. She had always planned to return to school for her M.B.A. and this year applied to and was accepted at six of seven of the country's best graduate schools. At the same time, she was offered a job at a higher level with a large salary increase. But because she is, unfortunately, quite masochistic, having these two excellent options left her feeling not elation but despair. Her sessions were flooded by tears; she felt her life was a disaster. A dream she reported to me was very expressive of her masochistic problems.

She was going on vacation on an ocean liner, but the day she was due to leave she delayed going home to pack and, after she finally did so and set off for the ship, she realized she had forgotten certain things and had to return home. Then she rushed to the dock only to see the boat pulling away. She called out, but no one heard her. So she jumped into the water and began to swim after the boat, seeming to gain on it for a while but then falling behind. She sank under the water and, looking down, saw herself lying on the bottom, drowned. In the second part of the dream, she was on the boat, which was filled with lots of young men and women. But rather than spending time with them, she was busying herself with organizational tasks, seeing that the chairs were placed right, that everyone had the proper stateroom, and so on.

The delay in the first part of the dream is a metaphor for this young woman's fear of life: She avoids, puts off, misses connections; she uses tangential, circumstantial actions (as well as speech) to keep herself from engaging with life. Then, filled with regret and remorse, she struggles to reverse her course, but it is too late; she has delayed too long. In the second half of the dream, which is an additional effort to solve the problem posed in the first segment, she places herself on the boat. Once there, however, her fear of others overcomes her again, and she is unable to involve herslf with the other people abroad. She is unable to be playful, to be accessible, to join in. She practices avoidance while endeavoring to disguise it with an overlay of busyness. One can assume several roles in the course of a dream and do things that seem irrational but that obviously serve an important purpose in the dream itself. This young woman was able to see herself drowned and then resurrected and on the boat.

The dream of an older patient of mine also featured self-destructive lateness as a key element. A paraprofessional who was approaching menopause, she saw in the first part of her dream a group of cheerleaders milling around on a football field, not properly dressed because they had not had time to put on their uniforms before the game began. In the second part of the dream she was to deliver a paper to her institution, but she arrived late. Standing outside was a group of dreary women, crying, suffering, looking dopey, a few of them drinking. The dreamer debated whether she should join them or go in to give her talk. Then she awoke with considerable anxiety.

When we began to discuss the dream, I said this seemed to make a statement about the American woman, but I wondered if I was imposing some of my notions on the interpretation. It shows a woman beginning life by having to look good and act out a vacuous role (after all, in a football game the players are doing what counts, not the cheerleaders) and ending up without men in an insipid group of women, trying to anesthetize herself. "That's exactly it," my patient exclaimed. "I was a cheerleader, and I spent, or rather wasted, a great deal of time in college trying to achieve some recognition that way. But a cheerleader isn't recognized as an individual, only as part of a group. And I'm afraid because I'm always late with whatever I do that I'll end up being of one of those drippy women. I have no confidence in what I do, no enthusiasm. I'm afraid it will only lead to failure and to being one of the castoffs."

Finally, I turn to the dream of a patient who was very aware of her masochistic problems but had yet to overcome them. This woman's mother had been a powerful and damaging force in her life since childhood, sometimes overprotective, other times brutal. My patient dreamed she was in a car with her mother who insisted on driving. "Let me drive, Mother," the woman kept saying. "You can't see." But her mother refused to stop and change seats, and at one point she veered from the left lane of the road over to the right and crashed into another car. The mother was thrown onto the road, which was strewn with crystal, and the mother's leg was broken off. When the woman looked up the stump of her mother's leg, she could see that it was hollow, as if her mother were a papier-mâché dummy. In a rage, and even though she knew it might hurt, the woman pulled her mother up from the pavement and said, "Why don't you ever listen to me? Do you see what's happened?"

This mother never let her daughter develop autonomy: She never let her drive. When the woman tells her mother that she cannot see, it reflects the reality of the mother's aging, as well as the fact that as the woman has become more mature she has developed a greater awareness than her mother. That she sees her mother as hollow, and no longer the powerful and threatening person she has always seemed is progress for this woman. Still, she continues to submit to her mother, and there is a suggestion that this causes great rage in her. When she yanks her mother off the ground, knowing it will hurt, and says, "Why don't you ever listen to me?" she is really saying that she is grown-up now and still not free of her mother's hold.

The day she had this dream, the woman had made a necklace for herself, combining the black and white crystals of two old necklaces. The broken crystal scattered on the road suggests that while she was able to remake the old necklaces into something new and pleasing, she was not capable of an equally successful effort in her life. Her masochistic sense of futility comes through in this image. It is as though she is saying: What is the use of making an effort if it is destroyed by my mother's refusal to let me take charge of my own life or to acknowledge that I am now the one who sees clearly.

"What is meant by reality?" Virginia Woolf wrote. "It . . . is what remains over when the skin of the day has been cast into the hedge. That is what is left of past time and our loves and hates." Although Woolf is speaking here of reality, I have always thought this passage was relevant to dreams as well. For they are what is left when the skin of the day is cast into the hedge, not emanations from an alien and mysterious place but essential pieces of our selves, our *innermost* reality.

13

Body Images

Several years ago, I worked with a young woman who was studying acting and beginning to get jobs in the theater. When I noticed she was getting thin, I questioned her about it and she gave me appropriate answers, most of them having to do with her career. I suggested, however, that it was now time to return to normal eating, her diet having been an obvious success. Shortly after this, when I saw that the weight loss was continuing and that she was beginning to look like a concentration camp victim, I told her so. She responded, "But I look *fat*."

This distorted body image is one of the most telling features of anorexia nervosa, a condition that is estimated to afflict over 300,000 people (mostly young women) in the United States. Anorexia was recognized as a disease a hundred years ago: it was considered an hysterical condition in which loss of appetite, constipation, amenorrhea (absence of the menses), weight loss, and restless activity prevailed, but its incidence was believed rare. Now it is widespread, which is perhaps not surprising in light of the enormous societal emphasis on thinness that exists today.

Our culture is plagued by a preoccupation with dieting, the tip of the iceberg that is composed of the compulsive quest for youth, a narcissistic concern with appearance, the dictum that women must be as slender as scarecrows to look fashionable in clothes, and the rejection of things "female" in an increasingly homosexual society. We are obsessed with what we are and are not eating, so much so that it is not unusual to hear even the slimmest of women waxing apologetic over nibbling on a cookie or eating a piece of chocolate. It has been suggested recently that anorexia nervosa might better be called a "fat phobia" or a "phobic fear of fat." That seems apt to me. The fear of being fat exists throughout the culture to an extraordinary degree. And in some people it takes on pathological, or phobic, proportions.

In her book *The Obession: Reflections on the Tyranny of Slenderness*, Kim Chernin writes movingly of the effect cultural forces have on women's feelings about their bodies. "The body holds meaning," she declares. "A woman wishing to make her breasts and thighs and hips smaller . . . may be expressing the fact that she feels uncomfortable being female in this culture. A woman . . . wishing to control her hungers . . . may be expressing the fact that she has been taught to regard . . . her passions and appetites as dangerous, requiring . . . careful monitoring. A woman obsessed with the reduction of her flesh may be revealing the fact that she is alienated from a natural source of female power and has not been allowed to develop a reverential feeling for her body."

Geneen Roth supports Chernin's notion that the culture puts pressure on women to reject their bodies. "I had only to look around me to see that desirable women my age were slinkly slim," she writes in *Feeding the Hungry Heart: The Experience of Compulsive Eating*. "All the Farrah mascara media maids who proclaimed that we must look like them to be attractive are bony. Their lean bodies are like powerless mockeries of the male physique. The models look male-weak instead of female-strong."

Obesity, which represents the swing of the pendulum to the other extreme, is also on the rise. And the obese person, like the anorexic, suffers from distorted body-image perception. In both instances, the sense of body image is delusional and represents a break with reality. I looked at my anorexic patient and saw someone who resembled a prisoner in a concentration camp. She looked at herself and denied that she was too thin; in fact, she did not think she was thin enough. The anorexic, no matter how thin she gets, always sees herself fat. Obese people, on the other hand, deny the reality of their size by trying to hide their heaviness. As one patient who was at least seventy-five pounds overweight put it to me: "When I look in the mirror, I only look at my face and it looks to me the way it always did. I see it as thin." Maintaining the delusion is difficult for the obese, however, and they hide their bodies in whatever way they can. They may drape themselves in clothing that is designed to conceal their contours. They are often reluctant to be photographed, knowing there is truth in the maxim; "The camera never lies." Some refuse to look in mirrors altogether.

Along with a skewed body image goes a distorted sense of body functions. The anorexic takes a few bites of food and feels full. The obese person, no matter how much she has eaten, always has room for more. Magical thinking often accompanies body delusion, especially in the anorexic. "If I am thin enough," she might think, "someone will love me." Or, "If I am thin enough, people will respect me." And anorexics and obese people have something else in common: Both believe that their thin self is their "real" self.

These eating disorders are really two facets of a single problem, flip sides of the same coin. They are primitive manifestations of masochism, expressions of self-hate and self-punishment that have crystallized around the issue of eating. The anorexic constantly punishes herself by avoiding food, often using laxatives to an excessive degree, and driving herself to keep up a level of frenetic activity that her lack of nourishment makes extremely taxing. The obese person punishes herself by constantly forcing more food into her body than it can tolerate, like a goose being force-fed for pâté de foie gras, a custom that was outlawed, by the way, because it represented such cruelty to the animal. Both the anorexic and the obese person may also suffer from bulimia, the binge-and-purge cycle of gorging on food and then forcing vomiting. And sometimes the two extremes of anorexia and obesity merge in a single person who veers from one to the other.

Such a young woman was the patient who began treatment with me immediately after moving to New York but only stayed a brief time before deciding to leave the city and return home. When she first came to see me, she was huge. Two years later, she returned to New York and began treatment again. This time I was startled to open the door to a painfully thin, sickly looking young woman. Observing my expression, which I apparently had not concealed successfully, she said, "I know it's a surprise, but don't I look good?" She looked neither good nor like a likely candidate for a photographer's model, a career she intended to pursue. She had obviously engaged in some magical thinking, believing that mere thinness qualified her for such a job.

The societal obsession with food and eating is itself masochistic. For today, even as people are eating, they punish themselves by analyzing their intake relentlessly, discussing weight gain and loss ad nauseum, denying themselves certain foods, feeling guilt-ridden if that denial fails and they, God forbid, give in. Rhoda Koenig wrote an article for *New York* magazine several years ago called "Living to Eat," that caught the essence of this obsession: "Though mother had always said it was bad manners to talk about your health problems at the table, at times seventies lunchtime chatter about proteins and carbohydrates and how 'Japanese is very Pritikin' made you think you had wandered into a nutritionists' convention." The increase in eating disorders occurs at a time of great nutritional sophistication and against the background of plenty our affluent society produces. We might be more inclined to savor the irony inherent in this if the disorders were not so desperately destructive. Both anorexia and obesity are life-threatening conditions.

Hilde Bruch, a psychiatrist famous for her work on eating disorders, stresses that hunger is not only a reflection of *physiological* nutritional depletion but also a *psychological* experience. In relation to this, she emphasizes the importance of the early mother-child interaction in the feeding process. The mother, Bruch notes, may not be able to distinguish whether or not the infant's cry is for food, but she may offer or force food on her child regardless. She may also reward the child for being "good" (that is, passive) with food.

The whole separation-individuation process that occurs, or fails to occur, between mother and child is acted out primarily in relation to food. And anorexia and obesity, two extremes of bodily masochism, are further enactments of this early experience. A mother may overfeed an infant or, in the case of a more overtly destructive mother (the same mother who, for instance, might batter her child), she may starve it. A mother may offer her infant what Harry Stack Sullivan called the bad, poisonous nipple. By that he meant that the mothering activities, especially feeding, are tainted by the mother's sense of anxiety, anger, or hate in relation to her child, or a combination of all three. A mother may attempt to maintain control over her child by either forcing or denying food. She may insist on certain kinds of eating, demanding a clean plate, for example, or requiring that a child sit at the table until a particular hated food is eaten. The former could lay the groundwork for obesity; the latter might elicit the angry defiance that leads to anorexia. This defiance serves the defensive purpose that is typical of masochism. Ruth Jean Eisenbud, writing about anorexia, notes how the anorexic somatizes her defiance by moving from I won't eat (a defiant statement) to I can't eat (a somatic manifestation). In both anorexia and obesity, the child punishes herself, however, using an instrument it is impossible for the mother to lay her hands on—the gastrointestinal tract.

Chernin also observes that the early experience between mother and child has a profound effect on how a woman comes to view her body. She suggests that women who try to cut down on their size and shape are driven by the desire to erase the memory of the primordial mother who ruled over childhood. Being slender spares them from looking maternally plump and thus reminding themselves of the helplessness of their own infancy.

Because "poisonous" circumstances have surrounded the experience of eating, the anorexic has unconscious fantasies that all food is poison. The anorexic is trapped between the need to eat to sustain life and her paranoid projection about food's toxic nature. Her dogged refusal to eat is more than just a compulsive pursuit of thinness. It also represents a phobic avoidance of poison.

The obese girl or woman, on the other hand, may need continually to retain food, as it represents to her a connection with the mother. Food serves as an umbilical cord without which she feels she will die. In such instances an unresolved symbiosis exists between mother and child. Obesity can also result, however, from a pattern of defiance to the mother. Perhaps the mother has forced food on the child or used food as a reward, only to cut back as she sees the child gaining weight. Obesity may be the child's way of stating that she refuses to have limits imposed.

This struggle between mother and child, with food as the battleground, begins in early infancy and increasingly becomes internalized and acted out solely within the individual. The anorexic is struggling against feelings of being enslaved and exploited and unable to lead her own life. She is struggling for *control*. Her compulsive perfectionism drives her to torture herself into starvation in order to be respected. She has no middle ground: She is either perfect or utterly worthless and completely vulnerable. The obese person is fighting to *hang on to* her parent, orally incorporating food-as-mother. This connection carries with it a sense of being a "good girl," of being loved and protected. In either instance, the involvement with food and eating is single-minded; it represents the only real "relationship" in the person's life. And the outcome of the battle may be the ultimate masochistic act of self-destruction, for both anorexia and obesity constitute ongoing passive suicidal activities.

Sometimes the urge toward suicide is more active than that embodied in under- or overeating—acts that after a time seem to involve no volition whatsoever. I think, for instance, of an obese young patient of mine who had as fixed and intense a symbiosis with her mother as I have ever seen. The mother, divorced for years from the patient's father, was saccharine in the extreme. The young woman was not especially attractive except for glorious hip-length red-gold hair, but she was bright and had a good sense of humor, qualities that accounted for her sizable group of acquaintances. She repeatedly regaled me with tales of her daily, lengthy stuggles in the bathroom, trying to force her body to relinquish the food she had compulsively crammed into it when she was not in the bathroom. As our work together went on, she did begin to make progress, developing some new interests, having a few tentative dates, and beginning to separate from her mother. At one point, however, as the necessity for this separation became increasingly apparent, she began to threaten suicide and was hospitalized. I could not help feeling when I visited her that her Mona Lisa–like smile signaled that she felt victorious. She avoided my attempts to discuss this, however, and shortly afterward her mother dismissed me.

Another masochistic element that accompanies these eating disorders is sexual deprivation. The anorexic, frequently amenorrheic as a result of starvation, generally suffers the loss of, or fails to develop, any sexual interest. The obese girl is less likely to be amenorrheic; when she is, it is more often for psychological rather than physiological reasons. She too, however, has diminished sexual interest.

Unquestionably, the pressure to be thin is on the rise in our culture. I have occasionally observed acquaintances of mine who are dedicated to being thin eating with a speed and intensity that indicate they are starving when they sit down to a meal. Bruch feels this emphasis on thinness and the concomitant hostility toward weight as something shameful or evil have had a powerfully destructive effect. I believe such attitudes have contributed to obesity's becoming a serious health problem. The obese person experiences society and its attitudes as a stand-in for mother who is saying, "Thou shalt not eat." Then she feels even more deprived and defiantly eats more. These attitudes push anorexics to starve themselves in the belief that thinness is all, the answer to life, its own reward. When this cultural climate combines with a personal history that causes someone compulsively to reenact the rudimentary struggle of her early infancy involving her gastrointestinal tract, the result can be the most primitive and self-punishing form of masochism there is.

Roth chillingly conveys the persistent, repetitive, punitive nature of the eating disorders in the following passage, a masochistic *cri de coeur* if ever I heard one: "I made myself vomit, using the practiced muscles of my stomach. Why do I do this to myself? Why do I stuff myself with self-hatred and shame, knowing I can never in this way get rid of the ugly anger and paranoia I'm filling myself with. Why can't I control myself? Why do I hate myself? I cried as I reached into the refrigerator and began eating compulsively again."

Anorexia and obesity represent masochistic retreats. People who suffer from these conditions turn from dealing with interpersonal relations to dealing with bodily, or somatic, functions. In this way, the disorders resemble other phobias that are also self-punishing and masochistic. A woman who suffers, for instance, from agoraphobia puts herself in a kind of self-constructed prison when she refuses to leave her home. Her fear is of open spaces, but this is a symbolic replacement of the real nature of her fear—which is that if she is out in the open, she is more likely to be confronted with people and to have to deal with them.

Another sort of somatic expression of masochism was evident in the behavior of a woman who came to consult me about the difficulty she was having in her marriage. Throughout the session, as she talked and cried, she dug the tips of her fingers into her leg or into the arm of the chair. At the end of the hour, she said to me; "You know, I often have skin problems with my fingertips, and I've consulted any number of dermatologists and gotten all sorts of cream, but nothing seems to do any good." This woman, who did not dare to get angry, took all her aggression out on herself, perpetually traumatizing her fingertips. When she sought help for this, and did not receive any, she heaped even more punishment on herself by wallowing in feelings of grievance and martyrdom.

Some years ago, somatic self-rejection was expressed in the extraordinary number of American women who had hysterectomies. These often needless operations constituted a kind of symbolic castration. Viewed psychologically, one could say that these women, at a very deep level, rejected themselves as women and/or rejected motherhood because of its feminine connotations. Today, the focus of this masochistic lack of self-acceptance is on the breast.

Throughout the centuries, breasts have been sexually interesting to men. In times past, they often have been emphasized by fashion, sometimes to the point of near exposure. In our own recent history, Marilyn Monroe epitomized the ultimate sex object, and a large part of the image she projected was based on her full breasts. That was the standard for what was sexually attractive. More recently still, that standard has been redefined by the unisex influence. As the emphasis on thinness has grown, breasts have been minimized. A patient of mine who had been a prostitute and later became a madam of a brothel, told me that in the past, men considered breasts an important part of a woman's attractiveness when selecting a partner. Today, she said, they focus on the derriere, another indication of cultural homosexuality.

Whatever the prevailing standard, women are constantly presented with images of how their breasts should look, a matter that is for the most part beyond their control. The breast is an organ that has its own genetic inheritance with regard to shape and form. Certain external events may have an effect on this (extreme obesity, extreme thinness, nursing an infant), but basically the size of a woman's breasts is genetically determined. That does not deter masochistic women from torturing themselves about their breasts, however. They complain that they are too big, too small, misshapen, ill-placed.

A patient of mine constantly agonizd over the fact that she did not have what she called "half-grapefruit" breasts, a term I have heard more than once since she introduced me to it. These are breasts that have a very wide attachment, resulting in their being rounded but not too full, gentle extensions of the body's contour that do not protrude too much. This woman had a lovely face, a seemingly attractive body, and a husband who was satisfied with her breasts as they were. But all that counted for nothing. Her narcissism and masochism were such that she constantly judged her breasts as inferior—especially after her regular visits to a health club where she compared her body to other women's. Another patient of mine, also attractive and also married to a man who had not complained about her body, insisted that she did not feel like a woman because her breasts were not large enough. She asked me repeatedly for the name of a plastic surgeon, and initially I demurred, urging her to discuss the matter further before she rushed into anything. Finally, I saw that she

was determined, and rather than have her go to someone unknown, I gave the name of a reputable plastic surgeon. She had
silicone implants in her breasts—and feels better for being able to
meet a social concept of attractiveness!

Sadly, a new torment connected with the breast has arisen as
the incidence of breast cancer has increased. Now, not only is the
breast an unsatisfactory object that fails to match the prescribed
stereotypical idea, it is also a threat. And women are constantly
made aware of the threat, of the danger their breasts may represent, by the self-examination that doctors advise. This worry
about breast cancer is often used masochistically.

I believe, and recent research supports me, that when organs
are not used for their proper physiological purpose, they are likely
to develop malignancies. Many women avoid nursing their children because they are fearful of spoiling their breasts. The irony
is that failing to nurse may increase their chances of developing
breast tumors.

The matter of breast cancer poses a terrible dilemma for
women. Constant self-examination, I suspect, may lend itself to a
masochistic emphasis on misery and potential suffering. On the
other hand, waiting for an annual examination by the doctor increases the risk that a malignancy may go undetected for some
time. I recognize that it may be controversial, but my inclination
is to advise women who do not tend to develop cysts in their
glands to avoid self-examination and leave the search to their
gynecologists whom they see once or twice a year. By doing this,
they can at least avoid the incessant worry that they may discover
a malignancy. I am not suggesting that there are any easy solutions in this troublesome area, and perhaps the most important
thing is for each woman to do what is least distressing for her.

I had occasion recently to view some anthropological films of
a New Guinea tribe in which female breasts were on full display.
The breasts of many of the older women had taken on the appearance of drained-out, empty sacks after years of nursing infants, while the young, nubile girls had full, rounded breasts. But
it struck me that the men did not seem especially aware of the
difference in these two types of breasts, nor did the older women

appear to feel inferior or self-conscious because of the shape of their breasts. I could not help but reflect on the contrast with our own culture, its narcissistic preoccupation with the minutiae of body shape and its demand that virtually every woman in every stage of life conform to movie-star standards.

14

Masochism in
Literature and Film

Virginia Woolf's story "The New Dress" offers us a truly remarkable portrait of the masochistic woman. Mabel Waring is thrilled to be invited to Clarissa Dalloway's party, but the invitation throws her into a turmoil about what she will wear. She settles on a choice that is within her means, one that is "original," if not fashionable. But from the moment she arrives at the party, she is awash in an agony of self-doubt, self-consciousness, and self-abasement. Her masochistic grandiosity tells her that everyone is concerned with, and making fun of, her new dress. When the cloakroom attendant simply does her job and attempts to be helpful, Mabel suspects she is rendering a judgment on Mabel's appearance. Then a guest she knows says, "It's perfectly charming," and Mabel detects a satirical pucker of her lips. Inundated by her lifelong feelings of worthlessness, she begins projecting these feelings onto others. They are all judging her mercilessly and maliciously; they are all false and deceitful.

But it is Mabel herself, of course, who feels that she is hideous and whose behavior is inauthentic. She sees herself set against the other guests as though the party were a competition: She is hopelessly dowdy and inept; they are all elegant and suave. She feels like a fly trapped in a saucer of milk with its wings stuck together. How should a male guest respond when Mabel says, "I feel like some dowdy, decrepit, horribly dingy old fly"? This bizarre remark (as inappropriate as that of the woman in Salzburg who told me she was "holding up the wall"), the product of

Mabel's enormous self-preoccupation, is hardly engaging and could only drive her listener away. And what if someone else had paid her a compliment? Would she have accepted it at face value? Of course not. She would have thought it a lie. Always anticipating attack, she has slapped herself on the cheek, punished herself, before anyone else has a chance to do so.

Mabel is masochism incarnate; few examples of such women in literature are as insightful, sensitive, or comprehensive. But if Mabel stands alone as an artfully and perceptively drawn portrait, she has a great deal of company when one considers her as the representative of a type. Literature is filled with suffering women.

Literary images of women tend to fit into one of four broad categories: (1) the woman who succumbs to the limits of the constricting cocoon in which society wraps her, the nice, good, and very often masochistic woman; (2) the woman who attempts to withstand these pressures to conform and has to pay a price for her resistance; (3) the woman who attempts to live vicariously since she is not permitted to live freely on her own; (4) the exception to the rule, the autonomous woman who displays self-assertiveness and courage and is not punished for them.

Josephine A. Ruggiero of Providence College believes that most women in literature serve essentially as conveniences for the resolution of masculine dilemmas. The virtuous woman is good and chaste and identified with the positive aspects of a man's life. The sensuous woman is bad, sexually experienced, and identified with the negative aspects. And at the core of the sentimental stereotype of women, says Ruggiero, is the view of woman as primarily emotional, helpless, and incompetent; at the core, in other words, is the image of the masochistic woman who has no power of her own and cannot solve anything for herself.

In a fascinating study of the French novel, Kathryn J. Crecelius notes the predominant pattern of the masculine lives portrayed. The heroes grow up, develop character, learn about the world, and finally achieve a place in society with attendant fame and fortune. The pattern of feminine development stands in stark contrast to this. The women in these novels are not happy or fulfilled. Even in novels of the last twenty years, Crecelius says, it is unusual to find a woman who leads a life that is satisfying but does not entail an enormous sacrifice of either her heart or her spirit. Because these women (or their creators) feel they cannot survive losing what happiness they already have, they are cut off in the flower of their youth.

Suffering Women: Feminine Masochism in Novels by American Women by Rosemary Morris deals with the work of Ellen Glasgow, Willa Cather, Edith Wharton, Gertrude Stein, and Mary Johnstone and studies all the novels of these authors that have a woman as a central character. "Horney believed, as do I," the author says at the outset, "that masochism in women is not an inevitable result of the female anatomy or physiological constitution. Rather it is a coping mechanism used by some women when the development of adequate aggressiveness has been discouraged."

Suffering was the central theme of life for Glasgow, Morris notes, and she "emphasized women who suffered or women who formed stoic defenses against anger." Cather, she continues, "a boyish woman, tended to show identification with two types of characters, the strong, capable women like herself, and with male characters who looked at certain women with romantic adoration." All the authors, Morris says, depicted some women who fit Horney's description of masochism and others who were strong, independent, and assertive. But only Johnstone "consistently identified with women and in her novels emphasized women with their own attitudes of purposeful activity and capability."

Lady into Fox, a stunning allegorical tale by David Garnett, shows the literal transformation of a woman into a victim. Sylvia Fox Teabrick, member of an old English family, fell madly in love with and married her husband after a short courtship. He was given to fox hunting; she had once seen a hunt as a child and when the fox was blooded, she vomited in disgust. Nevertheless, when the husband hears of a hunt, he persuades her to join him. As they near the place where the hunt is being held, Teabrick quickens his pace, while his wife hangs back. Holding her hand, he continues to drag her along, but suddenly, and violently, she snatches away her hand and cries out, causing him to turn around. "And there where his wife had been a moment before," Garnett writes, "was a small fox of a very bright red. It looked at him beseechingly, advanced toward him a pace or two, and he saw at once that his wife was looking at him from the animal's eyes." Now the wife is the victim, the object of the hunt, the creature who depends on her husband for her very life.

You will recognize here some elements of the sado-masochistic marriage: the brief courtship during which the masochistic woman deludes herself that ruthlessness and un-communicativeness are strength, the husband calling the tune while the wife submits—as defenseless prey.

One of the most familiar sado-masochistic marriages in litera-ture is, of course, that of Nora and Torvald in Ibsen's A *Doll's House*. Nora is dependent, passive, incompetent, masochistic; Torvald is charming to everyone else but coldly vicious to his wife. Nora, however, unlike Sylvia Teabrick, finds the courage to leave as life becomes unbearably painful. She takes the first step toward emerging from her masochism. But Nora operates at a great disadvantage even as she moves in the direction of au-tonomy. For she, like Emma Bovary, was not reared to be au-thentic. She has had no experience dealing with real problems; she has never learned to contend with them in an active and thoughtful way. Ruth Crego Benson points out, in *Women in Tolstoy*, that the ambivalence Tolstoy exhibited toward women in his own life carried over into his fiction. In the Russian intellec-tual life of the time, feminism was a real issue that was actively debated, part of the whole movement toward social reform. The consequences of anatomy, the nature of woman, the destiny of marriage, the possibility of true equality between the sexes—all these questions were in the forefront of the social consciousness of the day. And Tolstoy weighed in unequivocally on the an-tifeminist side. He bitterly resented feminist ideas and, Benson notes, was uncharacteristically superficial in considering them.

Tolstoy's notion of the ideal marriage was that the wife was, in effect, created by her husband in response to his teaching and instruction and, as a result, wholly identified with his interests and well-being. The husband, in turn, should provide the wife with a safe setting for her continued dependence and, Tolstoy believed, counter with stern discipline her need to control her own life. (Tolstoy's implacable hostility toward women was evident in a remark he made in his diary: "Women do not use words to express their thoughts but to attain their goals.")

In *War and Peace*, Natasha, after her first acquaintance with André as a suitor, says to her mother, "Only I'm afraid with him. I'm always afraid with him. What does that mean?" Whatever Tolstoy's intentions, he caught in these lines something very common for women: the beginning of their romantic life, their sexual life, signals the end of security and the end of the possibility of being authentic. When a woman is denied her sociological identity in Tolstoy, Benson says, she suffers the loss of her personal identity as well. The two are intimately related. *Anna Karenina* shows how a woman is molded by society, and Anna commits suicide at the end because, stripped of her identity, she has nothing left to live for.

It is impossible to examine the images of women in literature and not be struck by the difference in the treatment of men and women who have done essentially the same thing. Medea, who murdered her own children, is the mythic figure who stands for all that is horrible in women. The degree of passion, rage, and sense of abandonment that led her to act out her feelings is not really understood or taken into account. But Hercules, who committed incest and pedophilia and was thought to have massacred his entire family, is always presented as a symbol of strength and eternal youth. The atrocities he committed are ignored in the telling of his myth; Medea's barbarity is the centerpiece of hers.

In *The Scarlet Letter*, Hawthorne shows us the contrasting attitudes toward men and women who break society's code. Hester Prynne was treated with inordinate cruelty, her suffering was dreadful. Dimmesdale, a coward who did not speak up, suffered no external punishment at all. But this is not the usual tale of the suffering woman. Dimmesdale is the passive weakling in the story, Hester the admirable figure who has the strength to endure her pain. She withstands all the abuse heaped on her, and

Hawthorne even manages, with his extraordinary gift of perception, to fashion a reward for her: Hester, because she is alone, is everything to her child; her motherhood is as complete and satisfying as it could possibly be.

Literature can be, and has been, used by men to keep women in their place. It can be, and has been, used by women to write of their sufferings, to write of the ways in which they have tried to use their intellect, that forbidden element. It has also been used, though more rarely, to show that a woman can be a courageous protagonist just as surely as a man can.

A superlative example of a courageous woman who refused to be restricted by society is at the center of Jane Austen's *Pride and Prejudice*—Elizabeth Bennett, of course, who refuses to embrace the silliness that is her mother's forte or to marry just any man in order to be married. You will remember Mr. Collins, the pompous clergyman who decides that Elizabeth would make an appropriate wife for him. When she first refuses his proposal, he misunderstands because it is inconceivable to him that any woman would refuse him (a masculine notion not uncommon even in our own times). He seems to view her as the guest at a Chinese banquet who is expected to demur several times before accepting a delicacy the host offers, and her refusals spur him on to such windy confidences as, "I am sure you will add greatly to my future happiness." When Elizabeth remains adamant, Collins conveys to her his awareness that "an elegant female must refuse several times." "Please. Please," Elizabeth replies. "I am not an elegant female, but a rational woman." How delicious!

Shakespeare's women are extraordinary: They experience their share of pain, but there is not a true masochist among them. Cordelia suffers but she is authentic, nonmasochistic. When speaking would challenge her integrity, she remains silent, and only a woman who has attained a sense of identity could exhibit this kind of self-containment. On the other hand, when integrity demands that she assert herself, Cordelia speaks up. Gertrude also suffers, but the defensive style is absent from her behavior. Even Desdemona, though victimized, is not masochistic.

Kate in *The Taming of the Shrew* is an example of the degree to which wives were considered pieces of property in Shakespeare's day. But she does not accept her fate with docility, and she hardly fits the stereotype of the sweet, demure, compliant woman. When she is finally transformed into the model wife through torture and what could almost be considered a form of brainwashing, it is in a sense a victory for her as well as a capitulation. She learns the lessons of power well and comes to see that she will make her mark and achieve her status as the wife of a wealthy man, a bargain many women make. By doing this she revenges herself upon her father by proving him wrong, causing him to wonder if the huge dowry he offered was really necessary.

In *The Merry Wives of Windsor*, the women are aware of their limitations, but they are almost masculine in the way they play Falstaff for a sucker. Theirs is not behavior that fits the female stereotype.

All of George Bernard Shaw's women reflect different facets of the feminine personality; they have shortcomings, but they are far from masochistic. On the contrary, Shaw's women are flesh-and-blood creations endeavoring to maintain authenticity in the midst of struggle. Shaw, despite misogynist tendencies of his own, wrote heroines much more often than he did heroes, intelligent, active women capable of taking a hand in their own destinies, even though those destinies were necessarily circumscribed by the restrictions of the society in which they lived.

In a conversation with her daughter in *Mrs. Warren's Profession*, Mrs. Warren says that naturally she would rather have gone to college or been a lady than to have been a prostitute, but those were not options for her. "Respectable" poverty was, however, the kind she saw other women enduring: working in a factory twelve hours a day for a pittance and eventually dying of lead poisoning, or marrying a government laborer and keeping his house and taking care of three children with virtually no money, even less when he takes to drink. She vividly describes the degradation of such grinding hardship and then asks why she should not have made the choice she did. Vivie, her daughter, presses Mrs. Warren to make sure her mother would not advise her to choose the "respectable" course. "Of course not," Mrs. Warren replies indignantly. "What sort of mother do you take me for! How could you keep your self-respect in such starvation and slavery? And what's a woman worth—what's life worth, without self-respect? . . . The only way for a woman to provide for herself decently is for her to be good to some man who can afford to be good to her. If she's of his own station in life, let him marry her. If not, she can't expect it, and it wouldn't be for her own happiness. . . . If people arrange the world that way for women, there's no good pretending that it's arranged the other way." This is a clear-eyed, hardheaded assessment of societal conditions and, given them, Mrs. Warren did indeed make a choice that allowed her to keep her self-respect.

Candida is a different sort of woman, but she is equally forthright. When Marchbanks says, "May I say wicked things to you?" Candida is neither frightened nor aloof, and, because she is secure in herself, she is able to display respect for his passion. "No," she replies. "But you may say anything you really and truly feel. Anything at all, no matter what it is. I am not afraid, so long as it is your real self that speaks, and not a mere attitude—a gallant attitude, or a wicked attitude, or even a poetic attitude. I put you on your honor and truth. Now say anything you want to." A masochistic woman would never be capable of such a clear definition of premises. And toward the end of the play, Candida describes to Marchbanks her marriage to parson James Morell. Her clarity about how the world is set up for men and women and about her own place in that scheme is very like Mrs. Warren's. After telling Marchbanks about James's childhood as "the hero of [his] household," Candida says, "You know how strong he is . . . how clever he is—how happy! Ask James's mother and his three sisters what it cost to save James the trouble of doing anything but be strong and clever and happy. Ask me what it costs to be James's mother and three sisters and wife and mother-to-his-children all in one. . . . Ask the tradesmen who want to worry James and spoil his beautiful sermons who it is that puts them off. When there is money to give, he gives it: when there is money to refuse, I refuse it. I build a castle of comfort and indulgence and love for him, and stand sentinel always to keep little vulgar cares out. I make him master here, though he does not know it, and could not tell you a moment ago how it came to be so."

If in most of his plays Shaw recognizes that the best women can do is to live vicariously through the men they choose, there is one—*Saint Joan*—in which he pleads openly for women to be given a part in shaping the affairs of the world. His Joan is not a simple peasant girl who acts in response to visions but an intelligent, masterful young woman who spends time talking to soldiers, is fascinated by stories of combat, and "never [utters] a word that has to do with her being a woman." Shaw also gives St. Joan the last words: "O God, that made this beautiful earth—when will it be ready to receive its saints—how long, Lord, how long?" Women, Shaw might be saying, might even do better than men if they were in charge of things.

In Virginia Woolf's novel *Orlando* she makes a strong case against the restrictions placed on women when, midway through, the hero Orlando becomes a woman. The two are indistinguishable from one another, the woman being every bit as free, lusty, and appealing as the man. Mar, with whom Orlando, the woman, is having a romance, asks: "Are you positive you aren't a man?" Orlando replies: "Can it be possible that you are not a woman?" "Each was surprised at the quickness of the other's sympathy," Woolf writes, "and it was to each a revelation that a woman could be as tolerant and free-spoken as a man—and a man as strange and subtle as a woman." Sex is, or should be, irrelevant, Woolf was saying. Women and men share *all* human traits, abilities, and potentials.

The images of women in films also serve as models, as sources of informal learning, and they both reflect and influence women's ideas of themselves. Molly Haskell's remarkable book *From Reverence to Rape*, a study of films from the 1930s to the 1970s, conveys in its title alone what the attitudes toward women have been during this period. There used to be more independent-minded heroines portrayed than there are today, she points out, adding, however, that even these relatively strong women always suffered from a kind of vulnerability as well. They generally felt guilty about their self-sufficiency, apologetic for daring to lay themselves on the line. Today, Haskell says, we have regressed to portraying women as either bland young fashion plates or faceless, anonymous sex objects. Speaking of Garbo, Haskell says: "Her spirit leaped first and her body, in total exquisite accord, leaped after." About whom could we say this today? No one, I think. Today the appeal is almost invariably sexual.

Generally in films, Haskell notes, and particularly in the "woman's film," "a regular outlet for self-pity," women have been exhorted to relinquish everything for love, relegated to the home and to domestic chores, and denied opportunities for heroism. They have never experienced "a love that relishes separateness, grows stronger with resistance, and in the maturity of admitting dependence meets the challenge of being different but equal." On the contrary, their relationships have been characterized by passivity, dependence, powerlessness, and inequality. They have been, in other words, masochistic women.

In *Psychoanalytic Review*, Ralph Luce in some ways paralleled Haskell's book with an article called "From Hero to Robot: Masculinity in America, Stereotypes and Reality." Luce traces American male stereotypes from the cowboy hero to the military hero, folksinger hero, wheeler-dealer hero, and finally to today's robot hero in which superficial appearance is the primary value. This has evolved, Luce maintains, because of the deified computer and the exalted astronauts in whom technical skill and detachment of feelings in dangerous situations are the primary values. Marshall McLuhan called the electronic media an externalized nervous system, Luce notes, and without a nervous system inside him man is truly empty and devoid of feeling. Could this be one of the reasons man seems to need to keep on pushing woman into an inferior, nonthreatening, masochistic position?

The film *Rebecca* gives us a highly accurate portrait of a masochist in the young woman played by Joan Fontaine. Companion to a rich, aggressive, nasty widow summering on the Riviera, she lives in fear of the widow's reproaches and constantly chastises herself as well. "Oh, I'm so clumsy," she says, when she accidentally knocks over a vase of flowers. "Why can't I ever do anything right?" she asks herself time and again. The widow continually assaults the young woman's self-esteem; she in turn readily and repeatedly capitulates to the widow's demands. Once married to the character played by Laurence Olivier, who admits it is her very ineptitude that attracts him (certainly she is no threat), she is extremely vulnerable to criticism and feels herself to be a wretched replacement for Olivier's dead first wife, the Rebecca of the title. Interestingly, the Fontaine character does experience some growth during the course of the film, so that by the end she is more of a person than she had been.

Gaslight's heroine is another classic masochist. She has been raised by a father who hates her, is endlessly cruel to her, makes her feel completely worthless, and does everything he can to prevent her late-adolescent blossoming. She is a perfect set-up for any man who comes along and pays attention to her, and for the repetition compulsion to come into effect. When she marries, in defiance of her father, it is to a man just like him—one who attempts to drive her mad and, finally, to kill her.

The daughter has also been raised by her father in the film *The Heiress*, based on Henry James's *Washington Square*. The mother, in this instance, died in childbirth, a common enough occurrence in the past, and one that often left the surviving husband and father with a terrible sense of residual rage: He had lost the woman he loved, and his child was responsible. It was not surprising perhaps that men tended to project their rage onto the child. In *The Heiress* the father inculcates his daughter with a sense of her own worthlessness, ugliness, and lack of appeal. He makes it clear that no man will ever want her; he sadistically punishes her for her part in his loss of his adored, and perfect, wife. The daughter incorporates his judgments of her and internalizes his hypnotic suggestions so that when she does meet a man who is a fortune hunter, he quickly picks up the masochistic messages that indicate she is a prime candidate for victimization. She is easy prey. She has been *brought up* to be exploited.

The symbiotic tie between mother and daughter is all important in *Separate Tables*. The extremely masochistic daughter has been subjected to damaging treatment from her mother, a wealthy and formerly beautiful woman who would never let anyone—including her daughter—get in her way. She exacts absolute control, and one has only to see the daughter's posture as an adult to know that she has been disparaged and criticized all her life for how she looks, how she speaks, how she behaves. When the mother and daughter are at a seaside resort and the mother sees a friendship beginning to develop between her daughter and a retired army colonel, himself a very damaged creature, she immediately sets out to break it up. The mother's efforts to keep her daughter in a position of masochistic submission to her override all considerations of decency or fairness. She *needs* her victim. And so she arranges to bring into the open the colonel's past conviction for sexual molestation. But she has miscalculated; her masochistic daughter manages this one time to stand up to her mother and to support the colonel instead, taking one step in the direction of liberation.

The character played by Marlene Dietrich in *Witness for the Prosecution* is a woman perfectly capable of standing up for herself, making her own decisions, keeping her own counsel. Calm, self-assured, relying on herself rather than on unsympathetic men, she is presented as a decidedly suspicious figure whose femininity is suspect. And why? Because she acts like a man.

Ingmar Bergman's *Wild Strawberries* is set in a world in which men are the decision makers, the doers, and achievers, the ones who set the standards, the ones who are being served. What becomes of women in a world where they are either objects or servants; where they are raped by men, literally or symbolically, in or out of marriage; where they are deprived of the possibility of their own achievements and forced to bear children they may not want? Bergman shows that they become hateful wives and hateful, retaliatory mothers who, in turn, damage their own children.

Summer Wishes, Winter Dreams suggests the bleak results for a woman who enters marriage out of desperation, in the hope that it will offer a solution to her problems. Billed as the story of a "modern snow queen," that is, a frigid woman, played by Joanne Woodward, it presents some disturbing images of women. Miss Woodward's mother, a type I have heard dubbed "early West End Avenue," is a tasteless, empty-headed, self-absorbed woman who is mummified beneath layers of cosmetics, batting grotesquely false eyelashes. Miss Woodward's daughter, on the other hand, is ugly, aggressive, demanding, and overly sure of herself, a miniature "new woman." And Miss Woodward herself is the loser in the middle: a woman who made a meaningless match with a man she did not love in order to be supported and to have a home; in other words, she is a sexual domestic.

Haskell finds that films suffer from a fundamental inequity when it comes to treating the subject of age. Women are considered over the hill at forty (perhaps the age has even lowered a bit), while men of the same age are judged to be in their prime. This double standard comes through clearly in the ill-fated and misunderstood *Ash Wednesday*, in which the main character, played by Elizabeth Taylor, undergoes complete face and body surgery in order to win back a husband who has become involved with a younger woman. Her husband, the aging but still handsome Henry Fonda, has no need to rejuvenate himself in such an artificial and grotesque fashion. He can gain his new lease on life by connecting with a young woman, and he has found one who is willing to cling to him just as tightly as his wife did thirty years earlier.

While writing this chapter, I happened one night to see on television part of a Hollywood B-movie that startled me by the contrasts it presented to images I had been considering. The movie was lowbrow male-chauvinistic, and yet in two different scenes a woman was shown asserting herself in deft, unequivocal fashion. She is a gorgeous young woman, and when she sets up her beach chair on the sand, a man immediately approaches her with a pick-up ploy: "Having trouble?" he asks. Gazing at him without expression, she replies, "I wasn't." He changes tactics: "It's been a long time," he says. "We've never met," she counters. Seeing some suntan oil alongside her chair, he makes a third try: "Help you with your back?" "No," she answers, "but there *is* something you can do. Call a policeman. There's a man annoying me."

In a later scene, a man asks the same woman what her name is and she tells him it is Margaret. "Do you mind if I call you

Maggie?" he asks, chipping away at the formality that her full name suggests. "I don't like Maggie," she says calmly, settling the issue.

So vivid, and uncommon, were those instances of a woman standing up for herself that I found myself wondering if perhaps a film had to be grade-B in order to show something so subversive.

15

Digging Out

The rapid and prolific growth of assertiveness training courses in the wake of the women's movement reflected a recognition that women were unable to speak up for themselves in certain situations. Assertiveness groups addressed ways to deal with these situations and offered a setting in which women could rehearse the behavior they hoped to establish in their lives. Despite the intense focus on assertiveness, however, there seemed to be little or no attention paid to why women suffered from such a severe deficit of self-confidence.

In the last decade much has been written that touches on the underlying causes of women's inability to operate autonomously. The writers speak about stress, anxiety, depression. An article in *Vogue* by Barbara Langstern defined worry as a "pit of the stomach" feeling that something bad might happen, one that is more focused than anxiety but less definite than fear. Langstern offered the classic advice about worry: Separate those problems you can do something about from those over which you have no control. Inherent in this is the classic antidote to worry: Demonstrate that you have the capacity to influence something.

Carol Tavris, a psychologist for whom I have great regard, has written about what she calls "the language of tears" and the effect of crying on the spirit. She has also addressed "the impostor phenomenon." Women harbor negative feelings about themselves, according to Tavris, and fear that they will be found out. Even when they are uncertain that they will be found out about, they suffer from a feeling of being inauthentic.

In *The New Assertive Woman*, Bloom, Coburn, and Pearlman note that for generations femininity has been equated with being accommodating, passive, and nonassertive. And what is the price women have paid for this? The price, they declare, is that women have become anxious, inhibited, and emotionally dishonest.

I would not quarrel with any of these propositions. They are all accurate, as far as they go. But they address symptoms rather than causes. Worry, crying, feeling inauthentic, anxiety, and emotional dishonesty are all symptoms of masochism. *That* is the underlying cause of women's inability to assert themselves. That is the deep and damaging affliction of which all these symptoms are a part.

Worry is the masochistic torturing of oneself with irrational fears and anxieties; because they are irrational, it is not possible for the masochist to separate out those problems that can be solved from those that cannot. She is unable to make that distinction because she feels guilty and wrong about nearly everything. The message the masochist conveys with her tears is that she is pitiful and, therefore, she hopes, safe from attack. Masochistic people are not motivated by their natural, true feelings in interactions with others; *their primary goal is defense*. They are impostors in the sense that they have lost access to their genuine selves. They pretend to like and respect people of whom they are terrified; they regularly accede to people they would rather resist. And the more fraudulent their behavior, the more anxious, uncomfortable, and self-hating they become. It is important to recognize all these feelings and attitudes as part of the masochistic gestalt. For only when you have gone to the heart of a problem, only when you have identified the wellspring that gives it life, can you truly begin to overcome it. Only then can you start to dig your way out from beneath its oppressive weight.

Masochistic processes are both simple and complex, simple in that they can all be seen as defenses against feared others who are perceived as powerful; complex in that they can take on many different forms. Throughout this book I have delineated the myriad guises in which self-hurt can make its appearance. Now the question occurs: What can be done about it? Although masochism is far too complicated a problem to address with a "how-to" formula, I do intend this book to be helpful. And help is available if you, the reader, will put forth some effort in conjunction with the guidance I can offer.

Achilles was killed when Paris wounded him in the heel, his one vulnerable spot. Now is the time for you to examine yourself and identify *your* Achilles' heel, or heels, those masochistic weak spots that are threatening to your psychological life and health, those aspects of your personality that leave you vulnerable to self-damage. Ask yourself some searching questions. What have you learned about your own socio-cultural conditioning, early life experience, and upbringing that may have contributed to your developing masochistic tendencies? Did you recognize your own style among the masochistic messages outlined in Chapter 4? Are you able to recognize your own fearfulness in dealing with others? Are you able to acknowledge the low self-esteem that lies behind this? Attempting this kind of self-diagnosis may not be easy, but it will be well worth it if you are interested in overcoming your masochism.

Perhaps you feel you need help identifying your Achilles' heel. If so, a good friend, one you feel is trustworthy, may be able to offer assistance. Ask your friend if she or he has noticed aspects of your behavior that might be troublemaking. Have you seemed fearful, indirect, evasive, overly compliant, and so on? The answers you get can help to confirm your areas of difficulty.

Having determined those areas that are especially troublesome for you, there is another question you must ask yourself: Will self-help be sufficient to overcome your problems or should you seek professional help? Try to assess, as honestly and accurately as you can, the degree of alienation you feel. Do you identify at all with the woman in Salzburg who was "holding up the wall?" Try to evaluate just how fearful you are of those people you see as authorities. Are you, like Mabel Waring in the Virginia Woolf story, obsessed with and consumed by the judgments of others? Try to gauge the extent to which your masochistic problems keep you from living your life as you would like to. If you feel that your masochism constitutes a serious interference, then you must consider consulting a trained professional, either a psychiatrist, a psychiatrist/psychoanalyst like myself, or a psychologist who has been trained as a psychoanalyst. And make sure this person is someone you believe is knowledgeable about the problems of women and feminine psychology. The American Academy of Psychoanalysis, the American Psychiatric Association, the American Psychoanalytic Association, the American Psychological Association, your local psychiatric association, or local medical society may be able to suggest someone to you.

Women today frequently raise the question of whether or not they should undergo treatment with a male therapist. Generally, I would say that considerations of good training, sensitivity, and skill outweigh the matter of gender in choosing a therapist, most especially when the person being treated is seriously disturbed. On the other hand, certain gender-related nuances of behavior may be more comprehensible if one has grown up with them oneself. And men and women, as I have observed, grow up in very different worlds. Two vignettes come to mind in connection with this question.

The first involves a woman who entered treatment in the midst of a divorce action occasioned by her husband's affair with a woman he intended to marry. She was extremely distraught, and her husband agreed to pay for therapy. She found the male psychiatrist to be helpful. Once the divorce came through, however, her standard of living was considerably lower and she was concerned about the fee. Discussing it with a friend she was surprised to learn that her analyst's fee was much higher than that charged by others in the area. She told her doctor that she wanted to continue treatment but that she could not pay the present fee. And then she added, "I hope you can reduce the fee, especially since I've heard it's somewhat high in comparison with other analysts'." Enraged, he said to her, "What an aggressive woman you are!" Alas, he certainly had violated a primary principle of all dedicated doctors: *primum, non nocere* (above all, do no harm).

The second story concerns a patient of mine who, before coming to me, had spent seven years with a male analyst and had gotten progressively sicker. Early in our association, I told her that as she described those years to me I saw the image of a beautiful cathedral whose entire surface, including its brilliant stained glass windows, was covered with an accumulation of filth deposited on it by birds, pollution, and time. Our task, I said, would be to clean it up. The next session she reported to me a dream she had had of a big old house with many rooms, all of them empty. She climbed the stairs and, at the head of them, turned to the left, and there, to her surprise, came upon another room. It was lovely, filled with sunlight streaming through its windows, and in it there was a beautiful old oak desk. This dream, her own confirmation that there was something valuable about her, was the beginning of a difficult but productive collaboration between the two of us.

Women often experience problems that are difficult for male analysts to comprehend. In some instances, they may see the problems as trivial. A therapist must have a kind of prescience, an ear attuned to those subtle aggressions to which women have been subjected for years. This kind of well-developed radar may be more likely in a woman therapist, although there are men who possess it as well. But the masochistic woman who has problems that relate specifically to her femininity would probably fare best with a well-trained and perceptive woman therapist.

Whether you decide to work on your problems by yourself or to seek additional help from a professional, the effort to overcome your masochistic tendencies will require a great deal of work and courage. No psychic pattern yields to change easily or painlessly, and the deep roots of masochism go back to the very earliest days of life. Change takes time; there are no shortcuts on the road to surmounting the stubborn masochistic tendencies that may seem by now to be innate parts of your personality, fixed aspects of your character. When Thomas Edison was asked how he accounted for his remarkably prolific inventiveness, he answered, "One percent inspiration, ninety-nine percent perspiration." The same formula could apply here.

Perhaps you have discovered that you are inclined to lapse into tangential speech, an indication that you are fearful of getting to the point. You seek refuge in indirection because you have little confidence in your own judgments and perceptions. You fear abandonment, so you bind your listener to you by spinning out a seemingly endless string of words. It takes courage to resolve not to transmit this masochistic message any longer. It takes courage to summon up the determination to try something new. Courage does not mean that you are without fear; it means that you are willing to act in spite of it. And fears, I have come to believe, are often overcome by persistence, as well as by insight into their origins (persistence *and* insight should be an unbeatable combination in attempting to overcome your masochistic fears).

Urge yourself to express yourself directly, unequivocally, even if you are afraid of the response. Resolve that if you are uncertain of the worth of what you are about to say, you will at least keep your mouth shut and say nothing. This is extremely difficult for the masochist, but gradually, as you practice replacing an old, destructive pattern with a new, healthy one, the task will grow easier.

There is simply no doubt that it is always preferable to keep your silence rather than volunteering something that may be hurtful to you. Be aware of active masochistic expressions or actions that are certain to be troublemaking. I think of the mature woman who was visiting her rather overbearing mother with whom she had always had a difficult relationship. When she went to scramble some eggs for her own lunch, she noticed her mother's small frying pan was missing. Immediately she was afraid that she would be accused of having lost or misplaced it. But instead of saying nothing and scrambling her eggs in another pan, she mentioned to her mother that the pan was missing. "Well, I know it *was* there," her mother said, "so you must have misplaced it." Upon being predictably accused, the daughter was upset and began defending herself. Soon she and her mother were engaged in the same destructive parry-and-thrust act they had been doing together for years. Had the daughter said nothing, there would have been no incident.

Masochistic women often need to train themselves to be less prompt in responding to others. Just because someone asks you a question does not mean you are *obligated* to answer instantly. You are *entitled* to think your response through carefully. Try not to concern yourself with what the other person is thinking. Concentrate instead on what it is *you* want to say and wait until your statement is clear before you make it. Then speak as succinctly as possible. You will be, in effect, training yourself to exercise a new style.

Accepting the premises of other people is, as I have said, one of the prime hallmarks of the masochistic personality. Learning to question these premises, learning to substitute your own, is one of the biggest changes that must occur if you are to overcome your masochism. Consider the woman alone on the street who is approached by a stranger asking for a match and who stops to give one to him. She accepts his premise that he wants a match (heaven only knows what he wants) and that it is her obligation to give it to him, a hazardous attitude on her part. How might she turn this around? By responding to his approach with a counter-premise of her own: This may be a dangerous situation; I'm not going to risk my life for a match, or anything else; I have no obligation to stop and respond to him; I'm going to walk on—or run—instead.

Presented with someone else's premise, ask yourself if it is correct. If an accusation is involved, ask yourself if you are blameworthy or not. Gradually, as you move away from automatic acceptance, as you begin to question the way things are presented to you and whether or not they are valid, you will also begin to assert your own point of view. It will become easier to say no, I don't agree with that; no, that's unacceptable to me.

A young patient of mine had all her life been the focus of critical attacks by both parents. Nothing she could do pleased them; they constantly found fault with her. It was no surprise that her behavior was quite masochistic. But in treatment, she finally gained a grasp of her problems and was eager to begin putting knowledge into action. A voice student, she was making great strides with a new teacher. Although her parents had been critical of her music in the past, she determined that she would no longer suffer their fault-finding in silence, that she would beat them to the punch (not even let them get their premises on the record). At a family gathering, she sang to generally warm applause, and as soon as she finished, she turned to her parents and said, "Well, does this teacher do a bad job, too?" Her parents were speechless.

Another young woman also had spent a great deal of time examining her relationship with her mother and trying to understand the part she herself played in its destructive nature. She, too, was used to her mother's negative views of nearly everything she did but determined to change her responses. In love with a man she planned to marry, she knew her mother would not approve, so they were married in another town and she didn't tell her mother until the ceremony was over. "I have some good news," she said in a phone call afterward. "You have a new son-in-law." "I don't want anything to do with him," her mother replied. "That's too bad," the bride said, "because we hoped you'd be able to help us celebrate." In the course of the phone call, her mother came around considerably, and did in fact end up celebrating with the newlyweds. This was due in no small part to the positive way her daughter presented the news.

I recently watched a man being interviewed on television and, as is often the case, the interviewer took up an inordinate amount of time with his wordy questions and frequently interrupted the guest to paraphrase and interpret his answers. At one point the guest said quietly, "You're putting words in my mouth. I'd like to finish what I started to say." With these two short sentences, uttered pleasantly, the guest managed to challenge every one of the interviewer's premises—that he could express the guest's will, that his interpretation was the correct one, that he could behave in any way he wanted. The guest's behavior, his quiet assertion of his own rights, exemplified the essence of autonomy.

Perhaps during your self-examination you discerned that you have a tendency to inflict physical harm on yourself (running into things, cutting yourself with a knife, burning your fingers on a match, etc.) or by breaking or losing possessions. These are outward hurtful manifestations of an unexpressed anger within. Try to think back and examine what you may have been angry about when these "accidents" occurred. Try to discover why you were afraid to express the anger or to take appropriate action to dispel it. And when you next feel angry, try to be aware of it and acknowledge it at least to yourself. The more you are aware of things going on within you, the more choice you have in how to respond.

Ambiguity, as I have noted, is especially difficult for the masochistic person, and her tendency is to convert an unclear situation into a destructive, hurtful one. Feeling threatened, someone with masochistic tendencies would rather leap to a negative conclusion than to hover fearfully in uncertain territory. At least then the matter is settled and she need not live with her fantasies about the terrible things that might happen. But part of digging your way out of your masochistic suffering is to try to tolerate ambiguity. When something happens that causes you to feel wounded, question your interpretation of the incident. Is it correct? Might there be an alternative explanation? Have you rushed to place a negative construction on it and, in the process, perhaps overlooked something positive? Do you have to feel threatened by this incident? Very often positive things exist in the masochistic person's life, but she is incapable of acknowledging them, of giving them the same weight she assigns to negative occurrences. Busy defending herself against what is hurtful, and busy adding to the store of damaging interchanges, she is unable to see the positive aspects of her exchange with other people. They get lost in the negative shuffle.

Geraldine, a very masochistic patient of mine, had been out of the country for several years but now was reestablishing herself here. A friend she had not seen for some time invited her to spend the day with her and planned to pick her up by car. When she was a bit late, Geraldine got on the phone with an airline to arrange reservations for a trip she was planning. She was attempting to distract herself from the fear that the friend might not come and from the thought that she didn't value Geraldine enough to be on time. When the friend did arrive, Geraldine kept her waiting for some time, which annoyed the friend.

This was a very masochistic beginning to the encounter, and the day they spent together was not all that comfortable. Geraldine felt ambivalent about the friend and felt the friend was not all that fond of her. However, the friend invited Geraldine to spend an upcoming holiday weekend with her in the country. Despite the fact she had no definite plans, Geraldine declined and said she had already made arrangements for the weekend. Telling me about this, she reported that she was aware of a sense of victory when she was able to turn down her friend. But what an empty and destructive victory this was. Geraldine's relationship with her friend, as with other people in her life, was a power struggle, and she needed to feel that she could come out on top, that she could win out. This is sometimes the other side of the coin of feelings of worthlessness. The masochistic person pays insufficient attention to *what* it is she is winning; she just needs to feel that she can triumph, that she can be better than, that she is in control, no matter what the price to her.

Notable also in the interchange between these two women is the fact that at no time did Geraldine feel there was anything she could do to influence positively what happened between them. Because of her sense of helplessness and passivity, it never occurred to her that she could somehow contribute to making their time pleasant or to cutting down the distance that existed between them. As we talked further and she described their lunchtime conversation, she began to see that perhaps her interpretation of things was not quite accurate. It seemed from some complimentary remarks the friend made that, in fact, she thought highly of Geraldine and liked her very much. But this had been utterly lost on Geraldine until we unearthed it in a session after the fact. She had been so absorbed in her masochistic need to defend herself and one-up her friend that all the salutary aspects of their meeting had gone unremarked.

I described Geraldine's "victory" over her friend as an empty and self-destructive one. In contrast to this, I think of the feeling of victory that occurs when one begins to overcome one's masochism, when one puts into practice a new, autonomous response in place of an old, defensive one. That victory is a self-enhancing, self-sustaining one. And just as masochistic behavior generates more suffering and thus perpetuates itself, so a feeling of success breeds more of the same. You will begin to notice that your tolerance for discomfort decreases. You do not put up with things the way you used to.

A patient of mine bought a pair of shoes one day when she was in a hurry, and when she got home and put them on, she discovered they were too tight. Still mired in her masochism, she was fearful of confronting the salesman and could not take them back. He would, she was convinced, accuse her of having worn them or, at the very least, tell her she should have known they were the wrong size when she bought them. So she decided that she had to wear the shoes even though they hurt her feet, a masochistic punishment if ever there was one. Had this same incident occurred a year or so later when she had begun to overcome her masochistic tendencies, I have no doubt that she would have behaved quite differently. First, she might have attempted to return the shoes. If the store had not taken them back, she might have tried to correct the problem by having them stretched. If that did not work, she probably would have been able, due to her increased self-esteem and self-respect, to acknowledge that she had made a mistake and then simply to give the shoes to a friend with smaller feet.

The masochistic woman has wedged herself into a narrow behavioral mold that causes her a great deal of pain and suffering, just as a pair of too-tight shoes hurts the feet. In contrast, the woman who is beginning to dig out of her masochism and practice assertive, autonomous behavior feels the kind of comfort and ease that come with wearing a pair of shoes that fit just right.

Margaret arrived at a concert just as it was about to begin. There were no assigned seats, but she noticed in the first row of the balcony two empty places next to each other that had coats on them. "Is this seat taken?" she asked the man sitting next to one of the seats. "No, it's not," he replied, "but neither is the other one, and I want to leave my coat here." "I don't want to get involved in a battle about who will move a coat," Margaret said, "so would you please just move yours since that seat is closer to me." The man became quite angry, but Margaret quietly asked him to stop and then the concert began and put an end to the dispute. Although the incident was unpleasant, Margaret was pleased with her responses. In the past, she said, she would have fled at the first sight of the man's annoyance.

Margaret also told me of another incident that occurred at the lunch counter of a restaurant. She was in rather a hurry, and as she sat down, she signaled the waitress that she was ready to order. "Just a minute," the waitress said, turning her attention to a man who had come in after Margaret. After chatting with him for a time, she began to move away, but Margaret stopped her by saying firmly, "Waitress, come here please. Is this man's time more valuable than mine?" "He knew what he wanted," the waitress replied weakly. "So do I," said Margaret and gave her order. In both these instances, Margaret noted that she was particularly pleased she did not feel guilty when she asserted herself.

Margaret did not bring either of these situations on herself, but in the past, in passive masochistic fashion, she would have absorbed the slights and felt damaged by them. You may believe it is useless to protest every discourtesy you encounter. On the other hand, every injury you sustain reduces your sense of well-being and self-esteem.

A friend of mine in line at the food counter at Bloomingdale's had taken a number and was waiting her turn but stepped forward to get a better look at the fine assortment of cheeses. "You have to take a number, you know," the woman next to her snapped. "Yes, I have one," she replied. "Well, what are you elbowing ahead of me for?" her antagonist said nastily. "I just moved forward to get a closer look," said my friend. "I'm waiting my turn. It has nothing to do with you." Despite this, the unpleasantness continued, so my friend moved away. When her turn finally came, the clerk snapped at her as well, as if the attitude of the other woman were contagious. Refusing to be a passive masochistic victim of this unexpected and unwarranted rudeness, my friend asked if there was any reason for the clerk's unpleasantness and requested that he be more courteous. His manner changed, and she made her purchases in a much more agreeable atmosphere.

I witnessed another example of the refusal to be a passive victim while riding one day on the Third Avenue bus. A tall, somewhat surly looking young woman was sitting with her legs stretched out into the aisle. When a woman who was obviously well into her seventies approached, the young woman saw her but did not move her legs, and the older woman tripped and nearly fell to the floor of the bus, catching herself at the last moment. She looked over at the young woman who gazed back with a smirk and murmured, "I'm sorry." While the insincerity of this "apology" was evident, a masochistic person would have accepted it or, even worse, have said, "Oh, no, *I'm* sorry." Not this older woman. "What do you mean you're sorry?" she said forcefully. "What the devil were you doing with your feet out like that? You didn't even make any effort to move them. You damn well *ought* to be sorry!"

I am recommending assertion, not defiance, as one of the tools to help dig out of the masochistic morass. Often masochistc women have a great deal of secret anger and defiance, and they may veer from being overly compliant to being overly defiant. Neither extreme will serve to get them out of the masochistic position, however. Both are indications that the woman is still locked in a power struggle. Her behavior at either end of the spectrum is defensive.

Sometimes an incident is trivial, not worth the energy you would have to expend to address it, and you may decide that letting it go will not hurt your self-esteem. Other times, self-assertion may be imprudent or even dangerous. A friend of mine got on the subway and found it was crowded, but there was a section where several people were spread out, and she asked them collectively if they would mind moving over so that she could sit down. A large woman at the end of the row said, "I will not." "That's not fair," said my friend. "There's room for someone else to sit here and I don't want to stand." The large woman responded with a stream of invective. "Look," my friend insisted. "I have a right to a seat that I paid for where there is room. Please move over." Though there was still little effort to accommodate her, she shoved herself between two people, and gradually others shifted over to make room. Telling me about this afterward, she said that she felt everything she had done was appropriate, but that as she looked around the car and saw not one sympathetic face, she realized her stance might have been foolhardy in this situation. I had to agree.

When you experience one success in putting into practice new, nonmasochistic behavior, it leads to a second and then a third, in a domino effect. A new sense of self-worth helps you dig away at the tenacious foundations of the anticipatory defense system. All masochistic defenses are compulsive, that is, they recur repeatedly in order to avoid anxiety about expected attack and hurt. And anyone imprisoned in compulsive behavior necessarily suffers from rigidity and restriction. But when you begin to break through, there is an expanded sense of living and a new feeling of authenticity.

When you conduct your self-examination, I suggest that you keep a special kind of diary, writing down the ways in which you are aware of expressing your masochism. And as you continue the work of digging out, continue the habit of keeping notes. It takes only a few minutes and if there is not time when they occur, jot things down in the evening. Write down those occurrences that have been unpleasant or hurtful. At the end of a week or so, look over your notes and see if you can discern certain masochistic expressions or actions that turn up repeatedly. What do these reveal about you that you need to work on? Keeping a running log as you attempt to put new patterns into practice can help you to focus on the most troublesome areas and also to keep you abreast of your progress. It is also productive to keep a ledger on the credit side of your interactions. Note down those things you have said or done that you are particularly pleased with. See how they reflect improvements. This will raise your self-esteem and also show in what ways you have changed and suggest how you can continue to do so.

Another aid I would recommend to anyone having difficulty overcoming masochism is autohypnosis. The roots of masochism lie in good measure in the negative hypnotic imprints of early experience. Self-hypnosis, in conjunction with the other steps I have mentioned, may help to reverse the effects of those damaging imprints. The essential factor in self-hypnosis is to establish a kind of cue that will help you overcome a particular problem. Many people run groups that teach self-hypnosis, and you may want to explore that possibility. Or you can teach yourself by the following method, which is basically physical relaxation coupled with focused concentration.

The first step is to "write" a script. Fantasize a scene in which there are only positive elements. This would be different for everyone, of course, but for the purposes of illustration, let's say you are walking in the country. You feel the warmth of the sun, you note the way its rays sliver off the surface of the pond, you take in the lush, vibrant green of the trees around you and the colors of the wildflowers you pass. It is a truly glorious day, and you feel good just being a part of it. Then, let's say an attractive man approaches and says to you, "Isn't it a lovely day?" Try to think what response you might give that would allow you to continue feeling good. Construct for yourself a picture of how you would respond if you were happy, relaxed, comfortable, and enjoying a beautiful day.

Having written your script, practice sitting in a relaxed way in a comfortable chair, and each time you raise a finger in front of you and look at it, conjure up the image of the beautiful day and the pleasant encounter. Do this once a day, preferably at night. Allow yourself to experience the positive image, the good feelings, the sense that no one is criticizing you, and everything is all right. Gradually, with repetition (and that is crucial to make this work effectively), you will be able to sit back comfortably, raise your finger, and the pleasant feeling will be automatic. You are imposing new ideas on yourself—ideas of your own worth, your own acceptability, your own competence, and of your joy in life.

Now begin to address items you have written down in your notebook. Select a painful issue, an expression of your masochism that crops up regularly. Induce the hypnosis and, while you are in this positive frame of mind, think how you could behave in this situation. The response that comes to you from the midst of your good feeling will be very different from a response that is generated when you are feeling full of anxiety, self-hate, and guilt.

Another way to accomplish the self-hypnosis while sitting in a comfortable and relaxed fashion is to imagine two television screens in front of you. On one you project and see yourself acting the way you would ordinarily act out of fear, on the other, project the way you would behave if you were in harmony with yourself and not feeling threatened. Turn off the screen in which you act fearfully, and concentrate on the one showing how you act when feeling good about yourself.

Overcoming your masochistic tendencies is a demanding and challenging process that takes work, courage, and time. You will probably become discouraged on occasion, particularly when you find how obstinate these tendencies are. But if you persevere, the effort will be one of the most rewarding you will ever undertake.

Patricia Ball and Elizabeth Wyman, writing about battered wives in *Victimology*, proposed a list of entitlements that I believe can serve as a sort of bill of rights for masochistic women who are attempting to dig out of the masochistic defense system that has imprisoned them. These rights are listed below, and I suggest them as a framework for the effort of digging out.

Allow yourself:

1. to be angry

2. not to be abused

3. to change situations

4. to be free of *fear* of abuse

5. to *expect* assistance from policy and social agencies [or, I would add, from a trained, sensitive therapist, if you so desire]

6. to share your feelings

7. to want better communications

8. to leave a battering environment [any place where you are abused]

9. some privacy

10. to express thoughts and feelings [or, just as important, to keep them to yourself]

11. to develop your talents and abilities

12. to be less than perfect

13. to prosecute an abusive spouse [or to respond appropriately to anyone who injures you]

16

Masochism
on the Job

In the chapter about dreams, I described a young woman faced with a choice between attending one of the country's best graduate schools or accepting a high-level job offer with a substantial salary, enviable options but ones that caused her masochistic tendencies to burst into full bloom, leaving her distraught. She was beset by fears. She had made plans to enter school in the fall before the job offer occurred and feared reversing her decision. She was afraid, simulaneously, that she was not really qualified for the job and that she would be bored by it. She was afraid that as she came under closer scrutiny for the job that the offer would be revoked. She was afraid that if she took the job and delayed returning to school, her parents would be critical of her decision. She was afraid that the schools to which she had applied would not accept her in the future because she had turned them down. Each session we went over these fears as tears streamed down her cheeks.

Away from my office, meanwhile, she hurried from friend to friend, asking what they would do if they were in her place. At one point, she called her father, who had never been especially well disposed toward her, and asked him what she should do. Hearing that the job would pay her well over $50,000 his first remark was, "Boy, that's quite a salary." But he was no more helpful to her than anyone else had been. When I pointed out that the salary was probably higher than any he had ever received, and what a shock it must have been to hear that his pretty, "silly" little daughter (as he had always conceived of her) was thought to be worth such a substantial sum, she laughed and agreed.

We worked hard to discover the roots of her fears, of her sense of inadequacy. Her belief that other people would somehow have more valid answers for her than she could find for herself (she also noted that her repeated questioning of other people revealed her self-preoccupation and how annoyed people became with it). And we uncovered a piece of her early experience that accounted, at least in part, for her extreme disturbance.

Her mother's criticism of her had seldom been direct, and, as a result, it was difficult to detect. Her method had been constantly to compare Marjorie, my patient, to others, and always to Marjorie's detriment. "If Nancy were in this situation," her mother would say, "she would do thus and so." "Peggy would never do that." "Mrs. Andrews said *her* daughter would be doing this or that." And so on. This sort of subtle attack in which comparison is used to disparage the child is often more difficult to deal with than a direct onslaught. For one thing, it is harder to recognize. Marjorie did not realize what was causing her difficulty. It was as though she were shadow boxing rather than fighting a real opponent.

Despite these insights, Marjorie didn't really make much progress toward resolving her dilemma. One day in my office, extremely distressed and tearful, she began to rock back and forth, murmuring over and over, "What will happen to me? What will happen to me?" This reminded me of an experience of my own, and I recounted it to her. Once on a trip to Leningrad, I stayed behind at St. Isaac's cathedral after the group I was traveling with had gone on. I wanted some time alone with the lapis lazuli and malachite interior of that magnificent structure. When I eventually boarded the bus to return to my hotel, I suddenly realized I wasn't certain of its name, I didn't know at what street I should get off, and I didn't speak any Russian, so was in no position to make inquiries. Getting more and more upset, I clasped my hands in front of me and found myself saying aloud, "What will I do? What will I do?" Nearly everyone on the bus, it turned out, understood English, and a soldier helped me off at the proper stop and escorted me to my hotel.

Hearing this, Marjorie made an interesting and astute observation. "I said 'What will happen to me?'" she said. "It's so passive. But you said, 'What will I *do*?' You were searching for a solution—but I've been sitting and worrying about what would happen to me without my doing anything."

Marjorie's recognition of this was an indication that she had begun to overcome her masochistic problems. But I cite her story as an illustration of how damaging masochistic tendencies can be to a woman's professional life. Her behavior, if unexamined and unchecked, would almost certainly undermine, and perhaps even obliterate, the accomplishments that her gifts and her intelligence made possible.

The career woman must fight her masochism in both her personal life and in the competitive atmosphere of her professional world. In the latter, which turns on the axis of power—who has it, who does not—the stakes are especially high. The salary she will be paid, how far and fast she advances, the degree of respect she receives from colleagues—all these depend on how a woman comports herself. What she says and does takes on special significance. The "mistakes" a masochistic woman makes in her professional life, that is, those instances where she behaves in an unassertive, nonautonomous manner, will have far-reaching effects. Masochistic defenses, the masochistic communication style, are damaging whenever and wherever they occur. But when a career woman's professional conduct is shaped by these, the results can be devastating.

"If anything goes wrong, I immediately think it has to do with me. I spend a lot of energy trying to see how to avoid trouble, and I can't because it's unpredictable. I seem to be looking for the opportunity to make myself anxious. Sometimes I get all upset about things that don't even happen. Any change is threatening to me. Yesterday something happened that reminded me of my mother—or rather how I used to feel with her. My boss wasn't enthusiastic about a project I had finished. I immediately thought I would lose my job. Here I just got a promotion and an increase in salary, I knew he was upset about something personal, and yet I reacted as if it was my fault. I feel as if whatever I do, it's not enough."

It is not difficult to see the troublemaking potential of this young woman's outlook. Her passive grandiosity—dictating that she always puts herself at center stage—is unmistakable. She directs a great deal of energy toward activating anticipatory defenses, even though she recognizes that they are rarely effective. Rather than expressing *herself*, she tries to second-guess authority figures upon whom she has superimposed the images of powerful figures from childhood. She is inflexible and relentlessly critical of herself. She leaps to negative conclusions even in the face of evidence to the contrary. These masochistic tendencies are bound to interfere severely with her ability to function productively in her professional life.

To return for a moment to the tennis analogy, I would not describe her as having a very strong game. She probably wouldn't exhibit an effective return of serve, good reflexes at the net, or strong groundstrokes. She would be more likely to hit out blindly, miss the ball altogether, and then apologize profusely for her error. And all this because she is afraid of her opponent and is rendered ineffectual by that fear.

After some time in therapy, this young woman was doing much better but still had not left her masochism behind altogether. She started her own business, with partners, and one day in my office became aware that she explained her decisions to her partners in considerable detail, eliciting their opinions about them, while they informed her of their decisions after the fact. Describing her feelings of anger at this, she suddenly clapped her hand to her head and said, "I see what it is! I don't have to explain at all. But I do it to ward them off. I should make these decisions and act on them, just as they do. But I've been trying to avoid criticism, so I'm still acting as I did in the past but on a higher level." Obviously, it is gratifying to both therapist and patient when a sudden and important insight like this appears.

Considerations of power are paramount in business and career life, and power is the masochistic person's area of greatest vulnerability: she is quick both to attribute it to others and to disclaim it herself. This being so, the career woman with definite masochistic tendencies really ought to consider seeking the additional support and perception that professional help can offer.

But if you're going it alone, the first step toward overcoming problems is to focus on how your general masochistic tendencies are reflected in your business or professional life. What guises are your defenses most likely to take on in a career context? Only when you've identified and understood them can you go on to develop those special skills and strategies you will need to make your way ahead in business or a profession.

Even though it may not come naturally to you, expect respect. Try not to approach others fearfully but with confidence in what you have to say. And do not assume that what you have to say is any less vital or accurate or true than what someone else contributes.

Questioning someone else's premise is as important on your job as it is in your personal life. The other person's premise may not necessarily be wrong, but it is important that you examine it and decide whether or not you agree with it before you respond. Forgoing an immediate reply, taking the time to think something through, is extremely difficult for the masochistic woman. Because she anticipates attack, her instinct is to respond immediately in order to ward it off. She doesn't dare to wait and stay in that gray zone of ambiguity where her fate is undetermined. It has been said that "the certainty of misery tends to be preferred over the misery of uncertainty." And that aphorism could very well serve as the masochist's credo. But in career life, you must learn to take the time necessary to formulate an appropriate response. And it is up to you to do whatever is necessary to get that time for yourself. It might even mean saying to your boss, "I don't want to speak to you about this until the end of the day because I am working on something else now." Even the boss can be asked to adjust to realities.

One of Janet's partners, a man based in another city, was extremely competent in sales but knew very little about the creative side of their business in which Janet was involved. Nevertheless, whenever anything went wrong, he would call her up and launch into a harangue. "What's the matter with you?" he would ask. "You women just aren't to be trusted. You always slip up and make problems for me." At first, Janet responded to this by justifying herself, attempting to answer his specific complaints, and, by doing so, implicitly accepting his premise that she was at fault. Her early experience had conditioned her to expect censure even when she had done nothing wrong; she was an expert at assuming blame. But then she began to realize the part she played in permitting this kind of exchange to continue.

The next time her difficult partner was in town, she asked him to meet her for a drink. "I don't think you're really aware," she said to him, "of how hard I work, how much time I put in, and just how demanding the creative part of the business is. I'm as responsible as I can be, just as I'm sure you are at your end. And I don't want to receive phone calls that go on about women not being trustworthy. You're really defeating our purpose, which is to produce and sell goods and to do it well. When you tear me down, you're interfering with my ability to do my part, so I suggest you stop it." "You're absolutely right," he replied. "I know I get very difficult at times, and I'll try to be more careful about that in the future."

In finally speaking up and challenging her partner's premise, Janet defined the issue as she saw it and put the focus where it belonged: His behavior was counterproductive to the business. When she was able to point out that in fact the problem was *his* tendency to project blame onto others, the situation changed.

A woman with her own business took in a male partner who, with her masochistic collusion, was soon treating her as if she were his employee. One way she participated in this was to make remarks like, "I'm leaving a little bit early tonight because I have to get a manicure." The moment she volunteered that, he responded by twitting her. "I'm surprised you get any work done," he would say. "Obviously, you're more concerned with your fingernails than you are with the business." She gave him the opening; he took it. Gradually, however, she came to realize how she elicited such responses from him and began to change her behavior. She recognized that she was not accountable to him; she had no obligation to tell him where she was going when she left the office. It was, after all, her business. The only thing that mattered was that she be reachable if something important came up. "I'm leaving now," she began saying instead. "After five o'clock you can find me at such-and-such a number, if necessary."

Closely allied to challenging the other person's premise in a confrontation is the matter of timing. It is important to know that you can choose the proper time and place for a difficult encounter. You can decide when to act, and when not to.

Beva, a resident physician, was astonished and disturbed when an attending physician turned on her and said she was not a good resident. It was true that something had gone wrong that day but, in general, she was a capable and diligent doctor. She said nothing at the time and, in fact, retired as soon as possible to the ladies' room to cry (the right idea, because it's best to keep crying out of sight). This one negative comment made Beva feel she had been totally condemned. She spent a great deal of time working on this in treatment and did a lot of thinking about it on her own. She came to realize that this same attending doctor frequently made chauvinist remarks to her that bordered on a kind of sexual harassment. She began to understand both his position and her own more clearly.

Some months after the original incident, a similar remark was made to her. "Doctor," she replied this time, "would you mind giving me an outline of the things that lead you to say I'm not a good resident?" "Well," he said, "look at what happened today." "How about some other examples?" His silence indicated that he couldn't think of any. "Look," she said, "I've been on duty for sixty hours straight without a chance to sleep, and I've reached the point where it's very difficult for me to think. I may not have done the best possible in this instance, but that has nothing to do with the fact that I'm a woman. It has to do with the fact that I'm human and that there is a limit to one's endurance. Fortunately, nothing untoward happened. In the future, I'll thank you not to make unpleasant remarks to me. They don't help anyone." The doctor, to Beva's surprise, agreed with her, and their encounter ended on a positive note.

There may be times, of course, when you are caught by surprise and forced into an unexpected confrontation. Keep cool and remember that you are entitled to take time to think before replying. Try to decide if anything needs to be said or if silence might serve you best. If you decide to speak, ask the other person a clarifying question that will put him on the spot and temporarily take the heat off you. If you can use humor, do so—it's a great tension-reliever. Whatever the issue, present your side of it as clearly and simply as possible, and try to stand your ground.

Masochistic women must be careful not to fall back on knee-jerk excuses of gender or age when they encounter criticism in the work enviroment. Either of these factors may create trouble for you, but it is not helpful to rush to the conclusion that sex or age bias are at the root of all your difficulties. It is not helpful for a woman to begin a new job, for example, operating on the assumption that all the men in the company are against her. A them-against-us attitude will end up creating more problems than it solves. A woman who is not inclined to look for poor treatment, on the other hand, who is able to be generous in her judgments of her fellow employees, probably increases the odds that she will be accorded equitable treatment. When difficulty arises, try to stick to the issue at hand and deal with it on its own merits.

You may remember that TV anchorwoman Christine Craft charged that she was dropped by a Kansas City television station because she was "too old, unattractive, and not deferential enough to men." A jury awarded her $500,000 in damages. Despite a judge's setting aside this verdict and ordering a new trial, it seems obvious to me that Craft was *not* suffering from gender paranoia and that her difficulties did indeed stem from the fact that she was a woman who refused to meet certain male standards of appearance and conduct—and who rejected the idea of being old at thirty-seven.

In general, it serves a woman well to avoid controversy and keep larger goals in sight. A good way to bypass a clash over something unimportant is simply not to hear it. Ignore the provocative remark, the unjust implication, the inaccurate assessment. Don't get angry and sink into name-calling. This never settles an issue; it is only inflammatory. Choose to focus on the solution to a problem rather than on the "luxury" of venting emotion, for that is a luxury that may cost you dearly. Being reckless or defiant in an exchange with someone in a position of power is not self-assertive. It is destructive.

Tact does not come easily to masochistic people. Their energies are primarily directed toward the operation of their anticipatory defense system. Their self-preoccupation is enormous. Their narrow and intense focus on their own pain and their own problems often renders them incapable of concern for the feelings and sensibilities of other people. But in professional life, a gift for diplomacy is a great asset. Watch someone who is able to exercise diplomacy successfully. Use the energy you would ordinarily expend anguishing over your own mistakes to observe how tact works. It helps to shift the focus away from yourself and what is wrong with you and onto what is good and positive about someone else.

Maria is a researcher who works with a prominent scientist given to making rather oppressive demands on her, frequently, for example, asking her to attend to some minor busywork while she is in the midst of an experiment. The affirmative way she has learned to handle his intrusions is extremely effective. "Of course," she answers him, "I'll do it as soon as I finish this experiment." This response acknowledges his power by indicating that his request is reasonable and that she is willing to satisfy it. But, it also makes clear that her work is significant. Most important, it accomplishes both these things in a positive way that does not force a confrontation.

Masochistic dependence and an inability to trust one's own feelings and judgments can turn decision-making into prolonged agony. Masochists are fearful of making unilateral decisions and tend to seek support to bolster themselves. In one's career however, especially at higher levels, it is necessary to make judgments and settle problems on your own. As you begin to move toward autonomy and away from your masochistic defenses, as you learn to think things through alone and to create your own premises, you will be much better equipped to *act* independently. Margaret Thatcher, I am sure, consulted her ministers on the Falklands crisis, but she alone could, and did, make the decision to defend the islands. And she stood her ground in the face of criticism.

Learning to recognize and overcome your masochistic problems in the context of your work is half the battle. The other half lies in developing certain skills and strategies that can be crucial to professional success. Let me make some suggestions.

Try the truth. Suppose a masochistic woman is confronted with this dilemma: She is likely to put her foot in her mouth when she speaks up, but commitment to a career demands that she volunteer information. Opportunities for active masochism abound. My advice in this regard is to try the truth. Masochistic people learn early in life to sidestep it—evasions, half-truths, inchoate communications become their stock in trade. They can be quite unused to honest, direct expressions of information. The truth, if presented in a matter-of-fact way, is often much less troublemaking than the evasions you think will help you avoid trouble.

The effect of language. Language has been used for centuries as a subtle but deadly weapon with which to attack women. It is often used to denigrate them, confuse them, dupe them, and keep them in what men have deemed to be their place. Professional women must learn to recognize these attacks, however they are disguised, and to respond to them. They must learn to delve beneath the surface of the linguistic hypocrisy that is often characteristic of communications between men and women. They must learn to detect offenses and not let them go by unanswered. For each time an insult passes unremarked, it only leads to more of the same. Failure to respond to linguistic attacks constitutes a tacit acceptance of them.

The simplest form of linguistic attack occurs by attaching trivializing appellations to women. The most common of these is "dear." Anyone addressing you this way in a professional situation intends disrespect, you may be certain. The very use of the word is a denial of your professionalism, whether it comes from someone's secretary, an answering service, a client, or a colleague. I believe it often reflects the growing hostility that many men feel toward women as they are becoming more assertive and successful. Rather than absorbing this sort of assault and letting yourself feel damaged by it, try to respond to it, without anger, perhaps even with humor. Judge Shirley Levitan counterattacked in a most graceful and effective way when the lawyer who was trying the case before her addressed her as "dearie." "Correction," said the judge, "your Honor, dearie." (Of course, she was the one in power, which made it easier to be witty.)

A young physician reported that a doctor on the staff of the hospital where she was a resident frequently called her "honey." Eventually she was able to respond to this by saying, "Dr. So-and-so, I think it would be more helpful to me if you called me doctor. I'm just getting used to it at this stage in my professional life." She didn't attack him but enlisted his help and support instead.

Occasions may arise when it is difficult to respond to a linguistic attack. Perhaps the person addressing you is someone who holds great power: You are the newest member of a law firm and he is the senior partner. If the situation is such that it seems most prudent for you to accept "dear" or "young lady" without comment, be aware that you need not feel damaged by the slight, or obligated to absorb similar disparagement from the next person who comes along.

Another young doctor, a surgeon, was on her way to emergency room duty and passed the scene of an automobile accident. She stopped to help and was caring for the injured person when a second car stopped and a man rushed up and pushed her aside. "Stand back, lady," he said, "I know first aid." This happened to Dr. Jeanne Petrek, the first woman ever to receive a full-time faculty appointment in the Emory University Medical School Department of Surgery.

Another woman surgeon, Christine Haycock, recent President of the American Medical Woman's Association, accompanied by her husband, was driving a car with MD license plates. When a policeman stopped Dr. Haycock for speeding, he said to her husband, "Listen, doc, don't let your wife drive so fast." The conditioning that causes men never even to consider that a woman might be a doctor in these instances is the same conditioning that causes men to belittle women even when they achieve positions of status and power.

A microbehavioral study in 1955 by Margaret Mead and Helen

Wolfenstein concluded that an individual experiences between three thousand and five thousand transactions during the course of a day. I would estimate that for a woman probably five hundred of these are linguistic attacks generated by interpersonal exchanges, newspapers, television, magazines, etc. Fed into that remarkable computer, the human brain, what effect must these assaults have on a woman's sense of feminine identity and self-esteem? This kind of onslaught on another species would raise alarm. We would cry that it could not be expected to withstand such environmental pollution or encroachment on its territory, or slaughter of its young. We would designate it an endangered species. But when women are the object of such attacks, we barely notice. It just seems like business as usual.

A few years ago, I was to chair a conference at the annual meeting of the American Psychiatric Association, and part of my responsibility was to obtain and read beforehand all the papers to be presented. The conference was set for Monday, but on Saturday I still had not received a paper from one colleague. Then at *noon* on Saturday he called me. "Did I wake you?" he asked, a remark I think it unlikely he would have made to a male colleague. "Listen, honey," he went on, "I just couldn't get the paper done, but I'll have it at the meeting." I imagined the sort of judgments he would heap on a woman who was so late in delivering a manuscript. And I noted the "honey." "My dear Dr. So-and-so," I said to him, deliberately striking a tone of mild condescension by the counter use of the term of endearment, "since you're speaking to me in my office, I am hardly likely to have been asleep. As for the paper, it's unfortunate that you haven't been able to comply with rules everyone else was able to meet. It better be a good paper . . . and I'm sure it will be." I added this final remark to soften somewhat the tone of my admonition to him. After all, I had no desire to create an enemy. My interest was simply to rebut his derogation of me.

A compliment can often hide a linguisitic attack. In connection with the annual APA meetings, I had participated in a discussion on closed-circuit television. Afterward a colleague approached me and said: "Natalie, you looked great, just great."

"What did you think of what I had to say?" I asked. "I'm not interested in what I looked like." He obviously could not remember what I had said and was stunned that I had not graciously accepted his compliment. What more could any woman ask than to be told that she looked good? The professional woman, I cannot stress strongly enough, must ask a great deal more than that. She must ask that her work, not her appearance, be the focus of interchanges with colleagues.

Some years ago, I began paying attention to the jokes and stories that lecturers in academia used to "warm up" their audiences, and I was astonished at the number that were at the expense of women. These attacks are not readily discerned as such, veiled as they are by cleverness and humor; women may be just as likely as men to laugh at them.

When Professor Martin Roth, an expert on depression from England (he has since been knighted), spoke at the New York Academy of Medicine, he opened his lecture with this story. A group at Oxford was putting on a play about ancient Greece but found itself stymied by the setting, a Mycenean hut. Nobody knew what one looked like. The department of antiquities had two professors, one male, one female, and the drama group approached the male professor first and asked for his advice. "I can't tell you what a Mycenean hut would look like," he said, "because to the best of my knowledge there is no remaining record. But go to Professor Wetherall—you won't be able to *stop* her from telling you."

The following appeared in a newsletter called *The Executive Woman*, and it conveys superbly, I think, how the linguistic treatment of men and women differs.

How to Tell a Businessman from a Businesswoman

A businessman is aggressive; a businesswoman is pushy.
He is careful about details; she's picky.
He loses his temper because he's so involved with his job; she's bitchy.
He's depressed (or hung over), so everyone tiptoes past his office; she's moody, so it must be her time of the month.

He follows through; she doesn't know when to quit.
He's firm; she's stubborn.
He makes wise judgments; she reveals her prejudices.
He is a man of the world; she's been around.
He isn't afraid to say what he thinks; she's opinionated.
He exercises authority; she's tyrannical.
He's discreet; she's secretive.
He's a stern taskmaster; she's difficult to work for.

Sexual harassment. This is more common than is generally realized. It ranges from the bargain proffered by the boss, overtly
or covertly—you have sex with me and I'll look after you—to the
sexual innuendo of many male chauvinist remarks. Whatever
temporary advantage the masochistic woman may think she gains
by sleeping with her boss or by laughing at his chauvinist jokes
will be canceled out by the price she pays: further loss of self-
esteem. Sexual harassment should be seen for what it is: part of
the power struggle between men and women. Nothing serves one
better in a power struggle than the possession of self-respect.

Many women shy away from responding to sexual innuendo
because they fear they will be branded "libbers." I certainly can
think of much worse things to be called. In fact, I am proud to be
known as someone who stands for the liberation of women. But
suppose a man throws that label at you, and you are not comfortable with all its connotations. Perhaps he says, "You're not one of
those women's lib types, are you?" "Why do you ask?" you could
say, throwing it back to him, changing the venue, remaining
noncommittal yourself. If he says, "Well, they're all man-haters,"
you might answer, "It would be just as foolish to hate all men as it
would be to dislike all women because they want equality. Actually, I like men very much. But it's also true, since no one's perfect,
that there have been times when men have been very uncaring
and unfair to me."

What if an employer makes a direct sexual approach to you?
"Look," you could tell him, "I know you can find any number of
women who would be happy to oblige you, and all they would
want is a nice evening out, not a job. But I'm interested in the
job, and I know I can do competent work for you. Please let's

have a real business relationship. Give me a chance to show you what I can do."

A case of sexual harassment a few years ago in the Italian government can serve as a cautionary tale to career women everywhere. Aprile de Puoti, a journalist, was expected to become the first woman to serve as spokesperson for the Ministry of Labor, a particularly gratifying prize to her, as the upper echelons of the Italian bureaucracy are almost entirely male. However, she was not chosen, and she believed she was denied the job because she rejected the sexual advances of Labor Minister Vincenzo Scotti. De Puoti appealed to a higher authority, Prime Minister Giulio Andreotti, in the hope that he might override Scotti and see that she got the job. Andreotti refused to intervene, however, and added insult to injury by making the outrageous statement that de Puoti should recognize that he was not in a position to "control the hormonal discomfort of [his] cabinet minister."

This was a traditional male response, implying that the problem was in de Puoti, not in the Labor Minister, and also implying that her very legitimate discomfort was of no concern. (This same principle lies behind Arab women being garbed in the chador, the thesis being that if women are not entirely covered, men will be aroused and, ispo facto, need to act out their arousal. Therefore, *women* must bear the burden and discomfort of controlling men's temptation.)

Applying for a job. Many masochistic tendencies come into play here. My overall advice is to remember the tennis match: take the serve and *return* it. Ask questions and volunteer as little as possible. Your prospective employer already has your resumé, so he knows what you have done. Your aim should be to extract from him the maximum amount of information about the job. When you must answer a question, be sure you pick the most factual answer: "I *did* thus and so and *achieved* this and that," rather than prefacing your answers with "I believe" or "I feel." Keep your answers brief and don't volunteer anything extraneous—unless it is to cite some special achievement or distinction.

The matter of salary is often difficult for women to handle because they tend to underestimate what they are worth. Force vourself to tack on an additional amount to the figure you think is acceptable.

Once women are settled in a job, they are often afraid to ask for advancement or, if they do, they are not prepared to present a well-documented case for the change. They tend to say simply that they want the new job or need the additional salary rather than factually noting the accomplishments that lead them to think they are qualified for a promotion or to receive more money. Let me give an example, however, of a young woman who handled the question of advancement in a positive way, even though she had been masochistic most of her life. Recently divorced, Florence managed to get her M.B.A. while looking after her two young children and soon thereafter took a job that didn't pay very well but seemed to have promise. After only three months, it was apparent that she was gifted in her field and her immediate boss was pleased by her work. But because she was new to the job, she was very poorly paid. In the past, Florence would have accepted the situation as it was, telling herself she had no right to make waves as she had just joined the company. But she decided instead that her new life called for new behavior.

She pointed out to her boss that because she had been eager to get into the company she had taken a job with inadequate compensation, especially in light of the fact that she had a family to support. She realized she had only been there three months, Florence said, but the quality of her work suggested that she was worth a great deal more than her present salary. Her boss readily acknowledged that her performance had been outstanding and that she was underpaid. He was not in a position to pay her more now, he said; however, in a few months, the business was going to be reorganized, and his plan was to create a new job for her that would carry with it a higher salary as well as a new title.

Florence thought this over carefully. Had she been assertive enough? Should she accept what her boss said and wait to see what transpired when the changes occurred? In light of his generally positive response to her, she decided that it was worth taking a chance on waiting. She had approached this situation in autonomous fashion: She called her views and her needs to her boss's attention, she heard his response and weighed it, then she agreed to wait—a wise choice. She got both her increased salary and new job when the company reorganization went through.

Being noticed. When I was a first-year resident in psychiatry, my notion was that if I did the best I could and worked hard, I would be recognized and rewarded. Nothing could be further from the truth, I quickly learned. It is up to a woman to call attention to her work, something men seem able to do almost automatically. A woman who is shackled by masochistic fear will find this difficult, for it involves speaking up for herself. But be assured that if you don't do it, it's very likely that no one else will. When it's appropriate, put some effort into a little honest self-promotion.

What not to talk about at work. Women have been conditioned into overtalking as a kind of social style. Masochistic women in particular have a strong bent in that direction. Spilling, as I have said, frequently leads them into disclosing self-damaging information. My advice is to leave all personal matters at home. Talking about your outside concerns really can't do you any good in the office; it may do you harm. Conversations can be overheard; you can easily be misquoted. When I step into my office each day and shut the door, the rest of my world ceases to exist, and my focus is exclusively on the work I am there to do. Women who want to be successful need to learn to shut certain doors during work hours.

Networking. Much has been written about the necessity of making contacts with other women in your field, and I mention it here just to underline its importance.

Finding a mentor. This also has been much discussed but deserves mention. Having someone in your field who shows you the ropes and keeps you informed is an invaluable asset. Having someone important take an interest in you enhances your self-esteem. You need not wait for someone to choose you: Reach out and be helpful to someone you would like to learn from.

Time out for yourself. Although this category has nothing to do with professional relations per se, it may be the most important of all, especially for those women who are working at double or triple jobs: career, wife, mother. If you work very hard to address all these responsibilities, you may feel you're too busy to set aside time for yourself. But this time is crucial, even if it amounts to no more than an hour or two a week. You need to feel that you can give to yourself, as well as to those around you. You need to feel that you are not always on call, ready to respond to other people's demands. Women have very different ideas of how to spend such time: reading a novel, going to a health club, meeting a friend, attending a concert, cooking alone in the kitchen, sitting on a park bench and thinking. Whatever it is, schedule time for it and insist on using that time just to please yourself.

The feelings that animate the masochistic system of anticipatory defenses are those of fear, submissiveness, and powerlessness. Their roots are in early childhood, where the child's first experience of power relations is poisoned by the treatment she receives from significant others. These significant others very quickly become powerful others, feared and dangerous figures who take up seemingly permanent residence in the masochistic psyche, kept alive by the masochist's compulsive superimposition of them upon nearly everyone she encounters. She populates her world with powerful others and then suffers at their hands. Diseased power relations—the fear of power in others, the inability to exercise it oneself—lie at the heart of masochism.

Jean Baker Miller, feminist psychiatrist and psychoanalyst, in a paper titled "Women and Power," writes eloquently and insightfully about the problems women have handling power. And she gives some vivid examples drawn from the professional arena. When she attended a meeting of sales workers, Dr. Miller observed sharp differences between the conduct of male and female salespeople. A woman getting up to report on her successful record would say: "I really don't know how it happened. I guess I was lucky this period." Or: "This must just have been a good month." A man would describe his performance this way: "First I analyzed components and figured out the trends in buying. Then I analyzed consumer groups. And I worked very hard, putting in overtime three-fourths of the month."

Dr. Miller also describes a woman who was explaining a project she had initiated. The work seemed to be very solid and the project was going well. "I think I'm really on to something here," the woman said, then quickly added, "but everybody probably knows this anyway." Dr. Miller points out in these instances the women's work was just as effective as the men's, but their style was to put themselves down in spite of it. In the latter example, one can see the woman struggling to be autonomous, to recognize her accomplishment and take credit for it, and then one sees how her fear intervenes and causes her to cancel out her positive achievement. It is as though she had written something on a blackboard, clearly and boldly, and then picked up an eraser and wiped it away.

The dictionary, Dr. Miller notes, defines power as "the faculty of doing or performing anything; force; strength, energy; ability; influence; dominion or authority over others." Her own definition, which stresses creative power, is "the capacity to produce a change, that is, to move anything from point A to point B." Generally in our culture, the myth has been maintained that women should not have power of any sizable dimension, nor do they really need it. Since they are viewed as nurturers, it has been considered natural, and fitting, that they use such power as they possess in the service of others, fostering the growth of others, what Dr. Miller terms "using their power to empower others." But women, too, have a *right* to develop, and they must learn to use power in ways that are gratifying to themselves.

Selfishness, I would say, is putting one's own needs first at all times, a quite different matter from putting oneself first when it is important to do so and the situation calls for it. But when women focus on developing their own interests, they are invariably labeled selfish, and this is something they fear greatly. Dr. Miller, elaborating on the notion of power and selfishness, tells of a worker in the health field who sought help because she was very depressed. Her depression originated not when things were going badly for her but when she began to recognize her full potential. She began to see that there were ways she could use herself creatively, that she could effectuate change, that she could do more interesting work and receive higher pay, that she could become more "selfish." It was at this point that fear blocked her, and self-criticism and self-blame produced her depression. The superwomen of today, those professional women who feel compelled to take care of everything themselves—work, husband, home, children—are extremely fearful of being called selfish. They work hard to prove that they are not, and they pay a high price for it.

We are all aware of the kind of labels men have been inclined to attach to women who seek to develop themselves, who use their power not to empower others but to get ahead themselves. And many of these labels (perhaps epithets would be more accurate) make "selfish" sound mild. Women have been given the message that the use of power is disruptive. The weight of centuries, present cultural forces, and their own conditioning all tell them this. Women have come to fear that using their abilities and powers for themselves is *dangerous*. If they strive to achieve, they will be judged unworthy, be unloved, and, ultimately, be abandoned. Unwilling to face such a risk, they flee from power rather than claim it.

At this point in history, the power struggle between women and men is well recognized, and it is a very real one. But perhaps even more crucial is the less overt, but decidedly pernicious, power struggle between women and women. In the past, women used their power to foster the growth of others; they were the powers behind the throne. If they worked for the advancement of their husbands, certain advantages came to them in terms of social position, economic wealth, and so on. Some women today continue to operate as powers behind the throne and do not want to give up what they see as the advantages of their present position in order to function as independent, autonomous people. They fear they may not succeed as well on their own as they do by channeling their energies and ambitions through their husbands. Other women are eager to discard the constrictions and limitations of old role definitions and gender stereotypes and to assume power in their own right. Women are a house divided. And that fact, more than any other, militates against the eradication of masochism in women. For until women can agree on the strategies necessary for them to achieve autonomy, power and its use will remain a serious and damaging problem. Deprived of outlets for the development of their own power, women will continue to fear power in others, to turn their anger and resentment back on themselves, and to cope with the world through the development of masochistic defenses.

One of Shakespeare's sonnets begins, "Let me not to the marriage of true minds admit impediments." It is a love poem, but its opening line embodies the guiding principle I wish all women could embrace together: that they strive to adopt an honest, loyal, helpful attitude toward one another and endeavor to see one another's points of view. With this kind of union among women, autonomy and authenticity would be free to develop and grow—and the suffering and self-destruction of masochism could be left behind.

17

Reaching Autonomy

When Freud sought a model for the problems of adolescent maturation, he turned to Sophocles' drama of Oedipus, interpreting this phase of life as a time when the boy wants to kill his father and marry his mother, the passive prize awarded the victor. This focus on the male figure, virtually ignoring the other half of the human race, was a reflection of what his disciple Ernest Jones called Freud's unduly "phallocentric" view of humanity. In my search for a model for the autonomous woman, I also discovered what I was looking for in Sophocles' Theban plays about Oedipus and his family. Antigone, Oedipus' daughter and my model, did not fit at all with Freud's view of women or generally with women of Freud's time. She was self-reliant rather than dependent, active rather than passive, a young woman motivated by high ethical purpose rather than narcissistic self-involvement, a young woman willing to think for herself and take risks rather than blindly assenting to the established order of things.

In *Antigone*, the last of the three Theban plays, Eteocles and Polyneices, Oedipus' sons, kill each other in battle. Creon, who has taken over as king of Thebes, decrees that Polyneices, having fought against his own city, must be denied burial and left on the battlefield to rot. "He must be left unwept, unsepulchered—a vulture's prize," his sister Antigone observes, adding, "And anyone who *disobeys* will pay no trifling penalty, but die by stoning in the city walls."

Antigone, however, is concerned with the indignity of her

brother's body being unburied, the insult to his memory, and the threat to his afterlife. She decides to bury Polyneices in defiance of Creon's edict, a decision that is not impulsive but carefully considered, a decision that she knows may have grave consequences. When she appeals to her sister Ismene for help, Ismene, who is truly "Freud's woman," resorts to the dodge that "traditional" women have continued to use for centuries: "[We must] remind ourselves that we are women, and as such not made to fight with men. For might is right, and makes us bow to things like this, and worse. . . . I bend before authority. It does not do to meddle." ("And worse" suggests rape and assault, horrors which women rarely had the strength to resist and which led them to feel that deference to men was their only protection.) Ismene recognizes and accepts her own subjugation.

Not so Antigone. It is said of her: "Submission is a thing she never learned." Antigone is *not* resigned to things as they are. She is willing to grapple with the established order, to risk taking a stand based on ethical commitment. She sees her action as doing the gods' bidding; she calls herself "sinner of a holy sin." Her act has a spiritual as well as an ethical component, and it is life-affirming even though it may end in her death. "I go to bury him," she says. "How sweet to die in such pursuit! To rest loved by him whom I have loved. . . . I shall not abandon him."

Antigone's defiance of Creon's command is an act of autonomy and independence that constitutes a mature self-realization. She does not defy Creon out of self-centered murderous rage, such as Oedipus displayed in slaying his father. She exhibits, on the contrary, altruism and lack of self-concern. Her defiance is an act of love. "It is not my nature to join in hating, but in loving," she says.

Electra in Aeschylus' *Oresteia* furnishes an interesting contrast to Antigone and one that encompasses some characteristics of masochism. (Fortunately, Freud did not select her as a universal example of femininity, although you may recognize in Electra elements of his metapsychology of women.) She was a father-worshipper and, like Ismene, a woman unable to think for herself. She would not dare to challenge the existing order or to make a difficult decision on her own. She is not capable of acting autonomously. Facing the funeral of her father, Agamemnon, she says: "Bondswomen . . . give me your advice. . . . What words contrive to please my father's ear? . . . Shall I use the customary prayer . . . or pour [oil] in silence without ceremony? . . . I beg you to advise me. . . . Do not be afraid to unfold your thoughts to me." Agamemnon was the be-all and end-all of her existence, and yet this allegedly loving daughter does not know how to worship at his grave and turns to others for direction. The process of hero-worship has left her empty of substance, without identity or self-knowledge. She is passive; she is nothing. She does what the worshipped person tells her to do, and if he is not there, she turns to substitutes for instruction.

Antigone, on the other hand, is a person in her own right. Facing life's dilemmas, she doesn't need to cast about for someone to direct her. She knows what her ethical standards are, and she acts in accord with them. Is it masochistic that she undertakes an action that may result in her death? I think not. Antigone doesn't act out of fear and the need to defend herself. She is guided by love, and her action is assertive, not defensive.

Haemon, Creon's son and Antigone's betrothed, loves and respects her for the very qualities that lead her to make her difficult decision. His values are closely allied to hers; his persona is as strong a contrast to the intemperate youthful Oedipus as Antigone is to Electra. Threatened by his father, Haemon declares his love: "You know, my father, how I prize your happiness. For sons and fathers crown each other's glory with each other's fame." And he continues, speaking to his father as an equal: "Then, don't entrench yourself in your opinion, as if everyone else were wrong. The kind of man who always thinks that he is right, that his opinions, pronouncements, are the final words, when once exposed shows nothing there. But a wise man has much to learn without a loss of dignity." Haemon, too, would join in loving, not hating.

Antigone is not the average woman. But she is what the average woman might become: a person of autonomy and high principle, not narcissistically self-involved, not defensively suffering, but willing to take risks to live authentically. When Freud asked his famous question, "What do women want? Dear God, what do women want?" he would have had to look no further than Antigone to find his answer.

It is hardly necessary, of course, to go as far back as ancient Greece to find instances of women leading their lives with autonomy. Eleanor Roosevelt was such a woman, one who, I feel certain, had masochistic problems of her own to overcome but who learned to respond to life's challenges with autonomy. There surely was a great deal of pain in her life. She lost her mother at an early age; her adored father was an alcoholic. When she married her handsome cousin Franklin, they went to live with his mother, a controlling, imperious woman who could only have exacerbated Eleanor's feelings of being a plain and insecure young woman in an elegant and assured family. When Franklin became ill with polio, Eleanor's role as server and need-supplier was emphasized. When his political life took him away a great deal, she must have been lonely. And his long affair with Lucy Mercer had to have caused her terrible suffering.

Yet as life forced these painful circumstances upon her, it also presented her with the role of President's wife, and she used that as an opportunity. She did not accept the premise that a First Lady should simply look nice and serve as hostess at official gatherings. When her role as wife and mother began to recede, she used the role of First Lady to speak out on behalf of the disadvantaged of this country and elsewhere. She saw that they were plentiful and needed a spokesperson; her life's experience caused her to identify with them. She traveled widely in her efforts to help people, and, during the war, she was often in dangerous circumstances.

Mrs. Roosevelt was ridiculed by many Americans because of her shrill speaking voice. She was unable to move comfortably in the world, secure in the knowledge that she was an attractive woman. Nevertheless, she went out on her own, speaking up publicly for those who had no voice. Later on in her life, she continued to speak out in her capacity as the United States representative to the United Nations. Despite the price to her personally, she did what she believed was right. This took a great deal of courage, and it was through an exercise of courage that Eleanor Roosevelt became an autonomous person. Her life, as it evolved, was very reminiscent of Antigone's. It contained autonomy, high principle, and risks. Notable for their absence were narcissistic self-involvement and defensive suffering.

It may surprise some that I would choose Jacqueline Kennedy Onassis as another First Lady who exhibited self-assertive, autonomous behavior when she encountered new directions in her life. Once in residence in the White House, she saw that it was in deplorable condition and undertook to restore it in a manner that was tasteful, elegant, and historically accurate. This task was quite different from the one Eleanor Roosevelt chose for herself, but it reflected an independent and authentic course of action just as surely as Mrs. Roosevelt's did.

I also discerned an admirable and distinctly autonomous bent in the caring way that Mrs. Onassis raised her children. It was obvious that where they were concerned, she had clear priorities and abided by them. I once read a story that was critical of her for ducking out on a luncheon because she wanted to see a film before deciding if it was suitable for her children. I think she should have been applauded for showing such concern. She is also to be admired for her efforts to keep her children out of the limelight and to protect them from media exploitation. The criticism directed at her for her interest in clothes and money has been particularly vicious, perhaps due to envy After all, don't most women share such interests? That Mrs. Onassis had been able to indulge these interests more than the average woman is due to her life circumstances, and I think it is ungenerous to judge her harshly for those. She seems to me a woman who has been certain of what was important to her, and she has successfully built her life around those values.

One has only to read one particular story about Dr. Rosalind Yalow, the Nobel Prize–winning scientist, to know that she is without question an autonomous woman. In the story, which appeared in the *New York Times*, Dr. Yalow was recalling the difficulties her husband encountered when he took his doctoral exams. One of his examiners challenged Aaron Yalow's answer, told him he was wrong, and he worried that he might have been. "I took my doctorate exam in September," Dr. Yalow then said, "and the guy was stupid enough to try the same thing on me. And my answer was, 'Goldhaber and Hye taught it to me *this* way, and if there's anything wrong, you better talk to them about it.' " (The 1983 Nobel Prize–winner in medicine, Dr. Barbara McClintock, echoed this when noting that her research had been considered unacceptable for a time. "That was all right," Dr. McClintock said. "When you know you're right, you don't care.") Dr. Yalow's statement was an audacious one—bold and fearless. In that intimidating situation, I can think of few women *or* men who would have dared to respond as Dr. Yalow did. Obviously, she was extremely confident of her abilities in her field, and, coupled with that, she had the courage to insist on what she knew. The day after the story appeared, several of my patients mentioned it to me. They were impressed and inspired, as was I, to hear of a woman conducting herself with such authority. They also recognized that it would have been impossible for them to behave this way.

Dr. Yalow's action reminded me of the young Beethoven's when, at the beginning of his career, he went to study with Haydn. Haydn was then a revered figure, one of the premier composers of his age. When Haydn did not accept some of Beethoven's beliefs about musical theory, Beethoven refused to study with him any longer.

The shameless old lady in the film of the same name, based on a Günter Grass novel, developed the capacity for autonomy after she became a widow late in life. She began to believe that she was entitled to be free and to pursue those elemental pleasures that interested her, such as buying a few new kitchen utensils or having her hair washed by a young woman hairdresser with whom she becomes friendly. This occurs on a very simple level, but that does not make it any less autonomous. This woman, despite her advanced age, has discovered that she can define her own life rather than living the one imposed on her by the male-dominated Italian society. When her grown sons attempt to force her back into her old behavior, she stands up to them.

Rosina Lhevinne, the renowned piano teacher, might seem to be an example of autonomy abandoned, rather than achieved. Just days after marrying the great pianist Josef Lhevinne, she gave up playing the piano in concert although she was herself at the beginning of a promising career. Years later she explained, "I always thought there would be a certain rivalry, which would be absurd, because I didn't put myself on the same plane with him." Mr. Lhevinne, apparently, did not applaud her decision. When she would talk about her "little hands and little feet," he would correct her and say, "Nothing of the sort—regular hands and regular feet." Nevertheless, she stuck to her decision and always deferred to her husband's talent. At one point in their married life, they were invited to play a concert together. Afterward a friend told Mme. Lhevinne she was really the better of the two. "No!" she shouted, and insisted she would never play in public again.

But within these self-imposed strictures, Mme. Lhevinne did achieve a kind of autonomy in her career as teacher and developer of some of this century's finest pianists. She was nurturing the talent of others, but in doing this superbly she made a place for herself as someone other than just the wife of Josef Lhevinne, establishing for herself a life filled with all kinds of satisfactions.

Gloria Steinem could certainly be considered an autonomous woman. She recognized early how disenfranchised and subservient women were, how difficult it was for them to act with autonomy. But speaking for herself she said, "If you're willing to pay a price for it, you can do anything you want to do. And the price is worth it." And Barbara Honegger acted with autonomy when she resigned from the Justice Department after calling the Reagan Administration's efforts to eliminate sex discrimination a "sham." She is certainly an Antigone. She was willing to give up her job in order to speak out on a matter of principle and to do what she could to help women, despite the risks involved.

Most men do not need to struggle to achieve autonomy in the same way women do. It more or less goes with the territory of being male. And there is another quality men frequently possess that, I regret to say, I have virtually never seen in a woman. This is a kind of expansiveness or geniality that, I suspect, comes from having lived a successful life in an unrestricted, unhampered fashion. One definition of genial is "favorable for life, growth, or comfort." Men often grow up in conditions that could be defined thus, women rarely, as Virginia Woolf asserted in A *Room of One's Own*. There are many men who have felt, as the expression goes, that the world is their oyster. Very few women experience this sense of privilege. The world has not been eager to develop autonomy in women, to support and nurture their talents and abilities, to spend money or time to create conditions that will foster benign and joyous growth—and expansiveness—in them. And it shows.

I remember when Paul Robeson first appeared on the scene he possessed this expansive quality. Although he was black, his prodigious gifts as football hero, singer, and actor had gained him wide acceptance, and he obviously reveled in this. Robeson never set himself apart from other blacks, however, and he attempted to use his own good fortune for the benefit of his race, believing that acceptance for *all* blacks was possible. When he saw this was not so, and when people began to vilify him for his efforts on behalf of his race, when the red-baiters accused him of being a communist, he began to lose his wonderful expansiveness.

Being a woman in the world can have this same shriveling effect. Lack of power and lack of support erode what is magnanimous in a person. To possess this expansive quality, you must have had the following advantages: loving, caring parents who were delighted to have you from the moment of birth (males surely hold an advantage here); an environment that supports your growth; and a world that accepts you at the height of your creative abilities. The chances of a woman having all these things is indeed slim.

I have often thought that Golda Meir may have come close to enjoying such conditions in the course of her life. For her to have become the woman she was, she must have been welcomed, accepted, and loved by her parents. She never bore what could almost be thought of as the liability of physical beauty; undistracted, men simply responded to her competence. Her success may have come about in large measure because people virtually ignored the fact that she was a woman. Mercifully free of the sort of narcissism one sees in so many of today's political leaders, indifferent to the accoutrements of power, she had one overriding priority: to see Israel established and flourishing as an independent state. In her single-minded devotion to this one goal, she almost grew up like a man, she was virtually accepted as a man, she became Prime Minister of Israel as though she were a man.

Autonomy can appear in many guises, just as masochism can. But always, whether it shows itself in a political figure, a president's wife, or an elderly Italian widow, its cornerstone is authenticity, being true to oneself.

The Big Country, a huge, brawling, marvelous western film always sticks in my mind as a powerful illustration of this principle. Gregory Peck, who plays the hero, is a man from the East who has met and fallen in love with the daughter of a rancher, and they have decided to marry. When he goes West to meet her family, her father welcomes him warmly, but the foreman of the ranch, who had his own designs on the daughter, becomes an instant enemy who never passes up an opportunity to attack Peck. The brothers who own a neighboring ranch are cohorts of the foreman and one day they rope Peck and drag him through the dusty open spaces of the ranch. The father is incensed and vows to help Peck seek revenge. But when Peck demurs and says he does not think it is worth a big fight, the father brands him a coward, and it is clear that the daughter is beginning to make the same judgment.

There is on the ranch an ornery horse that no one has ever been able to ride successfully, and the foreman challenges Peck to ride him. No, Peck says, knowing what the foreman intends, but perhaps another time, maybe next week. The daughter becomes more and more disgusted by Peck's refusal to exhibit a macho style. During the week, Peck spends every night attempting to ride the horse, being bucked off and clambering back on, gentling the horse, finally teaching him who is master. He also during this period walks away from a brawl with the foreman, saying he does not believe in fighting. But the next time the foreman challenges him to ride the horse, he does so, and with authority, to everyone's amazement. The horse is gentle as a lamb. The daughter's interest in him is revived, of course, but he spurns her because their values are so different.

This film speaks of both the strategies of autonomy and its essence. It says that you can choose the time, the place, and the premises for any confrontation. You need not rise to the bait just because it is there. You need not be forced into "proving" yourself on someone else's terms. You can have your own definition of what a man, or a woman, is. And that definition is forged from those qualities in you that are authentic, those principles that are primary.

Aristotle's remark on dissent seems appropriate here: "Anybody can become angry—that is easy; but to be angry with the right person, and to the right degree, and at the right time, and for the right purpose, and in the right way—that is not within everybody's power and is not easy."

Autonomy is shaped by the determination to think for yourself. It is a freedom from tyranny, outer or inner; freedom from the tyranny of fear of exclusion or mistreatment; freedom from compulsion. The autonomous woman is not bound by the acquiescent, servile, secretly hating but outwardly conforming behavior patterns that result from capitulation to the prevailing cultural notions of what a woman should be. She is neither defiant nor imprisoned by defenses against a pervasive anxiety or by the anger, vindictiveness, self-contempt, and self-hatred that forced submission so often generates. The autonomous woman asserts herself as she *must*, not fearful of male power, not primarily concerned with male judgment. Her image of who she is and how she must live has been interiorized; it rests securely within her, safe from outside attack.

In the early years of this century the poet Rainer Maria Rilke described, in *Letters to a Young Poet*, a magnificent vision of the future of woman that might serve as a beacon for those women who are today seeking to move toward autonomy:

The girl and woman, in their new, their own unfolding, will but in passing be imitators of masculine ways, good and bad. . . . [The] humanity of woman, borne its full time in suffering and humiliation, will come to light when she will have stripped off the conventions of femininity in the mutations of her outward status, and those men who do not yet feel it approaching today will be surprised and struck by it. Some day . . . there will be girls and women whose name . . . will be something in itself, something that makes one think, not of any complement or limit, but only of life and existence: the feminine human being.

Bibliography

Abrahamsen, David. *The Murdering Mind*. New York: Harper & Row, 1973.

Aquinas, St. Thomas. Articles on the Production of Woman. *Summa Theologica*. New York: McGraw-Hill, 1964.

Ball, Patricia G., and Elizabeth Wyman. "Battered Wives and Powerlessness: What Can Counsellors Do?" *Victimology* 1977–78: 2:545–553.

Barbara Dominick A. "Masochism in Love and Sex." *American Journal of Psychoanalysis* 1973: 33:73–79.

Bard, Morton, and Dawn Sangrey. *The Crime Victim's Book*. New York: Basic Books, 1979.

Benson, Ruth C. *Women in Tolstoy*. Chicago: University of Illinois Press, 1973.

Bernard, Jessie. *The Female World*. New York: Free Press, 1981.

Bickel, Alexander M. *The Morality of Consent*. New Haven: Yale University Press, 1975.

Bieber, Irving. "Sadism and Masochism." *American Handbook of Psychiatry Vol. III*. Edited by S. Arieti. 2nd Edition. New York: Basic Books, 1974.

Bowlby, John. "Nature of the Child's Tie to His Mother." *International Journal of Psychoanalysis* 1958: 39:35–373.

———. "Separation Anxiety." *International Journal of Psychoanalysis* 1960. 41:89–113.

Bruch, Hilde. *Eating Disorders*. New York: Basic Books, 1973.

Chernin, Kim. *The Obsession: Reflections on the Tyranny of Slenderness*. New York: Harper & Row, 1981.

Crecelius, Kathryn J. "Do You Want to Grow Up like Her?" Lecture given at the Annual Meeting of the Society of Women Engineers, 1979.

Dalton, Debra, and James Kantner. "Aggression in Battered and Non-battered Women as Reflected in the Hand Test." *Psychological Reports* 1983: 53:703–709.

Dinesen, Isak. "Sorrow-Acre." *Women in Fiction Vol. 2.* Edited by S. Cahill. New York: New American Library, 1978.

Eidelberg, Ludwig. "Zur Metapsychologie des Masichismus." *International Journal of Psychoanalysis* 1935: 15:245–251.

Einstein, Albert. *The Born-Einstein Letters,* London: Macmillan, 1971.

Eisenbud, Ruth Jean. "Masochism Revisited." *Psychoanalytic Review* 1967: 54:561–582.

Erikson, Erik. *Childhood and Society.* New York: W.W. Norton, 1950.

Fine, Reuben. *The Hate Affair.* Lecture given at Symposium on Sadomasochistic Relationships, April 7, 1979, New York City.

Francoeur, Robert T. *Eve's New Rib.* New York: Harcourt Brace Jovanovich, 1972.

Freud, Sigmund, "A Child Is Being Beaten." (1919). *Collected Papers, Vol. II.* New York: Basic Books, 1959.

———. "The Economic Problem of Masochism." *Collected Papers, Vol. II.* New York: Basic Books, 1959.

Fromm, Erich. *The Anatomy of Human Destructiveness.* New York: Holt, Rinehart & Winston, 1973.

Garnett, David. *Lady into Fox.* New York: W.W. Norton, 1966.

Gelles, R. J. *The Violent Home.* Beverly Hills: Sage Publications, 1972.

Green, Maurice R. Review of *Understanding Sexual Attacks* by D. J. West, C. Roy, and F. L. Nichol. *Bulletin of the American Academy of Psychiatry and Law* 1982: 3:224.

Harlow, Harry F. "Primary Affectional Patterns in Primates." *American Journal of Orthopsychiatry* 1960: 30:676–684.

Haskell, Molly. *From Reverence to Rape.* New York: Holt, Rinehart & Winston, 1974.

Horney, Karen. "The Problem of Feminine Masochism." *Feminine Psychology.* Edited by H. Kelman. New York: W.W. Norton, 1967.

Krafft-Ebing, Richard von. *Psychopathia Sexualis* (translated from the 12th German edition by F. S. Klaf). New York: Stein & Day, 1965.

Langstern, Barbara. "Worries: What They Say about You." *Vogue*, December 1982.

Lessing, Doris. "To Room Ninteen." *A Man and Two Women and Other Stories*. New York: Simon & Schuster. 1958.

Levy, David M. "Maternal Overprotection." *Psychiatry* 1938: 1:564; 1939: 2:563.

Luce, Ralph. "From Hero to Robot: Masculinity in America, Stereotypes and Reality." *Psychoanalytic Review* 1967: 54:608–630.

Merriam, Eve. *The Double Bed (From the Feminine Side)*. New York: Marzani and Munsell, 1958.

Michaud, S. G., and H. Aynesworth. *The Only Living Witness*. New York: Simon & Schuster, 1983.

Mill, John Stuart. *On the Subjection of Women*. 1869; reprint, New York, Fawcett, 1972.

Miller, Jean Baker. "Women and Power." *Work in Progress*. Wellesley College Press 1982:82–01.

Morris, Rosemary. *Suffering Women: Feminine Masochism in Novels by American Women*. Ann Arbor: University of Michigan Press, 1975.

O'Connor, Frank. "Fish for Friday." *New Yorker*, June 18, 1955.

Pepitone-Rockwell, Fran. "Counseling Women to Be Less Vulnerable to Rape." *Medical Aspects of Human Sexuality*, January 1980.

Phelps, Stanlee, and Nancy Austin. *The Assertive Woman*. San Luis Obispo, Calif.: Impact Publishers, 1975.

Press, Shirley. "No One Wants Girls Except . . . " Letter to the *Journal of the American Medical Association* 1983: 249:2305.

Rilke, Ranier Maria. *Letters to a Young Poet*. New York: W.W. Norton, 1954.

Rioch, J. McK. "The Transference Phenomenon in Psychoanalytic Therapy." *Psychiatry* 1943: 6:174.

Rosenbaum, Mai-Britt. "Gender-specific Problems in the Treatment of Young Women." *American Journal of Psychoanalysis* 1977: 37:215–223.

Rosenman, Stanley. "Inner Promotings of the Victimizer as Illustrated in the *Psychodynamics of Anti-Semitism*." Lecture given at Symposium on Sado-masochistic Relationships, April 8, 1979.

Rossiter, Margaret H. *Women Scientists in America: Struggles and Strategies up to 1940*. Baltimore: John Hopkins University Press, 1982.

Roth, Geneen. *Feeding the Hungry Heart: The Experience of Compulsive Eating*. Indianapolis: Bobbs-Merrill, 1982.

Ruggiero, Josephine, and L. C. Weston. "Sex-role Characterization of Women in Modern Gothic Novels." *Pacific Social Review* 1977.

Sack, R. L. and W. Miller. "Masochism: A Clinical and Theoretical Overview." *Psychiatry* 1975: 38:244–257.

Scully, Diane, and Joseph Morella. "Why Men Rape." *Virginia Commonwealth University Magazine* 1983: 12:2.

Seidenberg, Robert. *Corporate Wives—Corporate Casualties?* New York: AMACON, 1973.

Selkin, J. "Don't Take It Lying Down." *Psychology Today*, January 1975.

Shainess, Natalie. "Psychological Aspects of Wife-Battering." *Battered Women*. Edited by Maria Roy. New York: Van Nostrand Reinhold, 1977.

———. "Psychological Significance of Rape." *New York State Journal of Medicine* 1976: 76:2044–2049.

———. "Vulnerability to Violence: Masochism as Process." *American Journal of Psychotherapy* 1979: 33:174–190.

Shulman, Irving. *Jackie: The Exploitation of a First Lady*. New York: Trident Press, 1970.

Spitz, Rene A., and W. Godfrey Cobliner. *The First Year of Life*. New York: International Universities Press, 1965.

Stolorow, Robert D. "The Narcissistic Function of Masochism and Sadism." *International Journal of Psychoanalysis* 1975: 56:441–447.

Sullivan, Harry Stack. *The Collected Papers of Harry Stack Sullivan*. Edited by H. S. Perry and M. Gawel. New York: W.W. Norton, 1953.

Tavris, Carol. "The Imposter Phenomenon." *Vogue*, December 1982.

Thompson, Clara. "Penis Envy in Women." *Psychiatry* 1943: 6:123–131.

Ullman, Montague. "The Social Roots of the Dream." *American Journal of Psychoanalysis* 1960: 22:180–196.

Walker, Lenore. "Battered Woman and Learned Helplessness." *Victimology* 1978: 2:525.

Wallerstein, J. S. and J. B. Kelly. "Effects of Parental Divorce." *American Journal of Orthopsychology* 1976: 42:20.

Weakland, John W. "The 'Double Bind' Hypothesis of Schizophrenia and Three Party Interaction." *The Etiology of Schizophrenia*. Edited by D. Jackson. New York: Basic Books, 1960.

Woolf, Virginia. "The New Dress." *A Haunted House and Other Stories.* New York: Harcourt Brace Jovanovich, 1944.

——. *Orlando.* New York: New American Library, 1960.

Zemlich, M. J. and R. I. Watson. "Maternal Attitudes of Acceptance and Rejection during or after Pregnancy." *American Journal of Orthopsychiatry* 1953: 23:570.

Index

255

'A passionate and gripping account of a famously
dysfunctional family. Haynes balances a fresh take on
the material with a deep love for her sources, wearing
her scholarship with grace, and giving new voice to the
often-overlooked but fascinating Jocasta and Ismene'
MADELINE MILLER,
author of *The Song of Achilles* and *Circe*

'Haynes's fascination with this long-vanished world
is evident in every line . . . Her Thebes . . . is
vividly captured: a place of hard light and sharp
shadows, dust, fountains and dry heat'
Guardian

'Glorious, gripping and brutal . . . I loved it'
VICTORIA DERBYSHIRE

'New life is breathed into a powerful ancient story
through Natalie Haynes's clever and vivid storytelling'
MARTHA KEARNEY

'Nearly every page of Natalie Haynes's *The Children
of Jocasta* could stand alone as poetry. This is a
visceral, engrossing and meticulously crafted
reimagining of two of the most important stories
of all time. A truly remarkable feat'
AMANDA FOREMAN

'In this gripping novel, Haynes takes us to the
breaking heart of one epically dysfunctional family
and makes heroines of those previously doomed to be
spectators of their own tragedy'
DAMIAN BARR, author of
Maggie & Me and *You Will Be Safe Here*

The Children of Jocasta

NATALIE HAYNES is a writer and broadcaster. She has written and presented six series of the BBC Radio 4 show *Natalie Haynes Stands Up for the Classics*. In 2015, she was awarded the Classical Association Prize for her work in bringing Classics to a wider audience. She is the author of two works of non-fiction, *The Ancient Guide to Modern Life* and *Pandora's Jar*, and three novels: *The Children of Jocasta, The Amber Fury*, which was shortlisted for the Scottish Crime Book of the Year award, and *A Thousand Ships*, which was shortlisted for the Women's Prize 2020.

Natalie Haynes

The Children of Jocasta

PICADOR

First published 2017 by Mantle

First published in paperback 2018 by Picador

This edition published 2021 by Picador
an imprint of Pan Macmillan
The Smithson, 6 Briset Street, London EC1M 5NR
EU representative: Macmillan Publishers Ireland Ltd, 1st Floor,
The Liffey Trust Centre, 117–126 Sheriff Street Upper,
Dublin 1, DO1 YC43
Associated companies throughout the world
www.panmacmillan.com

ISBN 978-1-5290-5713-3

7 9 8 6

A CIP catalogue record for this book is available from the British Library.

Printed and bound by CPI Group (UK) Ltd, Croydon, CR0 4YY

MIX
Paper | Supporting
responsible forestry
FSC® C116313

Visit *www.picador.com* to read more about all our books
and to buy them. You will also find features, author interviews and
news of any author events, and you can sign up for e-newsletters
so that you're always first to hear about our new releases.

For Dan

ὸ γοῦν λόγος σοι πᾶς ὑπὲρ κείνης ὅδε

Antigone, Sophocles

Author's Note

The ancient Greeks did not think of themselves as 'Greek' (the word Graeci is a later, Roman invention). They were Hellenes. They prized opposites – when ancient Greeks wanted to describe the whole world, for example, they would split it into two: both Hellene and non-Hellene, or both free-man and slave. But they also, perhaps predominantly, defined themselves as citizens of whichever city-state they inhabited. Thebes had a dense mythical history, as did its environs: a surprisingly large number of unpleasant deaths in Greek myth happened on or near Mount Cithaeron, where Actaeon was turned into a stag and ripped apart by his own hunting hounds, and Pentheus was torn limb from limb by his own Maenadic mother. Perhaps the moral of these stories is that the countryside can be more dangerous than the city. But not always.

The Children of Jocasta

Prologue

The man looked across the room at his son, who lay shivering on the hard couch. He took a step towards the boy, thinking he would wrap a blanket more closely around him to coax the shivers away. But then he stopped, unable to persuade his limbs to repeat the actions they had carried out the day before and the day before that. He had kept his wife warm when the shakes ran through her; her body like an axe-blade, juddering in the trunk of a thick, black pine tree. And then he had kept his daughter warm until she too succumbed to the disease. What was it the washerwoman had called it? The Reckoning.

He felt his cracked lips stretch into a mirthless smile. What kind of a reckoning did the citizens of Thebes believe this to be? Punishment from the gods for a real or imagined slight? The temples rang out with the sound of prayers and offerings to every god, by every name. Most often they called on Apollo. Mindful of offending him, they addressed him by one name after another: Cynthios, Delphinios, Pythios, the son of Letò. Everyone knew that his arrows carried the plague on their immortal tips and that his aim was always true. But what possible grudge could the Archer have held against this man's daughter, scarcely more than an infant? Or his wife, who had made her sacrifices devoutly with each new season? The god could not have resented her, but she had died all the same. Two days ago, he had carried her body into the streets himself, struggling with the weight not because his sickness-ravaged wife was heavy – she was sinew and bones, the skin hanging loosely from her arms – but because the plague had left him barely able to lift his own battered bones.

Carrying his daughter out the following day had been easier.

He looked over at Sophon again, and saw the convulsions ripple through his ten-year-old body. He felt a wetness beneath his eye and thought for a moment that he was weeping. But when he took his hand away from his face, he saw the raw crimson of fresh blood on his fingertips. The blisters were bursting, then. He had heard that men were losing their sight. Only a few heartbeats after he had silently cursed Apollo, he murmured a quiet prayer. Let me not go blind. A blind man was of no use to his young son. If the boy survived, he would not be able to take care of a blind beggar man. His prayers grew smaller: let me keep one eye, at least. One eye intact. And – they increased again without him noticing – let the boy live.

But should he really leave him to shake so? He had felt his own teeth drumming against one another when the shivering had consumed him a day ago. He worried he would bite through his own tongue. He paused, realizing that was not quite true; he had given no thought to his tongue when the fever rattled through him. Only afterwards, when the heat had broken and he lay spent on the ground, did he wonder how he had not injured himself. When the shakes came upon his wife, he had wrapped her up, and she had wrapped up their daughter. But neither had survived. He had placed all the blankets around them, so there was nothing left by the time he fell foul of the same cruel dance. Yet he was – so far – still alive. And so perhaps this was something he had learned about the Reckoning: it thrived in the heat. It might be driven out if it was denied warmth.

The boy moaned so softly that he wondered if he was hearing things. But he did not approach him, and he did not make him warm.

The Archer would take who he chose. But still, the man hoped – a tiny broken thing like a bird – that he would seek his prey elsewhere.

1

Sixty years later

I didn't hear him coming. I was in the old ice store, which lay at the furthest end of a forgotten corridor in a corner of the palace no one had used for years. Not since my parents were alive. My father loved ice, shaved with an iron pick from a block which dripped sullenly in this room, the thick walls protecting it from the constant sun which beat down on the white stone. How did it get here? I used to beg. Where did it come from? He would tell me a different answer each time: an angry river god had turned all the city's water into ice one day, and no one had ever found time to defrost this last chunk. It was an egg left behind by a huge frozen bird. Then it was Thebes's greatest treasure, and bandits had sailed across the oceans to invade the palace and seize it, like the Golden Fleece. This last story left me with nightmares of masked men, breaching one of the city's seven gates, climbing to the high citadel – fearless as they ran beneath the mountain lions which were carved into the stone gateway, golden stones embedded into their eye sockets to ward off our enemies – trampling along the colonnades and rampaging into the courtyard where we lived. My mother told him to stop frightening me. So the next time I asked him, he made me promise solemnly that I wouldn't tell her before explaining that he had won it in a bet with a Titan, who now cursed his name. I shouldn't be afraid of him, though, because he was fully occupied holding the weight of the sky upon his shoulders.

After my parents died, my uncle Creon had the palace extended and rebuilt. It needed to be more secure, he said, and grander. He added rooms and whole levels above the ground floor, so my home towered above every building in the city. The palace sat on the highest hill, and now it was the highest building too. Creon also insisted that the royal residence should no longer be kept ever-open to the city and her citizens, as my mother had liked it. There must be a space between us and them; we needed doors which could be bolted shut each night. Lessons had to be learned. And while all these works were being carried out, by teams of efficient and almost silent slaves, he decided this corridor might as well be abandoned. He didn't care for ice, the way my father did. So once the building works were completed, this room was no longer used for anything: it was too far from the new kitchens to be practical.

But it made a perfect place to read, on a bristling hot day. The light spilled in from two small slits, high up on the north- and east-facing walls. And with the door open onto the half-walled corridor outside, I could easily see to read the parchment roll I had taken from my tutor's office yesterday. I would return it as soon as I'd finished, like I always did. He didn't mind, so long as I placed it back on his dusty shelves in the exact spot from which I had removed it. I had learned to blow the dust across from either side to cover the tracks my fingers left on the wood. His eyes weren't as sharp as they used to be. The manuscript would be back in its place before he even noticed it was gone.

I often lost track of time in this room, which was one of its many advantages. The long days of summer were so hot and bright and dull. My uncle liked to say girls all across the city, across Hellas, wished to be in our place. But they must have imagined our lives to be other than they were, because no one would cherish these empty days. I longed to go down to Lake Hylica and swim with the frogs and the fish. But there was no one to go with, and I knew my sister would be annoyed if I took the maids with me. What if she needed them to help her change her dress or rearrange her hair? We couldn't all run around the palace like barbarians, she would say, not for the first time. I could almost imagine her petulant lower lip, protruding in annoyance at something I hadn't yet done.

The light only entered the ice store through thin strips, so it was easy to lose track of where the sun was in the sky. I would usually leave when I'd finished reading, or when I was hungry, or sometimes when I heard Ani or Eteo calling for me. They always knew that if I wasn't at lessons or in the courtyard, I'd be here. But no one was calling for me that day. It was always quiet in the palace in summer; anything important would be taking place in the public square at the front of the building. Perhaps that's what made me stand up and press my aching shoulders against the cool stone wall behind me. It was so quiet, I must have begun to think I was supposed to be wherever the rest of the palace's inhabitants were.

I heard his footsteps, I think, but I wasn't afraid. He wasn't walking like someone who had something to hide. I could hear heels striking the ground, a measured, easy pace. It didn't occur to me to be worried. Even so, I stashed the roll of parchment under my arm, in case it was my tutor, and covered it with the fine cloak I shrugged over my shoulders. I knew it wasn't his walk, though: he favours his right foot and drags the left one slightly. 'An old injury' is all he ever says if you ask him why. His eyes are dark and hooded, and they change if he doesn't want you to pursue something. The light disappears from them, and the subject is closed.

I walked out into the corridor, and the temperature rose pitilessly. Even wearing my thinnest cloak – a pale fawn colour, made of flax – I was too hot out here. I wished I could just wear a simple tunic, as I did when I was younger. But if my uncle caught sight of me dressed so informally, I would be in trouble. I could feel the sweat forming behind my ears and at the base of my spine. I almost turned straight back into the ice store. But I had decided I should go and find my siblings, so I kept walking.

With the increase in temperature came other reminders of the world outside the palace: grasshoppers scratching away beside the walls, darting sparrows chattering in their nests. Usually, a man with a long broom sweeps away the birds' nests from the walls, because their morning clamour irritates my uncle. But for some reason, they had been overlooked this year, and they chirruped away, gleeful at their reprieve. If the mountain eagles heard them, the sparrows would lose their fledglings.

The corridor twisted round to the left and then the

right, before it opened out into the family courtyard. My eyes were watering at the sudden brightness after the twilight of the ice store. I blinked away the tears and then licked them from my top lip. I realized I was thirsty; perhaps that was what had driven me out of my quiet corner. It must be Eteo I could hear, I thought, coming down the corridor to find me. Although he would surely be busy with his advisers at this hour. But the stride was much too long for Ani, and anyway, her shoes don't have those hard leather soles that slap the stones as you walk.

I followed the corridor around to the left, and saw the shadow of the man along the ground. Not Eteo, then, because this man was wearing a long cloak, and Eteo would be in nothing more than a tunic on a day like today. I heard a strange, metallic sound I half-recognized. And then I walked around the second corner and when he caught sight of me, the man stiffened, as though he were suppressing alarm. I had heard him, but with my feet bare, he clearly hadn't heard me. I was about to greet him when I realized his face was almost entirely covered, like the bandits of my nightmares. Only his eyes were visible: he had swathed the rest in a thin white fabric.

I tensed my arm against my side, to keep hold of Sophon's scroll. Behind the veiled man, I could see the courtyard, but it was empty. There was no sign of my siblings, my cousin, my uncle. I took a breath and decided I would rather run past him than walk. I am the second quickest of all of us: much taller than Ani, and Polyn – my oldest brother – would never deign to engage in a race with his little sister, so I would win against him by default. Only Eteo, with his long, lean physique, could outrun me, though my uncle would be horrified if he ever saw me hitching up my tunic to give my legs free rein. And when Eteo was busy with matters of state, there was no one I could prevail upon to accompany me somewhere quiet and spacious enough to sprint. So I was out of practice, but I still trusted my speed. Once I was in the courtyard, I could raise an alarm that a stranger was present in the family quarters. The household slaves must be somewhere nearby, surely.

I pushed my toes into the stone beneath my feet. I must have left my sandals in my room this morning: something else which would provoke my uncle to raise a weary eyebrow, if he saw me. I pressed forward and almost skittered past the man, but he stepped suddenly to his right, and I clattered into him. I felt a sharp jab under my ribs. He must have slammed the wooden end of the parchment roll into my side. I winced and said reflexively, 'I'm sorry.'

We were the exact same height, so our eyes met for a moment: his were a watery sort of grey, with two brown specks in the right iris. It made it look like a bird's egg. I should keep running into the courtyard, I thought, and then out the other side, and through to the next square where my brothers and my uncle would be. I could return the manuscript to Sophon and apologize for taking it without asking. He wouldn't mind. But even as I was thinking this, it occurred to me that perhaps my legs wouldn't carry me as far as the second courtyard. I was standing in the beating sun, but I was cold. The man looked past me for a second, though there was no one behind me, then his eyes met mine. Wordless, he turned and walked away. I thought perhaps I might sit on the ground for a moment.

I took a few more steps and fell to my knees, just before I was fully in the courtyard. A girl I didn't recognize – the daughter of one of the house-slaves, I suppose – was coming out of a bedroom, carrying a tray. The noise of me falling – my thick silver bangle crashing onto the ground – made her turn and she screamed, dropping what she was carrying everywhere. Hollow wooden things, cups maybe, or bowls. I heard them bounce and crash across the warm grey slabs. I hissed at her to be quiet, but she was too far away and besides, she was making so much noise herself, she wouldn't have heard anything I said. The light was so bright, it made me want to close my eyes. I saw the shadows of birds flying across the square, but I couldn't raise my head to see the birds themselves.

After a long time or perhaps no time at all, I heard voices, but they all sounded strange, distorted as though I was hearing them underwater. I blinked but my eyes wouldn't quite focus: there were guards and servants, and then my brothers, everyone running towards me. They were shouting – I could see from their flushed faces – but I could barely make out what they were saying. It sounded like, 'They've killed her.'

Killed who? There was only one person left in my family who they could possibly mean: my sister, Ani. Please don't let it be Ani, I thought. However much we argue, I can't lose her too. Please.

The last thing I remembered was looking down to see that Sophon's manuscript was completely ruined, covered in something sticky and red. I would have to apologize. It would be hard to replace. And then, of course, I realized they meant me. Someone had killed me.

2

As the pain coursed through her body, threatening to split her apart, Jocasta clawed at the bedclothes beneath her. If she could just get some air into her chest, she told herself, everything would be alright. Her lungs felt like an empty wineskin, trampled beneath a drunken soldier's boot. Yet she couldn't stop screaming for long enough to breathe. She felt Teresa's hand grabbing her own hard enough to squash the bones together. The secondary pain was so unexpected, she turned to look stupidly at her crushed hand.

'Breathe in,' said Teresa and counted her to four. 'And now out again.' The two of them counted the breaths, together but apart, because although Jocasta needed the older woman's help, she also knew it was all Teresa's fault that she was probably about to die, and she found that hard to forgive.

It had been Teresa's idea for the old king to marry. The city had gone too long without knowing its future. People were worried. If the king died without a son (even a daughter would be better than nothing), what would happen to the citizens of Thebes? They needed stability. Everyone agreed, the city had endured enough since the Reckoning had devastated them years before.

And it was strange, people said as they went about their business, that the king lived in a huge palace with courtiers, housekeepers, guards and cooks, but no family. He was past forty, past fifty almost: his habit of riding out into the mountains for weeks on end with his men – hunting deer or wild boar with their nets and short spears – was no longer as forgivable as it had once been.

Jocasta wasn't told how she was chosen. The whole thing must have happened so quickly: a group of men in a room lit by smoky candles, drawing lots to decide whose daughter would be elevated to royalty. One day, she had been at home – her parents' home, as she would soon learn to rename it – sitting in the women's quarters, thinking about very little. Five days later, she was standing in the public courtyard of Thebes's palace before an altar hastily dedicated to Ox-eyed Hera, pledged by her father to a man she had never met, before the eyes of a goddess who had ignored her prayers. She had no idea her father was considering marriage for her so soon, having expected to be at home for another year or two, at least. She was a dutiful daughter, careful at weaving and the other household skills her parents encouraged her to acquire. She would make a good wife. But surely not yet.

Her parents had acted with extraordinary haste. Jocasta felt foolish: she should have known what they were like. How else had they survived the Reckoning? Her father had a unique gift for profiting from situations that would fell lesser men. He had always been conscious of his standing: he was rich but he had earned his wealth, rather than inheriting it. Still he had earned plenty, and bought slaves enough to build a large house on the northern side of the city. It was not the most fashionable street (too far from the palace for that), but it was airy and the house was a grand stone affair, with the women's quarters tucked away behind the building's forbidding gates. His wife had slave women to do her weaving for her, though she still prided herself on the fineness of the cloth she used to make.

The particular pain of his behaviour this time came from the realization that he must have considered Jocasta – his only daughter, his first-born child – as nothing more than another problem waiting to be solved. It was one thing to be disliked by her mother – who had never tried to disguise the irritation she felt for her daughter – but another thing altogether to be rejected by her father, when he had always made her his pet, as if consoling her for her mother's indifference. After Jocasta's wedding – when she tried to defend him in her mind, so she could look back on some parts of her childhood fondly – she gave him credit for the fact that any father would be proud to marry his daughter to the king. Though she knew he had not thought about her, or what she might want, at all. Still, what man wouldn't seize a marriage connection to the king? And what father would jeopardize such a connection on the whim of his daughter? None. But he should have known she would have done whatever he had asked, if he had only asked. Instead of which, he organized the whole thing without telling her. The only possible explanation for such secrecy was that he knew how she would feel when she found out, and it saddened her that he had known but not cared.

He was a little drunk when he came home that night: the men had been drinking their wine too strong. Whoever had been master of the grape – pouring it into the krater and mixing it with insufficient water – had intended them all to get drunk before the flute-girls arrived. Jocasta preferred the euphemism to the word she heard her mother hiss: whores. But now she could hear her father whispering to her mother, who let out a sudden squawk of delight before the two of them began to laugh. Like children, she thought, in annoyance. She heard her brother murmur in his dream, and wondered if he would wake up. But as she stared across the room in the dim light, willing him back to sleep, he rolled over to face the wall and his breathing levelled out once again. She moved her head slightly, trying to hear what her father was saying. But she couldn't quite make out the words.

Would it have made any difference if she had? Would she have argued with him? She did that anyway, when she found out the next day, but it had no effect. Everything was already arranged, and there was nothing she could do. Would she have run away in the night, if she'd known sooner? Where could she have gone? Thebes wasn't a large city, and her father knew everyone in it. Would she have tried to escape from the city altogether? But how would she have made it through any of its seven gates, all of which were guarded? She had never thought of herself as a prisoner behind the city walls. But that was only because she had never wanted to leave before.

Still, when she asked them the next day what all the fuss had been about, she wished she had known sooner. Her father smiled luxuriantly, his pleasure slowly revealing his yellowing teeth, greying now at the gums.

'I have done the best deal of my life,' he told her. 'And you are to marry the king.'

The second sentence was so incongruous following the first. She had been waiting for him to say that he had discovered a new trading partner in the Outlying, Theban slang for Boeotia, the territory outside their beloved city, or to produce some rhyton that he had bought from a shipping merchant: her father loved the most ornate drinking cups. His favourite was a pointed vessel made from rock crystal, with smaller polished green crystal beads, wrapped in twists of gold, for a handle. She felt her face rearrange itself, from congratulatory to perplexed.

'What do you mean?' she said.

'King Laius needs a wife,' her mother explained, condemning herself forever in her daughter's eyes. 'You're very lucky.' Her father nodded.

'The king is an old man,' Jocasta said. 'He must be more than fifty years old.'

'Half-dead, then,' said her father, his eyebrows raised in a parody of amusement. 'He's only ten years or so older than me, you little brat.'

'So why would I want to marry him?' she continued. 'Instead of someone who isn't older than my father?'

'Sometimes,' her mother sighed, 'I think you take pleasure in being wilfully obtuse. I really do. So let me explain to you in words that even your little brother would understand: Thebes needs a powerful king. Laius is getting older, and people are growing nervous. What if something happens to him when he's away from the city? What then? The Elders will fight to succeed him. The city could fall into chaos.' She reached over to Jocasta and grabbed her shoulder, next to the fabric knots which formed the top of her daughter's tunic. She allowed her nails to rest on Jocasta's skin. 'That can't happen,' she said. 'The king needs a son. And, before that, he needs a wife, a young one, who could act as regent until the child comes of age, if something happened to him.' She shook Jocasta's shoulder with each alternate word. 'And that is going to be you, because your father is clever and lucky, which is exactly why I married him. Do you understand?'

Jocasta nodded, and her mother let go of her arm. 'It's an honour, you ungrateful little bitch. You'll be queen of the city. So run along to the temple of Artemis and dedicate your doll. And do it nicely, so she doesn't curse you, as you deserve.'

The ritual should have been only a part of Jocasta's proaulia: the time between betrothal and marriage when a bride prepared herself for her new life, but there was little time (and, on Jocasta's part, no enthusiasm) for more. When Jocasta was born she had been given a small clay figure of an Amazon girl, wearing brightly patterned leggings and a tunic top. She had played with it so much that the paint had rubbed away, only the odd fleck of red or green remaining from what had once been a parade of colour. The doll's left eye was still black, but the paint on the other had cracked, allowing the faded orange terracotta to show through. But married women could not have toys: she must take her doll to the temple and dedicate it to Artemis, praying for her to give Jocasta strength, like the warrior woman. After the dedication, the next temple she would enter would be sacred to Hera. Artemis would have no time for her once she was married.

Traditionally, a girl's family and friends accompanied her when she offered her doll to the Virgin Goddess. It should have been a party, a feast, an occasion for joy. But Jocasta's parents were too angry with her – and she with them – so she went alone, save for the slave girl who followed two paces behind her, to the temple only a few streets away.

She placed the doll in a small brown leather bag, and walked quickly along the dusty road, her feet reddening from the dirt that clung to the bottom of her shift. The rain would not come again for another month at least, and the sharp-pointed acanthus leaves at the side of the road were beginning to droop in the heat. She hitched her skirt up a little into her belt, but the disapproving stare of an old woman sweeping the steps outside a nearby house made her blush and drop it back to graze the dust once again. The temple would be cool inside, and she climbed the steps grateful to escape the glaring afternoon heat beneath the grand columns that ran along the front. She turned to her mother's slave and told her to wait in the shade beneath the temple portico.

Jocasta stepped inside and blinked into the darkness, but no one else was present. She took the doll from her bag and walked up to the large statue of Artemis – her serene face expressing mild pleasure in holding her bow and arrows – feeling oddly self-conscious. She knew she should issue a formal prayer as she left her toy for the goddess, but with no priestess to help her, she couldn't find the words. So she placed her doll carefully at the divine foot, propping it up against the cold stone. She murmured, 'Keep me safe', and turned to go. As she walked through a shaft of sunlight, her eye was caught by an angry red weal on her shoulder. Her mother's thumbnail had broken the skin, and when she raised her arm she saw four more gashes – the skin around them pink and inflamed – on the back of her shoulder.

She stopped and knelt on the ground, not wanting to go home again while her mother sat in the women's quarters, emanating spite. Her brother would be at lessons with his tutor, and her father would be in the market square, clutching the hands of florid men as he accepted their congratulations. She could see the gold rings which pinned back the flesh of her father's fingers, so they spilled fatly above the metal. He would consider this a very good day.

As she sat on her heels, she tried to imagine what it would be like to live in the palace, the citadel of Thebes. She had been there a handful of times when she was younger, always for festivals. She tried to separate the building from the occasions, but it was difficult. She could remember the overpowering smell of charred meat, tinged with cloying incense and the vinegary tang of wine. She heard the clamour of a crowd, all eating and drinking their fill. The priests in their finery, leading Thebes in their sacrifices and prayers. She had a sense of a big open courtyard, but she couldn't fill in any details of the rest of the building: the colour, the scale, nothing. Were there trees? She had half a memory of reaching up to touch silver-grey bark with her fingers. Above all, she could not place the king in his palace. She tried to remember whether he was clean-shaven or bearded, whether his eyes were light or dark, whether his hair was black, like most Thebans, or fair, as some were. Whether he was stocky or thin, tall or beginning to bend forward at the neck, like a tortoise. She bit her lip when she realized that whatever colour the hair had once been, it was probably grey now, or white. Or perhaps he was bald. She tried to suppress the sudden sourness she felt rising at the back of her throat.

She looked up at the statue of Artemis. The goddess sat placidly on her throne, her hair neatly plaited behind her head, a bow in her hand and a quiver at her side. The latter was decorated with deer, running between trees in bright green leaf. 'Please,' Jocasta said, looking up at the figure and reaching out to hold the cold stone hem of her robe. 'Don't let him touch me. Please.'

She stared at the painted eyes but received no reply. Zeus nods, Thebans said. If he assents to your request, he nods. But did Artemis nod too? Perhaps if she stared straight into the goddess's eyes and didn't blink at all, Artemis would understand how important this was. She held her gaze for as long as she could but eventually tears formed and she could no longer force her eyes to remain open. Did she imagine the head moving? She wiped the tears away with her small, pale hand. 'Thank you,' she whispered, just in case.

The dressmaker came the next day, her grey hair combed back so the bright sunlight picked out every wrinkle in her creased brown face. She had brought two bolts of fabric with her, in two contrasting shades of red. Jocasta wondered if her mother had chosen the cloth, which would make a thick, heavy chiton to wear on a warm summer day. Certainly no one had asked her. But she didn't question the dressmaker, in case it was all the woman had. Perhaps there hadn't been time for the dyers to begin work on new fabric. Besides, it was an unspoken rule of living in Thebes that no one complained about shortages. Everyone knew that the king and his Elders were doing their best to ensure supplies came into the city. But with the Sphinx in the mountains – right outside the city walls people sometimes said – no one could be surprised if there were interruptions and delays. She tried not to imagine herself in the shade of saffron she would have preferred, tried not to think how hot she would be dressed in fabric the colour of blood.

And at least the dressmaker's second bolt of cloth – for the cloak and the veil – was thinner and lighter, so she would not struggle to catch her breath. She said nothing, and stood obediently on a small wooden stool, while the old woman held the material around her waist and pinned the edges together. She kept the pins between her thin lips, her mouth puckering to keep them in place. She reached for each one without looking, but never scratched herself.

It was the first dress that had been made especially for Jocasta. Her other clothes had all been worn by a different girl before they came to her. She thought about how much she would be enjoying this process if the circumstances were different and she were not so afraid of what was to come. The dressmaker tapped her leg. 'Stand up straight,' she said. 'Or the hem will be uneven.' Jocasta pulled her ribcage towards her spine, and looked at the wall opposite. Their house was large by Thebes standards, built around a small courtyard with herbs and flowers growing feebly in the burning sun. But it felt cramped to her now, as though the building were readying itself to be rid of her.

The following day, the old woman came back with the finished dress. Had she been up all night, sewing? Jocasta shrugged it on, and the dressmaker's frown eased slightly.

'You'll do,' she said. 'Think of me when you're buying new clothes in future, won't you?' Jocasta felt suddenly awkward. It was the first time anyone had treated her as though she had something they might want.

'How did you make it so quickly?' she asked.

The old woman shrugged. 'I had to,' she replied. 'You need it tomorrow.'

*

When Jocasta awoke on the morning of her wedding day, she wasn't sure if the sun had risen or not. Weak light filtered through the thick curtain which covered her window. She peered round it to see if she could tell how early it was without waking her little brother. The sky was pale grey and there was only a faint trace of light, hinting that the clouds had built over the lake in the night, and the sun might not burn through until later. She could smell the fruit on the sweet almond trees outside, almost ready to be picked.

She lay back down for a moment, testing how she felt. At least she would make her journey across the city in the relative cool. But she would be too queasy to eat before she left. She could hear muffled sounds coming from her mother's rooms. They needed to set off early today, to travel up to the palace. She lay completely still for five more breaths, feeling the cool sheet wrapped round her calves and ankles, the warm, squashy pillow beneath her head. Then she sat up, placing her feet quietly on the floor in the hope of being alone a little longer. But she crept out and almost walked into her mother who had been preparing herself for the day ahead since well before it was light. Her hair was tightly plaited, then twisted into a once-fashionable style, and her eyes were lined with thick black paint. Her mother had perfected a way of talking to Jocasta without looking at her at all, so Jocasta had learned to do the same in return. She fixed her gaze instead on her mother's white dress, edged in bright blue stitching. The dress folds were too wide, puffing out from the thin leather cord that bit at her mother's waist and broadened her across the hips, but she knew there was no value in offering to rearrange it. The cord had been dyed specially to match the new embroidery on the dress, and Jocasta could see that it was already leaving a faint trace of colour on the sun-bleached white cloth. Her mother would be furious when she noticed. Perhaps she would have to have the whole dress dyed blue to hide the marks.

'We'll need to leave shortly,' said her mother. 'The slaves will help make you presentable.'

Jocasta nodded, but did not reply. Her mother's maid-servants had never offered to help her, taking their cue from her mother. So the morning of her wedding was the first time anyone had assisted her with her clothes since she had been old enough to dress herself. Jocasta disliked the women's hard, dry hands on her skin. She tried to banish from her mind any thoughts about the hands of the king – which would also be old and dry – touching any part of her.

A short while later, she was wearing her new dress – a simple red tunic with a plaited brown cord to draw it in – and her dark hair was loose. The red made her pale skin look paler still, but the dressmaker had made the stitches small and even. If she had worked the cloth by candlelight, she had not allowed it to affect her stitching. And even Jocasta's mother had once said her daughter had beautiful skin, never disfigured with blemishes or browned by the sun. The maid pulled Jocasta's hair into a knot at the back of her head, twisted it three times and bound it into the bright ribbons which held the style in place. She stuck a silver-and-ivory-tipped ebony pin into the back of Jocasta's knotted hair, jabbing it into her scalp as she did so. Jocasta winced, but she could see the woman knew her job: her hair would now remain fixed in place. For one terrible moment, she thought the woman would try to paint her eyes like her mother's, but the maid preferred to save herself the trouble, so Jocasta dipped her fingers in the rose-scented olive oil her father had recently given to her mother, in a lovely aryballos in the shape of a ram, his horns curling around his ears like ringlets. She fixed the stopper into the ram's patient head, and was about to return it to her mother's dressing-room. Then she reconsidered, adding the bottle to her own bag of clothes and other belongings.

She hurried to the front of the house where the rest of her family were waiting. Her mother looked her up and down, and said she supposed that would do. She gestured irritably at the doorway, hurrying her daughter along. Jocasta walked through the warped wooden door, noticing for one last time the tiny cracks between the panels where the wood had shifted apart. She had expected to feel wretched as she left her home for the last time, but instead she felt nothing at all except a faint pleasure at the thought of the little terracotta ram nestled among her things.

Across the city, she could see its outer walls glowering down over the rest of them. The palace sat atop the highest hill in Thebes, like a watchtower. The grandeur was undeniable, but it resembled a temple or a treasury, both of which it had within its walls; it was difficult to imagine anyone living there, impossible to imagine herself among them. Her little brother was hopping from one foot to the other. He was torn between the excitement of the trip across town, and the promise of a ceremony – a feast and dancing delighted his five-year-old self beyond measure – and a growing uneasiness at the incomprehensible idea that his sister would no longer be living with him.

'I'll come and visit every day,' he had said, throwing his arms around her neck, when she had explained to him that the marriage meant she would be moving away. She had nodded, pretending it was true. Jocasta was surprised to see a small carriage waiting outside the house, attached to a pair of truculent horses. Her brother was eyeing them with the wariness born of having already attempted to pet one.

'This is a fitting mark of the king's respect,' said her father.

'It isn't the best he has,' her mother replied, eyeing the carriage balefully. The king's household had, it seemed, forgotten that four of them would be travelling, and it would be a tight squeeze to fit them all behind the dark curtains which swung down from the wooden roof. Jocasta's father spoke briefly with the driver, and together they tied a strong-box to the carriage roof next to the bag containing her possessions: her dowry. She wondered how much of the weight was the thick wooden box and how much was the precious metals within. Would she be permitted to wear the jewellery, or would it go straight into her husband's treasure-house?

She climbed into the carriage, and sat herself down on the far side of the seat. Her brother ran around to sit opposite her. Jocasta felt a sharp stab of relief when her father pressed in beside her: at least she wouldn't have to look at his treacherous face all the way there. Her mother was much easier to ignore. She lifted herself up for a moment and rearranged her dress, trying to make sure the back wouldn't crease too much as she sat on it. But the driver was in a hurry, and he clipped the horses to a trot. As the carriage swayed into reluctant motion, Jocasta sat heavily back down. Her brother fell forward into her lap, and giggled.

The road made her teeth judder with every one of its many holes as they meandered down the long hill. Her stomach turned over and she found herself glad that she had eaten nothing. Even her brother – who had been so excited when he saw the carriage – realized it was barely quicker than walking when they reached the lowest point and began to go uphill again. Thebans usually reserved wheeled vehicles for transporting heavy goods around the city, and Jocasta hoped she wouldn't be expected to travel by carriage from now on. At least with her feet on the ground, however dusty it was, she could avoid the deepest troughs in the road. The carriage cracked over another one so aggressively that she wondered if the axle beneath her seat would survive the journey. She half-hoped it would not, that one of its wheels would crack and roll back down the hill behind them, so she would have an excuse to get out and walk. It was stiflingly hot, even with the curtains tied back, something her mother had finally agreed to after her brother had appealed to her twice.

They had crossed through the lowest part of the city, which was always busy unless the winter rains had caused flooding. Today, it seemed unusually quiet, though Jocasta knew the floodwater was long gone. When they finally reached the bottom of the palace hill, she thought she might recognize some of the buildings. But things looked different through the window of a swaying carriage than they did when you were on foot. It too appeared deserted, though it was surely now late enough for people to be bustling around the city. Many of the shop-fronts were shuttered, though their painted signs suggested that the food stalls and taverns would be opening later. As they climbed the hill, the buildings grew larger, and people finally appeared on the streets, though there was something strange about them which Jocasta couldn't place. It was her brother who noticed. 'Look,' he said, tugging at her wrist and pointing. 'Everyone is walking in the same direction. Isn't that odd?' And she realized that he was right: everyone she could see was walking up the hill. The further they went, the more the street began to surge with people. Men and women bustled through the crowds, giving a purposeful air to the city.

By the time the driver brought his horses to an exhausted halt, the sun was blazing high above them. It had burned through the clouds, just as she had known it would. Her brother pushed his fingers past the curtains and touched the roof, before drawing them back in exaggerated pain. Jocasta was desperate to get out and walk however far was left to travel, but her mother jabbed at her with one carefully filed nail. 'Wait here, and don't let your brother get out,' she said. She clambered down with Jocasta's father who never saw a crowd without wanting to stand in front of it. What could he possibly sell them today?

But the crowd wasn't looking at her father. They were staring behind him, at the dark carriage window, trying to see through the curtain which had swung free when her parents climbed out. It took her a moment to notice they had something else in common: everyone was wearing their best clothes. Torn cloaks had been patched and repaired, white tunics had been bleached to a brightness they didn't usually possess. She imagined them all stretched over rocks, their colour gradually eaten away by the harsh noon light. Leather shoe-straps had been tied symmetrically, and red dust had been brushed from feet and ankles. Those who wore jewellery had polished it: dark stones glinted in bright metal. These weren't simply passers-by, gawping at a carriage. They were, they must be, wedding guests.

'Come on,' she said to her brother, covering her face with her veil so no one could accuse her of impropriety. 'Let's get out.' His eyes glittered as she opened the curtain and let him step down. Her parents were deep in conversation with a small cluster of men. Jocasta blinked in the bright sun, and looked around.

She was standing right outside the palace, she now saw, at the top of the citadel. She wanted to stretch her arms and her neck, which were knotted up from bouncing over every uneven stone, but she was too self-conscious with so many people watching her. She looked back at the way they had come. A bumpy path curved up off the main street and formed a loop around a big square – Thebes's marketplace – outside the palace gates, where they now stood. There were more people than she had ever seen in one place before, even at festivals. Her brother, usually desperate to see and hear everything at once, was suddenly shy.

The palace was less imposing now she stood next to it. Its bright perfection was not so perfect up close: just like her doll, its paint was cracked and fading, and the ground beneath her feet was broken open. It was even bigger than she had remembered, though. She could not see all the way round it: only along the front wall, until the angle shifted and it disappeared from view. The palace must sit with its back on the hillside, in front of the olive groves and the vines which grew on the sloping rocky soil. Twisted old apple trees lined the walls, and while they must provide welcome shade for those inside the palace – and those waiting outside today – their roots had forced their way through the paths, leaving the stones cracked and distorted. The dark mountains which covered the miles south of Thebes rose high behind the palace, dwarfing it. Jocasta had never been close enough to see the individual pine trees on their higher slopes: they had only ever been a blanket of blackish green before.

She heard an odd sound, a rippling noise. She looked over to the palace, and saw it came from the crowd. They were clapping, more and more of them. Her mother turned sharply to find out what was happening, and began looking around to see what had prompted the sudden applause. Her eyes followed the eyes of the crowd, and saw that her daughter had disobeyed her instruction to stay inside the carriage. Jocasta felt a brief surge of alarm that she was about to be shouted at, humiliated in front of all these people. And then she realized that none of the wedding guests cared what her mother thought, or did. They were interested only in her, and there was nothing her mother could do while they were watching. She looked up and gazed intently at her mother for a moment – jolting her into eye contact at last – before turning to smile and wave at the strangers who applauded her. She could not change what her parents had done. But she would not be afraid of them again.

*

Jocasta would have almost no recollection of her gamos. The wedding faded from her mind almost as it was happening. She remembered the things which didn't matter: the dark berries which had fallen from trees and stained the ground with their purple juice. An ornate hair decoration made of spiralling gold and studded with blood-red stones worn by a wizened elderly woman which she longed to have in her own hair, where it would shine against her darkness instead of sparkling feebly against the old woman's thin white strands. The procession of unmarried girls – bright crocus-yellow ribbons tied into their hair – dancing around her in celebration of her arrival, and the dark, watchful eyes of boys the same age, admiring every step the girls took. Her father's tangible aura of self-congratulation. The smell of charred meat as the priest made his devotional offerings. Her mother's silver and gold bangles clanking together as she ostentatiously wiped away a non-existent tear.

But the gamos itself, the moment where she was sworn to Laius – a vulpine man with sparse white hair and ill-tamed brows – and presented with a slender gold diadem as a mark of her newfound status? The crowds of Thebans cheering their new queen as the priests mixed wine and water in a huge ceremonial krater? The taste of the wine she and her husband drank from a large kylix to seal their vows to and before the gods? She recalled none of it. In the years that followed, she would try to remember if they had stood on the north side of the courtyard or the south. If they had poured wine to the gods at the main altar, or one of the smaller ones. If the afternoon sun had streamed over the portico as the day dragged out, or if evening rain had fallen on the assembled crowd. She never came close to being certain of anything that happened between leaving the carriage and walking in through the front gates and the moment when she found herself alone again, many hours later, in what was now her bedroom.

Jocasta spent the day dreading the night. She knew something of what her husband would expect from her: she was not a fool, and nor was she completely naïve, even though she had been brought up in seclusion from boys, except her own brother. Girls talked, nonetheless. She was not wholly averse to this aspect of marriage. But she had always assumed that any man whose bed she shared would be one who was not so old that thick wiry hairs emanated from his nose and ears without warning. One whose skin glowed gold as the late afternoon sun caught him, and who could move without a percussive chorus of cracking joints and exhalations. Instead, she found herself able to think of little else but how his body repulsed her. An old man, one among many old men at the wedding party who winked and elbowed one another with delight at her evident discomfort. She hated them all.

The afternoon turned into evening, and the party continued. The old men – including the king – were drinking a great deal of wine, poured by slave boys all wearing matching charcoal-grey tunics. Jocasta was torn between wanting to ask questions of these boys – the only people her own age who treated the palace as familiar – and not wanting to look stupid in front of what were now her own slaves. She wondered if she would feel more confident if she too drank some wine. But the thought of tasting something sour and acidic made bile rise in her throat.

It had been dark for many hours when people finally began to leave: the torches had been lit for so long they were beginning to sputter. Jocasta had her arms and cheeks squeezed and prodded so many times that bruises were starting to form on her edges. No one, it seemed, could leave without touching the bride: they believed she would bring them luck. People believed all kinds of stupid things. Across the courtyard, she saw her mother teetering towards her father, and realized they, too, were leaving. Jocasta hurried towards the colonnade which ran around the outside of the square, stopping behind one of the broad columns so she could watch unseen as her family began to look for her. Her throat thickened at the sight of her little brother, crying when he understood that they really were leaving without her. But she stayed where she was, nonetheless. He was too young to understand anything she could say to him. It was kinder to leave him to her parents now, and hope he still remembered her in a year or two.

One of the boys dressed in grey caught sight of her, and walked towards her, carrying two silver rhytons. She had never seen such ornate cups: raised dolphins jumped around the base of each one, beneath painted azure waves which curled all the way up to the rims. She wanted to hold one and run her fingers over the design.

'Can I help you, Basileia?'

Jocasta looked around to see who he was talking to, this boy who might have kicked a pebble across her path a week ago, hoping it would bounce off her sandal and force her to look up. She would have blushed when she saw it had come from a boy she did not know, and looked back at the ground as she scurried away, so he did not see her smile.

'Basileia?' he repeated.

'Why are you calling me that?' she hissed. She might be the wife of the king, but she felt a long way short of being a queen. The word sounded ludicrous on his tongue. The boy frowned, and looked down at the cups he was holding.

'Would you like something to drink, Anassa?' he asked carefully. Perhaps the less formal title would please her. 'I can get you anything you like.'

'I don't want anything,' she snapped. 'Thank you.'

'Yes, Anassa,' he said. 'I'm sorry for disturbing you.' He began to turn away.

'Wait – do you work for my – ?' She couldn't frame the thought. 'For the king?' she asked.

'Yes, my lady.'

'Will everyone dressed like you call me Anassa?' she said. The boy nodded. His face remained solemn, but she saw a trace of amusement in his eyes. 'Once I tell them it is your preferred title,' he said.

'I should get used to it, then. That's what you're thinking?' she asked.

'I wouldn't presume . . .'

'Don't be stupid. Stop talking to me like I'm my mother. Or your mother.'

He looked at her steadily. 'I'm talking to you as though you were my queen.'

'I'm so tired,' she said, pressing one hand against her ear as if trying to expel the sound of revellers and musicians. 'Do you think they will leave soon?'

'I don't know,' he replied. 'Parties are usually all-night affairs at the palace. I mean, I think they are. We haven't had a wedding before. Obviously.' He blushed. 'I'm sorry.'

'What for? I'm sure it all seems obvious to you. But it isn't to me. I lived on the other side of Thebes until this morning. I don't know anything about the king, or the palace or the way you do things. I don't even know what you'll do if I ask you something.'

'I will do whatever you wish. Everyone will,' the boy said.

'Find me tomorrow. I want to know more about . . . well, about the palace and the citadel. The customs of the household. And whatever I ask, you have to promise now to tell me the truth.'

'Yes, Anassa.'

'You're not to laugh at me behind my back with the other slaves for not knowing. Swear it.'

'I would never laugh at you,' the boy said.

'Do you feel sorry for me?' she asked.

'Sorry?' His eyes bulged. 'No, of course not.'

'Good. Tell me where I'll be sleeping,' she said. 'I'm too tired to stay awake any longer. Can I go to bed, do you think? Before everyone leaves, I mean.'

'You're the queen,' the boy said. 'You can do whatever you want.'

Jocasta slept badly, and woke many times. She felt as if she were falling, although she was sleeping in the middle of the largest bed she had ever seen. When she finally came to the next morning, groggy from the interrupted night, she looked around the room in surprise. The flickering torches the night before had given her the idea that the room was dingy and oppressive. But now the light streamed in through lofty windows, she saw that she had been mistaken. The walls were a pale yellow colour, with a blood-red pattern of interlocking squares painted along the highest part. She had been tricked last night by the height of the lamps which were hung low, so the torches could be lit and extinguished without a ladder. A large, ornately carved wardrobe stood on the far wall, its doors a labyrinth of twisting inlaid lines.

Jocasta had not removed the bag from the roof of the carriage yesterday, where the driver had lashed it before they set off from her parents' house. But here were her dresses anyway, hung up carefully by someone else. There was no sign of her dowry, but she was not surprised by that. At least she had her diadem, which shone even without the torchlight to reflect back at her. She stopped for a moment as she reached out to pick it up: was she so vain that all she cared about was her jewellery? Jewellery which, for the most part, she had never worn, had not even seen before yesterday. She gripped the diadem until its sharp edges drove into her soft fingers. The gold was thick, not pliable. Jocasta might be new to the palace, but she was not so foolish as to think gold was a trivial matter. It was beautiful, certainly. But if things were ever so terrible that she needed to run away, jewellery would be the only thing she could bargain with. The delicate little crown represented more than her regal status.

There was no sign that the room had belonged to another person before she arrived last night. Had it been empty for years? A wooden dressing-table stood beneath the windows, a cracked, blackening glass offering her a view of herself: slightly puffy-eyed from sleep. Her hair was tangled, and she tugged it straight, before noticing a fine-toothed ivory comb in front of her. She picked it up, and tidied herself a little.

The room was large and well-appointed compared with the one she'd slept in at home. Although she had to stop thinking of it as that. This was her home now. She had always imagined that a room of her own would be wonderful, an impossible luxury not to hear the breathing of her brother – who whimpered through his nightmares and woke her – all night long. And now she seemed to have just that. Because one thing her bedroom was missing was the man who was now her husband. Not only was he not present himself, there was no sign a man had ever been in here. There were no men's clothes anywhere, not even a single robe. She had expected her husband to sleep in a room of his own, of course, just as her father did. But surely not on his wedding night?

There were three doors on three walls. The one behind her she had come through last night. It led to an open-sided corridor along the edge of a small courtyard which must once have contained a formal garden. Even by torchlight she had been able to see that the plants had run wild, sprouting up between the paving stones and forcing their way through the miniature walls designed to contain them. She had caught her sandal on the edge of a broken stone, and turned her left ankle over. She had said nothing, though, not wanting the boy in grey to know that she had tripped. She tested the ankle again now and felt only a small twinge. No harm was done. The door in the far corner of the right-hand wall was locked. She turned the handle quietly, but nothing happened. The door on the left-hand side of the windows led, she discovered, to a room containing a pump and several large bronze basins. Was it possible this was all hers? There was another door into it, from the corridor, but it too appeared to be locked. She tried the pump, and the water flowed freely. She washed her face and hands, before noticing a battered bronze cup on a narrow wooden shelf. She filled the cup, and drank. The water was cool and fresh, as though it came from somewhere deep underground.

She was nervous at the thought of leaving her room: the palace was quiet and she could hear no one outside, not even servants talking to one another. She was beginning to think of this corner of the huge building as hers, she realized: her table, her wardrobe, her bed. But she couldn't stay in there for the rest of her life, and the longer she waited, the more anxious she felt. She should go now, before it became unmanageable. She dressed quickly in a plain fawn-coloured linen dress. It hung shapelessly to her knees, and she belted it with a twisted length of undyed leather she found on the floor of the wardrobe. Combing her hair back behind her ears, she pinned it in place with the ebony pin she had worn yesterday. Jocasta took one last look in the dressing-table mirror and reminded herself that even today, away from everything she knew, she was the same person who had worn the pin before. She should not be afraid. She opened the door into the main corridor.

It was deserted. Was it really possible that all last night's guests had disappeared so completely? Or did the noise simply not carry this far through the palace? She still could not imagine its scale and layout. She stood for a moment, listening. She could hear nothing but the twin chirrups of birds and cicadas. She looked around one more time, making sure she knew which door led to her room – she paid close attention to the precise shape of the cracks in the shattered stones beneath her feet – so she could find her way back to this one familiar place without embarrassment. She turned to her left, wishing she knew where she was going. She soon found herself in a second, larger, equally empty courtyard, which she couldn't be sure she recognized from last night. Was this the way the boy in grey had brought her? There were frescos on the colonnade walls: horses riding towards centaurs who rode towards satyrs who ran towards wood nymphs who hid behind trees. They might not have been illuminated in the torchlight last night. Or perhaps she had come a different way entirely.

She decided to retrace her steps, and went back to the first square. This too had frescos, now she began to pay proper attention, but they were faded older paintings, this time of once-bright blue dolphins and fish. Was there another way out from this square? She could see a small doorway in the far corner: perhaps that led somewhere. But wasn't that the opposite direction from the main courtyard from last night? The disorientation vexed her. Where was everyone? Could a whole palace have lost its inhabitants overnight? Were they playing a cruel trick on her? Finally, she heard a brushing sound behind her. Someone was sweeping a floor somewhere in one of the courtyards, or in the corridors around it. She walked back to the colonnade between the two squares and stood still, trying to hear exactly which direction the sound came from.

Was it further away now? It seemed to come from the opposite side of this second courtyard, so she crossed it, and found herself looking onto the main square through decorative metal gates. This was where the party had been in full swing when she escaped to bed last night. There were several women at the near end of the courtyard, cleaning tables with wooden brushes and water. One of them looked across and saw her, then called out. The boy from last night appeared from a corridor on her right. The smart grey uniform was gone, and he was dressed today in a plain tunic, just like her.

'Forgive me, madam,' he said. 'I didn't realize you were awake.'

'Why should you?' she asked. 'Where is everyone?'

The boy looked at her face, but not her eyes, as he chose his words. 'Everyone is gone, ma'am. The guests all left around daybreak. The king and his escort have gone hunting.'

'Hunting what? Where?' She knew no one who hunted.

'In the lower reaches of the mountains,' he explained. 'They will be gone for around a week, I believe.'

'They go outside the city?' Like many Thebans, Jocasta had never left the city gates.

'Yes. They're out to catch a wild boar. The king has been trying to capture this particular one for some time,' he said.

'The king does this often?' she asked.

'Whenever the weather allows it,' he said. 'His retinue go with him, and most of the Elders go too. Those whose families can spare them.'

'He travels with a large party, then?'

'Yes, ma'am. The king is quite safe.'

She nodded, as though the king's safety was of any interest to her. He had made no effort to speak to her once the ceremony was out of the way. He had not said goodbye before he left. It seemed he had left no message for her.

'And you are part of the king's retinue,' she said.

'Yes,' the boy nodded.

'So why didn't you go with him?'

He smiled. 'You ordered me to stay, ma'am. Last night.'

And though she was affronted that the king had behaved so rudely, Jocasta thought she might hate her husband marginally less the morning after her wedding than she did the night before.

3

I didn't notice the pain at first, because I was too distracted by the thirst. My mouth felt like a piece of old dried-out parchment. My lips cracked as I separated them, tiny fissures of pain. I half-opened my eyes, though they were gravelly and itched so much I wanted to shut them again. But I didn't know where I was, and I needed to find water from somewhere. Everything was so bright. I lay on my back, trying to persuade my eyes to focus.

I turned my head to see Ani, my sister, sitting on a small wooden chair beside me. I was in my own bedroom, a large, high-windowed room on the west side of the palace, away from the city, overlooking the hills behind Thebes. She was working a small tapestry of some sort – I could see the light glinting off her needle as she took it up and down through the fabric. I wanted to ask her for water, but my throat was too dry and no sound would come. I tugged on the sheets to try and get her attention, though it fired pain through my left side. Eventually, I pulled hard enough to move the thin top sheet, and the rustling sound forced her to look up.

'Oh!' She put her hand to her chest. 'You're awake!' She leapt to her feet, and shouted, 'Isy's awake! She's awake!' She ran to the door to announce her news further afield. This was not what I had been hoping would happen. I heard quick feet padding towards me. My brother Eteo – king, for now – tall, dark-haired, always with a slight frown. He looked down at me and smiled. He looked at me for a moment, then stepped back. When he returned, he was holding a battered bronze kylix of water in his hand.

'You must be thirsty,' he said. 'Let me help you up so you can drink something.' If I had not been so desiccated, I would have wept.

He held my arms, and pulled me up and forward, stuffing an extra pillow in behind me. I felt another jolt of pain, but I didn't care. I reached out my hands and took the cup. I peeled my lips apart and took a sip, forcing it into every corner of my mouth before I swallowed. My throat hurt, and my tongue was swollen. I tried to drink it all, but Eteo reached over and took my hand.

'Easy,' he said. 'Don't drink it too fast. I'll get you some more in a moment.'

Ani ran back in with my oldest brother Polyn. 'Look,' she said, elbowing him hard in the gut. 'I told you. Why don't you ever believe me?'

'Well done, Isy,' Polyn said. He was stockier than Eteo, and his hair was a lighter, muddier brown. His eyes were light brown too, where Eteo's were so dark they were almost black. Without looking at his brother, Polyn reached over and ruffled my hair. 'We thought we'd lost you.'

'No,' I said, finally able to get the words out, now the water had released my voice, croaky but audible. 'You just misplaced me for a while.'

Eteo laughed. 'It was a while, Isy. You've been unconscious for three days.'

Three days. No wonder I was thirsty. 'What happened?'

Eteo opened his mouth to say something, but Polyn grabbed his arm. Eteo recoiled from the unexpected contact, but he said nothing. Ani reached over to the bed and picked up the sewing she had dropped when she saw I was awake. She fed the needle carefully in and out of the corner of her cloth to hold it in place, and stuffed it into the pocket of her green dress. She almost always wears green, to match her eyes. Virtually no one meets her without remarking on their extraordinary colour, so her strategy works. My sister has no intention of going unmarried, no matter what people say about our family. She knows that will be my fate, and she pities me, but not enough to condemn herself to the same thing.

Eteo took the cup from my hands and went to the table opposite my bed to refill it from an old jug painted with a faded harvest scene: men holding scythes and carrying sheaves of wheat. Polyn adopted an expression which was meant to convey, I think, fraternal concern: head tilted, lips slightly pursed, creased brow. And a moment later, the door swung open again, and my uncle entered the room. Four guards followed and stood just behind him. The clanking sound which accompanied them told me they were armed, even though they were inside the palace, inside the family quarters. This would never have happened before. We have always tried to keep the areas of the palace distinct: the public courtyard at the front, the royal courtyard in the middle, the family courtyard at the back. My uncle is solidly built: he never forgets that all adult men have an obligation to fight for Thebes, if any army declares war upon us. That is why my brothers and my cousin have been training with weapons since they were six or seven years old. Creon has always kept himself and his family in the proper condition to fight. Nonetheless, it was disconcerting to see his soldiers in my sleeping quarters.

'Isy,' said Creon. 'It's good to see you awake. We were worried . . .'

'Thank you,' I said. I didn't want to hear any more about people's worry. It was making me afraid for myself in the past, a position I could already see Sophon dismantling as foolish.

'You're safe now,' he continued. 'There are guards at either end of the corridor.'

I wanted to ask why, but there were so many people in the room now, I couldn't bear to tell them all that I didn't remember what had happened to me, and how I got hurt.

Then I heard the voice I always wanted to hear. 'Is she alright?'

My cousin Haem ran in, one hand pushed back through his hair to keep it out of his eyes. He wasn't looking at me. He was looking at Ani, of course.

'She's well,' my sister said. If you didn't know better, you would think they were talking about me.

'I'm glad to see you're recovering,' Creon said, ignoring them both. 'We have missed you at dinner, Isy. No one tells stories when you aren't there. I've been waiting to find out what would happen next with the Medusa. If you had slept through another day, I would have had to send someone to read your dreams and tell me what becomes of her.'

'That's why I woke up,' I told him. 'I knew you couldn't wait any longer.'

'Well, we shall let you rest now,' he said, smiling. 'Perhaps you'll feel well enough to continue the tale tomorrow or the next day.'

My uncle loves stories and songs. It is something we share. I learned to play the phorminx – a small lyre – when I was seven years old. Eteo plays too, but he rarely has time for such pursuits when he is ruling the city. Polyn has never played any instrument: as soon as Eteo showed interest in music, Polyn decreed it a worthless pursuit. Ani prefers to make things – sewing, weaving – but I have never had the gift for that kind of work. It requires a patience and attention to detail which I do not possess. She says the same is true for playing the lyre, but she is mistaken. Playing has never required my patience, only my concentration, which I give freely to music. My uncle loves songs about heroes and monsters, gods and men. I have played them for him after dinner for as long as I can remember, composing a little more of the story each day, or playing old songs for him again.

Creon beckoned Haem to follow him. My cousin flashed a pained glance at my sister and they withdrew, taking the guards with them. The room was suddenly huge, empty and safe.

'I don't know what happened,' I said to Eteo.

'What's the last thing you remember?' he asked.

I thought for a moment. Bright sun and blood on the papyrus.

'Someone stabbed me.'

'Yes,' Eteo replied. 'But we'll find him, Isy. I promise.

I have men interrogating everyone who was in the palace that day. Someone knows something and we'll soon catch him.'

'If I were king, the wretch would have been run through with my own sword a day ago,' said Polyn.

'Because you would have killed every man in sight, irrespective of whether he was involved or not,' Eteo snapped. 'Or tortured them until they named someone – anyone – to make you stop. How would that make our sister any safer?'

'Stop it,' Ani said. 'You can see you're upsetting her.' She shook her head. 'It's been so awful,' she said. 'I don't understand how someone could get into the palace to attack you. How are we supposed to stay safe if strangers can enter the palace unheeded?'

'But I'm alright. I mean, I will be.' I thought I was stating a fact, but as the words came out, I realized I was asking a question.

'Yes, you will be,' Eteo replied, his anger ebbing away. 'The blade caught your left lung, Is, so you ran out of air. The girl who found you was hollering for help – she made an extraordinary racket. She frightened the birds out of their nests: they all flew up in a great clamour over the palace. It was lucky she was there – and Sophon came running. He moves quickly for an old man, doesn't he? The moment he saw you, he knew what to do. You weren't in danger for long.'

'He was most worried about a fever,' Ani added. She would have enjoyed the drama of it all, I thought, even though she loved me. She would have enjoyed being the sister of an almost-murdered girl. I could imagine her tying her dark hair back, frowning and calling for hot water, with no real idea of what she might use it for. 'He stitched you back together and said we would have to wait and see what happened.'

I wondered what I would say to my tutor when I saw him. Should I thank him for saving my life? Apologize for bleeding all over his papyrus? It didn't seem right that another person had seen the inside of me, laid eyes on a part of my body that I could never see. I struggled to imagine his gnarled hands pushing a needle through my skin. Once Ani had mentioned stitches, I could feel a pulling sensation, quite separate from the pain of the wound. My fingers itched to explore it, to test how much it hurt and how neatly Sophon had sewn it up. But I knew I could not. The old man was right to fear an infection more than anything else.

'You were lucky, Isy,' said Polyn. It was true, even though I didn't feel very lucky. I felt like someone who was nursing a hole in her side, grit in her eyes and a sore throat.

I nodded, suddenly tired. 'I think I might rest for a while,' I said. 'Would you ask Sophon to visit me later? I want to thank him.'

'Of course,' said Polyn. He sounded relieved. 'We'll see you later.'

Eteo squeezed my hand, and followed the other two out. I did want to thank my tutor, of course. But not as much as I wanted to ask him what more he knew, about my injury and about the attacker. My siblings – even Eteo – tended to treat me like a little girl whenever something bad happened. But Sophon always told me the truth. He understood when you have grown up as I have, there is no security in not knowing things, in avoiding the ugliest truths because they can't be faced. There is only an oppressive, creeping dread that the thing no one has told you is too terrible to imagine, and that it will haunt the rest of your life when you find out. Because that is what happened the last time, and that is why my siblings and I have grown up in a cursed house, children of cursed parents.

4

Jocasta had assumed, from everything her mother and father had told her, that she was marrying the king because he wanted a wife. It now seemed to be the case that he did not, in fact, want a wife, or that if he did, he did not want her. It was oddly painful to be rejected by someone she didn't know. Had he decided on the hunting trip the moment he saw her? Before he saw her? She swept her hands down her dress, as if she could brush off whatever defects she apparently possessed. Because if he didn't want her, where was she supposed to go? She could hardly return home. She corrected herself, go to her parents' home. They could not take her back, even if they wanted to. She would be disgraced: a married woman running away from her husband. It was unthinkable. And anyway, she remembered her mother's claws in her arm. Even if her husband died (the only respectable way for her to cease being married to him), she would never go back to her parents. Begging on the streets would be preferable.

But she was getting ahead of herself. If she couldn't go anywhere else, she could at least explore the palace, and examine her new surroundings. It was easier if she forgot about the idea of home for now. The palace was where she was. The boy who had stayed behind – the one who had obeyed her – would take her into the marketplace later, with a maidservant in tow, so her propriety could not be called into question. And it would give her a greater sense of belonging, she was sure, when she knew the palace neighbourhood. But she would spend this morning trying to map out what stood where in the palace, so she didn't feel so lost.

She now knew, having walked through them in daylight, that the palace was made up of three courtyards of decreasing size from front gate to back walls. The huge public courtyard was the first square she had entered yesterday. As its name implied, it was open to any Thebans who had business in the palace. There were altars and a small temple enclosed on the west side, which – as she had seen last night – was the religious focus of the royal house. There were priests who came to the palace each day to maintain the sacred precincts and accept offerings from any citizens who brought them. The animals were kept in small pens near the back of the temple, ready to be sacrificed. On the east side were the king's treasurers, who also arbitrated in any disputes which arose outside in the market. As she peeked out at the bustling space, Jocasta saw two bearded men – so alike they must have been brothers, their black beards mirroring one another, and their curled hair bobbing in harmony – arguing in front of one of the treasurers, so loudly that she could hear them from where she stood, in the second courtyard, looking through the gates which sealed the public out of the rest of the palace. Or did they lock her inside? She tested the one on the right and found that it opened. But she did not dare to go out alone. The king might be absent, but the queen should avoid causing a scandal on her first morning in the palace, she supposed. She couldn't go wandering about in public without any kind of chaperone. She wasn't entirely sure what her duties would be – there was no sign of a loom anywhere in her quarters, so no one was expecting her to sit weaving all day, at least – but she knew it was her responsibility to behave respectably.

And there was plenty more to see in the two courtyards which were open to her. The middle square was a smaller copy of the public courtyard, with white stone paths bisecting each side and criss-crossing from corner to corner. They met in the centre of the square, which was dominated by a statue of the king atop his horse. Jocasta wondered if Laius had ever looked as tall and muscular as the sculptor had rendered him. She doubted it. But the sculptor had been clever; there was just enough in the statue's colouring to make it clear that it was intended to be the king: the brown curls of hair into the nape of the neck, the pale irises, picked out in a light blue stone. And perhaps he had been tall once, before his old man's spine began to curve in on itself. It was possible.

But this square wasn't filled with shrines or temples. The east and west colonnades were punctuated with closed doors. Some were obviously storerooms, but Jocasta could hear the sound of men's voices behind others. From what she could work out, as she stood eavesdropping in the colonnades, this was where the king's work was done in his absence. Or more politely, on his behalf, while he was off hunting. The corridor which housed the gates between the second and the main courtyards was also home to the kitchens. She could smell bread baking, and a sudden twist in her stomach reminded her that she hadn't eaten for more than a day. She walked towards the heat, and peered in to the dark room, her eyes taking a moment to adjust from the bright morning sun outside. 'Excuse me,' she said to a girl scouring dishes, when she saw she had found the main kitchen. The girl squeaked and ran out of another door in the far wall, reappearing a moment later with a pink-faced older woman. The woman was short but sturdy, and perhaps forty years old. Older than Jocasta's mother, but not by very many years, she wore her grey-brown hair tied back in a plain, unadorned knot. Her eyes darted around her domain: Jocasta could almost hear her counting the faults as she noticed them, one after another. The kitchen girl would be in trouble later. Jocasta was sure of it.

'Yes?' said the woman, wiping floured hands on her apron, before she looked to see who was bothering her.

'Could I please have something to eat?' Jocasta asked. The woman finally turned to see who was asking for her. Her hands moved up to push loose hairs behind her ears, a gesture which looked inappropriately girlish to Jocasta's eyes.

'Of course,' said the woman. 'Forgive us, we would have brought you something earlier, but no one knew where you were.'

'I was in my room, I think,' Jocasta said. 'And then I came looking for someone.'

'Oh, you were in your room?' said the woman, as though this were unlikely. 'Well, we'll know to bring food to you there tomorrow. Would you like to go back to your quarters, and I'll send something after you?'

'Would you mind if I stayed here?' Jocasta asked, looking across the kitchen to a large wooden table with several small stools sitting beneath it. She didn't want to admit that she was lonely, on her own in this strange new place. But nor did she want to go back to her room and sit there eating alone. Besides, her stomach was groaning at the smell of food, and the last thing she wanted to do was leave before she had consumed anything.

'Not at all,' said the woman, gesturing to the girl who pulled a stool out for Jocasta. 'I'm Teresa,' the woman added. 'I'm the housekeeper. And you're Jocasta, and we haven't even been introduced.' Her tone made it sound like this was Jocasta's failure of courtesy, though Jocasta couldn't see how the woman had arrived at that conclusion. The housekeeper should have been at her door this morning, summoned by the slave girl who should have been sent to help her dress. Teresa should have introduced herself to her new mistress and offered to show her around the palace. But Jocasta did not want to start her new life arguing with the king's servants and their lax manners.

'I'm sorry,' said Jocasta, taking the woman's hand, which was hard and dry, as though it belonged to a wooden statue. 'I didn't know where to find anyone this morning. It was all so deserted.'

The woman clicked her tongue against her teeth. 'We're not used to having anyone here when Laius goes away. But to forget all about you, when you only got here yesterday. You must think we're very disorganized.' Jocasta shook her head. She knew she had been set a test, but she couldn't tell if she had passed or failed.

'I suppose if I'd shown you to your room last night,

I wouldn't have forgotten,' Teresa said. 'Who did take you, if you don't mind me asking?'

Another woman's daughter would have missed the subtle change in tone, from apology to interrogation. Jocasta did not. 'One of the king's bodyguards showed me to my quarters,' she said. 'I didn't ask his name.' She did not mention that she had seen him this morning. She wasn't sure if it was him she was trying to keep from getting into trouble, or herself. But she knew it would be wise to say no more than she had to.

'Oh, that's Oran,' said Teresa, the tension slipping from her posture. 'The king left him behind to keep an eye on us all, I think.' This statement was so evidently ridiculous to her that she was smiling. Jocasta smiled too, anxious to keep on her right side, at least for now.

Blackened pots and pans were hanging from hooks above her, all around the table. Jocasta imagined her little brother leaping onto the stools so he could bang them all together to hear what sort of noise each one made. She pressed her lips together to quash the thought before missing him brought her to tears. Teresa bustled into the room she had come from and returned with two griddled flatbreads, one covered in olive paste, the other piled high with spiced chickpeas. Jocasta thanked her and began to eat. The bread was warm and fluffy inside, and the olive paste was dark and salty. 'You're half-starved,' said Teresa, watching her. Jocasta must be eating too fast.

'No,' she said, putting the bread back on its plate, though all she wanted to do was stuff the rest of it into her mouth. 'It's just that it's so good.' She hoped Teresa was susceptible to flattery.

The housekeeper smiled. 'I'm afraid we've been so busy clearing up after the wedding party, we quite lost track of you. It takes a lot of time to sort everything out when the king goes away, I'm sure you can imagine. But I promise we'll make up for it now. You must come and eat with us tonight – unless you prefer to be alone?' She raised an eyebrow, and Jocasta was reminded once again of her mother, who also liked to ask questions which weren't questions at all.

'No, I'd prefer to meet everyone and get to know you all,' she replied.

'That's good,' Teresa continued. 'We'll all know each other better by the time Laius gets back. He'll be delighted.'

Jocasta agreed, and listened as Teresa told her more about the palace staff she would meet, both slave and free. In addition to Teresa and Oran, there were various maids and gardeners and cleaners and cooks. She tried to keep track of the names as Teresa rattled through them all, but she could not. So she nodded and carried on eating, and wondered why Teresa's first action had been to lie to her. The housekeeper clearly controlled the household and it was inconceivable that she could have forgotten something as important as a new queen coming to live in the palace. So why pretend that she had?

*

It was something she wanted to ask Oran that afternoon as they set out for the marketplace. But the presence of a slave girl who accompanied them both – hovering behind her, holding a simple woven reed basket as though she had never been trusted with something so valuable before – made her wary of beginning a conversation about anything to do with Teresa. Instead she asked him about the public square, since they were walking through it.

'You mean the Great Court?' he asked.

'Is that its name?'

He nodded. 'It's the oldest part of the palace. It was here when this was just a citadel. The other courtyards were built later. That's why we're on the top of a hill, you know. It's the easiest place in Thebes to defend.'

'You don't believe all that?' she asked, watching with satisfaction as he reddened at her tone. 'That the oldest part of the city was built by dragon-men, sacred to Ares? And that we live here because an ancient hero followed a cow until she lay down and decided to build his city where she had indicated was the most propitious location?'

'Of course I believe it,' he replied. 'What do you believe?'

She looked at him in surprise.

'Forgive me, your majesty,' he added.

'I'm not angry,' she said. 'You needn't apologize. I don't know what I think, really. It just doesn't seem very likely that warriors rose from dragon's teeth and built a city. It doesn't even seem likely that a cow would wander up a steep hill of her own accord. A goat maybe. But not a cow. I've never seen anything like that happen. And don't pretend you have.'

'The plane trees were planted many years ago,' he continued, pointing to the gnarled branches that sprang up at irregular intervals along all four walls of the courtyard.

'By a dragon?' she asked, smiling.

'By a gardener, I imagine,' he replied. They walked towards the front gate, and Jocasta could hear the hubbub of the market on a trading day: stall-holders, bargain-hunters, gossip-mongers, butchers and fish-sellers, leather-workers, dyers, shoe-makers and smiths all vied for space. Chickens squawked and beat their wings against the bars of metal cages. Rabbits – crammed together in wooden boxes – looked fearful, and dogs barked as though they knew she was a stranger.

She felt as though she had been hiding in a back room, waiting for a festival to begin. The smell of freshly fried lentil cakes enticed her one way, but the sound of a flute being played in another direction made her want to go there instead. One stall was piled high with wooden crates that held pomegranates of such an urgent pink that she could almost taste the seeds. On another stall, her eye was caught by piles of clothes in every colour: bright dresses which she longed to touch, every shade of red between orange and pink, every shade of yellow between saffron and unripe lemons. She walked into the thronging aisle and reached out to feel the deep blue fabric of a simple shift dress. It was crisp and unworn and would be the right length without alteration.

'Nice colour on you,' said the owner, barely looking. 'I'll do you a good deal.'

Jocasta smiled and nodded. 'I'll be back later,' she said.

'You do that,' said the woman, her interest immediately switching to another potential customer. Jocasta wished she had brought something to trade, though she wasn't sure what the value of her possessions would be. She had entered the palace with a dowry, but that was technically her husband's gold now.

'Do you want it?' Oran asked.

'Yes,' she said. 'It's a pretty colour, and it would suit me.'

He jerked his head at the slave girl, who scurried up to the clothes-seller and spoke a few words. The dress was folded and handed over, and the girl placed it carefully in her basket. The clothes-seller bobbed her head to Jocasta as she walked away. 'We're here every day, ma'am. We make anything you want to order. Any colour, even the darkest purple. Come back whenever you want the highest quality fabrics in the city. We're always here.'

Jocasta now felt her own cheeks darken. Foolish, to be thinking of which of her pathetic belongings she might trade for a new dress. She was married to the king. And as soon as the locals learned to recognize her, she would be able to have whatever she liked.

*

Jocasta had been in the palace for nine days, and there was still no sign of the king. Teresa never mentioned him, unless to reply to a particular question. It was peculiar, Jocasta thought. It must take more effort not to talk about the man whose palace they all dwelt in, and in whose employ everyone but Jocasta worked. He was the centre of their world, but they all pretended it wasn't odd that he was always absent. And perhaps for them it wasn't. Jocasta had vague memories of her father complaining that the king was shirking his duty (spoken quietly in the privacy of his home, when no slaves were around to overhear, of course). But why had that been? Jocasta tried to bring the memory to the front of her mind, but she could never quite catch it.

Oran was not as discreet as Teresa. If Jocasta asked him about the palace when no one else could overhear, she sometimes learned more. That evening, Jocasta wandered into the family courtyard – as the slaves called it, though the only person sleeping in any of the quarters was Jocasta – and thought she would sit a while in the darkening evening. She told the slave who was hurrying ahead to prepare her room that she could go on without her. The girl scurried away and moments later, Oran appeared.

'Are you well, Basileia?' he asked. She rolled her eyes.

'How many times must I tell you?'

'I'm sorry, madam,' he said. 'Did you need anything? Water? Wine?'

'No, thank you,' she replied. 'I have everything I need.' She drew a new stole – spun from the finest wool she had ever touched, a dark purplish-red – around her shoulders.

'You're cold,' Oran said.

She shook her head. 'I just like wearing it.'

'It looks well on you,' he said.

'Yes,' she agreed. 'Why don't you sit down?' She patted the wooden bench which she had chosen. Oran walked to its far end and sat there. She turned and lifted her feet up, so her back rested on a cushion which she propped against the wooden arm, and she was facing him, curling her toes against the warm, smooth wood.

'It's not at all like I imagined,' she said. 'I thought it would be busier. People everywhere, rushing about, ruling the city. Instead it's almost deserted.'

'The Elders are keeping everything in order,' he said. 'They always do. It doesn't take much rushing about.'

'The king is away a lot, I gather,' she said. He nodded. 'It doesn't seem even a bit strange to you?' she continued. 'To go away the morning after his own wedding?'

'Well, no, of course not,' he replied.

Her eyes glinted in the half-light. 'Why is it obvious to you, when it seems so opaque to me?'

'Let me get you some wine,' he said.

'Please don't be so rude as to ignore me when I ask you something,' she said. 'Or to assume I am so stupid that I will forget my questions the moment you wander back with one of those beautiful terracotta jugs, covered in – what will it be today? Horses? Kingfishers? And by the time you have asked me to admire the intricate designs, and told me about the craftsman in the dark corner of Thebes who paints them, and how he sells them to the winemaker in exchange for all the wine he can drink so his wife must work for their children's food, and suggested we visit his shop one day, on the backstreet behind the hill up to the marketplace, our original conversation will have disappeared with the tail of Helios' chariot.'

'I could fetch another torch,' he said. 'If you are worried about the dark.'

'I am not worried about the dark. And as you well know, if you fetch a torch, we will soon be surrounded by insects. And then you can tell me you're worried I'll get bitten, and suggest I go inside, out of their reach.'

'I only asked,' he said.

'You avoided my question. Why is it clear to you, but not to me, that the king would leave the palace the morning after his wedding? Are you trying to humiliate me? Is it obvious he would leave because that is what kings do, and everyone here knows that except me, because I am a foolish girl from the other side of the city? Is it obvious he would abandon the palace because I am too ugly to be his wife? What, precisely, is clear to you?'

Oran looked hard at the darkening ground. 'It is obvious, madam, because the king is not interested in girls. In women. I thought you knew.'

'Not interested? Then I don't understand.'

'He prefers young men,' Oran replied.

'No, I understand what you are saying,' she said. 'Perhaps I haven't made myself clear. If the king is not attracted to women at all, I'm sure you can see that I might be perplexed as to what I am doing here. Men who don't like women don't want wives. At least, that has always been my understanding of it.'

'Men want heirs,' Oran said. 'All men need heirs. Or who will look after them when they are old?'

'Laius has a household of – what? – fifty slaves: cooks and maids and housekeepers and administrators and guards and grooms and the gods know who else,' Jocasta replied. 'I'm sure some of them will look after him when he's old. He's old now, and you're all still here.'

'But he needs a child,' Oran said. The small night-flies were descending on them as the darkness fell. 'Someone to guard his memory after he dies. No one can be immortal if their descendants decide otherwise. Or if they have none. He needs someone who will put up a statue commemorating him and listing his achievements as king.'

'Well, I'm sure if someone gave you a chisel, you'd give it a try,' she snapped.

'I am loyal to my king,' he agreed.

'Then perhaps you can explain something else to me. If Laius wants an heir, enough to marry, I presume he understands that he will have to spend at least some time in the same room, in the same bed, as his wife. Don't start blushing again. You're not a child.'

'That's not necessarily true,' Oran said. 'He wants an heir. It doesn't need to be his child.'

Jocasta tried not to allow her shock to show. A man would bring up another man's child? 'What are you saying?' she asked. 'That he expects me to . . . ?'

'Yes,' said Oran. 'He's waiting for you to become pregnant. It would be better, for him, if that happened sooner rather than later. So he can claim that the child was conceived on your wedding night.'

'And who exactly does he imagine I am cavorting with?' she hissed. She wished now that she had agreed to Oran fetching a torch. At least then she would be sure that no one was listening in to their conversation. But as it was, the colonnades were in almost total blackness, and anyone could overhear her, so long as they were quiet. Oran said nothing.

'You?' she asked. 'That's why he left you behind.'

'You asked me to stay,' Oran replied. 'I told him, and he was delighted. He'd rather you bore the child of someone you had shown a preference for.'

'Would he?' Jocasta asked.

'Don't be like that,' he said. 'Please don't. I promised him. He's my king. And he's your king too.'

'Hardly,' she said. 'We've barely even met. And what if I refuse?'

The silence was as wide and long as the night.

'You won't, will you?'

'Would it matter if I did?'

'It would matter to me.'

'But you would still obey your orders?'

'They are orders,' he said. 'I serve the king. I would have no choice.'

5

I felt pain again under my ribs when I lifted myself out of bed: duller now than it had been. When I placed my fingers gently on the dressing Sophon had used, I could feel the heat of the injury. But not the different, more intense heat of an infection. I knew when I peeled back the bandages in a day or two that the skin would be shiny and red, not swollen into the almost bluish-pink that characterized an infected wound. He had recommended I stay in bed for another day or two, but no one had come to visit me since yesterday afternoon, and I had woken far too early this morning, when I rolled onto my side and the pain jolted me awake. But if I were to tell Sophon that, expecting sympathy, he would smile and say that if my sleeping self had forgotten I was hurt, my waking self would follow in a day or two.

I would rather have taken the risk of ripping open my stitches than spend another hour on my own. I padded over to a wooden chest, and found an old shift dress the colour of freshly churned cream. The slaves had taken advantage of my period in bed to wash and mend all my clothes: I scarcely recognized the dress as mine. It was cut wide enough for me to lift it only a little way above my head. I twisted my neck to slide myself into it without using my injured muscles more than I had to.

I splashed water on my face to convince myself it was morning: my mind was still fogged from having woken too early. I couldn't reach down to put on my soft leather sandals, so I walked barefoot towards the door, relishing the cool stones. I could hear a faint murmuring from outside, and I was sure it was Ani. As I opened the door onto the colonnade at the side of the family courtyard, I saw her sitting by the fountain, its sides painted with leaping dolphins, holding hands with our cousin Haem.

My mother used to say that this was her favourite part of the palace. She didn't usually enjoy telling stories, it was something she preferred to leave to our father. But occasionally you could persuade her to talk about her life before she married him, before us. When she came to tuck me into bed at night, I would ask her to tell us a story about what the palace was once like. She would resist, saying it was time for me to go to sleep, or that she was tired. But sometimes, she gave in. This courtyard – she would say – was bare and sad when she first laid eyes on it. Scarcely any living plants in the ground, no water in the fountain. The frescos on the walls were faded, and chunks of the plaster had fallen off. Some of it still lay on the ground, like half-chewed lumps of meat. She didn't even think about how dilapidated it looked, she said. Until she met my father, who had spent so much time outside the city walls. He had grown up loving flowers and trees, she explained. Ask him to tell you the names of all the plants in the garden, she would say. He knows them all. When she saw him looking at the sad, dead courtyard one day, she realized she wanted to give him a proper garden. She found a gardener to fill the flowerbeds and repair the fountain. He brought three other men and they came at night, so it would be a surprise.

And so one morning, she and my father woke to the sound of the water, tippling down the sides of the long-parched ornamental stone. It was worth the effort, she said, just to see my father's face when he realized the gardens were filled with herbs and shrubs and new fruit trees. When you asked my father about the same day, he offered up a detail my mother always missed out: the first morning he looked at the thyme and rosemary, freshly sprouted from the new black soil beneath them, he claimed he had spotted the first butterfly seen in the palace of Thebes in hundreds of years. I always believed him. It took years before the almond trees first produced their fruit, or the figs. My parents never lived to eat them.

My sister looked so much like our mother: the same dark hair plaited around the sides of her head and bound at the back, the same pale skin. And the same tendency for dramatic gestures: every time my sister placed her hand on her heart, I wondered if she was copying our mother deliberately. But it never felt like the sort of question I could ask. She loved to sit by the fountain because she knew it was the perfect place for private conversations. No one could approach you from any side of the courtyard without being seen. No one in the colonnades could hear what was being said in the centre because the sound of the water masked the words being spoken.

Haem noticed me before she did and he pulled his hand away from hers. Only a small distance, just so you couldn't say they were holding hands. He knew – even if my sister pretended not to – that I wanted more than anything to be sitting where she was. His hair was a dark gold colour, lighter when he let it grow long and curl into his neck. And although it was many years since we had played together in this square – him carrying me around on his back, pretending to be a horse while I squawked with glee – I could still remember exactly how his hair smelled: clean and somehow warm, like spiced wine in winter. But of course he only cared for Ani. And now we were no longer children, he barely saw me.

I waved to them both as I walked along the colonnade. I wanted somebody to talk to, but I was too embarrassed to stop and speak to them now. My sister waved back and smiled.

'Are you going back to lessons already?' she called. I nodded and kept walking. I could make it to Sophon's study, surely.

I was the only one who still visited our tutor. Polyn had finished lessons when he turned fifteen, Eteo and Haem the year after when they reached the same age, both boys resenting that final year, when Polyn was spending his days with men as they were left to feel like children. Ani had never been interested in the classroom, unless my cousin was in it. She called Sophon a dry old man and said he had nothing to teach her. But once it was just him and me, Sophon began talking about more interesting ideas – history, philosophy – almost as if he had been waiting for the others to leave. I had never dared to ask him if he had deliberately bored them into removing themselves from his lessons, one after another. He was almost the only person who spoke about my parents at all (everyone else preferred to pretend they had never existed, even my uncle), and I wondered if he wanted someone to remember them to, as much as I wanted to hear them remembered. He was nearly seventy years old, and had lived through the Reckoning, when he was a boy, then through my mother's reign, and so far – he would say – he had survived my brothers. He liked to say that he planned to hold on till I became queen, and then he'd die happy. I would laugh, knowing this was a promise to live forever: as the poets would sing of me, I am the youngest of four siblings, cursed daughter of cursed parents. My brothers will marry because they are kings. My sister will surely marry Haem. But I cannot expect such a future for myself, and Thebes will never want me as her queen.

I knocked on Sophon's door and found him sitting in the thin early morning light on a battered old chair by the fire. It was cold in the courtyards at the beginning of the day. The sun took its time to clear the mountains behind the palace, and until it filled the open squares, it was never really warm, even during the summer. The hairs on my arms were standing up: I should have asked Ani if I could borrow a cloak or a shawl. My own cloak had disappeared. I asked one of the servants about it, and she told me that they had scrubbed and scrubbed but couldn't get the blood out of it. I was relieved to see that Sophon was also feeling the cold. He used to say the heat went out of him when he was thirty, so he had spent the last forty years lighting the fire.

His room was my favourite part of the palace. Its walls were lined with shelves, which were filled with carefully rolled papyri. There was nothing you couldn't find here, if you had the time and the inclination. Sophon didn't play favourites with the manuscripts he had acquired over the years: astrology and astronomy were next to each other, history and biography, agriculture and household-economy, and – most numerous and my favourite – stories about great heroes of the past.

The fireplace was on the far wall, surrounded by the shelves. Sophon's desk was under the high windows, but he preferred to sit closer to the heat. He was white-haired, balding on the top. He had a neatly trimmed white beard, and I never saw him wear anything which wasn't brown. I had asked him once why he liked brown so much, and he said it was easier. Long ago, before the Reckoning, he was a doctor, and lived at the temple of Asclepius, son of Apollo, down in the belly of the town. People would travel from all over Thebes and the lands outside to be treated by him. But he moved up to a house near the palace when he met my mother and she asked him to be Polyn's tutor. She couldn't think of anyone better, she said.

'Isy – you look cold. Come and sit here.' Sophon waved at the chair opposite his, and I hurried over and sat down, trying not to wince. 'I'm not sure you should be up yet, should you?' he asked. He pointed to the back of the chair, where there was a woollen blanket. I pulled it down and wrapped it around myself.

'I woke up so early,' I told him. 'I was bored.'

'You wanted something to read, I imagine,' he said. 'This might be what you're looking for.' He stood up with a suppressed groan and walked over to his shelves. He was a cacophony of bones: a joint creaked or snapped with every step. He reached up without a moment's hesitation and picked out a new papyrus from the crammed stacks.

He gave it to me, and I saw it was a replacement copy of the one I had been reading before. The one I had covered in my blood.

'I'm so sorry I ruined it,' I said.

'Isy, it doesn't matter,' he replied, though his eyes were filmy, as though it mattered very much. 'And the scribe was pleased to have the work.'

'Thank you.'

'Is there any news on your attacker?' Sophon asked, as he sat back down. I looked across at him. His chair was in front of the window, so it was too bright behind him for me to see his face in more than silhouette.

'I don't know. Eteo is searching for him. What have you heard?'

'I've heard your brother will find him,' he said quietly.

'I don't understand.'

'I believe your attacker will be found shortly. It has taken several days now, long enough to make it appear that it has been a difficult job to track him down.'

'You're not saying that Eteo . . .'

'I don't think so, Isy, but I can't be completely sure. I think someone else is responsible, but – as far as I can tell – Eteo is as much their target as you.' The fear must have leapt across my face because he corrected himself. 'Not a target of an assassin. The target of a plot. Someone is trying to destabilize his kingship. Killing you would have been an extremely effective way of doing that. The king can't be responsible for keeping his city safe when he can't even keep his own household safe. Do you see?'

'But Eteo will only be king for one more month,' I said. 'Then it is Polyn's year.' My brothers alternate the kingship. In other cities, Polyn would have become king, because he is the eldest. But the age gap between my brothers is very small: barely more than one year. And my uncle decided that sharing the kingship would be a better solution for our city. He believes in prophecies, and he was persuaded by a fortune-teller that our city could easily descend into civil war otherwise. The king of Thebes, whoever he is, is cursed, Creon believes. Lots of Thebans believe it. So by splitting the power, he hoped to divide the curse. And half a curse can't possibly be as bad as a whole one. One day, I would like to ask him if he really believes this or if he just believes he should pay heed to it in public. My uncle is not an easy man to read.

'Yes, that's the most confusing aspect of things,' Sophon said. 'Only a month . . .'

'What do you expect to happen next?' I asked.

'I think they will find someone who appears to be guilty. But if he is the perpetrator – which I doubt he will be – he will only be the most visible element. The real plot is still hidden from view. You must be careful.'

'I was careful before,' I said, although I knew this wasn't true. I hadn't been expecting a masked man to in- filtrate my home. We have guards everywhere. I thought I was safe and I had behaved accordingly.

'I'm not blaming you, Isy. I'm trying to protect you.'

I nodded. I had come to Sophon to try and feel better, and if anything I now felt worse. I wanted to go back to my room, but my side was throbbing too much for me to stand.

'Do you have any old parchment?' I asked him. 'That you aren't using?'

'Yes, I think so,' he replied. 'Are you too old for wax tablets now? Your words need some permanence?' He smiled. 'How old are you today?'

'Fifteen,' I reminded him. He knew perfectly well when I was born.

'It feels like a year or two at most since you were a baby,' he said. 'It's only because you've grown so tall that I believe you when you say that.'

He opened a cupboard door beside the desk and pulled out two small rolls of parchment. 'Here you are,' he said. 'Will this be enough for now?'

'Yes. Do you have any ink?'

'There's ink and everything else you need in the cupboard over by the door,' he said. 'You can pick it up when you go back to your room. Save me walking over there.' He crunched his way back to his chair and sat down again.

I thought of something Eteo had said, about Sophon running to help me, when I was stabbed. The man who supported his way round the room leaning on the furniture could not really have run, surely? Not even if there was a fire behind him. But my brother has never been prone to exaggeration: like me, he prefers to leave that to Ani.

'What do you intend to use it for?' Sophon asked.

'I want to keep a record,' I told him. 'Of what's happening. When we talked before, about history, you said I must always bear in mind who composes it. And I thought about that a lot when I was in bed. I thought about how my story would never be told if I didn't tell it.'

Sophon said nothing.

'An official history of Thebes would mention my

brothers and my uncle. It might even mention Ani, because she will end up marrying Haem.

Sophon nodded. 'Yes, I think she will.'

'But no one will remember me, the youngest daughter. I don't matter, do I?'

Anyone else would have told me I mattered very much to them. Sophon sighed. 'No, Isy, I'm afraid you don't.'

'So I should compose my own history, shouldn't I? Or it will be lost forever.'

'Yes,' he agreed. 'You should.'

'Is it better to start at the beginning?' I asked him. 'Or to start now and work backwards?'

He thought for a long moment. 'You should try to compose it in your head first,' he said. 'And then you will know how to begin when you write it down. I think, perhaps, you should start now, and then try to understand what will happen in the light of what has happened so far. Do you see?'

'Everything that is to come has been decided by what has already occurred? You sound like Creon: the gods decide everything, and we are their playthings.'

'Not the gods, Isy. The gods do what they will. I doubt they have much time for us: why would they? Don't they have more important things on their minds than the fates of a few mortals?'

'Of course they do. You know I think the same. That's why I don't understand what you're saying.'

'Because events are decided by other events. Aren't they? If someone ran in through the door now, and shouted that a pack of wild dogs was tearing through the main courtyard, what would happen?'

'We would shut the door and lock it. We might push some of the furniture against it, too. Then if the lock doesn't hold, the chairs might keep them at bay.'

'And if no such messenger arrives, what happens to the furniture?'

'We leave it where it is.'

'So the fate of the chair today is decided by the decision of a pack of dogs that have – at this moment – never set eyes on it. Who could not begin to understand that it even exists. Do you understand?'

'Yes. I think so.'

'No one would believe the gods had nothing to do with what happens to us, Isy, but we surely can't believe they would intervene in the existence of a simple chair, or even a dog.'

'And a human life is more complicated than the life of a chair,' I said, wishing I had thought this through for myself.

'Of course. Can you even begin to count the myriad ways in which your life might be affected by the choices other people – people you have never met, whose existence is utterly hidden from you – are making every day?'

'So how can I write my history, when there is so much I don't know, which might cause a profound change to things I think I do know?'

'Well, that is the difficulty of writing it,' he said. 'The ink is by the door. I told you, didn't I?'

He closed his eyes. This is typical of our conversations. I end them knowing more than I did when they began. But I am somehow less sure of things.

6

Jocasta had been in the palace for almost a month now, and the king had yet to return. She often woke in the night, disturbed sometimes by random noises of a large household but more often by the sense that someone was nearby, wishing her ill. She had no proof that this was so, but she knew it to be true. Her bedroom door had a lock, but no key. Or if there was a key, she did not have it. So many doors in the palace were locked to her, but not even in sleep could she close herself off from anyone who wanted to walk in. She had asked Teresa about the absent key, but Teresa had blinked slowly, and said she wasn't sure she had ever seen it. It was at this moment, when Jocasta thought she would reach out and slap the woman right across the face, when she wondered if she might be pregnant. She didn't know what made her think of it.

Oran still visited her every night. He took his duty seriously. And although she knew he didn't need to, he tried to make her happy. He told her she was pretty and that he liked the way her hair – released from its daily plaits – flowed across the pillows, like seaweed on the lakeshore. He had tried never to hurt her, and if she expressed any pain, he stopped. But still she stared into the darkness when she wanted to fall asleep: this was the boy she had believed her only friend and ally in the palace, and he too chose to obey the king's perverse whims.

Her days were less terrible than her nights, though the sleeplessness left her blurry and exhausted. She liked to walk around the agora with her slave girl and look at all the stalls and the people who came to buy. If she had married anyone else, this would have been her daily routine: carrying a basket to fill with fresh onions and lettuces, cheeses and bread. But she had no such responsibility. The palace was managed entirely by Teresa and their food was managed by the cooks. So Jocasta wandered the market aimlessly, stopping to look at whatever she pleased. She chose dresses in pale colours, knowing she would never have to worry about keeping them unmarked: whoever was in charge of the laundry was someone she would never meet. And if a dress was damaged, she could pick something else in a different shade, perhaps this time with serried lines of contrasting embroidery around the neckline and shoulders. The stall-holders soon recognized her, and kept aside their best cloth for her. Though she liked the market, she wished that the palace was not quite so high in the city. It meant there was only ever one road she could take, and that was down and into the bustling streets, when she would sometimes have preferred to go somewhere quiet. Not contained, tamed quiet: she had quite enough of that in the palace. But she would have liked to visit the lake or wander out past the city graveyard onto the hillsides, and hear the goats and sheep bleating as they grazed. She would have enjoyed walking around the hill beneath the back of the palace, but she had not yet found an exit from the palace into the wasteland outside the city walls. She wondered what would happen if she announced to Teresa that she wanted to visit her husband in the mountains. But she didn't wonder for very long.

One morning she planned to go to the market as usual, but when she woke, she felt feverish. Her room was cool, but her hair was pressed damp against her scalp and the sheets were sticking to her back. She wiped the sweat from her forehead and realized she was also queasy. She refused breakfast, in the hope that the nausea would pass. She sat for a while in the shade, too uncomfortable for the bright sun. She ate only an apple for lunch, and noted Teresa's beady pleasure in her sickness. Of course Teresa knew about Oran. Jocasta had no doubt that the whole thing had been the sly housekeeper's idea.

Eventually, she decided that she would go out in spite of the shakiness which radiated from her belly to her feet. She summoned her slave and insisted they go to the market now, even though it was the hottest part of the day. The girl said nothing, but picked up her basket and followed her mistress through the courtyards. With every step, Jocasta knew she was making a terrible mistake. The sickness threatened to overwhelm her. But she could not lose face in front of this girl, in front of the palace. She put one brittle foot in front of the other, and wished that she had a parasol. She decided she would search for one among the stalls.

She didn't recall seeing parasols in the market before, but then, she hadn't been looking for one, and sometimes these things slipped past the eyes of the uninterested. Perhaps she had half a memory of a vendor of curved sunhats, made from elaborately woven straw. That might do. She took a different route through the square, hoping to notice them again. But although she wanted to give the stalls her full attention, she soon realized she needed to concentrate on her feet, kicking their way through the sandy dust beneath her sandals. She felt a small piece of grit wedge itself between her foot and her shoe, and the pain was as intense as if someone had driven a sharp metal blade into her heel. She grabbed at the foot, and fell heavily onto her knees. The maid stood behind her, useless.

A dark-haired man, greying at the temples, rushed out from behind piles of papyrus, and reached down to help her up.

'Fetch me my stool,' he cried, and another stall-holder brought the man's folding wooden seat out into the aisle behind her.

'Here,' said the man, and lifted her onto the seat. 'Try to take deep breaths. You—' he barked at the slave girl. 'Fetch water, now.' The girl ran off.

'Is she entirely hopeless?' he asked Jocasta. 'Or does she do what she's asked?'

Jocasta thought for a moment. 'She usually does what she's asked,' she replied. 'Though she might have been quicker if we'd told her where to get the water from.'

The man pursed his lips and glanced across at the stall-holder – a middle-aged woman with stringy nut-brown arms – and asked a wordless question. She produced a flask and poured water into a small wooden cup which she held out to the old man, who took it and brought it to Jocasta's lips. He tipped it carefully towards her mouth, and she felt its coolness wash into her.

'Thank you,' she said, to him and the woman who had given her water away.

He looked at her, lips still pursed. 'You'll be well again shortly,' he said. 'But you need to rest. How far did you walk to get here?'

'From inside.' She waved at the palace behind them.

'Hmm,' he said. 'I'll take you back there in a few minutes.'

She sat watching dully as he engaged the woman at the next stall to keep an eye on his papers and scrolls. He picked up an old leather bag which he swung over his shoulders, and offered her his arm. She smiled at the kindness, in spite of the sweat she could feel crawling over her scalp.

'Thank you.' She took his arm and they walked slowly back to the palace. They were entering the front gates when they almost walked into the slave girl, who was carrying a small kylix of water, most of which she had already spilled.

Teresa caught sight of them as Jocasta entered the third courtyard. She hurried over, frowning.

'What's going on?' She pointed at the stall-holder. 'Who's this?'

'Are you her mother?' asked the man.

'I – no.' Teresa wasn't used to being questioned, Jocasta saw. And certainly not by someone who wasn't afraid of her.

'She needs rest. She shouldn't be on her feet, especially in the afternoon heat. Where can she lie down?'

Teresa was torn between telling him to leave, and wanting his help to move Jocasta into her room. Need won out, and she took Jocasta's right arm while the man continued to support her left. Together they walked to her room, and led her to bed. The papyrus-seller reached behind her, rearranging her pillows with one efficient hand.

'Take off her shoes,' he told Teresa, who obeyed him in silence. He helped Jocasta to sit back on the bed, and placed more cushions beneath her legs.

'I'll check back on you tomorrow,' said the bookseller, once he was satisfied. 'Until then, don't go further than you have to.'

'Thank you,' Jocasta said.

'You're comfortable?' he asked. She nodded. 'Good. Tomorrow, then.' He strode off, walking far more quickly now. Teresa shot a baleful glance at Jocasta, and hastened after him.

By the time the king heard this story, on his return from the mountains, Jocasta had no doubt that it would have been Teresa's idea to find a doctor to keep an eye on her. As her pregnancy became more visible, so did the king. But she never saw him alone, and he barely spoke to her, even when others were present. Every man in the palace would toast her and Laius, and wish health to his heir. 'A son!' Jocasta grew weary of hearing. She secretly wished for a daughter, just to serve them right. The king looked no more enthusiastic at the prospect of a son than she felt, though he never spoke about it to his wife. 'So long as the child is healthy,' he would announce to whoever asked, trying to avert the evil eye. 'I wouldn't mind at all being the father of a daughter.'

She almost preferred it when he ignored her, or went

back to the mountains, because the alternative provoked a black-eyed, wrathful stare from Teresa, who resented any time he spent with his bride at all. Jocasta tried to puzzle it out, but could not: if the housekeeper was so devoted to Laius, who had no interest in Jocasta, why had Teresa not married him herself? She could have had children once: no one was born old. So why had she not done so, instead of embroiling Jocasta in the whole hateful deceit?

At least Jocasta had found Sophon, the man who ran the papyrus stall. He had been a doctor for several years, before deciding to indulge in his primary pleasure of reading and dealing in manuscripts. But he was happy to have one more patient: he began to visit Jocasta, checking up on her, answering her questions about the dizziness and the sickness. He brought herbs which quelled the latter and advised rest to battle the former. As the weeks dragged by, and her body felt more treacherous with each day, she asked him if he would be there when she gave birth.

'Of course I will be nearby,' he replied. 'But you know a midwife will attend you. You need someone who has been through it herself.' Jocasta asked Teresa if she would find someone, and the housekeeper nodded.

'Of course,' she said. 'It's all in hand.'

*

After seven months of persistent, sometimes crippling nausea, Jocasta was desperate to be rid of this parasitic child which persecuted her from within. She was not precisely sure when she had conceived it, but she knew it must be due some time in the next few weeks. She was terrified of what was to come. She was barely sixteen years old, slightly built, and afraid her body would soon be split in two by an infant who cared nothing for damaging her, but whose only determination was to be born. She wanted to ask Sophon the one question she could not: was it rational to hate a part of your own body? And what if it wanted you dead? For the last time in her life, she wondered if it was too late to send a message to her mother. But she could not bring herself to do so. News of her pregnancy must have spread across Thebes by now. And yet she had not heard a word from her family. She lay on her bed, propped up by cushions, wishing the whole thing was over. And then, of course, it was.

The pain was indescribable, and more than once she found herself pledging every possible offering to the divine Eileithyia if it would abate. When she understood that it would not stop until the baby was out or she was dead, she screamed into the uncaring air that she would give anything, everything she had if the goddess would ease her pain. She reflected, between the worst pains of contraction, that this particular goddess – a daughter of a vengeful mother – should be her ally, above all others. But still the child of Hera did not come to her assistance.

She asked and asked for Sophon, but no one could find him, or even guess at where he might have gone. Jocasta was so upset that one of the palace guards brought in the woman who looked after the stall next to Sophon's. She said he had received a message from home yesterday which required an immediate response, and he had yet to return. Looking over at Jocasta – who was red-faced and gasping for air, her hands clawing at the sheets she was lying on – she asked if she might be excused, and ran from the room. A dead mother was a bad omen. So in the end, it was just Jocasta and Teresa, as the housekeeper must have always intended it would be.

Teresa was solicitous, pushing Jocasta's hair out of her eyes and behind her ears, murmuring that all would be well. Jocasta soon lost track of time: she wasn't sure if she had been struggling for hours or days, and Teresa would not tell her. Shutters were drawn across the windows and she found herself dozing in the half-light, waking up anguished and confused. In the whole awful process, it never once occurred to her that anything could be worse than the pain. And then eventually, after time had slowed or perhaps stopped, after she had pushed and struggled and panted and wept, she made one final impossible effort and heard Teresa exhale loudly as the pain receded a little.

'Is it a boy?' Jocasta asked. In a single moment, she found she no longer hated the parasite which was trying to kill her. She had a baby, and she wanted nothing more than to hold it in her arms and keep it safe. She had survived the birth. She had lived to be a mother.

Teresa replied that yes, it was indeed a boy, and Jocasta was so happy that she didn't notice Teresa's expression or hear the warning tone in her voice. Jocasta knew Teresa had little time for her. But she had never seen a look of pity on the woman's face until now.

'Give him to me,' Jocasta begged. There was something purple in the woman's hands, like offal at a sacrifice. Where was her son? And why didn't he make a sound? Babies cried, didn't they?

Teresa turned away from her, and walked out of the room.

'Give him to me,' she shouted, though her lungs ached and her throat was scratched raw. She tried to get up and follow Teresa, grab her baby and hold him tight. But her legs wouldn't support her, and she simply lay there for what felt like forever. When Teresa returned, she was holding nothing. She looked at Jocasta and shook her head.

'He wouldn't have let you keep a boy, even if the child had survived. Do you understand?'

Jocasta shook her head, wordless.

'The king cannot have a son, only a daughter. There is a prophecy which said he would be killed by his son. He won't allow that to happen. So I couldn't allow it to happen either.'

Jocasta thought she must be hallucinating from the exhaustion. A prophecy? Was Teresa mad? It was one thing to pay reverence to the gods who controlled the affairs of men, but another thing entirely to believe that they gave out messages for the future. To their priests and most devout followers, perhaps, but to ordinary men? Even to kings? It was almost blasphemous to suggest it.

The rational part of her mind, if she could have reached it, knew that after the Reckoning, plenty of people had sought meaning in messages from the gods. They had preferred to see it not as a disaster, but as a warning, or something foretold. People wanted priests and fortune-tellers, entrail-readers and diviners to prove that they had seen it coming. Most of all, the survivors wanted to believe that they had been saved because of something, or perhaps for something. Blind chance was too frightening for any-one; who could feel safe if their survival was simply down to luck? And who could grieve for the crushing losses they had experienced, if none of it held any meaning?

'The king believes in prophecies?' She was clutching at sense.

'Devoutly,' Teresa nodded. 'He refused to have a child, for years. Eventually, he was persuaded that he could have a daughter, because the prophecy said he would be killed by his son. I hoped you would have a girl, you see. Because I could only have sons and I couldn't leave a third one on the hillside to die.' Jocasta gazed at her, wondering if she was hearing the housekeeper's dulled tones correctly. Had Teresa borne healthy sons and then exposed them on the mountain to avoid a prophecy? The woman must be quite mad.

'I want to see my baby,' said Jocasta.

'He didn't survive.' Teresa looked at the floor. 'He was too small, and the cord was wrapped around his neck. He went too long without air. It happens often.'

'I need to see him.'

'It wouldn't help,' Teresa said quietly. 'Your doctor will be back tomorrow or the next day. He'll say the same thing. There is nothing to be gained by holding a dead baby, and wishing life into it. Believe me.'

And with this, she walked out. Jocasta was too bloody and exhausted even to cry.

7

I now felt uncomfortable only when I reached upwards, though I still couldn't twist my body: if someone called my name, I would feel a stiffness under my ribs as I tried to turn. Even moving my neck pulled out echoes of leftover pain below. But the stitches were gone, leaving me with a puckered red triangle beneath my ribcage. I stood in the sunlight beneath the high windows of my bedroom, and raised my arms to shoulder height. Ani ran her fingers across the scar, and said doubtfully that it would probably fade over time, and that no one but me would ever see it anyway. I didn't tell her that I liked it: I was drawn to its symmetry and the way it marked me out as someone who didn't die when they were supposed to. It was like the tattoos of an Amazon warrior, the mark of the victor. But I was alone in perceiving it that way. Only when the stitches were gone did everyone stop behaving as though I were a breakable object. I saw myself as bronze while my family viewed me as a delicate piece of terracotta which had already broken once and been carefully glued back together. It was hard to feel like myself again until everyone stopped treating me like someone else.

I had begun to think about composing my history, and decided it would be best to begin the story with what was happening now. In a few days, Eteo would be giving up the kingship to Polyn. It was a huge occasion every year, when Thebes gave thanks to her ruling family for providing the city with not one, but two kings. Thebes, Sophon says, is an anxious city: she always fears for her future. It is the only place I've ever lived, so I don't know if things are different in other cities. And it seemed reasonable to me to fear for the future of Thebes, but that was because her kings were also my brothers, so my fate was woven into the city's well-being.

The dual kingship was my history as well as my future. My mother was queen of Thebes for many years. When she had two sons, and then two daughters, everyone has always said the city gave a sigh of relief. The ruling family was in place for another generation. It was only when I came to think about this for my history that I realized it was strange that Polyn had not yet married. He was almost twenty; it was more than time. He and my uncle must be considering potential brides. Perhaps they were waiting until Polyn was king again to give the city a royal wedding she would enjoy: a formal ceremony with a grand sacrifice, a feast and songs through the night and into the next day. And then Eteo would marry the following year, and he would never be here again, splashing in the fountain with me in the warm summer evenings. He would be with someone else, a stranger I might not even like. And then there were further consequences to us having dual kings: whose son would take precedence? Polyn's, because he was older? Or Eteo's if he was king when his son was born?

I had set myself the task of writing about the past, but it seemed I could only think about the future.

———

Eteo had asked us all to stay inside the palace grounds until my attacker was caught. Polyn scoffed at the idea that he should modify his behaviour for any reason. Ani went wherever Haem was, wherever they could meet in private. So although we were all supposed to be in the same place, the family quarters were deserted except for the increased number of guards and slaves. I understood why Eteo was worried, but I was growing bored of being stuck here on my own. I found myself peeking through the gaps in the outer walls, trying to imagine myself on the hillside, sitting beneath the shady pine trees that dappled its lower slopes. Or, looking out the other way, I could just make out the edges of Lake Hylica from the east wall. I could see children diving in, their muscled bodies like dolphins against the glinting water.

How I envied them. But I couldn't sneak out to join them, even if I hadn't made a promise to my brother to stay in the palace. Sophon would never forgive me if I swam with a still-healing wound. And though he was right to tell me I had to keep it dry and clean, I wanted to feel the weeds beneath my feet and the cool water on my skin. It was so hot in the palace: dipping my toes in the fountain made little difference. The water was too shallow, and it soon grew warm in the afternoons. Besides, I wanted to see the kingfishers and frogs, hear the insects buzzing around me. I wanted to watch the water-skaters dancing across the surface as they tried to escape my splashing arms.

And on top of the boredom was the strange atmosphere in the palace. Usually, we marked the changing of the kings with celebrations. Preparations took several weeks, as the public square was decorated and a calf was sacrificed every day in the temples. The priests burned incense to the gods and the whole city participated. But something was different this time. Instead of a sense of excitement for renewal, Thebes was like a snake sloughing off its old skin too soon, and crawling – still soft and vulnerable – into the light. We were fearful rather than exuberant. Nothing was safe.

Even my uncle, who was usually so calm, had been touched by disquiet. The day before, he had had a statue delivered for his rooms, which were across the courtyard from ours. He had decided to redecorate his quarters, as part of the new year celebrations. It was the second delivery of this likeness, because when it first arrived, it was a rather nondescript representation of him: plain, almost austere. Even the stone looked to be of lower quality than the other statues in the palace. The marble was veiny and held a strange pinkish colour. Creon was disappointed with the piece, even more so when Haem snorted at the likeness.

My uncle had obviously expected something more impressive. So the sculptor was commissioned to improve upon the original before bringing it back. The man painted detail into the clothes and hair – applying a handsome pattern of interlocked blue squares around the hem and neckline of the reddened tunic – which had left the face strangely bare in comparison. Creon still felt the statue failed to reflect his status, as well as his appearance. So the sculptor agreed to make further improvements on site rather than carting the statue back to his workshop a second time. He decided to replace the blandly painted eyes with ones made from lapis, which is extremely prized in our city and all across Hellas. He must surely have believed that my uncle could find nothing to complain about then.

The sculptor could not find two pieces of the bright blue stone which were large enough to use in their entirety, so he smashed several smaller stones onto a palate covered with adhesive paste to create a glittering blue that he could paint over the irises. He stood on a ladder – the statue was slightly larger than life-size – and coated the dead stone eyes of my uncle's likeness with a layer of sparkling blue dust. When he came down the ladder and looked up at his work, he wasn't quite satisfied with the symmetry of the result. He climbed back up and pulled a chisel from his belt, to tidy the right eye which offended him. At this precise moment, Creon walked in from the courtyard, and saw the sculptor jamming a metal shaft into the statue's eye. My uncle – who never shows weakness or fear – gave a horrible cry and ran out of his rooms, out of the courtyard altogether. Palace guards came running from the second square when they heard the awful sound and marched the offending craftsman away.

The statue was removed, but no one knew where. Sophon has asked around but even he cannot find out what happened to the sculptor.

*

And then one day, they found my assassin. My would-be assassin. When everyone called him a killer, they seemed to have forgotten I didn't die. He was one of the new young recruits for the palace guard. Sixteen years old, the same age as Ani. The recruits live in dormitories, with twenty boys to each room, in the barracks down the hill from the market square in front of the palace. Their training-grounds and gymnasium are all part of the same complex. They are taught to defend the king, his family, and each other, in that order. They spend many days learning drills and practising with their weapons. They start with wooden swords, just like my brothers did when they were first taught to fight. Only when they have proved they won't injure themselves or their comrades are they given the heavy bronze swords they have earned. It is a source of enormous pride to be the first boy to graduate from his practice-weapon to a real one and a corresponding shame to be the last.

The evidence was easily found: this boy had not progressed yet to the bronze. He was still practising every day with wooden sticks. Yet he had a knife, a real one, stashed beneath his blanket which he had folded to use as an extra pillow on his pallet. The blood – my blood – was still visible on the blade, a dark rusty coating which he should have known to wipe off.

He was marched up the hill to stand before the king and explain himself. The rumour raced around the palace more quickly than the guards could drag him through to the main square, where cases of treason are heard. Thebes's traders were hard at work in the agora in front of the palace, so the guards lost time going around the outside. If not, I wouldn't have been able to squeeze my way through the crowds which had formed when my brother and his advisers strode out into the main square to sit as judges. I knew if Eteo saw me, he would be angry that I had ignored his request to stay in the secluded part of the palace. But surely he would understand that I had to see the man who had tried to kill me. If I didn't, I would forever be plagued by the nightmare vision of a masked man. I needed to see the face which had worn the mask.

The crowd were jeering and shouting so loudly I could scarcely hear what was being said. The accused boy had the same difficulty. He was too frightened to speak until he was punched hard, once in the ribs and once in the side of the head, by one of his erstwhile trainers. Eteo sat in front of him – his advisers on both sides, my uncle in the most prestigious place to his left – and asked the boy to explain himself. The boy could not. He had never seen the knife before, he didn't put it there, he didn't know who had, it hadn't been there last night or this morning, he hadn't ever been to the palace, he would never hurt a member of the royal family. He wept as he gave his answers. Perhaps he was younger than Ani after all.

My uncle leaned over to advise my brother, and the men huddled together for a moment. Eteo nodded and turned to the boy. The crowd fell quiet.

'Thebes finds you guilty,' said my brother in a stranger's voice. 'The sentence is death.'

There was a scream but it didn't come from the boy. It came from a woman in the crowd. She was his mother, I suppose. Her cries were quickly hushed by her neighbours.

I didn't see the boy's face until the guards turned to march him away. I had pushed myself around the edge of the crowd to catch sight of him, and I knew from a glance that they had the wrong man. He was nowhere near tall enough, he must have been a hand's width shorter than me. The man who attacked me had been my height, and his eyes were grey. This boy had brown eyes, like a calf about to be slaughtered by a priest.

I pushed my way through to the front and shouted to Eteo.

'I need to speak to you,' I called. Annoyance and worry flashed across his face, one after the other. But he knew why I had come.

'I'm not glad to see you, Isy,' he said, stepping down from the wooden platform so he could hear me. 'I wish you'd stay inside, where you're safe.' I watched him realize the folly of his words. The palace was the place where I had been least safe.

'It isn't him,' I said. 'He's not the one.'

Eteo looked at me so sadly that I wanted to reach over and hold him. 'I know, Isy. But there's nothing I can do.'

'You can't mean that. He's innocent. You're sending an innocent boy to his death.'

'It's him or me, Isy. Not just me, us.'

'The man who did it is still out there. Out here.' I waved my arm at the dispersing crowd. They had seen executions before, but many of them were still wandering out of the courtyard towards the barracks where the boy would be killed: strangled, probably, or bludgeoned by his former comrades.

'I know,' my brother said. 'Stay beside me until we're in the second courtyard. The guards will escort us back inside. You have to trust me. It's better this way.'

8

A year after her baby had died, Jocasta looked at her hair in the blackening, pock-marked mirror, and wondered when she had begun to look so haggard. One day she had been ripe, her belly stretched taut like a peach around its stone. After that, she had ignored her reflection as the days slid into months: her torn skin and rent garments were nothing she wished to see. And now, after a year, she saw that somehow she was no longer young. And although this seemed like a minor loss after everything else, she felt the pain of a fresh wound rushing up from her gut to her throat and she opened her mouth to scream.

*

Two years later, Jocasta wondered if Teresa would replace the mirror which (having hated it for as long as she could remember), she had finally smashed against the hard stone floor of her bedroom. The housekeeper, often so quick-tempered, had not even shouted when she saw the floor covered in dark shards. Slaves had come running from every corner of the palace courtyard; even Jocasta had been startled by the noise it made as each piece sprang free from its bonds. She laughed as she watched the glittering angles spin around her feet. It was not until later, when Sophon was picking splinters of glass from her legs with a pair of small silver tweezers, that she even realized she was injured.

*

The following year, Jocasta spent every day kneeling before the shrine which Teresa had arranged to have built in the courtyard. Laius had refused his wife, when she had petitioned him, but the housekeeper had eventually persuaded him that Jocasta would be quieter if he gave way. Laius was himself a pious man, and he made his offerings in the temples in the main courtyard of the palace. But his wife was no longer able to walk among the people of Thebes to pay her devotions: the eyes of strangers overwhelmed her and she was swiftly reduced to tears. Even the women turned away from her, fearful that her ill-fortune might be contagious, might afflict their own future children. Once, she saw a woman make the sign to avert the evil eye. She would have sworn she had no evil in her, but at the same time, she knew she must have affronted a powerful god; why else was she punished so cruelly?

*

After three more years, Jocasta no longer trusted she would one day see a grave marker for her son. She had dedicated years of her drawn-out life to pleading with Teresa but the woman was obdurate. She insisted there was no grave, no stone to signal the place where Jocasta could take a lock of her hair to her beautiful boy, and pour wine into a wide, shining dish for him. Jocasta did not believe her: how could she have simply disposed of the boy, as though he were nothing but refuse, like mouldering cabbages thrown away from a too-warm kitchen?

She demanded to see her husband and ask him the same questions. But Laius, who had long since given up speaking to his wife, and now avoided the palace almost entirely – preferring to live out on the mountains in all but the harshest weather, rather than find himself within earshot of Jocasta – had no consolation for her. He either did not know or did not care what had become of the baby. Once it was dead, he was satisfied. The opposite was true for his wife, who would never be satisfied again.

*

In the eleventh year after her son's death, Jocasta began sending messengers to the Oracle. Although Delphi lay several hundred stades away, across territory which was rarely safe, she had concluded that the Pythian priestesses offered her the only comfort she might find. Making offerings to Apollo in her home was no longer sufficient. The wine was poured, the entrails were burned, but she was no closer to happiness. Fear and revulsion still coursed through her whenever she thought of her own body almost tearing in two. The mere sight of a pregnant woman left her panting for breath. She longed for her missing child, but she could not imagine having another. Even Teresa had stopped suggesting it. The grief it caused was too disruptive for the whole palace.

The Oracle returned Jocasta's interest with gnomic utterances but only occasionally. There was no certainty her messenger would survive the journey there and back:

bandits, robbers and mountain lions all fed on her slaves from time to time. And those who did return brought messages whose meaning twisted away from Jocasta, like snakes in her hands. She would take the message gladly, and when she first heard it, she felt better, somehow lighter. The Oracle was benign, it offered sage advice.

Then, over the next day or two, she would reflect on its hidden meanings and on the Oracle's possible motives. How could she truly know what it meant when it was so vague? Was it really saying that her son was alive, when it referred to him as 'cursed'? Or was his death the curse itself? That she too was cursed she had no doubt. Almost more cruel than the loss of her child was the terrible, suffocating uncertainty. After several days, she would demand that another messenger be sent to request clarification. But the clarification, when it came, if it came, was no less vague than the previous message.

*

By the fifteenth year, she was given a new mirror, and was shocked to see she had grown old. She had a mesh of fine lines around her eyes that she had never seen before. Her mother had died that spring. When her brother arrived with the news, he had been tentative, not wishing to add further grief to a sister bowed down by the weight of what she had already borne. But, if anything, Jocasta had been relieved. She had taken the carriage across Thebes to attend her mother's burial: it would have been impossible to do anything else. And as she cast the damp earth over her mother's grave, murmuring the ritual words to grant her mother safe passage to Hades, she felt no grief. She said the words again, beneath her breath, for her dead boy, and cast an extra handful of dirt over his imagined corpse.

*

The following winter, her father followed her mother into the boat of Charon and across the River Lethe. Again, Jocasta scattered earth and poured offerings to his shade. Although she conducted the rituals as was proper, she rent her garments and tore her hair because custom and the gods demanded it, not because she felt any fresh pain. In her own mind, she had been orphaned fifteen years earlier, when they gave her to the king. And then orphaned again when her baby died. Why was there a word to describe the child of dead parents, but no word to describe the mother of a dead child? The question had plagued her for years: there should be a word for her, for what had happened to her. Yet there was not.

*

It was sixteen years since her son had died, and only Creon existed as the bridge between her past life and her present existence. She found her brother's visits both reassuring and difficult. Firstly, there was the problem that he had grown up. He was twenty-one now, and she found it disconcerting when he arrived a stranger: taller, darker, his face lengthening and hardening as he left childhood behind. Only his voice stayed the same: calm, deep, measured. His voice and his pale blue eyes.

Jocasta wished her brother would move into the palace

and keep her company all the time, so she would have someone to talk to, someone who connected her to a time in her life when things had been easier, happier. But he wouldn't agree to it: on his last visit he had mentioned a girl he was hoping to marry. Perhaps once they had married, they might consider moving nearer to the palace and the hub of the city. Jocasta thought he should hurry: Creon was no longer a boy. It began to look peculiar if men went unmarried for too long.

She thought she would send a messenger to ask him to visit her. But were the only reliable slaves all away in Delphi? She could not think when she had last received an oracle. Perhaps one was due back today. Or perhaps he had been due back yesterday or the day before, and she had lost another man to the perils of the Outlying. The anxiety rose in her: if her messengers kept dying, she would soon have no one left to trust. And then what would she do? How could she find someone else who wasn't in Teresa's pocket, telling Jocasta not truths which emanated from the god, but stories which came from the old housekeeper? How could she be sure the slaves she had already sent were loyal to her rather than Teresa? She could not.

Her hair had grown wispy and lifeless. It hung down behind her ears, when once it had – she was sure – curled over them. Realizing she hated it, she opened one dresser-drawer after another until she found what she needed. She bundled the hair in her left fist, and hacked into it with a blade that should have been sharper. She placed the offending hank on the table and immediately wished someone would take it away, so she couldn't see it any more. Once it was no longer attached to her, she was revolted by it.

*

Two days later, when a messenger, a foreigner, arrived and asked to see the queen, the palace staff were perplexed. There must be some mistake. Did he want to see Teresa? She was in the agora somewhere, and would doubtless return before nightfall. She had left no instructions for what they should do if someone asked for Jocasta. No one ever did except her brother, Creon, and they all knew him. But the man – or he was really nearer a boy – stood firm: he must speak to the queen, immediately.

There was some quality in his manner, his urgency, which spurred them into an action they did not want to take. Two slave women – who usually acted as Jocasta's maids – hurried him through the courtyards, each one noticing that the messenger had clearly travelled in haste: his boots were mud-spattered, his cloak had a small tear on the lower back, as though he had caught it on a branch, and wrenched himself free. They entered the private courtyard and found Jocasta kneeling before the shrine, as she often was these days. She was murmuring something to herself, a prayer to the god who tormented her.

'Forgive me,' said one of the slave women. She had the wit to know Teresa would probably have them both flogged if she found out that they had allowed a stranger into the company of the queen. Looking across at her fellow slave, she jerked her head in the direction of the kitchens. They should disappear into the bowels of the palace and then they might be able to deny their involvement later.

'Excuse me, madam, but this visitor needs to speak to you.'

Jocasta turned. Her eyes darted to the stranger and she noted his dishevelled appearance. She reached one hand to the altar, to support herself as she stood. Then she bent down and brushed the dust from her dress. 'What is it, sir?' she asked.

'It is the king,' he replied. 'I'm very sorry, madam. He is dead.'

'Dead?' Jocasta asked. The messenger nodded, his face a mask of mute sympathy. 'Good,' she said. 'So what happens now?'

9

It was the morning of Polyn's coronation and, getting dressed in my room, I could hear the preparations taking place throughout the palace. The market stalls had been removed from the agora outside the palace gates, and the sand had been swept into a racetrack. Once the ceremony had taken place in the throne room, fifty youths – who were known as the aristoi, the best of Thebes's young men – would be competing in the celebratory games. They were all Polyn's age or thereabouts. Many of them had been his friends for years. They were the sons of Thebes's leading families, and Polyn, Eteo and Haem would compete alongside them: Polyn and Haem in the wrestling and Eteo in the foot-race. It was a chance for my brothers and my cousin to show off, and Thebes would be disappointed if no one from the royal household won an event.

I was making my preparations alone. My sister and I would both be wearing crocus-yellow dresses: the colour worn by girls at Theban ceremonies. It was a colour which Ani said suited me, bringing out the golden tones in my usually mousy hair. My sister was far less happy about wearing it herself, saying that yellow made her look sallow and plain. She wanted to wear a beautiful blue-green dress – the colour of the lake we never visited any more

– which she had recently acquired (a gift from Haem, I imagined), but she could not prevail on either my uncle or my brothers to let her disregard the traditional colour and wear what she chose.

She was so angry that – to placate her – I suggested she had the slaves help her to make herself presentable (she would allow no more than that, in such a horrible dress). My sister has never looked anything but beautiful to everyone else. The intricate hairstyle she was planning required at least two women to plait and wrap. I reassured them that I could dress myself without assistance – as I did most days – and Ani threw her arms around me with gratitude. She knew my hair would look the same no matter how many people tried to ambush it with combs and pins. But that was not why I preferred to dress myself. I could not bear to hear the slave girls gossip. The palace was buzzing with details from those who had watched the boy – my supposed assassin – die. Everyone except Eteo thought I would want to know what had happened. It was meant to reassure me: no more danger, now the man who attacked me was gone. Instead, hearing them was like joining a conspiracy. The soldiers had beaten him to death, before carrying his bludgeoned body to a wooden pole in front of the palace gates and stringing him up as a warning to other criminals. Even by staying away from the main courtyard, it had been impossible to avoid him: the smell, sweet and rancid, permeated the palace. I wondered how long they would leave him there, beckoning the crows and wild dogs to ruin him completely.

When I refused to go and look at the broken boy, Polyn laughed and said I was too squeamish. But I could not stand to see another person dead. My parents died within hours of each other, years ago. I was five years old, Ani was almost seven, Eteo nearly nine and Polyn ten. And the only thing which comforts me, when I think back to that whole terrible day, has been the certainty that my parents loved one another in a way that most couples do not. If one of them had to die, it was better that they both did, because neither of them could have survived without the other.

No woman has ever gazed at her husband with the urgency that filled my mother's face whenever she looked at my father. When he left a room, even if it was just for a brief time, her whole body slumped, as though her soul went with him and she could do nothing but sit and wait until he returned. It might have been pitiful, had he not loved with equal fervour. If he had to go somewhere without her, you would see him almost sprinting across the courtyards on his return, just to get back to her a moment sooner. When the aristoi run in their foot-race today, each competing for the glory of victory over his peers, not one of them will have such focus in his eyes as my father, hastening across the palace to my mother. She used to wait for him like a dog, her head lifting every time she heard footsteps that might be him, coming home. This never struck me as odd, because it was all I knew. If I thought about it at all, I just believed everyone's parents were like this: anxious when they were not together. As long as my mother could hear us playing, she was content. The sound of her children was sufficient for her to know we were safe. But with my father it was different: she needed to see him, to touch him, as though only then could she persuade herself that he truly existed.

So when she died, the idea that he might live without her was unthinkable. His heart broke on the spot, so people used to say, and he simply gave up and died himself. As a child, this seemed to me not only plausible, but necessary. But now I can no longer resist the knowledge that people rarely die of broken hearts, except in the stories poets sing.

I have only the most fractured memories of the day they died: the rest I know from my siblings. My parents were buried over by the city walls, a little way down the hill from the palace. I remember the funeral because so many people were crying and tearing their clothes. I didn't understand why my uncle was weeping and holding Haem so tightly in his arms. My brothers had tried to explain to me that our parents were gone and would never come back, but I still thought they would walk into our rooms at any moment, holding each other and laughing. Once it became clear that no one thought this except me, not even Ani, I indulged in this belief only when I was alone in bed. I cried when my uncle snapped at me that they were dead forever, and then Ani would cry too, because she hated to see me cry and we both hated to hear what he said. So on my own, in my head, in the darkness, I would imagine their return: how we would hear two sets of sandals clipping the stones in the courtyard, how the splashing water would be interrupted when my father ran his hands through it and splashed it into his face to cool off. How they would block the light for an instant when they stood in my doorway and smiled at me. I knew exactly how it would be, but it never happened.

I still remember the smell from the temple grounds where offerings were made after the funeral: the pungent incense – pricking my eyes with its sweet, suffocating smoke – which the priests burned in their honour. There were gleaming white calves with fillets tied around their heads which were sacrificed to the shades. Their small clean hooves clattered against the cobbled ground as the blade cut through their undefended throats. I remember that too.

But so much is lost to me. I have always felt that if I had been even a little bit older, I would have known more. No one ever spoke about my mother after she died. Perhaps they believed that we would forget about her if no one mentioned her. In fact, the opposite has happened. She seems more real to me now than ever, as though I could walk through the door into her bedroom and see her sitting up with pillows all around her, patting them for me to spring up and kiss her, even though I would now be taller than her. I still wake up sometimes, thinking I can hear her shutting the door as quietly as she can, having checked I am safely asleep.

There is one more memory I have from that day, one I am certain of. One I cannot forget. My mother was carried across the palace on a stretcher by two men, one much taller than the other. They had placed a sheet over her, as a sign of respect. But as they hurried through the square, the disparity in their heights meant that my mother was tilting downwards. The cloth shifted as they shuffled along, and the one at the front could not see: he was facing the wrong way. So he didn't notice when the sheet uncovered part of her face.

Ani and I were standing in the colonnade, trying to understand what was happening: so many people – slaves, guards, our uncle, Sophon – had been rushing in and out of our mother's room. We knew something was wrong, but could not imagine something so terrible. And even when we saw the stretcher, we didn't think it could be her, because why would our mother be lying on a litter with her face covered? That wasn't how she behaved at all. Even when I saw what I now know must have been her face, I didn't realize it was our mother because it was not her: the person I saw was purple and puffy and broken, barely a person at all. Then our father walked out into the courtyard and caught sight of her. The sound he made – a wordless howl of anguish – is one I could still hear now, if I allowed myself to do so. He ran over and flung himself onto the stretcher, crashing with her down to the ground. Within moments, my uncle had intervened and my father was lifted away from her.

I have tried and tried to remember what happened next, but I cannot. Nonetheless, I am as certain as I can be that this moment was the last time I saw my father. And how am I supposed to compose my own history without including this part of my story? I am the daughter of a king and queen, the sister of two kings, but I will remain unmarried and will grow old alone. What Theban family would ally themselves with one as cursed as mine, unless real power and wealth was at stake?

Perhaps I should leave here one day, and settle in another city, where the curse is not common knowledge.

But I doubt if even Eteo would agree to his sister wandering Hellas like a vagabond. My parents were disgraced and died in so short a time. I was the same child from one year to the next (or the changes I underwent were minor: a little taller, my hair a little longer), yet I metamorphosed from princess to burden in the cessation of a heartbeat. No wonder the philosophers say that a river is always in flux, never staying the same. So a person cannot step into the same water twice.

10

The messenger looked at the queen and then back at the slave woman who had accompanied him through the palace. But the woman said nothing, her eyes fixed on the ground in front of her feet. He turned towards the queen once again.

'I worry I may not have made myself clear, highness,' he said. 'I was trying to convey to you that the king of Thebes is dead.'

'You made yourself perfectly clear,' she said. 'It's hard to imagine you could have been any clearer. Laius is dead. I understand. My question, which you perhaps misheard in your quest for clarity, was: what happens now?'

'What happens now?' The messenger was flummoxed. 'Well, the king's body will be brought back to the palace, I should think, and then—'

'I'm sorry.' Jocasta flashed him a gleaming smile. 'You seem to be struggling to comprehend what I'm saying. What I mean is, am I in charge now?'

'Er . . . yes, I would imagine so,' said the messenger, trying to dispel doubt from his voice. 'Yes.'

'Thank you,' she said. 'My husband had financial advisers, didn't he? And political ones? Where are they? They didn't all die too, I suppose?' Her voice was almost wistful, and the messenger looked more perplexed than ever.

'No, I don't think so,' he said. 'If they were the men who journeyed with their king, they are now accompanying him back to the city. He travels in state, of course.'

'It can't make the slightest difference to him now, whether he travels in state or not,' Jocasta said. 'You could tie him facedown to the back of a mule for all he'd know about it.'

'Madam?'

'Unless he isn't dead at all? Are you sure he's dead?'

'Madam, I regret to say that I am completely sure. He was stabbed by one of the Sphinx, and then . . .' His voice tailed off as he saw that Jocasta was only half-listening.

'The Sphinx?' she said. 'I can never quite remember who they are.'

'Why, they're . . .'

'No, don't tell me,' she said. 'I have enough to worry about without thinking about things that can't be changed and don't affect me. You will stay here, at the palace, I hope. Put him up in the guards' barracks,' she said to the slave woman. 'And when the late king's advisers arrive, which will be tomorrow? The next day? We'll have to see how eager they are to reach me, won't we? When they arrive, you will please show them to me in . . .' She turned to the servant again, 'Which of those rooms in the second courtyard would be the right size? I'm sorry, I don't know your name.'

'Phylla,' said the woman.

'Which room did the king use for his most important meetings? One of the big ones in the second courtyard?'

'Yes, madam. The blue room, on the east side.'

'You will show them to the blue room when they arrive,

please. Then you will fetch this gentleman and bring him to find me in the private courtyard. He will escort me to them. Understand that I will accept no excuses if you fail to do precisely as I have asked.' The girl nodded. Teresa could not punish her for obeying explicit instructions from her mistress. Jocasta turned back to the messenger.

'You will be my ally in that meeting, do you understand?'

'Yes, madam,' said the messenger, confusion still playing across his face.

'For every day that they are behind you,' Jocasta continued, 'I will give you a plain gold ring.'

The messenger blushed, greed suffusing his cheeks along with the colour. 'Thank you, madam.'

'Do you know why?' she said, and he shook his head. He was not confident about anything the queen was saying. 'Because the longer they take, the more it proves that you were trying to reach me as soon as you could. The more it proves that you were hurrying here to make me the ruler of this city, while they dawdled behind you, excusing their indifference to me behind their proper respect for the dead.'

The messenger thought for a moment, and decided it would be better for him, at least economically, if he agreed. 'Yes, madam,' he said.

Jocasta turned to walk away to her room. She seemed taller than usual, Phylla thought, when she lifted her gaze from the ground. Perhaps her strange haircut had added to her height, with spikes of hair sticking up at every angle.

'Excuse me,' the messenger called after her. 'Please

don't go. I didn't introduce myself, madam. And I have only told you half of the story.'

Jocasta slumped a little. This was the longest time she had spent speaking to a man other than her brother since – she couldn't remember. Oran? But she didn't like to think of him. She was growing tired and fretful, and wished she could scratch at her forearms with her nails, because they were beginning to itch intolerably. Nonetheless she turned back to face the stranger and raised her eyebrows.

'In your tongue, my name is Oedipus, ma'am,' he said, and she looked at him properly for the first time. He was young, this boy, with beautiful long dark hair and glinting brown eyes. His mouth was set in a serious line, but she couldn't shake the thought that he normally laughed a great deal. He was tall and slender, and though his clothes were torn, his skin was golden from the sun, rather than brown from the dust. He reminded her of ripe apricots.

'Have you worked for my husband for long?' she asked.

'I don't work for your husband at all,' he said. 'I am not from Thebes, madam. I come from another city.'

Phylla gave a small choke, and covered her face with loose fabric from the top of her tunic.

'Don't be ridiculous,' said Jocasta, brandishing her arms about her. 'There hasn't been an outbreak in over twenty years, for hundreds of stades in any direction. Not one. And anyone can see this man isn't sick. Look at him.'

Phylla did as she was asked, but she didn't remove the cloth from her mouth. 'Leave then,' Jocasta shouted. 'If you're so afraid. I will direct him to the barracks myself. Or perhaps I will invite him to stay in our guest quarters.' Phylla scurried away.

'Come and sit down, sir,' Jocasta said, gesturing to a bench. She sat beside him, and smoothed her hair with an anxious hand. She found herself suddenly wishing she hadn't cut it all off two days earlier. 'I'm sorry,' she said. 'I just assumed you were one of Laius's boys. You look like them.'

'No, I'm sorry,' Oedipus replied. 'I should have made myself clearer from the outset. I came across your husband and his men in the mountains. They were pegged back by the Sphinx – is that what you call them?'

'I think so,' she said. 'I've never really known very much about the land outside the city. Just enough not to believe that every other city in Hellas is afflicted by the Reckoning, except ours.' She jerked her head in the direction the maid had left. 'They think Thebes is special. Blessed. They don't understand that it is the opposite.'

'Have you lived here all your life?' Oedipus asked, gesturing around them.

'In Thebes? Yes. In the palace? No. I've been here for almost seventeen years. But I lived on the other side of the city before that. My father was a trader so I was brought up not to fear the Outlying.'

'So you've never been to the mountains? That's a shame. They're beautiful in the summer.'

'Are they?' It had never occurred to Jocasta that the mountains were beautiful at any time. As a child, she had thought of them as an impassable green wall behind the city. As an adult, she had seen them as her husband's territory. She had never thought of them as an actual place, with characteristics of their own.

'Where do you come from?' she asked.

'Corinth,' he said. She looked blank. 'A trading city on the other side of the mountains.'

'Is that right? What do you trade?'

'All sorts of things. Minerals, metals, oil, grain: whatever you need. We trade with everyone. We're well located, on the isthmus.'

She nodded, but he could see she didn't know what he was talking about. 'We're on the sea,' he explained. 'So everyone comes to us.'

'And you're a trader?' she asked.

'Not exactly.' He smiled at her. 'My father is an important man. He wanted me to stay in Corinth and learn the trade. But I wanted to see something of Hellas first. And the mountains are less dangerous at the start of the year, so they say, so I decided to try my luck. My parents know I can take care of myself.'

'And they are right, because here you are,' Jocasta said. It took a moment before she remembered that he had probably been about to tell her of her husband's death when they got sidetracked, talking about the mountains and distant trading posts. She wondered if he had just realized the same thing, for his golden confidence dimmed slightly, while he tried to find his next words.

'You found my husband and his men in the mountains?' she reminded him.

'Yes, they were in a bad way,' he said. 'They were pinned into a dead end. The mountain is full of them, you have to learn where they are. I don't know how they got themselves into such a position. His scouts should be hanged, if any of them survived.'

'You're not very forgiving,' Jocasta said.

'No.' He shrugged, unapologetic. 'They led your husband into a trap. They were either incompetent or treacherous. There is no excuse for either.'

'But you tried to help?'

'I think I did a bit better than that.' He smiled again, the sudden anger of a moment ago disappearing. 'The Sphinx are very much less terrifying than people make them out to be, in their stories. They aren't a mythical fighting force, they're just a gang of mountain men. They know the paths and secret routes through the peaks better than anyone alive. But they aren't an army; they have no discipline. If one of them is hurt, the others panic, or they get angry. Either way, it makes them weaker. People say they are numberless, but I doubt they are more than forty altogether. They seem to come at you from all sides, but that's just because they know shortcuts that are hidden from the ordinary traveller. Of course they do – they have been born and raised on the mountains, they are practically goats.'

'And how do you know the mountains so well?' Jocasta asked. 'I thought this was your first trip to Thebes.'

'I don't know the mountains all that well, but there are other mountains nearer Corinth which are not so different, and which are home to similar men. So I have the good sense to move carefully on unfamiliar terrain. And I don't travel with a huge retinue, making a racket and drawing their attention. Your husband – forgive me, madam – was practically begging to be attacked by brigands.' She waved his apology away. 'Besides,' he admitted, 'I had something more important than knowledge on my side. I had luck.'

'What do you mean?'

'I came up behind the Sphinx, completely by accident. Their attention was focused entirely on your king. No one was keeping watch behind them, because they were embroiled in a skirmish ahead. Your husband's men outnumbered them, even though they weren't well prepared for a fight. So the mountain men had their hands full, fighting. It was easy to pick a few of them off, one by one.'

'But people say the Sphinx can't be killed,' she said.

'People say all kinds of nonsense,' he replied. 'I told you, they're just men.'

'So if you killed the Sphinx, what happened to my husband?'

He coloured. 'That is harder to explain, madam.'

'Perhaps you might try,' she said.

'It was an accident,' he replied. 'Your husband was distracted by the carnage around him. He saw one man after another fall. And he was injured himself. He had taken a knife wound to the right shoulder. You can't imagine how that must feel. His whole arm would have gone numb.'

'You know a lot, for someone so young,' she said.

'My city is not as civilized as yours, Basileia.'

'Don't call me that,' she snapped. 'And my city is a great deal less civilized than it appears to you.'

'I'm sorry,' he said. 'But I'm afraid your husband was disorientated. He was slashing at anyone who came near him with a knife. The sweat was pouring into his eyes; I doubt he could see very much.'

'So what happened?' she asked again.

'I approached him to tell him that the threat was over, that many of the mountain men lay dead, and the rest had run away. He lashed out with his knife.' The boy raised his left hand and she saw a long cut down the leather guard he wore on his forearm, the bare skin beneath it flaming red. 'Lucky I move faster than your husband, or I'd be bleeding out in the mountains instead of talking to you now.'

'He tried to kill you.'

'Yes.'

'So you killed him.'

'Not intentionally,' Oedipus said. 'I shouted at him to stop, but he wasn't listening. He backed away from me to prepare for a second attack. And he lost his footing.'

'He fell?'

'Not very far, but he landed horribly. Like I said, he couldn't see. He broke his neck – it would have been very quick,' he finished.

'And so you came here to tell me that you are responsible for my husband's death?' Jocasta asked.

'In a manner of speaking,' he said. 'I saw his men collect his body and decide to bear him home. That's how I found out he was the king: I was watching them from the rocks above. If he'd stayed with the main party, he would still be alive, Basileia, I swear it.'

'I said not to call me that,' she said. 'Did you not think it was a risk? Coming here to a strange city to tell me you'd killed the king? What if I decided to have you executed?'

'From what I overheard, madam, your husband's men didn't seem to think you would be unduly saddened by his death. They seemed to think you could be removed from the palace quite easily.'

She nodded. She had never been popular with her husband's men. Of course they would want to replace her.

'And I suppose I took a chance. Your husband deserved to die, madam. He was foolish and vain. He should have been more careful and he should have hired better scouts, and treated the mountains with more respect. But I couldn't see that you had done anything wrong. I thought I would ride ahead of them and tell you what had happened. So you could prepare yourself.'

'That was kind,' she said. She reached over and touched his arm.

'And then, when I told you he was dead, you said I was your ally.'

'I thought you were one of his boys,' she said again.

'It doesn't matter,' he said. 'Just, when you said it, I decided it was true.'

'My hair doesn't normally look like this,' Jocasta said, wishing she had not hacked it off with a blunt blade two days earlier.

'I don't imagine it does,' he replied. 'It suits you, though.'

11

The flutes were playing a loud, clear song, regal and imperative. They had rehearsed for many days to prepare for the coronation. There was no longer any hope of ignoring it: I opened my door and almost stumbled over my sister, who had found a way to wear yellow which did not make her appear sallow. Her dress was paler than crocus, closer to the shade of ripening lemons. Only the sash was the crocus colour of my own dress, and I wondered how she had managed to change it. Her hair was woven into plaits which spiralled around her head, and she had rubbed perfumed oil on her limbs so they shone white, like an alabaster statue. She looked me up and down.

'That's a pretty dress,' she said. 'You look lovely, Isy. You'll catch plenty of eyes, especially if you stand up and stop slouching.' She noticed one of my uncle's guards walking through the courtyard behind her. 'Not that you would want to,' she added, her eyes following him. 'Your only desire is to be an ornament to your brothers and the royal house.' And as she spoke, she winked at me. My uncle would be too busy today to listen to tales from an eavesdropping guard.

I put my arm through hers, and we walked through into the second courtyard, which was full of our brothers' many advisers and associates, all scurrying around trying to look important as they went about the palace. There was an air of anxiety about these men each summer, when the kingship changed hands. Half of them worried they would lose whatever influence they had cultivated under Eteo when Polyn took over. The other half were hoping that was true, and that they might be able to grease their own way into a position of greater authority. It was this dynamic of constant unease which appealed to my uncle: if the king was permanent, Creon was sure the administrators would grow lazy and complacent.

We walked across to the gates on the far side of the square. The main courtyard was a clamour of noise and colour: every citizen of Thebes must have been there. The guards at the gates smiled and stood aside for us to pass. They held silver-tipped spears, having exchanged their usual weapons for ceremonial ones in honour of the occasion. A thick cloud of perfume surrounded us: it was being poured in offerings around the square. Thebes liked to honour all the gods on coronation day, so none would ever feel slighted and turn their immortal wrath against the city.

Ani and I were just in time. The doors to the throne room – a small, gilded corner of the public square, which was kept locked except for this day each year – had been opened. The room shone like a statue of Zeus himself, as the sun caught its chryselephantine adornment. My brothers, both sweating in their ceremonial robes – bright red and trimmed with so much golden embroidery that they were stiff, like wooden mannequins – were waiting for us. My uncle and Haem, similarly attired though with a little less pomp, were already seated to the right of the throne. Ani and I climbed the steps and took our seats on the opposite side of the altar which was placed directly before and below the throne. Finally, the flutes reached their high note, and were silenced. The ceremony could begin.

Muttering priests surrounded us: my uncle loved a religious ceremony. It was not enough to have a feast and a ceremonial handing-over of the crown. He wanted vows to Zeus and Apollo, followed by multiple sacrifices and offerings of wine. He enjoyed sitting in the sweltering heat hearing the prayers and nodding his solemn promises to guide the new king as he had guided the old one. Ani, I could see, was focusing most of her attention on Haem, who was studiously trying not to look at her. He must be hoping his father was unaware of their increasing closeness, though that seemed unlikely. My uncle might have been pious, but he wasn't blind.

I was only half-listening to the priests. We had done this ten times before: we knew when we had to bow down before the majesty of Zeus and when we could stretch ourselves back up. We could have completed this ceremony while half-asleep, which was fortunate, given the heat. I was grateful to be in a simple linen dress – its belt kept loose to allow a little air onto my damp skin – rather than the formal garb the men were wearing.

Finally, the droning ended, and the priest reached his right hand into the pocket of his white robes. He was nearly finished. The crowd looked on, bored now of the excessive religiosity. They wanted more music, they wanted the meat to start cooking and the wine to start flowing, not just for the gods but for them too. And most of all, they wanted the games to begin. Although the chariot-races, the sprint and the wrestling were sacred to the gods, there would be many men who wanted to place bets on the outcome, discreetly enough to avoid the attention of Creon and his priests. An abundance of property would change hands before the sun set this evening. Bottles of oil, terracotta figurines, weapons and jewellery: no one could be certain who would take treasures home tonight.

The priest removed his hand from his pocket and held it aloft, as an acolyte brought the calf – too docile for this noisy occasion, as though he had been drugged with the leaves the priests were always chewing – to the space in front of the throne room. Perhaps they had stunned it with a quick blow to the head before bringing it outside. They would deny it – sacrificial offerings were supposed to have their wits about them when they went to the gods – but religious men are not always honest. The priest took the calf tenderly, holding its head by the nascent horns. As he brought his hand down to its neck, the sunlight reflected off his gleaming silver blade. And then everything became impossibly loud, as though every word and shuffling foot-step were happening all at once, next to my ears.

Then my sister was holding me around the wrist, squeezing it tightly. Her nails jabbed into my arm and brought me out of the noise and back into my skin.

'We'll get you out of the sun in a moment, Isy. These endless prayers and offerings. It's too much, almost blasphemous,' she said.

I wanted to tell her that the heat wasn't what was making sweat pour down my back, nor the dizziness threatening to knock me to the ground. It was the knife, and all the blood. Somewhere in this huge gathering was the man who had stabbed me. I could feel his eyes on the priest, assessing the efficiency of his blade, and the elegance with which he drew it across the neck of the beast, whose huge eyes gave no sign of the spurting horror beneath them, though his legs kicked frantically at the ground. Out there in the crowd was a man who had looked at me in the same way as we looked at the dying calf. A sacrifice for a greater good.

That was why I was shivering in bright sun.

The ceremony was finally over. Polyn had sworn to protect Thebes for the duration of the year to come, and Creon had lifted the crown from Eteo's head and placed it on Polyn's. The crowd cheered wildly, more because this was the end of the formal ceremony than because my oldest brother was more favoured than the other. The mass of people poured out into the market square, which was unrecognizable today. Every stall had been folded down flat, and wheeled into tight-packed rows by the city walls. Fresh sand had been swept into a racetrack which was marked out with round white stones. There were wooden benches on every side of the course for the spectators quick enough to reach them. Palace guards stood at either end of a raised bier with individual wooden seats placed in a neat row upon it. This was where Creon, Ani and I would be sitting. On the other side of the square, workmen had erected a temporary palaestra, where the wrestling would take place later in the day.

The aristoi were already preparing themselves in the palaestra. They had stripped naked, and were covering themselves in oil and the red dust that keeps their skin from burning in the harsh sunlight. The sprint would be the first competition today, and Eteo was running as always. The crowd was humming with excitement. The priests were still attending the remains of the sacrifice inside the palace courtyard, and spectators were taking advantage of their absence to mutter their bets. By the time the eight competitors lined up at the starting rope, people were jostling one another for the best view of the finish line.

At the crucial moment, the two slaves who held the starting rope dropped it to the ground. The youths sprang over it, and pelted down the track for one complete circuit. The dust sprayed up so high it was impossible to tell which boy was which: all of them were dark-haired from the oil which they had slicked over their bodies before wiping their hands through their curls to keep their hair out of their eyes. All were red-skinned. Only when they cornered the furthest bend and began to sprint back towards us could I see it was Eteo ahead of the others, running with all his might. He took a long, loping stride which looked almost effortless. I saw how hard he was pumping his arms: he was determined to win. There was a boy on his heels, but my brother ran so easily, it must have crushed his rivals. The second boy was frantically trying to keep up, his arms and legs splaying in every direction, as though he were frightening the birds from the crops before the harvest.

The other boys clustered behind them, running as a pack. The one at the front of their group was a friend of Polyn's, I thought. He usually ran a faster race than this: he and Eteo had been competing in the sprint since they were both children. Perhaps he was holding something in reserve for the final straight, hoping Eteo and his rival would tire each other out and he could race past them and take the crown. Eteo had done exactly that to the boy last year, and he was surely hoping to take his revenge now. But he had misjudged the race and it would cost him the victory: Eteo was extending his lead, and showing no sign of slowing down, or even struggling to maintain his pace. The boy just behind him, to his left, looked like he was about to pull back. His face was almost as red as his dust-coated limbs.

But as they turned the last corner, the boy in second place suddenly tripped and fell forward, his arms tangling themselves in Eteo's legs for just long enough to knock my brother off balance. Eteo was too graceful an athlete to fall, but he lost momentum as he was forced to extend his arms to stay on his feet.

'I thought we'd have to wait for the chariot-race to see this sort of thing,' shouted one man, laughing. The chariot-eers often fell from their cars when their horses clattered into one another on the tight bend of the racetrack.

Eteo saw his chance was gone, as the loss of speed had allowed his rival to spurt past on his way to claim the victory. So confident was the boy of his win that he took an almost comical zigzag route to the finish line, laughing and raising cheers from the spectators. Meanwhile, Eteo stopped to offer his comrade a hand up. The crowd cheered this kindness almost as loudly as they cheered the winner. The royal prince would cross the finish line in last place, but his honour would be intact. My clever, kind brother.

The boy couldn't lift himself at first: Eteo's arm was too slippery with oil for him to get a good grip. Seeing him struggle, my brother reached out two hands and heaved the boy upright. But when the boy stood, his left leg buckled immediately. He grabbed at it, crying out in pain. Mingling with the orange sand beneath his feet and the red dust on his body was the unmistakeable crimson of blood, dripping from the boy's foot onto the sand beneath him. Eteo reached down and picked up a sharp iron spike, which must have been hidden beneath the surface of the sand. All the boys ran barefoot, so whoever placed it there knew he would injure one of them.

A gasp went up from the spectators, followed by a groan when my uncle declared that the race result would not stand. No one would receive the crown of olive leaves. The winner began to protest, but seeing the anger of the crowd as their bets were nulled, he sensibly decided to accept things without making more fuss. The slaves who had set up the track were summoned before my uncle, who ordered them to stand in a line, remove their shoes and walk across every finger-width of the course.

The limping boy was helped off the course by Eteo, and Creon signalled to the charioteers that they would compete as soon as the course had been checked. The atmosphere improved as the spectators realized their pleasure was merely postponed rather than cancelled. The charioteers checked their horses' hooves, and readied themselves to race, each one tying himself to his car with leather straps. But it was hard to concentrate on their preparations when the injured boy was trying to clean his wounded foot, and bind it closed. The gash was huge, right across the sole, so it would tear open again whenever he took a step. Eteo summoned one of his guards and sent him away: a short time later he returned with a stick which the boy could use as a crutch. But the bandages still reddened as the day wore on.

The crowd were so involved in their next series of bets that they had already lost interest in the injury and how it might have occurred. Had one of the boys laid a trap for his rivals? Was it an attempt to hurt Eteo? Everyone knew he was quick: he was likely to be at the front of the sprinting group. I tried to dismiss the thought of sabotage.

But what else could it have been? The slaves found four more sharpened iron spikes wedged into the sand at different points on the course. It was pure luck that none of the other boys had been injured. Or perhaps the boy who won the race had known which parts of the track to avoid. Perhaps they had all known.

12

Jocasta had never enjoyed being married to her husband more than at his funeral. She loved everything about it. She ordered a dress to be made in a dark reddish-purple – the most expensive dye she could have chosen – knowing that if anyone suggested it showed insufficient respect for the dead, she could simply remind them that she married Laius wearing crimson. There was no more fitting tribute than wearing a more flattering shade of the same colour at his funeral. She had her hair neatened into a simple style which made her look younger. She had ribbons plaited into it, so it appeared more ornate for the funeral. And – once the slaves had polished it to its former shine – she placed her wedding diadem on top, lest anyone forget who she was.

The prettiness of her dress and hair were only a small part of her delight, however. She radiated pleasure at having seen off her husband's friends and their attempt to depose her. Not realizing that Oedipus had ridden ahead and told her everything, the men made no hurry in returning to Thebes. They were three full days behind Oedipus and even – this was their crucial mistake – one day behind Laius's guards. The commander of the guard was happy to swear loyalty to Jocasta, as were his men. She bribed them all with nuggets of silver – mined in the Outlying many years ago – which she had found in one of the store-rooms next to the treasury, opposite the formal reception rooms in the second courtyard. Perhaps she had known before that it was there, and had simply forgotten. She couldn't now remember. So much from the past seventeen years had lost its separateness, as though it had been writ-ten on papyrus which had suddenly rolled itself back up so individual parts of the text were lost within the whole. But the presence of Oedipus, so determined to help her fight off the threats he had overheard in the mountains, focused her attention on matters of importance.

So – in the three days between Oedipus's arrival and the return of her husband's body – she hunted around in the state rooms of the royal courtyard, most of which she had never previously entered. She didn't wait for Teresa to tell her what to do, and she didn't wait for word to come from the Oracle. For the first time in as long as she could remember, she gave very little thought to what the Oracle advised at all. After all, it hadn't forewarned her about Laius dying, or Oedipus arriving. Perhaps it was less powerful than she had thought.

In Laius's bedroom, she found a small wooden box filled with keys, all in their own divided spaces. These turned out to be everything she needed to open the treas-ury and a host of other rooms which had been hitherto forbidden to her. Had she really lived in such a small part of the palace for so long, trotting between her bedroom and the shrine and occasionally the kitchens? It seemed ludicrous to her that the keys had been here all along – presumably Laius had always left them behind – and she had never gone looking for them. But then, what would

she have done with them before the king died? Teresa
would never have let her walk into Laius's rooms while
he was alive. But the announcement of the king's death
(so welcome to his wife) had devastated his housekeeper.
Teresa withdrew to her quarters for two days when Phylla
gave her the news. Had she known that the messenger had
come from abroad, and was now staying with the queen
under Hellene rules of guest-friendship, Teresa might have
postponed her grieving. It was one thing to offer food and
a warm bed to a stranger for a few nights, as the gods
demanded, but it was another thing to allow him to stay in
the family courtyard, in a room which had only ever been
occupied by the queen's brother for a few days each year.
But Phylla never thought to mention what she perceived
as these less important details, and by the time Teresa re-
appeared in the palace, her previously unassailable position
was too damaged to be repaired. The stranger had wormed
his way into the queen's trust.

Jocasta smiled to herself as her husband's corpse –
tightly wrapped in white linen as was respectful – was
carried out through the three courtyards of the palace, in
a long, slow procession. As she walked at the head of the
procession – head bowed appropriately, crown glinting in
the dawn light – she remembered the insufferable smug-
ness of his closest friends and advisers, each one arriving
back in Thebes determined that he was the man to replace
Laius as king. Perhaps if they had all been less ambitious,
and had thrashed out a compromise before they returned,
they would have been more dangerous. But much as they
disliked the queen, none of them wanted to see his rivals

promoted. And they didn't have the discipline to set aside personal gain for the good of their factions.

She had welcomed them coolly when they arrived, then instructed Laius's guards to carry his body into the palace where it would lie in state for one day, not from a lack of respect but because the delay in bringing him back to the city meant that he now needed to be buried as soon as possible. She had immediately assumed a position of reli- gious authority: who was responsible for the delay, if not these men who had made such slow progress to the city? The gods would not forgive Thebes if the king lay un- buried for days on end. He must go beneath the earth, and offerings must be poured. While they dallied along the lower reaches of the mountains, her husband's shade was stranded on the banks of the River Lethe, unable to pay Charon to carry him across. The men shuffled awkwardly, eyes fixed anywhere but on their queen. They could make no defence against the charge of religious impropriety.

And then Jocasta told them to leave. Surrounded by the armed guard, who had appeared in full ceremonial dress to pay their respects to her late husband, the queen was not the woman that they had spoken of so scornfully over her husband's still-warm body. She thought she might interview one or two of them in a few days, and see if they could be civil. She might need advisers herself, after all.

Throughout all this, the boy Oedipus remained with her. She gave him, as she had promised, three small gold rings for his arrival three days before her husband's men. But although Oedipus had his reward, he seemed in no

hurry to leave. In fact, he appeared to relish his new surroundings. His eyes gleamed when Jocasta found the keys
to her husband's treasury, filled with serried ranks of gold
and silver, bronze and jewels, tapestries and perfumed
oils. Oedipus offered to help her make sense of what she
owned and what she needed. He only left her to go to the
market outside, from which he returned a short while
later, carrying a fine leather string, which had been dyed
a vivid magenta. He fed it through the treasury keys – one
for the door to the main room, one for the door to the
treasury itself – tied it into a knot, then stood behind her
to place it carefully over her shorn head.

'So no one can take them off you,' he explained, his
warm breath raising the hairs on her neck as he sounded
the first word. Jocasta wondered when anyone had last
thought about what she wanted, or worried about her
safety.

Teresa had always been quick to act as an intermediary
for her, with the Oracle. But now that Jocasta thought
about it, the Oracle had rarely made her feel better about
anything. That was not what it was for, of course. It spoke
the truth and saw the future. But she couldn't shake the
sense that it had been better at seeing her future when it
was unchanging – as it had been for so many years – than
recently. Her mind returned to its suspicions: if the Oracle
was all-knowing, it should really have predicted her dramatic change in circumstances. And of course she knew
that oracles were riddlers, only to be understood by those
versed in their opacity, like the priests, or Teresa. But it
had said nothing about the king's death, not even when

Jocasta thought back to its recent utterances with the clarity of hindsight. She could scarcely remember why she had wanted the shrine to be built. Or had it been Teresa's idea?

It was built soon after the death of her baby; that she could remember. Her poor dead son was still now beautiful in her imagination. She had watched him grow up in her mind: heard his first words, seen his first tumbling steps. She had taught him to count and draw, she had watched him go to his tutor in the early mornings and come home each afternoon. It had become harder to imagine his voice cracking into adulthood, as it surely would have done last year. But she had kept him alive nonetheless in this dual existence – a dead baby she had never set eyes on, a living son she saw every day.

Teresa had realized that Jocasta was spending a great deal of time alone, with her child. She had proposed the shrine as what? An alternative to a grave marker? Jocasta had asked Teresa, in the beginning, where her child was buried, but Teresa refused to give her an answer. She lost patience with the question: babies were exposed or buried all the time, living and dead. Of course, it was more usually girls than boys who were robbed of their new lives, but that hardly mattered. Other women accepted it, and so should Jocasta. It was not regal, or reasonable, to make such an extravagant fuss about something which could not be helped or changed. Eventually, Jocasta's howls and screams had forced the truth from her: the child had never been buried. It had simply been disposed of, along with the rest of the refuse which was taken from the palace each day. There was no grave to visit. So her shrine – a miniature copy of the temple where the Oracle dwelt – was, perhaps, a peace-offering. Something Teresa proposed to give Jocasta somewhere to focus her prayers and attention.

And it had helped, at first. Designing it and building it took time, and that gave Jocasta something to think about. She could watch it grow larger, more finished with each day. Then, once it was built, she had to learn which offerings she should make, to which gods, in what order. If she could just get everything exactly right, Jocasta had thought, things might improve. Perhaps Teresa would suddenly confess to a mistake: the baby wasn't dead at all, but was being raised with a family nearby. A kind, loving family who would nurture her son until he arrived one day in the palace to reclaim his birthright. She would only find out the truth if she did everything exactly as the gods required.

But the day never came, no matter how hard she prayed, and no matter how carefully she made her offerings. She was never good enough to receive the truth she wanted to hear. Sometimes, Teresa would tell her that the Archer god was looking on her favourably, and that this was an appropriate time to embark on a new project (Teresa was always careful not to say 'pregnancy'). Jocasta refused even the suggestion with such screams and horror that no one tried to force her. In the months and years that followed her nightmare, she often felt close to losing her mind, but she retained enough of it to know she could not go through that whole horrifying process again. She could not.

Besides, she didn't want some other child, she wanted her child, the one she had already given birth to. She couldn't simply replace him with another baby. What would be the point? She would know from the start that it was an impostor. So instead of believing that the god – answering her prayers at the shrine with his cryptic messages from the Oracle – was guiding her towards something better, she felt that she was being punished and re-punished for wrongs she had never committed. Why did her child not arrive one day at the palace, having been alive all along? There were only two explanations, one of which she couldn't countenance. Which meant that the only possible reason was that she was somehow being found wanting by the same Oracle which had persuaded her husband that a son would kill him, and therefore couldn't be allowed to live. Was the Oracle punishing her? And if so, what for? But, of course, ignorance was no excuse. That was not how the Oracle judged things. She knew that, because (whatever its reasons) it had taken her child from her, without her ever being able to touch him.

'Thank you,' she said to Oedipus, as she placed the keys beneath her clothes. 'That's perfect.'

'Don't take it off,' he said. 'Even at night.'

She felt the metal burn against her skin as he spoke. 'I won't,' she said. 'Will you still be here when I get back from the funeral?' The crowds were gathering before the palace, and she knew she needed to leave.

'Of course,' he smiled. 'I'd come with you, if I didn't think it would cause a scandal.'

Jocasta felt a twinge of delight. 'You should come,' she said. 'The more mourners attend the dead king, the greater the respect we are showing him. No one could argue. And besides, I want you to.'

Oedipus shrugged, stood up, and offered her his arm. 'Madam,' he said. 'It would be my privilege.'

*

If any of Laius's friends thought it odd that his widow was now accompanied by a young man who none of them had ever seen before, they didn't dare ask any questions. Laius's guards, now Jocasta's guards, stood behind her, armed and quiet. Jocasta saw eyebrows rise, as one man looked at another, all asking the same unspoken question and receiving the same wordless reply. No one knew who he was or where he had come from. He didn't look quite like a Theban: his skin was paler, his build narrower, and his hair fairer than the majority of their citizens. Oedipus walked alongside her until they reached the burial mound, a short distance outside the city. He helped her over the uneven ground, where the path had been blistered by tree roots. And he stepped back, perfectly proper, when the moment of interment came. Jocasta stood for a moment with her head bowed, then scattered earth over the late king. The city seemed to let out a collective sigh: the king was properly buried. The gods would be satisfied that Thebes had conducted itself well.

And then she led the funeral procession back to the city gates. She continued to the marketplace outside the palace, which today had suspended business, in a gesture of mourning. Many Thebans had gathered there, preferring not to go outside the city walls, even for a funeral. Jocasta walked to the palace gates, then turned to face the crowd.

'Thebans,' she shouted. 'My husband is dead and I am now your queen.' A roar went up from the people. Jocasta could not quite judge if it was positive or negative: were they endorsing her position or calling it into question? 'I want to thank you for the support you have shown me in this difficult time,' she continued. 'My husband's funeral games will be held in the main courtyard in one hour. You are all invited to attend.' There was another shout, this one louder and more certain than the first. Funeral games were a worthy mark of respect.

Jocasta turned to Oedipus, who escorted her through the gates. 'That was well done,' he murmured.

'Thank you,' she replied. 'You have to give the people something, that's what Laius used to say whenever he held a party.'

'He had to be right about something,' said Oedipus.

Jocasta squeezed his arm. 'Shh,' she said. 'I can't be seen laughing. Not today.'

'Forgive me,' he said. 'Let me tell your housekeeper you've just invited three hundred people into the palace.'

Jocasta looked ahead of them, and shook her head. 'It's already done.' She pointed to a boy who was scuttling towards the kitchens as fast as his short, dirty legs would go. 'He's the kitchen boy and her little spy,' she said. 'She'll hate to open the wine jars again, but she won't complain. She can't. It's for the late king, after all. And Teresa was,' Jocasta paused as she searched for the right word, 'devoted to him.'

As the evening sky gave up its last trace of red, Jocasta thought that the games had been a great success: most people were drifting away now the wine had run low, and they were leaving without any doubt that she was now the regent of this city. She had felt Oedipus's eyes upon her as she spoke to one person after another. She had never spoken so many words in a single day. But, for the first time she could remember, she was not afraid of anything. She simply did what she needed to do: shook hands, squeezed elbows, patted shoulders, accepted condolences. Most people, it transpired, thought she had cut her hair in a moment of profound grief for her late husband. They were moved by her sacrifice, and she saw it made her queenly in their eyes.

After the games had finished, and the shadows were lengthening across the courtyard, she looked over the square to see her brother approaching – tall, with his dark hair receding slightly, though he was not yet old – accompanied by a small, pretty girl who reminded her of a fearful mouse. Her small hands clutched at a little leather purse, like a tiny creature's paws might curl round a nut. This must be the girl he had mentioned; Jocasta searched her memory for the name – Euly? Euny? She walked towards her brother, turning a smile on the girl.

'Creon,' she said. 'Thank you for coming. And how nice to meet you,' she added. The mouse-like girl must have tried to say something, but all Jocasta heard was a squeak.

'This is Eurydice,' said Creon, with an expression that Jocasta could not place for a moment, before realizing it was shyness.

So she took the arm of her brother's friend, and said, 'Tell me all about yourself. Let's go and find you some wine: I know exactly which servant has the best grapes, and you deserve something special. If my brother likes you, you must be wonderful.'

She only half-heard the girl demur and then go on to talk about how she and Creon had first met when he had admired the stole she was embroidering as she sat with friends in the afternoon sun – the stole she was wearing this very day – and asked how she could make such tiny, neat stitches. As she nodded and smiled at the girl's prattling, Jocasta continued to bestow a charm she had forgotten she ever possessed on every courtier of her husband's she met. Yet all the while, she found herself looking around for Oedipus, always making sure he hadn't left.

As the palace slaves encouraged the last guests out of the gate, she felt his eyes upon her. He was leaning against the courtyard wall, almost invisible in the darkening twilight. She turned towards him and he peeled himself away from the stone, straightening up and smiling at her.

'You did well,' he said. 'Wonderfully well.'

She couldn't imagine why she was so pleased to have his approval. She had not wanted anyone's approval but the Oracle's in as long as she could remember. 'Thank you,' she said. 'Maybe it will all be alright now.'

'It'll be much better than that,' he said. 'It'll be perfect. Do you think they realized you were considering them for a position?' He jerked his head at the last few stragglers, a group of men who had worked for her husband.

'Was I?' she asked.

'Of course. You've placated everyone for now. But you don't want them plotting against you in the future, do you? You've decided you'll have to marry one of them. He'll owe his position to you, so he'll be impossibly grateful and will likely shower you with all kinds of gifts.'

'I don't need gifts,' she snapped. 'I have the keys to the city treasury around my neck. Now my late husband isn't around to spend it all on wine and horses and foolish hunting trips, I'm hardly short of resources.'

'It would still be better to ally yourself with someone, though, don't you think? Otherwise they will all keep vying with one another for your attention. It's inevitable. And it's bound to cause problems sooner or later.'

Jocasta felt her shoulders droop at his words. She wanted to tell him he was wrong, but she knew he wasn't. The men were all very loyal and sympathetic to her today, but they hadn't intended to be. They had simply been outmanoeuvred by her. By her and by Oedipus, and his quick journey from the mountains. Once the dust had settled over her husband's grave, they would soon begin plotting again. But she had already spent seventeen years married to a man she didn't love, who did not love her. Surely she could spend a little while without the exhausting burden of a husband?

'I should issue a notice that I don't intend to remarry,' she said. She wondered how long she could get away with. 'For at least a year?'

'Good idea,' said Oedipus. 'That will give them something to aim for.'

'You aren't at all sympathetic,' she complained. 'You can see I don't want to marry another old man and it's not very kind of you to laugh about it.'

'But I can afford to laugh,' he said. 'Because I know you aren't really going to marry any of them.'

'You just said—'

'That you should remarry. Yes.'

'Well, there you are then.'

'I didn't say you should marry one of them.'

'You said they'd fight if I didn't. They'll destabilize the city.'

'They'd back off if they saw that none of them had a chance.'

'And how do I achieve that?'

'By marrying me,' he replied.

'That's the most ridiculous thing I've ever heard. How old are you?'

'Old enough. Come on, Basileia. I'm much more handsome than anyone else you know.' He preened at her and she laughed, in spite of her annoyance.

'What would your parents think? You came here to help your father's business, didn't you?'

'What better help than becoming a king? Everyone wants to do business with the father of a king.'

She heard the unconscious echo of her father's reasoning for marrying her off, all those years ago.

'Your mother will be expecting you home,' she said, trying to inject a tone of finality into her voice.

'I'll go back and tell her myself,' he said. 'The mountains are safer now, you know. A brave traveller killed a few of the Sphinx. On my way back through, I'll cull the rest.'

'You want to leave me?' she asked.

'Temporarily,' he answered. 'I'll be gone for half a month. Fourteen days. That's not long at all. And when I come back, I will have my parents' blessing, and my name will be sung from every corner of your city, because I will be the man who made the mountains safe again.'

'The same mountains which took their previous king from them,' she said. She had to admit, it would be easy to persuade ordinary Theban traders that Oedipus would be the perfect king. 'When did you start thinking about this?'

'About what?' he said, his face shining with false innocence.

'When did you start dreaming up this plan?'

He reached over and kissed her on the cheek. She knew she would feel the heat of his mouth for the next fourteen days.

'It hardly matters, does it? I've thought of it, and it's so brilliant even you can't find fault with it, and you are an extremely clever woman, though hardly anyone but me has realized it,' he said. 'I'll see you in half a month, Anassa.' And with that, he sauntered off into the city, as though he had all the time in the world.

13

The races had finished, and we had all moved across the square to the palaestra, built by the palace slaves in recent days. It was not a formal structure, just a neat sand square with sides as long as the track was wide, enclosed by a simple wooden colonnade for the spectators to watch from the shade. There was a small area at the back of the ground for the wrestlers to change their clothes and rub white chalk onto their hands and feet, in readiness for the bouts. My brother Polyn was an excellent wrestler: he possessed the short, stocky build that made him virtually impossible to knock off balance. And he was wily too, which made him all but unbeatable (although Ani once asked him if his run of victories might have any connection to the fact that most of the aristoi would not wish to dishonour the past and future king by knocking him on his back. He didn't speak to her for days).

An old man had just drawn a wide-toothed rake through the sand in neat lines, the semicircles where he turned back on himself still visible at the edges of the arena, so we knew the boys could fight safely. Although the raking had occurred while we were all over by the racetrack, so I didn't know whether sharp objects had been left in the sand but had now been removed, or whether it had only been the running track that was sabotaged. I whispered this to Ani as we took our places in the stands, but she shrugged as though it didn't matter.

I wished that Sophon were present: he no longer attended the coronations. He said the first five had delighted him sufficiently for one lifetime. Ceremonies and public festivals didn't interest him. He preferred to stay in his study, protected from the brightest glare of the sun, reading his most recently acquired manuscripts. Yesterday, he received two new treatises on farming and the proper way to maintain olive groves. He has never owned an olive grove, but he said he enjoys imagining how he would tend to the trees he doesn't have.

'Which one will you read first?' I asked him that morning.

'Which one do you think, Isy?' Sophon replied. He had always done that: answered a question with another one. He says it makes me measure my thinking. I say it makes every conversation take twice as long as it needs to, but I don't mind very much.

'I think you should read this one,' I told him, holding up one of the papyri. 'It seems to be full of advice on how to keep your barn in good repair.'

His rheumy eyes brightened at the thought, though he has never owned a barn either.

'Very good advice, Isy. We would all do well to think about such things. You may read it as soon as I have finished with it.'

'Thank you,' I said. 'I'd rather read about fishing, though.'

'Fishing?' He leaned forward to make sure he had

heard me correctly. 'You want to go down to the lake and fish?'

My siblings and I used to do this when we were small: my father would take us. He loved Lake Hylica. He had grown up by the sea in Corinth, and it was the one thing he missed in Thebes, more than a hundred stades from the water. I barely remember going there with him, only flashes of silver scales and slippery white bellies, leaping and gasping on a rock by the side of the water. After he died, my siblings and I would go together each year in the first warm days of the spring. Creon never allowed us to go in the summer: he said it was not safe then, because of the Reckoning.

'I haven't been to the water since before,' I said. Sophon knew before what. First I had been injured, then I had been healing, then I had been forbidden to leave the palace, and then the ceremonial days had begun. I was desperate to get away from the city for a day, to leave behind the sand and dust and the harsh sun. I needed to walk through the grass and watch the grasshoppers leaping across my path. I wanted to see the turquoise-tipped kingfishers which nested by the water, and the frogs which would leap out of the water onto the shore, ten at a time, if you arrived at the right moment. The trees by the lake offered a broken shade even in the hottest part of the day. Most of all, I wanted to feel water on my skin.

'I think you prefer swimming like a fish to catching them.' Sophon could hear my thoughts.

'The day after the coronation,' I said. 'I'll go then. Eteo will be free to come with me once the ceremony is completed.'

'Yes,' Sophon agreed. 'I would guess that the day after he ceases to be the king is the longest day of your brother's year.'

The coronation falls almost two full moons after midsummer, but I didn't bother correcting him.

Even though Sophon would doubtless have responded to my questions about the metal traps concealed on the running track with more questions of his own, I would have preferred that to Ani's indifference. She seemed not to have realized how badly Eteo might have been hurt, and how likely it was that he had been the intended target. Only my uncle, ordering the slaves to examine the sand themselves, shared my concern. Ani would have felt differently if it had been Haem who almost had his foot sliced open, I thought. But since our cousin was a wrestler, like Polyn, she showed almost no interest in the foot-races.

Wrestling bouts were enormously popular in Thebes. Sixteen boys would fight one another in the first round, the pairs chosen by lot. The eight winners would go on to fight one another, again chosen by lot. This would continue until there was one winner, who could wear the olive-wreath crown for the day, and the title of victor for the whole year. Polyn had a pile of these crowns – the leaves dried and curled so you could barely tell which plant they came from – stacked on top of one another in his quarters. But he would always fight for another.

The referee (one of the older palace guards, who had probably trained every boy in the competition at some point) produced an earthenware jar, into which each boy dropped a small wooden block which he had previously engraved with a rough symbol or picture. The referee shook the jar once all sixteen blocks were inside it, smiling as the spectators cheered the rhythmic sound. He reached into the mouth and pulled out the first two blocks.

Like the runners before them, the boys had already covered themselves in oil and red dust, and now they took their places in the centre of the palaestra. They stood a few feet apart: wrestlers cannot be close enough to touch one another before they begin. The referee reminded them of the rules – no gouging, no kicking, no biting – before announcing the start of the bout. The boys grappled with one another but it took no time at all before the taller of the two had been tripped onto his back three times: an automatic defeat.

Polyn's bout was next, but he did not need to go as far as knocking over his opponent three times. He pushed the boy off balance then took his legs out from beneath him. Once the boy lay winded on the ground, Polyn leapt onto his back and grabbed him round the throat. The boy tapped the ground twice in quick succession: he conceded, and my brother had his three points.

I tried to stifle a yawn. It was hot and the day had already been long. But the pairings were well matched: all but the first two took time to play out. Gamblers were watching intently, trying to assess which boys were likely to be a safe bet in the next round. There was a tempting smell of onions coming from the other side of the market-place: someone had begun frying herb pastries by the running track. I turned to see if the stall-holder had a tray he would be bringing over to the spectators soon, but a sudden shout drew my attention back to the palaestra. The first quarter-final was being contested, and the boy who had just been declared the winner had done so by grabbing the wrist of his fellow combatant and forcing back his fingers, until he cried out in pain. There was a lot of hissing from the audience, who believed this to be cheating. The referee shrugged and allowed it. But the boy facing us was nursing his hand in pain: one of the fingers was sticking up at a horrible angle, clearly snapped. As his taller opponent advanced on him, the boy backed off and conceded defeat.

There was something about the naked fear in the boy's eyes, and the way the taller boy moved, which made me want to join in with the booing of the crowd. But the victor swaggered off the sand, to be punched affectionately on the arm by my brother Polyn. They were friends then, he and the cheat. My brother won his quarter-final without such tactics, and began preparing for his next opponent: re-chalking his hands and feet so he wouldn't lose his grip. The pastries smelled so good, I could feel my stomach growling. My sister elbowed me when I turned to look again at the food-seller. We were supposed to be paying attention to the games, no matter how long they went on for, or how much of a foregone conclusion they seemed to be.

Polyn and his tall friend were the finalists, and the audience cheered enthusiastically. Many of the men watching would have bet on my brother as the winner: the real surprise was that they could find anyone to wager on a different outcome. But the taller boy was talented, and perhaps he would put up a more vigorous contest than

Polyn's earlier opponents. I leaned down to ask my sister how much longer they would be.

'It's all about your stomach, Isy. Why didn't you eat this morning? You know how long these days are,' she snapped. She was right. I did know that the coronation days were long. I'd just forgotten in all the noise and fuss.

Polyn was now facing us, and his friend reached forward to begin the final bout. They wrangled for a few moments before Polyn made a grab at his opponent's leg, trying to draw him off balance. But his rival was not going to fall for anything so obvious. He skipped back out of Polyn's reach and wrenched Polyn's outstretched arm as he went. It was just enough to pull my brother forward onto his knees. But he was up again in an instant: no danger of hitting the sand with his back, and losing a crucial point. They approached each other again, and this time my brother needed to defend himself against an attack at his ankles. If you could take out an ankle, the wrestler almost always hit the ground square on. It was the easiest way to win a point. But Polyn transferred his weight to the other leg, bent forward, and head-butted the boy back. The crowd cheered.

The taller boy was losing patience now, and he circled Polyn, looking for another opportunity. He hadn't noticed how far from the centre of the ground they now were, so when Polyn ran at him and shoved him with all his might, the boy stepped back in surprise. This was a foolish tactic that would take my brother off balance and leave him vulnerable to an easy attack. The boy was already reaching forward to grab Polyn's foot and pull him over. But the referee stepped in and declared my brother the winner. The boy looked down in horror to see that his back foot had strayed outside the fighting square. It was an instant defeat.

Polyn raised his arms in victory, and his friend looked on with a weary amusement. He was the better fighter, but my brother was more cunning. Only when he turned to watch Polyn receive his olive-leaf crown did we finally see his face: the whole bout had been about showing off the king to his people, so it was always Polyn who held our attention and the prime place in the square.

'Good match,' said my brother, grabbing his rival by the arm and raising it for the applause of the crowd. Polyn was a far more gracious winner than he was loser. The tall boy nodded and smiled and took the applause of the crowd, his eyes finally taking in the spectators, where previously he had been focused only on his opponent. For the briefest moment – no longer than it takes to blink – his eyes met mine, before he turned to receive plaudits from the other side of the square.

It was all the time I needed. The man standing on the sand, next to my brother – his friend and competitor – was someone I would have recognized anywhere, as soon as I saw his eyes. I had seen them before, once in the courtyard of the palace, and many more times in my mind when I woke up with my heart racing, knowing I was in danger but unable to do anything to keep myself safe.

My brother's friend was the man who had embedded a knife in my side.

14

If there was one thing Jocasta knew how to do better than anyone, it was endure days of waiting. When Oedipus left, she found herself wishing he would return almost immediately. How clever of him, she thought, to have insinuated himself into her life so completely that after only a few days of knowing him, she missed him. And missed him in a dense physical way, as though she were nursing a profound and worsening injury.

He had been gone for little more than a day when she began to feel a faint, familiar echo of the panic which had so often overwhelmed her in the years after her child died. Her mind jumped from one unpalatable thought to another: what if he never came back? What if he was killed coming through the mountains? He had to travel through them twice, going to Corinth and coming back again. What were the chances that a man could travel through the mountains three times in less than a month, and not be killed? She couldn't begin to imagine the likelihood. Thoughts flitted around her mind like trapped birds. What if he had been lying to her? Perhaps he had no intention of coming back. Perhaps it had all been a strange, cruel joke. She wanted to believe him, but how could she, now he wasn't standing in front of her, allowing her to judge his intentions from his frank, open expression? What kind of person arrived in a city for the first time and told the queen that she would marry him? He was probably mad, she now saw. Though he hadn't seemed mad, when she was with him. He had seemed all sorts of things: impulsive, passionate, impetuous, quick-tempered, but not mad. Still, she reasoned that he must be mad: how else could she explain his behaviour? When she looked at things like this, it would almost be a blessing if he didn't return. A lucky escape, as her mother would once have said.

By the fourth day, Jocasta was beginning to make pacts with the gods. If she could make the perfect sacrifice of a pair of dappled kid goats, Oedipus would return. Then she reasoned that a paltry two goats was insufficient tribute to Apollo. So she painted the altars with the blood of white bull-calves, but still it was not enough.

On the tenth day, she calculated that he could have returned to his city and arrived back in Thebes easily by now. He had simply said half a month to allow himself the extra time at home. But he must have known she would be worrying: how could he be so cruel as to idle away time in the city where he had spent his whole life, when he knew she was here alone, waiting for him?

By the twelfth day, she knew he was dead. The journey might not have been possible in ten days, but it was more than possible in twelve. The only reason for his continuing absence must be his death. It was easier to imagine him dead than cruel. Sorrow descended and she wrapped it around herself.

On the fourteenth day, Oedipus returned exactly as he had promised. But even he – who travelled so quickly through dangerous territories, as if he were strolling along to the marketplace – couldn't keep up with the rumours which raced ahead of him: a man, this stranger, had killed the Sphinx. By the time he reached the palace gates, a small band of people clustered around him. Some of them were travellers he had picked up on the other side of the mountains. He had encouraged them to accompany him through the risky terrain, and had dazzled them with his strategy for dealing with the Sphinx, which amounted to little more (so he explained to Jocasta when they were finally alone) than moving through the mountains in total silence – without pack animals or anything which slowed them down or made any noise – and always being armed and ready to fight assailants who might appear from any direction, particularly from above. The Sphinx may have been fearsome once, but they had become – in Oedipus's opinion – lazy. Too many people made it easy for them by travelling in large groups, which left stragglers and scouts alone to be preyed upon. They announced their presence with noisy conversations or clattering hooves. Oedipus made none of those mistakes. When faced with a group who were determined not just to survive them but to attack them, the Sphinx were easily outclassed. They had already lost men on Oedipus's first trip through the mountains. And it wasn't long before he had masterminded a successful attack on the rest. Giddy with excitement and thrilled by the bloodlust, the travellers were soon telling everyone they found on the road to Thebes. They had killed the Sphinx, and it had all been the strategy of this one man, of Oedipus.

Even Jocasta, cut off from most city gossip in the palace, heard the news that the Sphinx were gone and their killer was coming to Thebes to be rewarded for his work. She knew it must be Oedipus, but she refused to believe it until she saw him. Unable to wait any longer, she walked out into the main square to receive him. When he entered through the palace gates, his clothes stained with the blood of the mountain men for a second time, she felt her breath become quick and shallow. If only all these people weren't here.

'Welcome to my city, sir,' she said, and the travellers and Thebans he had gathered along the way began to beat their hollowed hands together in applause. 'I hear we have to thank you for your remarkable bravery and cunning.'

'You don't have to thank me, your majesty.' He bowed low, smiling, enjoying the audience and the performance they allowed him to put on. 'It was the least I could do to impress the city of Thebes, as I knew I must.'

'Why would you need to impress our city?' asked Jocasta, above enthusiastic cheers from his supporters. These were not Laius's wealthy friends, Thebes's elite. They were ordinary men and women who had heard of the traveller's exploits, and come along to see what all the fuss was about. They didn't know the rules of palace etiquette, it seemed, so they cheered whenever they felt like it, rather than waiting to be invited. Oedipus's eyes glittered as they met hers. No one had ever enjoyed himself so much as he did in that moment. He paused until the noise had died down, determined he would be heard by everyone when he spoke. He had, she realized, no doubt that she would agree to anything he proposed.

'Because I intend to ask their Basileia for her hand in marriage,' he said.

Jocasta looked at him, far too young but handsome and – so far – a man of his word. She thought of the time she had spent in the palace alone, and she felt the treasury key nestled beneath her collarbones on the cord he had bought for her.

'She says yes,' she said, turning and walking back into the royal courtyard leaving Oedipus, a vision of confidence, to chase after her.

The news spread through Thebes faster than the Reckoning once had. People were asked to repeat it, because it didn't seem possible. The queen, widowed less than a month ago, was to remarry? A foreigner? He looked how old? It took very little time before the self-appointed Elders of the city – mostly the same men who had travelled back from the mountains with Laius's body, expecting to depose the queen with little difficulty – arrived at the palace in a sweaty, disconcerted mass. Amphion, a man who had always irritated Jocasta because of his superior manner and florid dress, had been chosen as their spokesman, or perhaps he had appointed himself. They couldn't have made a worse choice: the Secretary of the Treasury of Thebes bore a marked resemblance to her late father, and she loathed him.

Still, she couldn't ignore the frantic scrambling of her servants, racing across the cobbled courtyards to tell her that Amphion and his friends demanded an audience with the queen. She told them to take back the message that the queen was currently engaged in other business, but that she would receive them the following morning. It was time to teach these men that they did not own her and could not simply expect her to put everything aside to meet with them.

The following morning, they were standing waiting for her in the public square. They nestled together, gossiping like the old women who hung their faded laundry over the steep, narrow streets outside.

'Gentlemen,' she said, walking up behind them. She saw the shock in their faces: the small, pale girl they had laughed at with their king was not afraid of them. And she was no longer a girl.

'We've heard the most ridiculous story,' spluttered Amphion, and Jocasta wondered how a man could be so self-satisfied that he didn't feel the slightest embarrassment at the way saliva bubbled in front of his teeth when he spoke.

'I'm sure you've heard lots of ridiculous stories,' she replied. 'It's probably the company you keep.'

Amphion's face darkened. 'This particular story is one you must refute. Immediately.'

Jocasta smiled. 'I'm sure you can't mean to give the impression that you are walking into my home and giving me orders.'

'I—'

'And I'm sure when you began speaking, you meant to say something like, "Good morning, your highness",' she continued. 'Because to start barking orders at your queen, without so much as a greeting and a wish of good health, is – I think we can all agree – rude.' She looked round at the cluster of old men, some of them beginning to realize that Amphion's influence might be ebbing away. There was a subtle shifting of position, as the more pragmatic ones edged back, realizing they didn't want to ally themselves too closely with their spokesman after all.

'Forgive me, your majesty,' he said, sarcasm dripping from every consonant. 'I thought we had something urgent to discuss, and that we might dispense with niceties for now.'

'Dispense is an odd word to choose, isn't it?' she said. 'It makes it sound as though you normally speak to me with the respect and courtesy that I might expect, given my position. And yet, I can't remember ever hearing you speak to me by name, let alone by title. Though I'm sure you know both my name and my position. You see, I've overheard you speaking about me occasionally, and – I'm sure you won't mind me being honest, since I know it's a quality you prize – you didn't come across well at all.'

He flushed so red that she wondered if he might be about to collapse to the ground, clutching at his chest.

'I am trying to reassure the people of Thebes that their queen is not about to act in a foolish and hasty manner,' he said.

'I'm just not sure that's true,' she replied. 'I think you've come here to tell me that I should marry one of you, so you can be king of the city, instead of the man you think I intend to marry.'

Tiny beads of sweat had coalesced on his temples to create small rivulets which were now running down the sides of his face. 'Do you mean to tell us that you don't intend to marry some foreigner? Have we been misinformed?' He gestured around him to include the men who were sidling ever further away.

'It's hard to imagine how that could be even the smallest part of your business, isn't it?' Jocasta said.

'I am the Secretary of the Treasury,' he snarled.

'Were,' she said.

'What?'

'I said you were the Secretary of the Treasury. Now you're just a rude old man who used to be important, and then wasn't any more, because he couldn't keep his spittle-flecked mouth shut. Guards.' Jocasta gestured to her men, who approached Amphion. 'This gentleman would like you to escort him from the grounds,' she said. 'And any of his friends who would like to leave as well. Gentlemen?'

The Elders looked at the ground and shook their heads. She had a sudden memory of Creon and his school friends, aged four or five, caught stealing figs from a neighbour's tree. Guilt was a great deal more endearing in children. The guards removed Amphion with an easy efficiency.

'Did anyone else have a question?' Jocasta asked, looking from one awkward face to another.

'Only one, majesty,' said a grey-haired, pinched-face man who she thought was called Taron.

'Yes?' she said.

'When might we meet the new Basileus?' he asked. She smiled.

'Clever boy,' she said.

The people of Thebes viewed Oedipus as their champion. Jocasta had never noticed, during her years in the palace, that the city was split into two unequal halves. Laius and his men were not especially popular with ordinary citizens: he was absent too often, and the common perception of him was that he was uninterested in the city, and tended towards snobbishness. His advisers, meanwhile, were viewed less favourably still. It was not only Jocasta who had seen them as a cabal of old men with no common touch. She, on the other hand, had a romantic appeal. A beautiful girl, married to a king whose sexual proclivities were the source of constant gossip, speculation, and more than a few drinking songs. She had spent so much of her time in the palace after the death of her child that she was perceived as a tragic figure, trapped in a court filled with aloof, unpopular men. Ordinary Thebans were rooting for her to marry again, but someone younger and more like them. And Oedipus fulfilled both criteria.

His entry to the city as its saviour – even though most Thebans had never travelled through the mountains – was the real reason they loved him, of course. Everyone knew someone who knew someone who had been lost to the Sphinx. It was easy to turn a now-vanished threat into something more serious than it had been. People didn't ask how dangerous the men of the Sphinx really were or how much of an impediment to trade they had been. They just celebrated the fact that the Sphinx were gone, and they had this handsome visitor to thank. Finally someone had done what their own king had failed to do for many years. And were the rumours true, that he had proposed to the queen the moment he arrived at the palace? You couldn't deny that he had charm. Exactly what the queen needed, everyone agreed. Was he too young? Better that than another ossified old fool.

The wedding was arranged with a haste which shocked the Elders and delighted the commoners. Jocasta was a widow for less than two months. She married Oedipus at the start of spring, just as the earliest fruit trees were coming into blossom. Thebans saw the flowers as auspicious. But Jocasta refused to consider auspices any more. The only thing that worried her about the day of her gamos was the absence of Oedipus's parents. She couldn't decide whether she would like to meet them or not. With every day that passed, she wanted Oedipus more, and more than wanting him, she desired him. She longed to consume him whole, and have his youth and vigour shine out from her pores. She wanted to wrap herself around him like a cloak and never let go. And she wanted to know everything about his past: his city, his home, his family. But she couldn't leave Thebes without a ruler, while she travelled with him to Corinth to meet his family and visit his home. It would be unsafe for her, as well as deeply unpopular with her citizens. So all she could know about her new husband was what he brought with him to her city. In the evenings before their wedding she begged Oedipus to repeat stories, so she could learn the names of everyone important to him. Of course she must meet his parents.

But at the same time, she felt a twinge of relief when he said they wouldn't be able to come. His mother's health was poor: she was confined to a chair, and could only travel short distances by litter. She could never make the long journey across uneven terrain that would be necessary to see her son in his new home. And his father was always loath to leave his mother for a few hours, let alone a few days: they were, Oedipus assured her, inseparable. And of course she wanted to hear this too, to know that he was the son of a couple who were so devoted to one another.

The notion of his chair-bound mother brought her another, different kind of relief. In their absence, she could render them old, much older than her. It was the only question she never asked him: how old are your parents? Because what if the answer was one she couldn't bear to hear: oh, about the same age as you. And her imagination took her further still. What if he hadn't mentioned her age to them? She spent terrible moments imagining a scene where his aged mother looked around for someone young enough to be her son's betrothed, before her puzzled eye eventually lighted upon Jocasta. It was unthinkable.

'Tell me again,' she said, as he lay on her bed, the golden strands of his hair glowing in the candlelight. He propped himself up on one arm, and ran his hands over her skin. She reached out to touch him, but the sight of her hand – every knuckle bearing the marks of every time she had bent every finger – next to his flawless skin made her draw it back so she could look at him unspoiled.

'You've heard it all,' he grinned. 'Let me keep a bit of mystery, so you don't get bored of me as soon as we're married.'

'Is there anything you want to know about me?' she asked. Oedipus's finger was tracing a silvery mark on the right side of her stomach. Did he know what it was? Should she tell him? Again, she found herself split. She wanted to share the terrible story of her loss, and have him hold her while she wept one last time for her missing boy.

Because she was determined that with this new marriage, the one she had chosen, she would finally put aside the grief which had crushed her through the last seventeen years of her life. She wanted to begin again, and she would. But wouldn't that be easier if she didn't tell him the whole wretched saga of the past?

'Tell me what you did, when Laius abandoned you,' he asked, quietly.

Jocasta was surprised. The only thing that had ever mattered to her about her dead husband was his refusal to have a son. Everything else had blurred away over the years. She was not now sure she knew Laius's eye-colour, if she ever had.

'I was relieved,' she said. 'It meant he didn't want to have anything to do with me, and the feeling was mutual.'

'It's peculiar that he wanted to get married, isn't it? Keeping up appearances, I suppose.'

'I think so,' she said. 'It was what Thebes wanted for him. He just didn't want it for himself. He resisted it as long as he could.'

'So he married you and then moved to the lower slopes of the mountains to live as he actually wanted to?'

'Essentially, yes.'

'And what did you do? Did you have endless affairs?'

'You are so rude,' she said, swatting him with a cushion. 'No, I didn't. I took my position seriously.'

He began kissing her neck and she felt her stomach contract. What was the point of explaining Oran, the father of her lost child, after all this time? What was the point of even remembering him, when he was so long gone, and Oedipus was so entirely present?

15

The morning after the coronation, I tried to leave the palace, but there was no one available to accompany me. I asked my sister if she wanted to go down to the lake, but she made some excuse about a headache from sitting in the blistering sun the previous day. I tried to remind her of the dappled shade by the water, but she waved me away, a damp linen cloth on her forehead. It was more likely she had planned to meet Haem in some quiet corner of the palace and was waiting for me to leave so she could begin to get herself ready. There was no one else I could ask to come with me: Sophon would not welcome the suggestion that he clamber down the uneven, rock-strewn paths with his stick. And I could not ask Eteo, because I didn't know what to say to him yet. That was one of the reasons I needed to go down to the lake: I wanted to swim away from the palace, and find my thoughts somewhere in the water. The painted dolphins which decorated the sides of the fountain in the courtyard were taunting me, swimming happily in their blue shallows.

In the end, I told one of the slave women that she would have to accompany me, and though she sighed and said she might be missed by the housekeeper, I pleaded with her until she agreed. We walked together through the courtyards: the sight of men scurrying around the second courtyard to do Polyn's bidding would have amused me on another day – each man so intent on his own importance as he followed his route, like ants swarming around a nest – but today it made me feel more afraid. I had no way of knowing how many of these men, of the aristoi, were a danger to me. Or if the danger had ebbed, now that Polyn was ruler of Thebes once again. Sophon thought the attack had been organized to discredit Eteo. So was I safe now that Eteo was no longer king? The fear which had paralysed me at the coronation ceremony when I saw the priest's knife had ebbed away today: I wanted escape.

The slave woman and I hurried through to the doorway which led into the main courtyard, but there we found the gates were closed and barred. Looking through them, it appeared that the front gates – from the main courtyard into the market square – were locked too, although the traders would certainly be at work by now. There were no guards standing by the gate. Only when I hammered on them did one appear on the other side.

'Open the gates, please,' I said.

He shook his jowls to and fro. 'Not today.'

'What do you mean, not today?'

'By order of the king,' he said. 'The palace gates are to be kept locked.'

'Until when?' I asked. The sun was still low in the sky, and if they opened the gates again soon, I would still have time to walk down to the lake before it grew too hot. The guard shrugged and walked away. The maid looked at me, waiting to see what I would do now.

'You can go back to the housekeeper and tell her our

plans have changed,' I said. She began to walk away. 'Wait.'

She slowed and I caught her up. I preferred to walk with her across the second courtyard than go through it alone. Once on the other side of it, she disappeared into the kitchens, and I walked back along the colonnade into the family courtyard. The fountain was spluttering in the middle of the square, and I decided to go and sit beside it. I should find Sophon and ask him if he knew what was happening. Why would Polyn have closed the palace off from the city? Was he keeping the rest of Thebes out, or keeping us in?

I sat on the edge of the fountain and unlaced my sandals: I had spilled water on them yesterday and now the leather had hardened and was biting into my hot feet. I swung my feet into the pool, while I bent the leather straps to and fro in my hands, trying to soften them again. I could smell the honeysuckle and thyme from across the square: my father had planted both, hoping to attract wild bees to the garden. His plan had worked. One summer when I was small, they swarmed across the courtyard and built their hive in a dead tree just outside the palace walls. We had honeycomb that summer, dripping it onto hard brown bread and soft white sheep's cheese. My difficulty with these memories is that I can never quite be sure that I've caught the right one from the mass of them flying around inside my head. I tie these two events together – my father planting the shrubs and the bees producing the honey – but I don't know if I'm right to. I don't always remember things in the order in which they happened, I don't think. I remember individual moments: my father dusting the soil from his hands and picking me up so I could see the flowers on the honeysuckle and the bees nuzzling their way inside the petals. But did those two things happen on the same day? Surely he would have planted honeysuckle before it came into flower, or the blooms would have fallen when the plant was moved? As for the honey: I remember eating it – sweeter than anything I'd ever tasted before – but I don't know who drizzled it onto my small, fat fingers. Were my parents still alive then, or was it my uncle who offered me the treat?

I sat by the fountain for a while, trying to tie the memories together in the right order, until Eteo's door opened and he walked into the courtyard, running his hand through his ruffled hair. He had clearly woken late. I waved and he walked over to join me. He didn't need to remove his sandals, having bare feet already.

'What's going on?' he said. 'Why aren't you and Sophon busy composing some epic tale together, on the glory of my kingship?'

I shoved him. 'I wanted to go down to the lake,' I said. 'But the gates are locked. On Polyn's orders, according to the guard.' I had been worrying that I would find it difficult to talk to him today, but it turned out to be easy.

'Why?' asked my brother. I shook my head. 'You could sneak out the back way,' he said. Eteo and I are the only ones who know about the door on the way to the ice store. Well, that isn't entirely true. Plenty of other people must know where it is: the palace staff, for a start. But it had been locked for so long that no one else ever thought about it. A door that doesn't open for a long enough time becomes the same thing as a wall, Sophon once said. I'm sure it was this kind of remark that provoked my siblings to stay away from his lessons. Still, I knew what he meant. Eteo had been with me when I found the key, years ago, hiding in a dark recess between a wooden chest and the bottom of the colonnade wall, outside our rooms. It was only visible because I was lying on the floor at the time, watching a bright green lizard scuttle along the ground. Lizards are usually brown or a dull, dusty green. But this one shone like a jewel. I was hypnotized by its radiant colour; Eteo by how it had avoided being eaten by a sharp-eyed bird when it was so bright.

The light glinted off something behind the emerald lizard and I reached under the chest to see what it was. The lizard scurried away in alarm, but I had this strange, ornate key to remember it by.

Eteo and I had no reason to keep the key secret, but we did anyway, because we both loved secrets. We waited until the others were occupied elsewhere, and carried the key from door to door, hidden in a pocket, testing it furtively, until we had exhausted every lock in the palace. It must have taken us a month. Only then did I remember the door that was not a door, in the ice-house corridor. We waited for days until there were no servants around, and our uncle wasn't in his rooms, which were close to the entrance of that corridor. The key seemed to fit, but we couldn't turn it at first, because the lock had stiffened with age. Then Eteo took a small bottle of olive oil from the kitchens that night, and we dipped the key into it, feeding oil into the lock to loosen the mechanism.

After all that, when we finally opened the door, we found it opened out onto nothing, the height of a man or more above the ground, which cut away beneath the palace because of the hill. There were no stairs or even a trace that there once had been any steps outside. We meant to make a rope ladder, so we would have our own secret exit from the courtyard, but we must have been distracted by something and we soon forgot about it. Once the mystery of the key was solved, we weren't so concerned with using it. We just wanted to know what the key was for. Besides, we'd always been able to leave the palace before today.

'I could sneak out that way,' I said. 'But doesn't it seem odd that we should have to?'

'You didn't go to Polyn and ask him what was going on?'

'I couldn't.'

My brother turned to look at me. 'Why not?'

And the noise of the fountain covered the sound of me telling him that it was because I was afraid of our older brother, and afraid of the friends he had chosen.

*

It was now half a month at least since Polyn's coronation, and I was no closer to leaving the palace, not even for one day. Polyn was no longer spending the nights in the family courtyard, in the rooms he had as a child. I didn't know where he was sleeping: perhaps one of the storerooms in the royal courtyard had been converted into the king's quarters. I wanted to ask the servants if they knew, but I could not bear to lose face in front of them, to have them gossiping about the fact that I didn't know where my brother was. And I didn't. He had so often been absent that it took me a few days to notice that I hadn't seen him at all since the coronation games. But there it was: he had not been in the family courtyard since he took the crown.

Eteo had not left his rooms since discovering that he had sentenced an innocent boy to death. Although he had always known that the boy with the knife was an unwitting victim of the same conspiracy which nearly cost me my life, there turned out to be a difference between knowing something terrible might be true, and discovering it was definitely true. He could not forget the cries of the boy's mother as her son was marched from the palace grounds, sentenced to death by the king. By him. And until he emerged from his seclusion and returned to the fountain, I couldn't talk to him. There was nowhere else I would feel safe discussing something so dangerous. Nowhere else where I would be certain we couldn't be overheard.

Meanwhile my sister, who should have been talking to Polyn on our behalf, since they had always been closest – me and Eteo, her and Polyn – seemed entirely unconcerned by his absence, and wouldn't have even noticed unless I'd asked her about it. Unless Haem mentioned something to her, or someone else talked to her about Haem, she paid no attention at all.

And then there was the problem of the palace gates. It was just for one day, the day after the coronation, that the front gates were barred. After that, the main courtyard was opened again to the people of Thebes. But the inner gates – from the royal courtyard into the public one – remained locked, and only Polyn's advisers and friends seemed able to come and go as they pleased, the guards stepping smartly aside for them. I could see slivers of this from the family courtyard, because the gates from there into the second courtyard were now shut and barred as well. There wasn't even a guard. There was no need for one. The gates had been closed for days, so they had become, as Sophon would say, no different from a wall. I could not go to my tutor in his study either. I didn't know if he was still sitting there waiting for me or if he had given up and left the palace. Or even if he had been told to leave.

I tried asking my uncle about the locked gates, but I achieved little. I told him I wanted to visit Sophon and borrow a manuscript. He replied that I was surely too old for lessons now, and could already read and write, sing and compose and play the phorminx – the five-stringed lyre that the older generation of Thebans prized above all other instruments – better than any other girl in the city. Flattering as this was, it did nothing to help. I asked again about something to read, and he said I could tell him what I would like and he would send someone to fetch it from Sophon's room and bring it back with him at the end of the next day. He and Haem were still able to come and go between the courtyards, though I hadn't yet seen the gates open for them. I wondered if I should just sit beside the gates for one whole day, and then at least I would force whoever came and went to explain why I could not. But I sat there for a while, and no one tried to enter. They could just wait me out. I thought perhaps when Eteo came out of his room, we could share the duty, and then it wouldn't require such perseverance. When I asked my uncle why he could move around the palace but I could not, he said that the security of the royal family was of unsurpassed importance, so we needed to accept these new measures to keep us safe. He thought I would understand that, after everything that had happened. But I didn't feel safe; only trapped.

I tried to comb out this tangled state of affairs so I could compose verses for my history, verses which Polyn would not enjoy hearing me sing. But I could not successfully unravel it all. I had to work things out in my head before I could start trying to write anything down. I didn't have enough parchment to make mistakes, and I didn't know when I would be able to get more. Sophon would have expected me to use reasoning to understand my predicament, and I was trying. After much thought, this was what I believed to be true.

I could not accept that my oldest brother had wanted me to die. But equally, it was inconceivable that his friend had infiltrated the palace and attacked me without Polyn being, at the very least, aware of it. Sophon had suggested Polyn was part of a conspiracy intending to disrupt Eteo's kingship, and it was true that my brothers had become virtual strangers to one another. Or perhaps it was always thus. I couldn't remember them being friends even when they were very young. Eteo always had more in common with Haem than with Polyn. So I had two contradictory beliefs: that my brother was involved, and that he could not have been so heartless. I could not maintain them both. But without further evidence, I would not condemn my brother.

I didn't know what kind of evidence I was expecting to find next. Would Polyn announce that the wrong man had been condemned for the attack on me? That would have weakened Eteo's standing with the people of Thebes, certainly, but not by very much: the boy was not from one of the elite families, and anyway, he was dead now. Besides, it might well discredit Polyn, too. Ordinary Thebans spent far less time thinking about which of my brothers was king at any one time than they imagined, at least if Sophon's judgement on the matter was correct. Prince, king: he often observed that the distinction was far smaller from the outside than it was on the inside. Both were a world away from being a market-trader or a cobbler or a smith. So though I understood why Eteo needed time alone to contemplate what he had done, I believed he was being eaten up by a baseless fear: people would not find out that he had condemned an innocent man. Apart from everything else, if the boy was publicly exonerated, Polyn would need to find another scapegoat. He was hardly likely to lay the blame where it belonged, on his own friend.

The courtyard gates were not, I believed, kept closed to keep us safe. The only danger I had ever been in was at the hands of my brother's friend, the aristos with the knife. If he was back inside the palace now – as he probably was – it could only be at my brother's invitation. And it was not credible to think Polyn would invite someone dangerous into our home and then worry about the danger. He was the king: no one could come into the palace without his knowledge and approval. The only other possibility – which I had discounted – was that Polyn himself was being forced to accept things he didn't want to accept, just as I had been forced to accept that I was locked into the smallest courtyard of the palace. But who could force their will on the king? The idea was absurd.

So my conclusion was that I was a prisoner in this part of the palace, for whatever reason and for however long Polyn decided. When Eteo emerged – if he could put aside his guilt – he would help me to work out what to do next. The guards ignored me, and I could have hammered on the gates all day without provoking one of them to come over and speak to me. But they would not ignore the man who was king until recently and who would be king again once the four seasons had passed.

The problem with my theory was that I could think of only one plausible reason why Polyn would behave as he had. There was one explanation which encompassed all the information I had considered: Polyn had no intention of sharing the kingship any longer. He had replaced Eteo for good this time, and he would not give up the throne again.

It was impossible to conclude anything else.

16

Jocasta lay on a couch covered with fatly stuffed cushions in the middle of the courtyard, her eyes closed. She could pick out the voices of both her sons and her daughter, as they squawked at one another in the shade of the east colonnade. In a moment, the coos and squeals of delight would no doubt be transformed into howls of pain and rage, but for now, the children were playing together as she had always imagined they would, and she delighted in ignoring them. She had never managed to explain to Oedipus that so long as she could hear the children, she was happy.

Even when she had a crippling headache – which happened sometimes now her belly was so swollen she could almost hear the baby's voice murmuring into her ears – she liked to be able to listen to the children, to be able to hear each one separately from the others. It had been easy when there was just Polynices, who screamed at the top of his lungs every day for months. Then, when Eteocles arrived, she had been astonished to discover that there could be a smaller baby than Polynices. She could see that her older son had grown longer, and heavier, and finally taller, as he sat up looking at his surroundings as though he might one day approve of them but not yet. Still somehow, he remained a tiny baby in her mind until Eteocles was born,

undeniably smaller. The same thing had happened when
Antigone was born, but with the added delight that now
she had a girl. Two sons and a daughter. She could hear
the difference in every sound they made: Polynices did
everything noisily, even breathing. Eteocles was quieter,
but snored like a cat. Antigone raged at the slightest
provocation, and could never keep still. Even when she
was just a few months old, she watched her brothers with
vast green eyes, determined to escape the cage of her crib
and join them in their adventures. And the new baby, what
would she be like? Jocasta stroked her hardening stomach
to see if she could feel a kick. This one was nowhere near
as restless as the other three had been. She – Jocasta knew
it was a girl from the way everything tasted somehow
metallic, though she could not explain this to Oedipus –
lay still for hours at a time. Just as Jocasta began to worry,
the baby would give her a reassuring shove. Hand touching hand, with only her own skin between them.

She could hear her husband kicking a soft leather ball to
Polynices, as Eteocles demanded they let him play. Would
he be the first to crack the tranquillity with a scream?
No, Antigone as usual was suddenly wailing at some real
or perceived injustice. Jocasta listened to Oedipus scoop
her up and tell her she could play on his team: the two of
them versus the boys. Everything was as it should be.

She lay half-dozing in the sun, trying to remember
what she needed to do today. But she had little to fret
about: her brother was in control of things. He had
become increasingly helpful as her children arrived, taking
on more responsibilities each year. Creon wanted to ease
her burden, he had told her when she was pregnant with

Polyn. He always rushed to put a stool behind her, as if her legs could not possibly hold the weight of her and her unborn baby. She had thought then what a good father he would be, when he and Eurydice had a child; once they did, she saw she was right. He doted upon his little son, who now came to the palace so often with his papa.

Eurydice and Creon had moved into a neat little house, just down the hill from the market square, near the palace gates, three – or was it four? Jocasta struggled to remember – years earlier. The smell of rotting vegetables behind the grocery stalls had made Eurydice queasy when she was pregnant, and for a while she clearly felt that the move across the city had been a mistake. She stopped attending the palace with her husband and withdrew into her own household. But once Haemon was born, she saw the virtue of the location. Creon could walk to the palace in a matter of moments, and Eurydice could come and go as she pleased, with the baby. If she wanted more time to herself, she dropped him off with Jocasta's brood. One more child made no difference in the palace, where plentiful nursemaids were always on hand. Eurydice was never the sister that Jocasta had hoped she would be, but she made Creon happy, and their son was a delight.

Jocasta thought she should ask Creon if he and Eurydice were planning to have another baby. She had been sure they would have armfuls of them when she saw them with Haemon. But first months and now years had passed, and still there was no second child.

She heaved herself off the divan, shedding cushions in her wake, and waved across the square at Oedipus and the children.

'I won't be long,' she called. She walked into the middle courtyard, and wished she had stayed where she was. Lying in the sun was pleasant enough, but walking in it, even this short distance, left her over-heated and exhausted. She could feel the sweat form beneath the linen tunic that pressed against her back. She opened the door to the treasury room, and found Creon sitting in the ornate wooden chair that had been a gift to Jocasta from a visiting ambassador from Athens.

'You look comfortable,' she smiled.

He leapt to his feet. 'Forgive me, sister. I was just—'

'You don't need to apologize,' she said. 'I must sit down.' Jocasta dropped onto the nearest couch, which was covered in hard padding: was it animal hair? She wished again she had stayed in comfort on the divan, and summoned Creon to her. She dimly recalled that one of the other children had made her as tired as this, but she couldn't remember which one. 'This baby is determined that I spend nine months lying on my back,' she said, accepting a small metal cup of water which Creon brought over, concern in his pale blue eyes.

'Should I send for some ice?' he asked. 'I know you like it.'

'No, thank you. I do like it, but the baby doesn't. It must be too cold for her. It makes her kick.'

'Ah, that's a pity,' he said. 'How are you feeling otherwise?'

'Puzzled,' she replied. 'Why don't you and Eurydice have another child? And why haven't I ever asked you before now?' His face coloured. 'Don't blush,' she added, smiling. 'Only one of us should be bright red and sweating, and it can't be you, because I came into the room that way.'

He thought for a moment. 'I did want more children,' he admitted. 'I would have liked three or four. But Eury . . .' He lost the words, and she forced herself not to fill in the silence, uncomfortable though it was. She would never know the truth if she allowed herself to be tactful.

'Eury was so sick when she was pregnant, she said she couldn't face going through it all again. And I was worried for her. It can't be safe for a woman to be so sickly.'

'Was she that ill?' Jocasta felt a sharp twinge of guilt. She knew her sister-in-law had suffered from morning sickness at all hours, but she didn't realize it had been quite so debilitating.

'She was sick all the time,' he said. 'Every day. She grew so thin in the early weeks – don't you remember? She could barely eat a thing.'

'Of course,' Jocasta said. But she was lying. She already had Polynices by then, and was expecting Eteocles, who was only two months younger than Haemon. She had felt for her sister-in-law, but hadn't been paying her particular attention. She had simply assumed Eurydice was sick sometimes, in the same way as Jocasta and every other pregnant woman was.

'Eury didn't want another child enough to be that ill again. I felt guilty even for suggesting it, to be honest. As if I was asking her to put her own life at risk again.'

'Well, if she felt that strongly . . .' Jocasta said. 'You have Haemon, that's the important thing.'

'I know,' he said. 'I do know. But I would have liked a daughter, too. You know I would have.'

'I'm sorry,' she said. 'I wish I hadn't asked. It was rude of me.'

'No,' he replied. 'It's good to be able to say that out loud. I wouldn't say it at home, you know. Eury would think I was criticizing her. Or expressing some sort of dissatisfaction with Haem, who – of course – is the perfect son. She has given me an heir: it's all I could have asked for. But it's quite separate from him, you know? Wanting a daughter. You understand.'

'I think so,' she said. 'This one will be a girl, I'm sure of it. Will you promise to take care of her?'

'Are you planning on exposing her on the mountain-side?' he laughed. He was looking across the room at the strong-boxes which contained Jocasta's gold, and the new tapestry she had asked him to acquire for her – blood red, shot through with gold, and woven so carefully the Fates themselves could do no better – so he did not see the shudder run through his sister's body.

She swallowed and replied in a light voice. 'Of course not. Oedipus loves having daughters, you know that. He prefers Ani to either of the boys, even though she fusses all the time. I'm just worried this one might get over-looked. She's quieter than the others.'

Her brother turned to look at her. 'How quiet?' he asked.

'No,' Jocasta said. 'She moves. Just not as often as I'm used to. Antigone punched and kicked me every day – do you remember?'

He nodded. 'It was driving you mad. The gadfly, you called her, because she stung you so often.'

'She'll never be short of attention,' Jocasta agreed.

'Which is why you must always look out for this one. She'll be the baby of the family, so she'll need someone to make sure she isn't ignored. Say you promise.'

'Don't you want to ask Oedipus?'

'Why? He would think it was a good idea, just like I do. I know he would.'

Creon looked at her flushed face, framed by damp brown hair which was now flecked with grey.

'I promise,' he said. 'I won't let you ignore her, no matter how noisy all your other brats are.'

'Good,' she said. 'Now will you bring the tapestry over here so I can look at it? Is it as beautiful as we were promised?'

'It is,' he said.

By the time they had finished, Jocasta was relieved to accept her brother's arm as he walked her back to the rest of her family. 'Will you stay for dinner?' she asked, as she watched Haemon run the length of the courtyard before flinging himself into his father's arms. 'I could send someone to fetch Eurydice?'

Creon's biceps bulged as he swung his gleeful son around him in a circle. At the same time, the tension in every other part of his body seemed to disappear.

'You're getting too heavy to do that,' he said, as he hurled Haemon round one more time before placing him on the ground. 'When did you get so tall?'

'I don't know,' squealed the little boy.

'Was it this afternoon?' asked Creon.

'No,' Haemon said.

'This morning, then? It must have been this morning.'

'No,' the boy shrieked with delight, running to look in the water beneath the fountain, to check if his reflection had grown taller.

'I think we'd better go back,' Creon said to Jocasta. 'Eury will have planned dinner by now.'

Jocasta tutted. 'Of course. I should have thought of it sooner. Polyn! Eteo! Come over here!' The two boys ran over, but stopped carefully before they crashed into her. They had learned to do this when she was expecting Ani. 'Will you go and pick some herbs and flowers for your Aunt Eury? So she knows we miss her and long to see her for dinner tomorrow,' Jocasta said. 'While your uncle has iced water with me and Papa.'

The boys nodded and bustled off, filled with sudden seriousness.

'There's no need,' Creon said.

But his sister patted his arm, and walked back to her divan, which still lay in the afternoon sun. She turned the hot cushions over, so she could lie on something cool. Oedipus walked out of the shaded portico where he had been sitting, and waved to Creon, pointing at a plain wooden chair he was welcome to use.

'I cannot stay for much longer,' Creon told him, sitting down. 'My wife is expecting us home.'

'You can stay for a little while,' Oedipus yawned. 'They'll start scrapping before they've done as they were asked. It never takes long.'

'They're not that bad,' Jocasta said, just as Eteocles shoved his brother aside to reach the rosemary. 'They're just boys being boys.'

But Oedipus was right. The boys were at war again,

and were no longer picking herbs. A moment later, Polynices brought over a mangled bunch of thyme stems, bent and broken from being pulled by competing hands. Haemon came over to take a look at the sorry bouquet. 'I'll do it,' he said, and took himself off to look at the plants. One of the gardeners was working in the far corner of the courtyard, and seeing Haemon's intense concentration, hurried over to assist him.

'Why can't my sons behave like yours?' Oedipus groaned. 'Little monsters.'

Eteocles and then Polynices, seeing that things were progressing more successfully without them, scurried over to help rather than watch their cousin carry out the important task alone. 'You see?' Jocasta said. 'They're not so terrible.'

Conversation between the three parents dried up, as it so often did. Jocasta wished her brother and her husband would at least feign the friendliness they couldn't feel. Creon had never liked Oedipus, though he had never said a critical word about the king. But Jocasta remembered the expression on her brother's face, when she first introduced him to her husband. He had obviously been warned to expect someone young, but her brother's shock had been vivid and ill-concealed. He was used to being the youngest man in his sister's life: she was ten years older than him, after all. And then he met Oedipus, and had to readjust his role accordingly: he couldn't be the baby brother if her husband was six – or was it seven? – years younger than he was. And he was no longer the only man Jocasta relied on, once she had a real husband, a proper marriage. It was an abrupt awakening.

And Oedipus was a proprietorial man. It was this kind of thing Jocasta occasionally wondered if she might have noticed before they married, had things moved less quickly when they met. Oedipus was the opposite of Laius, never happy in the company of men. He preferred to be alone with her, and his possessiveness stretched backwards in time. He disliked the presence of anyone from her life before he arrived in it. Teresa had barely continued in her employ at the palace for a month after Laius died. Jocasta had felt sure that her housekeeper – a free woman – would prefer to leave. But upset though Teresa was about Laius, she seemed to want to keep her position. Still, she could not have made her dislike of Oedipus more overt, nor her delight when he left Thebes a few days after he had arrived with news of the king's death: Teresa's spies must have been slacking, Jocasta had thought, because the housekeeper had been more surprised than anyone when Oedipus returned a half-month later to ask the queen to marry him. Teresa's response had been furious, and Oedipus had ordered her out of the palace within the day. She had turned to Jocasta, expecting the queen to overrule this upstart and tell him that Teresa was not to be argued with. But Jocasta had done nothing of the kind. Rather, she had taken her husband's arm, and told Teresa that things were changing at the palace, so perhaps it was time for her to move on. Teresa had spent a day holed up in the kitchens, waiting for the queen to reconsider. But when a new housekeeper arrived – Oedipus had put out word that the position was vacant and dozens of Thebans hurried to offer their services – she had been obliged to pack her things and leave. Jocasta thought about her occasionally, and wondered where she'd gone that day. After all those years living in the palace, would she have had anywhere else to stay? But it didn't matter. Jocasta had made her choice, and that was Oedipus. After so much of her life had been decided for her, she was determined to stand by her decisions now she was finally allowed to make them for herself. And soon, Oedipus was asking why the courtyard didn't have flowers and suggesting they knock down Teresa's ugly little shrine and replace it with an almond tree. And a few years later, when the tree came into blossom for the first time, Jocasta had forgotten that the square had ever looked different from the flowering place it had become.

If Jocasta was honest with herself, she knew that even if Creon had offered a boundless welcome to her second husband when they first met, Oedipus would probably not have warmed to him. Oedipus had always loved her jealously. He was irritated when he had to share her attention with the children – much as he loved them – and he certainly didn't love her brother. He always found the older man both condescending and excessively protective. 'Where was all this concern when you had a husband who hated you?' he once asked. Jocasta shrugged and reminded him that Creon had been a child when she was married off, and had known little about her life in the years that followed. She couldn't blame him. But she also couldn't focus too much on Creon's comparative youth, because he was several years (she rounded the number down in her mind) older than Oedipus, who had defended her against her husband before he even met her.

Jocasta had long ago decided that the best course of

action was to refuse to allow that there was anything wrong between them. She had learned never to be too fond of Creon when Oedipus was there, as jealousy only made him more impatient. Her husband needed to be unrivalled in her affection, and he was. She had always hoped they would warm to one another one day and things would become easier. She had tried to enlist Eurydice as an ally – encouraging her brother to marry the girl as soon as he could – but even when it was just the four of them (Creon and Eurydice living so close by) it made no difference. Jocasta tended to elide the status difference from her thoughts, but the others never did. Creon prickled to hear Oedipus called 'king'. And Oedipus relished Creon's lack of official position, choosing to refer to his work as 'helping your sister'.

Jocasta heard the children come running over with the flowers and herbs, tied with a neat little plait of grasses. 'That's beautiful,' she said to the three of them. 'Will you take it carefully to your mama?' she asked Haemon. He nodded.

'Time to go,' Creon said, and raised himself from the chair. 'See you tomorrow,' he told his sister.

Perhaps the flowers would persuade Eurydice to visit, Jocasta thought, as she waved her brother a lazy goodbye. But she knew she was the only one who wanted the four of them to be friends. And that was never likely to be enough.

17

I don't think about my parents every day, but I miss them more than I remember them. Growing up without them has left me with an uneasy sense that I have been careless with something fragile and irreplaceable: a precious bottle of perfume, perhaps. I can't reach into the past and take better care of them. But the one consolation I have always had is my three siblings. There are traces of my parents in all of us. Ani looks very much like our mother, and always has: the bright, birdlike eyes, the thick, dark hair. She is small, like our mother was, and delicate. Even her hands could be our mother's: the neat, sharp nails that she digs into the soft flesh of a ripe fig. Polyn is a compact version of my father: he has the same quickness in his expression, as though he is waiting for you to catch up. But Eteo has my father's build, and his long, ranging gait is so evocative that sometimes if he catches me unawares, I lose myself for a moment, thinking it is Papa.

But not any more.

Finally, Eteo came out of his room. He had always had these dark periods, even when he was a small boy. There was no consoling him when he was angry or upset: you had to leave him be until he was ready to talk again. I knocked on the door and called his name, quietly, in case he was asleep. I had done this every day, but he had not replied. Then one day, he opened the door and came out, blinking into the bright sunshine of the square. His eye sockets were puffed up, swollen like blisters. I reached over to embrace him, but his arms squeezed me back emptily.

'Come to the fountain, Isy,' he said. I saw no value in telling him that, as far as I knew, we were unlikely to be overheard anywhere, as we were the only people in the courtyard. Ani was somewhere with Haem, I guessed: I didn't know where. The slaves had come in early this morning with toasted barley grains and sour goat curds but they were long gone now.

'Where is everyone?' Eteo asked, looking around.

'It's been like this for days,' I told him. 'I've asked our uncle when they will open the gates again, and he shrugs and says we're safer like this.'

'Safer?' My brother raised a weary eyebrow. 'We'd be safer wrestling a mountain lion than in this place. I'm sorry, Isy, I abandoned you. I had to think about things.'

'You're here now.'

We sat by the fountain and I reached out to dip my hand in the water. 'What happens when you try to leave?' he asked.

'No one comes to open the gates.'

'What if you shout and hammer on them?' he asked, smiling tiredly.

'Not even then,' I said.

'But the slaves have been coming in and out?' he asked, jerking his head at the food which remained on a table under the colonnade, a fine linen cloth draped over it to keep the flies away.

'Less frequently than before. But yes.'

'Through the gates?'

'I suppose so.'

'When do they come?'

'Before I'm awake. They come back each night to take the plates and dishes away and refill them.'

'So we're stuck here,' he said. I nodded. 'Where's Ani?' he asked. I shrugged.

'With Haem, I think,' I replied. 'I don't know. I haven't seen her for days. They plan to announce their betrothal soon, I am sure of it.'

'You've just been here on your own?' he asked.

'Since the coronation,' I said. 'Ani is here sometimes, but she's always with him, so I can't talk to her.'

'You don't trust Haem.' Eteo nodded slowly. 'Or Ani?'

'I don't know who to trust except you,' I said.

'Then you're lucky I'm here,' he smiled. 'The slave boy has brought food into my room every morning. I couldn't face seeing any of them: Polyn and Creon and the others. Not once you'd told me about Lynceus. It didn't occur to me that you were out here on your own. Forgive me.'

'Lynceus? Is that his name?'

'Polyn's friend? Yes.'

'Polyn can't face seeing you either,' I said. 'He hasn't come back here at all.'

'I don't think he's ashamed of what he's done, Isy. Are you still thinking the best of him now, even when you have so much evidence against him?'

'I don't have any choice. The only alternative is to think the worst of him. And how does that help me?'

Eteo shook his head. 'Be realistic.'

'I am being realistic,' I said. 'What would you have me believe? That my brother agreed to have me killed, and it is just good luck and the skill of an old man that means I am alive today? Is that truly what you think?'

'I didn't mean to upset you,' he said. 'I'm sorry. Let's not talk about him any more.'

He stood up, and walked over to the table. He picked up two figs and threw one over to me. His aim was off and I had lean right back to catch it. I almost fell on my back, but my balance just held and I righted myself again. Finally I saw my brother smile properly. The weight of things seemed to shift from his brow bones and his face opened up, like an unfurling leaf.

*

I should have guessed he was planning something. It is how Eteo has always been: whenever he is upset about something, he withdraws from the world until he has thought things through. Only then does he act. There was no reason for him to behave differently now.

He was more determined to leave the courtyard than I was, which was hardly surprising. I couldn't go outside the palace, or even into its public areas, without an escort. If one of the slaves or one of my relatives didn't accompany me, no one would let me out as far as the main courtyard. So even if I had made an almighty racket hammering on the gates, I could only have reached the second courtyard, and that was where Polyn's friends, Lynceus included, would be. Eteo had no such restrictions on his movements, of course, so he had a great deal more to gain.

One of the odd things about my brother is that people

forget how quick he is. They watch him each year at the races, sprinting at full pelt, and they know he is fast. But because he is tall and has a lazy, sinuous way of walking, they don't remember that when he's away from the race-track. Perhaps, too, they had forgotten that he wouldn't stay in his rooms forever, although that would obviously have been more convenient for them.

The next day, long before it was light, a slave came in carrying fresh fruit and cheese. He did not need a torch, because the moon was large and full that night, and the clouds covered it only intermittently. Besides, his arms were full with the dishes he was carrying. He had done this every night for days, he was not expecting anything unusual to happen. So he wasn't looking in the darker recesses of the colonnade, where Eteo was hiding, waiting.

I heard nothing, which can only be what my brother intended. The slave was not found until the next evening, tied up on Eteo's floor. He had been carrying in the new dishes, he explained (though by then no one cared), when a hand had clapped itself around his mouth and a blade bit at his throat. He did not resist, though he claimed he did not know it was the royal prince who was accosting him until he was bundled into his room. Eteo must have picked up yesterday's used dishes and taken them with him, to keep anyone from guessing that something was amiss. The guards weren't manning the gate very atten-tively, that much was clear: Eteo was a hand taller than the slave he had imprisoned, and more muscular. He left the crocks outside the kitchens and if anyone thought this was strange, they said nothing. The kitchen boy took them (no doubt complaining to himself that his fellow slave had slacked off) and washed them, as he always did. No one knew where Eteo was until after it was light. He must have hidden somewhere: my guess is that he went into one of the state rooms, which were rarely used, unless ambassadors were visiting from another city. The night-watch would not have checked those rooms more than once at the start of the evening, if they even bothered to do that: they would not have seen the point. It scarcely needs mentioning that every man on the night patrol is dead now, clubbed to death by the royal bodyguards.

Eteo was cleverer than me, so he had already worked out that Polyn was living in the old king's rooms in the second courtyard. No one has used them for as long as we have been alive, but apparently the old king (the one before my father) slept there. Eteo could have crept in to speak to Polyn before it grew light, but he did not. Instead he waited until the king rose and washed and ate and walked through to the treasury to begin the day with his advisers. Eteo then crossed the courtyard to the state rooms on the west side of the courtyard. No one stopped him. The guards would perhaps not have known that he was supposed to be locked in the family courtyard with me. He had been so quiet for days, perhaps they had forgotten he was there. They either did not see or did not question the fact that he was carrying a sword. It was hardly an unusual thing, to see a prince with a ceremonial weapon. But just because the hilt of Eteo's sword was studded with polished agate gems did not make the blade any less sharp.

He opened the door of the treasury, and walked inside, letting it close behind him. Polyn must have been shocked to see him, but perhaps he was not. He must have been expecting this, or something like it, sooner or later. It would have been unlike him to underestimate Eteo: the two of them have been squabbling since Eteo was born. My uncle was also in the room, as were two slaves, from whom I heard all this. I bribed them with honey-cakes so they would tell me, though they had sworn to my uncle to keep their silence.

'Resign the kingship,' Eteo said. He didn't shout.

'What can you mean, brother?' Polyn asked. 'Your turn is next year. You must be patient.'

'You are responsible for what happened to Isy. It was your man who stabbed her. How could you do such an appalling thing? The gods themselves must have stolen your senses, and they will surely punish you for such an impious crime.'

Guilt settled on Polyn's face for a moment, before flying away again like a weary bird. 'I don't know what you mean,' he replied. 'You were king when our sister was attacked. She was your responsibility.'

'She still is,' Eteo replied. 'And she is yours, too. We both swore to protect our sisters long ago. Father would have been ashamed of you. I am ashamed of you. To set a grown man to attack a girl, and your own sister. I tried to believe anything else before I could accept that you were capable of such behaviour.'

'How dare you?' Polyn leapt to his feet.

'I told you to resign,' Eteo said. 'I will banish you from the palace, and the city. You will leave Thebes before nightfall. You can beg Isy's pardon before you leave. I wouldn't give it to you, but she is soft-hearted and wants to think well of you, so she might. But you deserve nothing from her, or from anyone.'

'Get out,' Polyn whispered. 'I will not tell you again. I will call the guards and have you locked up in the caves beneath the palace. You think I fear the scandal? I don't.'

'Polyn, Eteo, calm down,' said my uncle. He said nothing else.

'I don't think you fear any scandal,' said Eteo. 'What kind of man could agree to an attack on his own sister? You filthy coward.'

Polyn reached for his own sword, but he wasn't wearing it. Why would he be, when he was sitting in the treasury with my uncle and his slaves? He stepped backwards, groping behind him for an ornamental weapon: a valuable silver knife which was usually used by the priests during their sacrifices. The blade was sharp, but the metal was soft, designed for killing a helpless victim, rather than for combat. He jabbed at Eteo, and drew blood from the arm my brother raised to ward off the blow. He cannot have believed that Polyn would really attack him. It is this which I think reveals the truth: Eteo took a sword with him – I don't deny it – but he did not intend to use it. He was trained to fight; he knew he could not defend himself against a knife with his bare arm. It was the behaviour of a brother, who believes his sibling is feinting, and will not really hurt him. He put up his arm, not his sword.

Eteo saw his own blood dripping from his slashed forearm onto the stone floor. And only then did he shake his head like a wounded boar, and raise his sword in anger. Polyn swiped at him again, and this time Eteo parried the attack with his sword. The tip of Polyn's knife shattered with the force of Eteo's defence. Polyn cursed as he looked at the blade: it was shorter, jagged now from the damage, but still sharp. He made one final attempt on Eteo, stepping in and stabbing at his neck. There was no mistaking his intent. Even a short blade will kill a man if it pierces him in the neck. He took such a large step that it confused Eteo, who was preparing to parry the knife again, expecting a blow to be aimed at his torso.

Eteo's sword – so beautifully kept, as the armourer had taught him when he was still a child – cut right into Polyn's chest. My oldest brother fell to his knees, dropping the knife as he went. Eteo must have been horrified by what he had done, because he dropped his sword too, and reached out to catch Polyn, who slumped forward into his brother's arms.

It cannot have been Polyn who shouted for the guards, because he would not have had the strength, as he lay, his head on Eteo's shoulder, his blood pouring out over them both. And it cannot have been Eteo, who would have called for a doctor, for Sophon, but not for the guards. So it must have been my uncle who shouted with a tone of such urgency that the guards ran from all over the courtyard – most with their heads still half-filled with sleep – and pushed the treasury door open, almost falling over one another in their haste to obey Creon's summons. They saw my brothers tangled on their knees and looked at my uncle for instructions.

'The king is dying,' he said. 'Here is his assassin.'

Thebes does not have many laws. But the guards knew what they must do. They picked Eteo up by his shoulders and dragged him outside into the courtyard. They pulled back his hair to expose his neck, and slit his throat like a bull.

Ani and Haem had run into the courtyard from wherever they had been hiding. The shout and the sudden stampede of feet had pierced even their solitude. And so it was the sound of my sister screaming which drew me to the gates to see what on earth had happened. Only when I put my weight against them did I find they were now open, as Eteo must have left them when he slipped through, earlier in the morning. I ran into the royal courtyard, my eyes on Ani, frantic because I thought she was hurt.

I stood in confusion, because she seemed uninjured, and Haem was beside her, also safe and well. Finally I turned my head to follow her gaze, and saw the guards bringing Polyn out of the treasury on a litter they had fashioned from one of their cloaks. My brother's clothes were blackened with blood and he lay limp and lifeless on the stretcher. I looked back at Ani, hoping she would find a way to tell me I was mistaken. But her eyes were not on me, they were on the guard I had almost run into, who was brandishing a knife with a rusty blade in his left hand.

Only then did I realize that the blade was not rusty, and that the lake of blood pooling beneath my feet belonged to Eteo. Only then did I see that I had lost both my brothers. Everything had gone in a few beats of my heart. Everything but my sister.

18

Jocasta would never know what had been the first sign of the new Reckoning. No one did. The first Reckoning had ravaged Thebes many years earlier, a few summers before Jocasta was born. Her parents had survived it because her father was away trading in other cities and, because they were young and yet to have children, her mother had accompanied him. Thebes had closed its gates, and all admittance to the city was prohibited for a month or more. When they returned, only a day or so after the gates were finally reopened, they were startled to see that things were worse than the rumours had warned. The disease had been merciless, and more than one in eight of their fellow citizens were dead.

Some areas of the city had suffered greater devastation than others: the lower district, in the centre of the town, had a higher death toll than anywhere else, but no one knew why. Jocasta's parents lived high up on the hill on the far side of the city, but they had still lost seemingly numberless neighbours and relatives. People learned not to ask, if someone didn't appear at the market for a few days, or if their shoes went uncollected from the cobbler. The answer was always the same. Whole families had died, because those who tended the sick were more likely to fall ill themselves. If one child developed the early symptoms, their parents knew they too would have little chance of survival. Their only hope was to throw the sick child out onto the streets, and hope that they had acted in time. The child would die wherever it was, so parents tried to save themselves and their other offspring. Hopelessness was one of many symptoms of a disease which began with a headache and so often ended, seven or eight days later, in death. There was no way of knowing who would survive and who would die. Healthy young people were culled as efficiently as in a war, while their ancient parents – so frail before the Reckoning came – somehow withstood the ravages of the plague.

The sickness afflicted different people in different ways: all had a raging thirst and an unceasing sensation of burning from within. The inner heat was so terrible that people fled the city, clambering over its walls to throw themselves into the lake. But they felt no cooler, no matter how long they lay in the shallows and no matter how much water they drank. And when they tried to return to their homes, the gates were still barred and they could not enter. So they lay dying outside the city walls, their groans a wretched hymn for those guarding the gates.

Despite the intense internal heat, the sufferers' skin was not hot to the touch at first. The disease moved downwards starting with a cruel, vice-like headache. Most patients would then begin bleeding in the mouth, from the gums and the ulcerated tongue. Then the chest would tighten and an awful hacking cough would develop. By then, many of the sick would be overcome by the desperate state of their plight. They could no longer raise themselves to eat. Only those who were nursed – and hydrated – had any chance of survival. Those who lived in smaller houses, which grew unbearably hot in the summer months, had no hope at all. The disease descended to the digestive system, and the death toll at this stage was highest of all: the weakness caused by vomiting and diarrhoea was impossible to fight.

Those who survived suffered further indignities: the disease penetrated their extremities, and often they lost all feeling in one or more fingers or toes. Many could no longer practise the trade they had worked in all their lives, unable to work the leather or cloth which they had previously cut without needing to look. And even a minor cut, now painless and so unnoticed, could quickly became fatal. Pain was a warning, and the warning had been taken away. Some lost sight in one or both eyes; some lost hearing; others lost even their memories and could not recognize their friends or remember their own names.

In the months after the Reckoning, Thebes lost something of itself. Its people had always prided themselves on their steadiness, their ability to take everything which befell them in their stride. But they no longer felt this way. Too many had died and too many rules had been broken. The dead had not been properly buried while the Reckoning ravaged the city. No one could leave Thebes and inter their loved ones in graves outside the walls, as they used to. So people built funeral pyres and burned the dead instead. Some were too weak or weary to build a pyre, so they simply threw their dead on one already burning. Some used ropes to drop the bodies of the dead or terminally sick over the city walls. But everyone noticed that the vultures and dogs did not eat the corpses of the plague-dead. Even when the ribs of a dog were poking through his mangy fur, he would go hungry before he would chew on the polluted flesh.

The city had a proud history of welcoming strangers and traders from all over Hellas. The rules of xenia – where a traveller could expect food and lodging from strangers which he would one day reciprocate – had always been sacrosanct. But those too had gone. The gates were kept locked during the summer months for many years afterwards. Only those who could afford to bribe the guards could get into the city during the hottest part of the year. And the bribe needed to be a handsome one: the penalty for allowing someone from the Outlying into Thebes when the gates were closed was death. Each spring, Thebes would look nervously at its omens and wonder if this would be the year the Reckoning returned. Parents frightened their children, telling them stories of the terrors that presaged their birth.

Gradually, the fear subsided. But this was largely because those who had lived through the Reckoning were dying, not from the disease but from simple old age. By the time the disease struck Thebes for a second time, it was fifty years after the first blight. Only those who had been children the first time were still alive. And people had long since forgotten the symptoms, lost beneath layers of exaggeration and rumour. So Jocasta did not know, could not have known, that when the first of her citizens began to complain of a vicious spiking pain in the head and an unquenchable thirst, Thebes was at the beginning of something far worse than the usual summer sickness.

It was the summer of Isy's fourth birthday, and it was

Sophon who came to the palace asking for Jocasta. He was tutoring Polynices and Eteocles in their letters and geometry, having long since retired from treating the sick. He was sixty years old and his hands were too shaky, his eyes too weak for dealing with people who were frightened by whatever ailed them. But no doctor could really retire, especially not him. People still turned up at his door, begging for advice on one ailment or another. The past week had seen the numbers increase at an alarming rate: parents worrying about their children, children fearful for their ailing parents. On this day, he told the boys that he needed to see their mother before they could recite the verses they had learned for him. The slaves took one look at his dishevelled appearance, and took him straight into the second courtyard to speak to the queen.

'There's something wrong,' he said, as he hastened through the doorway into the treasury. Jocasta turned in surprise to greet her old friend. She was sitting with Oedipus and Creon, discussing the provisions the city would need to import during the coming winter. They had expectations of a good harvest: the grapes and olives were ripening on the hills outside the city. As usual, they would need to import grain. Jocasta looked well, perhaps a little tired, Sophon noticed. Motherhood suited her. Her greying hair betrayed her years, of course, but it was a clean, metallic grey, and her face lifted as she smiled at him.

'What's the matter?' she asked. 'Are the boys arguing in your class? I know they can be a nuisance.'

'The problem is not in your household,' he said. 'It's outside. In the city.'

Oedipus swept round behind him and pulled up a light wooden chair. 'Sit,' he said. 'Get your breath back.'

The old man sat down heavily, banging his elbows on the carved flowers which covered the arms of the chair. He sat for a moment, looking at the stone floor. 'My queen,' he said when he raised his eyes again. 'Too many people are falling ill. It reminds me of before.'

'Of before?' she asked. But she knew what he meant.

'Of the Reckoning,' he said. 'The headaches, the fever. Those who fell ill first are now developing the cough, four days in. It's the same as before.'

'You were alive during the Reckoning?' Oedipus asked. 'But that was a lifetime ago.'

Sophon eyed him. 'That's hardly an accurate system of measurement,' he replied irritably. 'It is more than your lifetime, than any of your lifetimes.' He looked from husband to wife to brother, and his tone softened. 'But somewhat less than mine. I was a child when it took the city the first time.'

'How did you avoid catching it?' Oedipus said.

'I didn't.' The old man's shoulders heaved. 'I caught it, but I recovered. So did my father. My mother died of it, as did my sister.'

'And you recognize the symptoms again now?' Jocasta asked.

'I'll know for sure in three days,' Sophon replied. 'When they start to die.'

'What can we do?' Creon asked. 'How did they stop it before?'

'They didn't stop it,' Sophon said. 'No one could. It

consumed the lower city. It devastated us. And there was nothing we could do to contain it or prevent it. Everyone fell sick, no one was safe. Eventually, people either recovered or died. Those who recovered didn't catch it again.'

'We can't let that happen now,' Oedipus snapped. 'There must be something we can do. In Corinth,' he paused, thinking about the stories he had been told as a child, 'they said it came from the water.'

Sophon nodded. 'The same belief arose here. It was nonsense, of course. People who lived near the wells died because sick people congregated near the wells. The disease makes you thirsty.' His eyes were cloudy as he remembered drinking everything he could find, and still feeling his furred tongue and cracked throat, desperate for water. He saw again his father offering him the last cup of water in the house, though his own lips were split and bleeding.

'Does water cure them?' Jocasta asked.

The old man shrugged. 'Many of them will die even if they can get enough to drink. All of them will die if they can't. Or if they refuse to.'

'Why would they refuse?' asked Creon.

'Fear,' Oedipus said, before Sophon could reply. 'They will avoid the wells if they believe the water is tainted. People aren't rational when they're afraid.'

'They closed the city,' Jocasta said, snatching at the memory she didn't know she possessed. But she remembered her parents talking about it: their grand adventures in the Outlying, while Thebes was bolted shut.

'The disease must have come in from somewhere,' Sophon agreed. 'A traveller, a tradesman, someone brought it in with him, this time just as before. But shutting the gates can't help you now. The disease is already here.'

'It might prevent more travellers bringing it in,' said Creon. 'You should close the gates.'

Jocasta looked across to her husband, her eyebrows raised. He nodded.

'The gates will be closed in the morning,' she said. 'Only one announcement beforehand. If Thebans are away, they will have to manage until we reopen the city. Foreigners in the city will be able to leave if they wish.'

'They might be no safer out there,' Oedipus said.

'That's not my concern,' his wife replied. 'I am only queen of my own citizens. How do we persuade the people that the water is safe?'

Sophon sighed. 'I'm not sure you can,' he said.

'We can make an official pronouncement,' Creon suggested. 'Telling the citizens that the water supply has been checked and is harmless.'

'What would you think if someone said that to you?' Oedipus asked.

'I'd think they had something to hide,' Jocasta said. 'But what else can we do?'

The four of them sat in silence for a moment, until it was broken by Oedipus.

'Put guards around the wells,' he said. 'Order them out there now. Two guards on each well from sunrise to sunset.'

'The heat of the day is when people will need water the most,' Sophon protested.

'They will store water to use during the day,' Oedipus replied. 'If the guards are seen there all day, drinking the water as they please but preventing ordinary citizens from doing the same, Thebans will be furious. They'll wait till the guards leave, fill every vessel they have, and carry it back to their homes.'

'That's clever,' the old man smiled.

'It's infantile,' said Creon. 'Thebans will believe their queen is deliberately withholding water from them.' He turned to his sister, his hands spread in supplication. 'They will never forgive you. They'll blame you even if they survive,' he said. 'Follow this advice, and they will hate you. You can't win.'

'I don't want to win,' she replied. 'I just don't want them to die. Alive and hating me is better than dead.' She addressed the old man again. 'Is there anything else we could do?'

Sophon nodded slowly. 'The Reckoning was fast,' he said. 'Impossibly fast. It went through the city like a blaze. People were dead or recovered in a matter of days. If they recovered, they didn't catch it again. Those people must help us nurse the sick: first the old, who survived it last time. And perhaps, once they have recovered this time, the young. And it is not just nursing we will need help with. Bodies must be buried or burned, as soon as they are dead.' He ignored the horror which spasmed across Creon's face. 'The stench of this disease is nothing compared to the smell of the dead, piling up behind the closed doors of houses. The Reckoning wasn't the only thing that killed people the last time. Corpses are dangerous, and they carry their own diseases. We need somewhere outside the city walls. A lime pit. Do you understand?'

'So we need to have men ready to dispose of the dead,'

Jocasta said. 'That shouldn't be too difficult. My guards can organize that.' She thought for a moment. 'There are a few older ones. And those without children, after them. Their commander will arrange it.'

'They should cover their faces,' Sophon said. 'With scarves. It makes it easier to breathe if you can't smell the dead.'

'Very well,' she said. 'What else?'

'Nothing that will help,' the old man sighed.

'What else?' she asked again, reaching over to her friend and patting his arm so he understood that she needed to know everything, even if it would frighten her.

Sophon thought for a moment, and spoke again. 'Even if they have water to drink, and somewhere cool to sleep, even if this heat breaks and the disease breaks with it, and even if we can get rid of the bodies before they contaminate anything else, it might not be enough to save everyone who could have survived. Because people stop trying when they've lost too much. It's not something you can prevent. I survived because my father survived. I had him to live for and he had me. So although my mother was gone . . .' He paused to wipe away a tear which had sprung from his eye, pushing his hand into his face as though he wanted to punish it for its weakness. 'I had someone to feed me and look after me. And my father had someone to look after. He couldn't just lie down on the ground and weep for everything he had lost, though I'm sure he wanted to. And that's the one danger you can't guard against. The more people die, the more people have lost their reason to live. Do you understand?'

Jocasta nodded. Of course she did.

19

Everything happened so fast, but also too slowly. Someone – one of the guards, I suppose – reached around me from behind. His hands were covered in wiry hair, and the knuckles were swollen and calloused. He held me in a strange, clumsy embrace, and lifted me away from Eteo. I could hear Ani sobbing on the other side of the square, and Haem murmuring words of comfort. I looked up to see she had turned into his chest, her back heaving, one small hand clenched on his tunic. I stood alone as people walked around me: the guards carrying Polyn on a litter, reverently, because he was the king; the ones who walked past Eteo without noticing his precious body, as though he were a pile of refuse; my uncle, walking out from the shaded colonnade in front of the treasury and into the morning sun, which illuminated what would have been better left in darkness. I saw Creon's mouth move as he spoke to one of the guards, but too quietly for me to hear. There was a rushing sound in my ears, as though I had dived underwater. Everything else was muffled and distant.

Slaves rushed into the square from all sides, and stood waiting to be given orders: my uncle directed them calmly to remove Eteo from the courtyard stones. He didn't use my brother's name. He said 'this' and gestured. I stepped forward to help them, because it was my duty – mine and Ani's, as their sisters and closest kin – to prepare both my brothers for burial. But the slaves bustled past me, as if I were no more than one of the statues which stand in the four corners of the square. Both brothers would need to be washed and wrapped in white cloths. And we would need to place some small piece of gold – a ring or a thin chain – into each one's hands or around his neck. Thebans believe the ferryman will not take someone across the river of the dead without some payment for his trouble.

But even as I was thinking about all this, a part of my mind wanted to shout out that it was all ridiculous. How could my brother be buried, when it was impossible that he was dead? He was alive a moment ago; he could not now be something else. I was looking around the square, expecting Sophon to arrive and explain that he could revive Eteo, stitch him back together as he had done me, shaking his head and tutting about how we got ourselves into such scrapes. But he didn't come.

The slaves carried Eteo away before I could touch him. It was only later I realized they were taking him the wrong way: out towards the main courtyard, when he needed to be carried to the family square, so we could lay him out and wash him. I knew something was wrong at the time, but it seemed so minor, after everything else.

My uncle finally noticed me and my sister, and directed a slave girl over to each of us. She told me that I must go to the family courtyard, and wash my brother's blood from my feet, from where I had blundered into the square, too late to save him. Only then did I look down and see she was right: my feet were covered in Eteo's sticky black-red blood. I wanted to clean myself of such a terrible pollution, but simultaneously, I wanted to kneel down and rub my hands in the blood: to run my fingers through it and paint it over my face.

But as I felt my knees collapse beneath me, the guard who had lifted me back from Eteo a moment and a lifetime ago stepped forward and caught me. He glanced over at my uncle, and swung me up into his arms, as though I were a child. He carried me away from the scene of my brother's death towards the family square.

Not just the scene of one brother's death, the scene of my both my brothers' deaths. The loss of Eteo was so enormous, I could barely see around it to Polyn. I could not take in what had happened: my whole family gone except Ani. I heard the words of the slave girl, as the guard put me down carefully on a bench by the water pump in the corner of our courtyard, but I couldn't think how to do what she was saying. Soon, more slaves approached me, all carrying water and cloths. One undid my sandals and slipped them off, before wiping my ankles and feet with her cloth. She rinsed it out into a small wooden bucket, and I watched the water darken with Eteo's blood.

'Where's Ani?' I said to her, as she finished, folding her cloth in half and placing it on the edge of the bucket. My sister was still with Haem, I supposed, and I needed her. When she finally came through the gates, I stood and ran to her, forgetting I was barefoot until I was standing on the sharp stones beneath the colonnade. She held out her arms and, clinging to one another, we stumbled away from the courtyard to be alone together with our grief. We sat on one of the couches in her room – a puffy, cushioned thing which our mother used to lie on when she was tired. Ani's face was streaked with tears: her hair was sticking to the salt left on her cheeks. She reached over and squeezed my hand.

'Did you know what he was planning to do?' she asked.

'Of course not,' I told her. Though at that time, I did not know precisely what Eteo had done, only what my uncle said he had done, and I knew better than to believe everything people said in the palace. 'I knew he was angry with Polyn. I knew he wanted to get out of the courtyard. You'd know this too, if you hadn't disappeared.'

She blushed, knowing the accusation was fair. 'I'm sorry, Isy. I didn't think about him.'

'Or me.' I wasn't in the mood to make her feel better about how she had behaved.

'No,' she agreed, fresh tears springing from her eyes. 'I just wanted to be with Haem. He was planning to announce our betrothal today.'

I stared at her. 'He might have to wait until our brothers are in the ground.'

'I know. I'm sure he will. I didn't mean to suggest that . . .' She paused. 'I'm sorry, Isy. I know you've always admired him.'

Now it was my turn to redden. I had tried so hard to avoid letting them see that I cared for our cousin at least as much as she did. I had always known he would choose her. It would have been unthinkable for him to do anything else: quite aside from her beauty, she was the elder sister. I could not be married before she was.

'It doesn't matter,' I told her.

'It does,' she said, gulping. 'Who will want to marry you now, Isy? After what our brothers have done? I know I've told you before that you would be hard to marry off, but I thought there was at least a chance. You know how people have gossiped about our family since . . .' She refused to say the words. She always had, ever since she and I had watched our mother be carried through this courtyard on a litter. 'This will just confirm that what people say about us is true,' she said. 'That our family is cursed, has always been cursed. For two brothers to kill one another . . .'

'Cursed? What does that even mean?' I asked. 'Polyn and Eteo have never been close. Sharing the kingship was the only way to keep their dislike of one another in check. And then Polyn changed his mind about sharing Thebes with Eteo, as he has done with everything else since I can remember. The only curse is that Polyn should have been born an only child.'

She looked startled. 'Are you saying this is all Polyn's fault?'

'Ani – open your eyes. Or at the very least, use them to look at something other than your intended. Polyn is the one who tried to throw everything into chaos. Polyn is the one who tried to turn the people against Eteo. Polyn is the one whose friend attacked me.'

'You can't mean what you're saying.'

'I saw the man again, Ani. I saw him at the coronation games. I recognized him straightaway.'

'But you said the man who stabbed you had his face covered.'

'His eyes weren't covered.' Ani opened her mouth but

she did not argue. She knew that I would not have made a mistake about something like this.

'And that's why Eteo . . . ?'

'Of course. What did you think?'

'I thought he was seizing the throne, Isy.'

'But he's your brother. You know what sort of a man he is. Eteo isn't at all ambitious.'

'I know,' she said. 'But you must see what it looked like. Eteo attacked Polyn.'

'I don't believe that.'

Ani looked at me for a moment, and pushed her hair back, shifting the strand which had stuck itself to her face. 'It doesn't matter what you believe, Isy. It matters what everyone else believes, and they will all think Eteo was the aggressor.'

I knew she was right. 'We need to tell people that they're wrong,' I said.

She patted my arm. 'We will. We can do all this once I am crowned queen.'

I was so startled by her words that I could find nothing to say. How long after she saw our brothers dead did she decide she should succeed them?

*

I was in my own room now. There was a basket of raw, greasy wool which had been in the corner for so long it had acquired a thin coating of dust. I hated spinning, and always had. It was the appropriate task for women in the royal household, my uncle once said, when I asked him why I should work wool badly when we had a palace full of slaves who were skilled at spinning and weaving some of the finest cloth in Hellas. Creon knew I was happier in lessons, or playing the lyre, and he did not press the point.

But today, I needed to do something with my hands, or I would lie on the ground and scream my brothers' names until my throat was raw. I could not play the phorminx: there were not yet words or music for what had happened. There would be elegies to come. But not yet.

I sat on the floor next to the basket, pressing my back against the wall. I took a handful of wool and began to turn it over, picking out the burrs and seeds which had caught in it. I piled them up on the wooden stool, and began twisting the wool to make a thick, lumpy thread. It unravelled itself so quickly: how did the slave women keep theirs from returning to a puffy cloud of fibres? I pulled on the thread with my other hand, tightening it to keep it straight. Ani was right, of course: she would be queen now. No one would expect us to share the throne, as our brothers had. She would be queen, Haem would be king, and Thebes would be unchanged for most of its citizens. But the palace would be changed, and I would be changed.

Where would I go, when Ani and Haem had this court-yard for their own family? Would I stay in my rooms, as her unmarried sister? Ani was right about my chances of marriage now, but she always had been. I had spoken about it with Eteo many times, and he had always promised that I could live in his court, no matter how many children he produced. They'll need their wise aunt, he used to say, and I felt a wrench through my gut at the loss of my brother and his future. I tried to concentrate on protocol, so I could staunch my tears and catch my breath. The appropriate match for me was a prince from another city. But to be the sister of two murdered brothers was a curse in itself. People would believe the cruel tales about the gods persecuting the children of my parents: and who would want to ally themselves with someone who came from such a wretched house, of which stories could never be told without sadness?

I felt the grease spreading across my hands as I carried on twisting the wool, and saw the dirt was discolouring my nails. Eteo couldn't have known that Polyn would fight. He could not. He must have believed that our oldest brother would stand aside when presented with the truth: that his siblings knew what he had done. But had Eteo been foolish? If Polyn was so shameless that he could enlist a friend to attack me, he was hardly likely to be shamed when he was found out. Eteo should have foreseen this, and then he would still be here with me now, watching me and marvelling at how I could ruin a whole sheep's worth of wool in a matter of moments. My brother had made a simple error: he had assumed that Polyn would behave as he himself would have behaved. But Eteo was never like Polyn, could never have been so devious. So how could he think Polyn would behave like him?

I dropped the thread and watched it unfurl back to its unwound state. Why was the courtyard so quiet? The slaves should have brought Polyn and Eteo in to their rooms by now, so we could wash them and wrap them with the other women of the household. Where were they?

We should have known what was coming. Especially me; trying so hard to find the story that made sense of our home and our family, imagining myself a historian, an astute chronicler of events. I fell so far short of what I imagined myself to be. I was no historian, no poet; merely a fool, failing to understand every single thing that happened until it was too late. The humiliation of realizing this was terrible. Who was I, if I wasn't the clever, observant creature I had always imagined myself? I was no one. I was the stupidest of us all. Because I was watching so closely, and still I was tricked, like a gullible fool trying to spot which cup the ball is under: so confident in his prediction, so risible in his confidence.

In the time that I had been sitting with my spindle and my worthless woollen yarn, thinking only of my future, the palace had changed irrevocably. The neat destiny my sister had spied for herself was not to be hers after all. She was the heir in line to the throne, but the throne was no longer vacant. At the precise moment that I was wondering why the slave women had not summoned me to wash my brothers' corpses, I heard a distant, tinny peal.

I knew immediately what it was: a herald's horn, sounded for an official pronouncement in the main square. I stood up and ran to my door. They were announcing the death of the king. Ani's door swung open too, and her eyes met mine. She frowned, and reached out her hand. We scurried along the side of the family square, and then through the second courtyard, both of us trying not to look at the bloodstains which still covered the ground. The guards should probably have prevented us from crossing to the gates into the main square, but they were nowhere in sight. It was much later when I discovered they had all been marched out of the palace and executed, the standard punishment for failing to prevent the death of a king.

The final squawk of the horn had barely died down before my uncle stepped forward on a podium and reached out his hands to quieten the small but excited crowd which had gathered. Rumours about my brothers must have been racing across the city from the moment Eteo walked into the treasury this morning, and the murmuring was growing louder. My uncle stood waiting for them to realize that he would not speak until they were quiet. Eventually, their curiosity overwhelmed their desire to deliver gossip dressed as fact.

'Men of Thebes,' Creon said. 'The king is dead. Slain by his brother, cut down by bitter rivalry.'

The murmuring began again, more intensely than before.

'I stand before you a bereaved uncle,' Creon continued. 'Not one but both my nephews died today, each by the sword of the other.' I felt Ani's hand squeeze mine. She wanted me to keep silent, even as we heard him lie. 'It is a dark day for Thebes,' my uncle said. 'And it must also be a new beginning. It was never my desire to inherit the mantle of power from my sister; you all know me and you know this to be true. I was content to be the adviser of kings, I have never sought kingship for myself.'

The crowd of strangers nodded, flattered by the suggestion that they were party to decisions made in the royal household, when they simply happened to be in the market square as the news erupted.

'But I can shirk my responsibility no longer,' he said. 'Today I accept the role I now acknowledge I was destined to perform.' A priest in a hastily tied robe stepped up behind him with the bright gold crown which had last been placed on Polyn's head. My uncle bowed slightly, and accepted it over his own balding pate. The crowd cheered: one king was much the same as another to them.

So my sister did not become queen. And I realized at last – too late – that Polyn had been the victim of a conspiracy, just as much as Eteo.

20

Jocasta looked up at the sky. How had the sun moved so quickly? Sophon and Creon were somewhere in the city, carrying out her orders. She had asked them both to return to the palace before nightfall. Before the gates were closed for the duration of the Reckoning. Sophon had said nothing, only squeezed her arm as he left, smiling. She knew he would not be back until the sickness had passed through the city. The stubborn old man would be treating everyone he could, relying on his immunity to the disease, disregarding his age and increasing frailty. But her brother would return, bringing his family with him. If she could just keep them all safe, it would be something to cling to, while her city was battered by the vicious storm.

When the two men left this morning, Oedipus had wandered back to the family courtyard alone. When she returned there herself, she found him working in the garden, even though the midday sun was punishing. His grey tunic was wet, and his hair had furrows running through it, where he had pushed it back from his face with damp hands. He looked so beautiful that she paused to admire him. Her husband was twenty-seven years old, and to her eyes, he looked the same as when he arrived ten years ago. His eyes still glittered with flecks of gold, his unmarked skin still shone like ripe apricots. His muscles had retained every defined curve. Unable to avoid the comparison, she looked down at her own body and wished for the thousandth time that carrying each of her children had not left its traces on her. She had aged so much more than her husband, though ten years was a larger proportion of his life than of hers.

Every morning Jocasta woke up wishing that time might flow backwards at night, just for her, so she could stay where she was, a summer or two past forty until he caught up with her. She never complained of the backache she had when Ismene wanted to be picked up and carried. She never mentioned the soreness she felt in her hips and knees when she bent down to pick up a discarded wooden toy. She knew Oedipus would sympathize, would offer to rub her aching muscles, but she couldn't bear for him to think of her as old enough to have painful joints. She knew what scorn she had felt for Laius, who always had some niggling injury. So she ignored the discomfort, in the hope that it would disappear. But it never did: it simply moved to a different sinew or bone, to torment her anew.

'You have slaves to do the gardening for you,' she smiled, as she walked over to him. The children were too hot even to quarrel, and were drowsing under the colonnade.

He looked up from the plants he was cutting back.

'They're dying back a bit from the heat, but don't worry. The roots are healthy.'

'I'm glad,' she said.

'I'll go and talk to the night-watchmen after we've

eaten,' he said. 'They need to know what's going on, so they can drum up some extra men.'

'People aren't going to storm the gates,' she protested. But she knew there was no point.

'It's best that we're prepared,' he told her. 'My parents told terrible stories about the last time. They used to frighten me with them when I was a child, tell me to hurry up to bed because the rats were coming. That's what they called the plague orphans, in Corinth.'

'We don't need to close the palace because your parents terrified you with bedtime stories,' she said.

'Your doctor told you to close the palace,' he reminded her. 'What's your brother doing?'

'He's organizing men to guard the wells and prepare to bury the dead,' she said. 'He'll be back here before it gets dark.'

'Are you sure they should stay here?' Oedipus asked. 'Eurydice, Haemon: they're definitely not ill?'

'Would it matter if they were?' she said.

'Yes,' he replied. 'Of course it would. My darling, I don't want to see you go through the pain of losing your brother or your sister-in-law or your nephew. But you must know,' he took her shoulders and shook her gently, so she raised her eyes to meet his, 'I would see them all die before my eyes, rather than let them anywhere near you or the children. You know that.'

And she nodded, wondering how he could make a declaration of love sound so much like a threat.

Jocasta had tried everything to distract Oedipus from the setting sun, but as she looked across at him from the divan where she was pretending to sleep, she saw him glance up in irritation: he was finding it hard to see as the evening drew in.

She stood up and walked behind him, reached around her husband, draping her hands on his chest. 'Have you finished with your plants for today?' she asked.

'I'm just thinking about all the things we need to do,' he said.

'There's nothing to do.' She feigned a languidness she didn't feel, but she had done all she could for her city. At dawn tomorrow, criers would walk through the streets announcing that Thebes would close her gates, for as long as was necessary. Any travellers needed to leave immediately, or they would be locked in regardless. When the weather broke, she would consider allowing the gates to be opened for people to leave, although there would be no admittance to the city for two months, at least. The plague had come in from the Outlying; she could not take further risks.

'What do you mean, there's nothing to do?' Oedipus tugged her wrists, pulling her hands away from him. 'I want to be sure the children are safe. How long do you think the illness takes to show itself? We need a quarantine period for anyone who left the palace today or yesterday. They can't come near you or me or the children until they have proved themselves healthy.'

'That's a good idea,' Jocasta murmured into his ear, knowing this was her best chance of diverting his attention from the sinking sun. She felt him squirm a little from the tickling sensation of her breath in his ear, and gently kissed the lobe. He took a deep breath, but then moved away, saying, 'That'll have to wait, my queen.'

'No,' she said, as he turned to face her. 'Nothing has to wait.'

'The gates need to be closed,' he said, gently unhooking her fingers from his arms. 'I'm going to order the men to do it now.'

'They know when to shut the gates.' She tried to laugh. 'They do it every night.'

'But tonight is different, lover. Tonight they need to be locked and barred. No one in, no one out. They need to understand that there are to be no exceptions.'

Jocasta loathed arguing with her husband. They hardly ever raised voices against each other. He was impetuous and could be quick-tempered, but she rarely allowed things to escalate into a full-scale disagreement.

'I'm not sure Creon's back yet,' she said. 'They need to wait for him.'

Oedipus reached down and cupped her chin in his hand. He had beautiful hands with long, slender fingers like a musician. He rarely played the lyre these days, but she loved to watch him when he did. He shook his head gently. 'They can't. We need to lock up, whether your brother is here or not.'

'He's only away because he's doing the job I asked him to do,' she cried. 'You can't punish him for that.'

'He should have sent Eurydice and Haemon up here before he left,' Oedipus said. 'I wonder why he didn't.'

'Because he thought he'd be back in time,' she said. 'Please.'

'Are you really begging me to allow your brother into

our home?' he asked, wrenching his hand away from her face so quickly that she felt her head lurch on her neck, and winced from the pain. 'When he's been all over the city today? Do you think that's wise? When he might bring in the plague and infect you, or me, or our children?'

'He's my only brother,' she said, tears falling from her eyes. Oedipus had never planned to wait for Creon, she realized. She hated crying in front of her husband; she knew it made her look old. She turned her face away from him.

'He should have come back sooner,' Oedipus said, and stalked off to the front of the palace. Jocasta listened to the pebbles crunch beneath his anger, until he was too far away for her to hear. She sat on the edge of the divan and heard the distant grate of iron on stone. The gates were closed. Then a loud thud, which took her a moment to place. It was the sound of the thick bars of black pine – rarely used – sliding home across the inside of the gates. She strained to hear the sound of Haemon, squealing with excitement because he and his parents were spending the night at the palace and he had just found out. But the sound didn't come. They hadn't arrived in time. She felt a stabbing pain in her left temple, and knew it would soon be followed by a similar pain on the other side. She walked over to the fountain and dipped her hands in the water, then drew small circles around her throbbing brow. Sometimes the coolness eased the pain, but not tonight.

*

A month later, they reopened the palace gates. The plague had danced through the city this time. It did not annihilate everything it touched, and was – according to those who remembered its first incarnation – less ruinous this time. Many Thebans had boarded up their windows and stayed inside for the duration – darting outside to collect water in the darkest portion of the night – and most of them had survived.

Of those who were infected, many more lived than died. This Reckoning was more predictable than before: it picked off the very young, the very old, the sickly and the weak. But it did not cull the healthy with the same careless vigour it had shown before. Once again, it fed on the lower reaches of the city. But it was not catastrophic, only terrible, so the city did not descend into anarchy, as Jocasta had feared might happen, with their queen locked behind the palace gates. There was anger that the water supply was guarded for the duration of the sickness, but none of the guards was lynched, as had looked likely at one point. The citizens did not like their queen withdrawing from her city when it was in crisis, but most were honest enough to admit that they would have done the same themselves, if they had been able.

Jocasta sent her criers through the city, proclaiming the end of the Reckoning and asking her citizens to continue their vigilance against the symptoms of the disease in future. On the day the palace and city gates were reopened, she hoped her brother would appear, but he did not. She knew he must be angry with her. She had asked the guards – discreetly, when Oedipus was busy elsewhere, playing with the children in the garden, as the heat had finally broken – whether her brother had arrived at the palace on the night the gates were closed. They had arrived much too late, she had discovered. Long after sunset: Creon and Eurydice, the latter carrying Haemon on one hip, his legs swinging as they walked. Creon held a torch in the thickening night, to light their way across the uneven stones and old vegetables left rotting in the market square.

Creon had carried out every task Jocasta had entrusted to him. He had travelled across the city, speaking to her men directly. He had warned Eurydice that she would need to pack their essentials while he was away, but when he returned he found she had ignored him, saying she preferred to stay in her own home, no matter what was coming.

A bitter argument had followed and he had hurled clothes and valuables into two large cloth bags as quickly as he could. But Eurydice refused to leave the house. What about looters, she asked. What if people broke into their home and moved themselves in? How could they prove it was theirs? Eurydice was more afraid of losing her home than her life, Creon told her. But by the time he dragged her and Haemon from the house, darkness had fallen. They walked in silence the short distance up the hill to the palace. Even Haemon – usually so talkative – was quiet. He knew his parents were angry with one another, and was fearful of making things worse. When the family reached the palace gates, the guards, who had known him for more than ten years, refused him entry. The gates were barred, one of them shouted from inside the courtyard. No exceptions.

Creon was unlike his brother-in-law in almost every regard, not least in the way they each expressed anger.

While Oedipus radiated his annoyance, conveying to anyone who could see him that he was displeased, Creon was contained. He did not attempt to reason with the men, but simply turned around to take his family home. Only his closest friends could have deduced his feelings.

'Where are we going? Why aren't we going in?' asked Haem.

'I told you. I said they didn't want us there,' Eurydice hissed. 'Everyone can see it besides you: your sister doesn't care a jot for anyone but herself and her husband.'

Creon was too weary to argue with his wife. He walked back to his house, and unbolted the doors. He used his torch to light a smoky candle, then extinguished the larger flame with a handful of sand.

'I'll get food and more water tomorrow,' he said. He took his son's hand, and half-carried him to bed, the candlelight flickering on the walls.

His wife sat alone in the darkness until he returned.

'We were too late,' he said. 'That's all.'

'We're their family,' she said. 'That should be all.'

He nodded. 'I thought they would let us in. We should have left earlier. If Jocasta had been there . . .'

'If Jocasta wasn't there, it was because she didn't want to be,' Eurydice snapped. 'She knew you were coming back tonight. She hides behind Oedipus, you know that. She won't criticize him or disagree with him, even when it means throwing us to the wolves.'

Creon smiled. 'I'm not sure we should add wolves to the list of things we need to protect ourselves against,' he said. But Eurydice wouldn't take the cue and ally herself with her husband against the world.

'You always take her side,' she said. 'Always. She uses you, and then she ignores you when it suits her. You're the only person who can't see it.'

Creon turned away from his wife and went to bed. The next morning, he rose to find she had not come to bed herself. When he walked into their living space, he was surprised to find it empty. He looked around for a sign from his wife, something to indicate where she might have gone.

Eurydice had been taught her letters by her father long ago, but she rarely used them. So it was several moments before Creon noticed the wax tablet on the table. It belonged to Haemon, who used it in his lessons at the palace. Sophon must have let him bring it home to practise scratching onto the wax without pushing through and damaging the wood beneath. It was a challenge for a childish hand. Even when he saw the tablet, he didn't notice the writing at first, assuming the ill-formed letters must be Haemon's. Only when he had looked everywhere else and found no hint of Eurydice's whereabouts did he look at the tablet more closely.

'I have a headache and the thirst,' she had written. 'Look after him.'

21

On the day of Polyn's coronation, I had thought the
only thing I wanted was to feel safe again in the palace.
In my home. But I was mistaken. We had never been
safer, my sister and I. No one could now enter the palace
without prior consent from my uncle. None of the aristoi
– Polyn and Eteo's friends – had been allowed in since the
day my brothers died. They had been replaced by their
fathers: Creon preferred older men for his advisers and
colleagues. But we were now prisoners in what used to be
our home. Every door and gate had been locked. I hadn't
seen anyone but my sister and the servants for days.

I finally persuaded my uncle over dinner the night after
they died that I should be allowed to see Sophon. I told
him my lyre had fallen out of tune, and I had broken
one of the strings retuning it. He told me I should be
weaving, behaving as though he had always been king,
as though nothing terrible had occurred only a day earlier.
Ani produced a sample of the cloth I had made: a rich,
red wool, woven into a lumpy, scratchy, ill-shaped piece of
fabric, and he decided it would be foolish to waste such
expensive materials on me. I could keep trying to spin my
own threads, but what I produced would not sell on the
cheapest market stall. It was – Creon sighed – an embarrassment to the royal household to have produced women

so unskilled in fine work. But he didn't say what anyone else would have: who will want to marry you with such a lack of the wifely skills? He had no need.

'I need my lyre or I cannot sing at the wake,' I told him. Thebans understand that paying our duty to the dead is more important than anything which happens while someone is alive. The announcement of deaths in the royal household meant that the city was in mourning, and would remain so for five days, until the burial was held. There would be fires and feasting, sacrifices and music played that night, as a sign that we had paid the dead their dues and were then allowed to re-enter the world of the living. Until the burial, Ani and I were in a liminal state: tainted by the dead, unable to fit in to normal life.

My uncle nodded his head in weary assent, and told me he would send Sophon into the family courtyard the next morning. 'You must use your time to compose a song for your brother,' he said. I thought I must have misheard the final word.

'I will,' I told him. 'I am already trying to think of the best way to twine their two stories together.' We were sitting around a small table, and Haem was reaching out to take a piece of flatbread, still warm with griddle-marks stamped across it, like a brand. Creon was holding a bowl of chickpeas in one hand, and scooping them onto his plate with a spoon.

'The song will be only for Polynices,' Creon said, and Haem froze just for a moment. Creon turned his head slightly to look at his son – who was sitting opposite Ani, rather than next to her, as usual – and Haem flickered back into life, picking up the bread he had been reaching towards.

'I could write a song for each of them,' I said, as though I were agreeing with Creon's suggestion. Sitting next to Ani, who had dropped her head, allowing her hair to hide her face, I could hear her shallow breathing.

'Just for Polynices,' he repeated. 'Eteocles will not receive a wake. He was an enemy of the city.'

'Don't be absurd,' Ani said, looking up at last. She had forgotten that arguing with Creon is never the best way to change his mind. You have to persuade him to do things differently, over time. Contradicting him only drives him to occupy his previous position more immovably. I saw Haem's eyes flash a warning, but too late. Creon turned his gaze from me to my sister.

'You will apologize for speaking in such a way to the king,' he said. 'You are no doubt distressed by the loss of your brother.' Ani has never been able to resist provocation.

'Two brothers,' she said. 'We have lost two brothers.'

'And you will mourn one,' he told her. 'Polynices was the king of this city, and Eteocles tried to overthrow him. It was treason. Thebes does not don her mourning garb for traitors.' The last word was almost spat onto the table, as he slammed the earthenware bowl down. I jumped, even though I was watching him do it.

'We can have a private, family funeral for Eteo,' I said quickly. 'I will compose a song for Polyn's wake. Ani and I will bury Eteo together, away from the rest of the city, if it pleases you.' My sister looked at me as though I were an imbecile.

'We must bury both of them together. In death as in life,' she said. 'You know that.'

'They were not close,' I reminded her. 'The burial is what matters. Everything else is just . . .' I ran out of words. I did not wish to be disrespectful of Theban traditions, or insult my uncle. But Ani should have known what I was saying was true. If Eteo didn't receive a fine white linen shroud woven by the best craftswomen in the city, it didn't matter. We were both shrouded in grief. That would suffice. He just needed to be buried, to be safe beneath the earth, so his shade could pass into Hades, and rest easy.

'You can't mean what you're saying,' she said. 'They must both be interred in the family grave. Eteo was not some peasant farmer, to be buried in the earth by his sisters. He was king of the city. He must be paid all due respect, not just for his death but for his life.'

'Niece,' said Creon, 'I can only imagine you are sick with grief. You will do me the courtesy of silence, or I will lock you in your room for a month until you are cured. Then you will miss Polynices' funeral, which I know cannot be what you want.'

'Why don't you say something?' Ani cried at Haem, who had been examining his plate during this whole conversation, his reddened ears the only hint he could hear them.

There was a pause. Haem did not look up, but only said, 'My father is right. Traitors and heroes are not the same. They cannot be treated as though they were.'

I wondered if these were his own thoughts, or those of his father. Ani could not have been more appalled if he had reached across the table and slapped her.

'So no one will stand up for Eteo,' she said, pushing back her chair.

'Ani,' I said. I wanted to take her to her room and tell her to stop this, before she pushed Creon into doing or saying something more dreadful. If he confined us both to our rooms, neither of us would be there to mourn our brothers at their funerals, a disgrace too terrible to contemplate. We needed to be patient, and work on my uncle over the next few days. Haem had agreed with his father, that was a valuable beginning to our bargaining: our views did not even taint our cousin, so surely we could be left to bury our brother. I was exasperated with Ani. On top of our grief she had added further difficulty.

'Sit down,' Creon said, without looking at her. She stood, uncertain whether she would make her point better by continuing to argue or by storming off to her room. A moment later, she decided on the latter. The slam of oak on oak as the door smacked into its frame echoed around the courtyard.

My uncle stood up. 'Very well,' he said to me. 'Your sister is incapable of civility or common sense. She would see the city celebrate a man bent on its destruction, it seems.' I bit my cheek, knowing I could not reply without worsening matters. But it was too late for that. 'So I shall make my point quite clear,' Creon said. 'Polynices will be buried as our traditions and family duty requires. He was – as Haem says – a hero. Eteocles will not receive a state funeral, as I have explained. As your sister seems unable to comprehend why, I shall explain things to her in a language she understands. The traitor will not receive a burial of any kind.'

With those words, he stalked out of the courtyard. Haem leapt up and followed him, casting a guilty glance at me as he went. And the next morning, you could have heard my sister's scream all the way up in the mountains, among the black pine trees.

*

She was shaking when I burst into her room. There were old curtains on the windows of the sleeping quarters on this side of the palace, because it faced east and without them it would have grown too hot in the mornings. I rarely used mine: I liked to see the sun at the start of each day, as it crested the mountains outside, and I have never minded the warmth. But Ani was a light sleeper and always drew hers at night. So when she had woken, she pulled back the curtain as usual, and looking out onto the hillside behind the palace, she had seen what no one should ever have to see. I gasped when I saw it myself, horror pushing all the air out of me. I put my hands on her shoulder and turned her around. I held her face against my chest and closed my own eyes, so I couldn't see either. When the slave girls ran in shortly after me, they screamed and drew the curtains closed again, and left without speaking, one clutching at the hand of the other.

I took Ani into the courtyard, and beckoned one of the servants over to us.

'Prepare a room on the west side of the courtyard for my sister,' I said. 'She'll sleep there tonight. And send someone with some wine for her now.'

The maid returned moments later with wine, water, honey and herbs from the kitchens. I used the honey to counter the bitter taste of the herbs, and gave the drink to Ani, holding it for her between sips. She drank it slowly, and gradually the shaking stopped. I took her to the newly prepared room – which was plain and dull but comfortable enough – and watched over her until the wine and herbs soothed her to sleep. Then I walked across to her room on my own, and pulled the curtain back. Terrible as it was, I could not do my poor brother the disrespect of refusing to see him.

At first glance, it looked almost like he was sitting against the rock, his head lolling as though he were dozing in the warm morning sunshine. But of course he was not. He had been propped up, his head rested against the rock for support, its second mouth gaping, black. One of his legs was turned at an impossible angle, and his sandal was only half on his foot. It must have been loosened when he was dragged outside. I tried to tell myself that he was just asleep, but he looked further from sleep than anyone I had ever seen.

I felt the sobs shudder through my body, now I was alone. Ani's grief had been so loud, I couldn't hear my own. So I let it consume me for a while, sitting on the floor of her room, looking out at the ruins of the person I loved most in all the world. I cried myself past thinking, past words. But after I had shed every tear, I knew what I needed to do. I had to bury him, of course.

I could not leave him to rot outside the palace, pecked at by birds and mauled by stray dogs. That my uncle could even consider allowing such a thing was horrifying. He knew his duty to the dead, as did we all. But there was nothing to be gained from speaking to him: Ani's outburst last night had seen to that. Creon would bear any disapproval from his subjects rather than change his mind. The one thing he had never been able to tolerate was any hint of weakness in himself. So having forbidden a burial for Eteo, he would not reconsider. But I had to find a way to put my brother beneath the ground. I could not leave him, casting about on the banks of the River Lethe, watching as his brother crossed into Hades, and he was left behind. The dread king and queen of the Underworld would never forgive such a slight.

I tried to think what I could do now. I remembered that my uncle had given me permission to speak to my tutor today, and decided I should do what I had asked to do. I stood up and drew the curtain across Ani's window again, begging my brother's forgiveness for leaving him, for turning away from him. I went back to my room to put on my sandals (a new pair had been placed in my room; the bloodstained ones had never been returned). I changed into a long, formal tunic and picked up a dark red shawl to cover my shoulders. I plaited my hair into a neat braid, and pinned it up behind my ears. My uncle would no longer permit us to walk around the palace dressed like children, I was sure. He used to chide me before, when Eteo was king, for not taking due care of my appearance. And since I wanted to go into the second courtyard to find Sophon, I knew my best chance was to behave as he wanted me to. After everything he'd done to become king of my city, it would be foolish to imagine that he didn't intend to use that power in every aspect of his rule, however petty.

It took me an age to persuade the guard that I had the

king's consent to leave the courtyard, but eventually – after checking with my uncle's advisers that I was truly allowed to walk through to a room I used to visit every day – he unlocked the gate and allowed me out. I skirted around the south then west side of the square, trying not to look at the faint pink discoloration which still marked the stones beneath Eteo when he died. I knocked on Sophon's door, and opened it carefully.

My tutor seemed to have aged years in the days since I last saw him. He stood slowly from his chair, supporting his weight on the sticks he had propped against his legs.

'Jocasta,' he said, and tears sprang from his eyes.

'You can't have forgotten me so quickly,' I said. But I wasn't sure he even noticed that he had called me by my mother's name. He opened his arms and I ran into them and embraced him. 'I don't know what to do,' I told him. And he patted my hair, as I had stroked Ani's earlier.

'You must not antagonize your uncle further,' he said, when he released me and sat back on his hard chair. 'And that goes twice over for your sister. She misjudges her situation. How can she not understand?'

'I'll make her understand,' I told him. 'She doesn't realize it was Creon who orchestrated all this: Polyn and Eteo at war with one another. She doesn't think like that.'

'No,' he nodded. 'Your sister has always been so open. She thinks everybody is the same as her.'

'Creon has forbidden us to bury Eteo,' I said. I let the words sink into the crags of his face. 'Is there anything you can do to persuade him he's mistaken?'

Sophon shook his head slowly. 'I doubt it. Your uncle is a difficult man, Isy. I have worked with him for many years, and I would never regard him as a friend. He is closed off from other people. He loves Haemon. And you, of course.'

I thought I must be hearing things. 'Me?'

'Creon was devoted to your mother for many years. He never liked your father. But it took something terrible for him to give up on your mother.'

'Do you mean Aunt Eury?'

'I do. But even though that soured his relationship with your parents, he kept coming here every day, after the Reckoning. Partly because he always wanted to be where the power was.' He swung a shaky arm around the room. 'And partly because he liked to see you. He used to tell you stories when you were very little. Perhaps you don't remember.'

I did not.

'Your uncle longed for a girl of his own, and you were the daughter he could not have. Your father was thrilled when Ani was born: how could he not be? Everyone told him how much she looked like your mother. Your father's great regret was that he had come into your mother's life so late. He always wished he could have met her when she was young. So Ani was enchanting for him: he felt he could finally see what Jocasta looked like before he knew her.'

'Ani was my father's favourite,' I said. People had told me so many times that it scarcely hurt any more, like pressing an old bruise.

'No,' Sophon said. 'No, she wasn't his favourite. He loved you all. If he had a favourite, it was your mother. He adored her from the day they met to the day she died.

But he always wanted children. He would never have been satisfied without you. But your uncle was devoted to you.'

'If that were true, he would let me bury my brother,' I said, angry.

'Go to Polyn's funeral tomorrow. Do everything he asks. Perhaps you'll be able to persuade him as the days wear on,' Sophon said. I began to cry again, thinking of poor Eteo being bitten and pecked while I could do nothing to put his body out of reach of scavengers. 'But if you're asking me for my opinion, it is this: your uncle is unlikely to change his mind. Still, the priests will tell him that he is committing a terrible wrong, against your brother and against the gods. They cannot pretend otherwise: they would fear to be struck by lightning for their perjury. All is not yet lost.'

I knew he was right. I wiped the tears from my face with the edges of my shawl before I stepped outside Sophon's study again. My uncle might be persuaded. I would have to pin my hopes to that.

22

The heat of the summer was fading but the memory of the dead burned ever brighter. Once people had stopped fearing for their own lives, they started to ask questions. No one doubted that the Reckoning had come back to claim another generation. But why? And why now? No one wanted to articulate their darkest fear: if the disease had been gone for fifty years, and returned, perhaps it could never be outrun. Thebans wondered if they had made a mistake all those years ago, when they unlocked their gates after closing the city against the first plague to ravage their world.

Whose idea had it been to open the city gates again? People argued for days about it. Some said it was the fault of Laius, the late king. But where was the satisfaction in blaming a man long dead? Others thought the order to unbar the gates had come from the queen. But the most popular view was that it must have been Oedipus's idea. The queen's husband came from the Outlying, didn't he? So of course he would want to open up the city to others like him. But it couldn't have been his idea, someone argued. The gates must have been open before he arrived in the city, or how did he himself get in? This was dismissed as sophistry by most. Besides, even if the gates had been open for the odd foreigner to enter the city, Oedipus had encouraged Thebes to look beyond her walls. He had championed trade with his own city, Corinth, and the opening of further routes both north and south. He had changed Thebes from fortress to market. And now look where they were: placing offerings on the graves of their dead children.

Jocasta was partially aware that the mood of the city had turned against her. She had never thought very much about her popularity because she had never needed to. Laius hadn't been a popular king, and he had lived and died exactly as he would have wished. Well, perhaps he had not died exactly as he had wished. But close enough. Still, as the days grew shorter, Jocasta felt the city turning cold.

She indulged in brief self-pity: she had done everything right, and followed the advice of her friends and experts. But because they had used subterfuge to persuade the citizens that the water supply was safe, she could not now claim credit for having lied to them. And she had closed the palace gates, which had perhaps contributed to her citizens' sense that she had cut herself off from them in their moment of crisis. But she had four children, and Sophon had warned her that the young were especially at risk. Surely people would understand that? Thebans would know – the women would know – that she had to keep her children safe. But a tiny voice in her ear told her that a woman who had buried her own infant in baked-dry ground sprinkled with lye would have little sympathy left over for a woman with four healthy children running about the palace grounds. She had locked down the city to prevent further contamination coming in from outside.

But how could people measure what hadn't happened? If the gates had remained open, many more cases of plague would have devastated her city, she was sure. But there was no way to prove it. People only counted the deaths there were against how many fewer they wished there had been.

Jocasta wished, more than anything, that she could talk things over with her brother. But the distance between them could not be traversed. Creon had come back to the palace a few days after the gates were reopened, and begun working on the tasks he had been forced to abandon during the plague. He had never reproached his sister for allowing the gates to be barred against him, never asked her how she could have abandoned him and his family, never shouted at the unfairness, never wept over the loss of his wife. He continued to offer advice when she sought it. But he never discussed anything personal, and he left promptly each afternoon. He no longer brought Haem to play with his cousins, but kept the boy at home. Jocasta had tried to apologize for their enforced separation, tried to express her sorrow for what had happened to Eurydice (though Oedipus was quick to remind her that her sister-in-law had already been carrying the sickness when he had closed the palace, and that she – and the whole family – were lucky the plague-riddled woman had remained outside). Jocasta could not find the words to bring Creon back to her. She wanted to touch his arm and beg his forgiveness, but after the contagion, the city had lost the habit of touch and so, she found, had she.

—

One morning, when the leaves were beginning to drop onto the ground and scratch her feet as she walked through the courtyards, Sophon arrived, asking to speak to her. She could see he was upset. He looked to have aged ten years since the start of the summer. Purplish-brown shadows were painted beneath his eyes, and his expression was oddly sympathetic. She stood up and wrapped her hands around his.

'Thank you for coming,' she said. 'What a terrible summer.'

'You did everything you could,' he told her, the words she had been longing to hear from someone. 'You are alive, your children are alive. You did well.'

Tears sprang from her eyes, and she wiped them away with her fingers. 'Do you honestly believe that?' she asked. 'I feel as though everyone hates me, and I don't know why. I thought I'd done everything right.'

She took him across the square to the padded chairs by the fountain, which were piled high with cushions. Jocasta waved away a servant who sprang up to arrange them comfortably for the old man. She picked up a pillow in each hand, and propped them behind Sophon's back as he settled himself onto the seat.

'You're going to tell me something horrible. I can tell.' She took the seat next to his, leaning forward, her hands gripping a cushion so hard her knuckles were white.

'How?' he asked.

'I've known you for over half my life,' she said. 'Longer than I've known anyone but my brother, and he . . .' She couldn't finish the sentence. Sophon took a moment to phrase his reply.

'I don't agree with your diagnosis that everyone hates you,' he said. 'But I must tell you the truth: the Thebans I speak to every day are not happy. They think you should have done more to help them. I always ask: what should the queen have done? Most of these people don't know I am your friend. So they are not trying to spare my feelings. I ask them because I want to know what they say, what they believe. And none of them has an answer. They all say the same thing: they just feel that you didn't do enough to help your people in their darkest hour.'

'Should I have been by your side?' she asked. 'The queen, mopping brows and checking fevers? Would that have saved lives? Even one life?'

'Of course not,' he replied. 'Your place was here. But the rumours that are swirling around the city . . . You would hate them.'

'What rumours?' she snapped. 'I suppose they all think we spent the summer eating and drinking and laughing in the palace, while they faced death alone.' She coloured, as she realized that this description was not entirely in-accurate. Oedipus and the children had spent a blissful summer, much of it in this garden. If her brother and his family had been with them, Jocasta might have enjoyed it too. But she could not weep for every Theban lost to dis-ease or anything else. She was the queen: she could not allow herself to be consumed by pity or sorrow.

Perhaps people thought she should have sealed the city years ago, when Laius died. But the Reckoning had been gone for decades by then: how could she have known that it would one day return? Besides, Thebes had more press-ing needs, for food and trade. The city was self-sufficient for some months of the year, but it would never be able to feed its population without importing some foodstuffs. Besides, Jocasta had always thought her city had a tendency towards self-importance. It needed the Outlying, however much its citizens preferred to imagine it did not.

'I don't want to upset you,' Sophon said. 'But you should know. You need to combat the gossip-mongers, and you can't do that if you don't know what they're saying. Has no one said anything to you? Your brother?'

She shook her head. 'Creon has not spoken much since the gates reopened,' she said. 'His wife died. He grieves for her. You must tell me. What are people saying?'

The old man looked at the ground for a moment.

'They say that the plague is your doing,' he said, the words spilling quickly from his mouth.

'My doing? How on earth could that be?' She laughed at the ludicrousness of it all. 'Have I poisoned the water supply? Who could possibly believe such nonsense?'

His rheumy eyes met hers for a moment, before she looked away. 'They don't think you are causing it on purpose,' he replied. 'But they nonetheless think you are the cause of it. They believe the city is being punished by the gods.'

She let out a snort of annoyance. 'I sometimes believe the city is being punished by the gods,' she said. 'Or why would stupid, small-minded people survive, when so many innocent children have died? You can't be serious.'

'I wish it was a joke,' he said. He reached out and touched her hand. There was worse to come. 'People believe you are committing a terrible crime against what is right and decent. You and Oedipus. They think that you have both affronted the gods, and that the plague is the consequence of your behaviour.'

'How have we affronted the gods?' she asked. 'Because Oedipus knocked down that ugly shrine and replaced it with a garden? Because I no longer prostrate myself before an unseeing oracular god, day after day, for no purpose? Since when did Thebes become a hive of religious devotion? I didn't see many of them going into the temples when I was a child.'

'You would now,' Sophon told her. 'People have become increasingly,' he paused, to think of the appropriate word, 'superstitious over the past few years.'

'Because they're afraid,' she said. 'I understand that.'

'You won't understand everything they're saying,' he said. 'Maybe you should send for Oedipus.' She was about to refuse, then realized the old man was trying to protect her. So she stood up and walked over to her quarters, returning a few moments later with her husband.

'What's this about?' Oedipus asked, as he perched on the edge of the fountain, facing them both. 'Jocasta said there's something you think we need to know.'

'Please believe that I would very much rather not be telling you any of this,' Sophon said. 'But in my experience, rumours don't disappear merely because their object doesn't know about them. Gossip is spreading and it can't be stopped by me. People say you have angered the gods with your marriage. With your children.' He exhaled, and his shoulders slumped forward.

'How?' Oedipus scoffed. 'That's ridiculous.'

'They're saying you can't be married,' Sophon said,

looking up to meet two appalled faces. 'They're saying you're mother and son.'

Oedipus gave a hard bark of laughter. 'That's the stupidest, most unpleasant thing I've ever heard. You can't be telling me that anyone is taking this seriously?'

Sophon nodded. 'I'm afraid so.'

'They know I came to the city ten years ago, for the first time?' Oedipus asked. 'And that Jocasta had her first child nine years ago?'

The glance between Sophon and Jocasta took less time than a beat of her heart, but it gave her away, just the same.

Oedipus didn't speak to her for three days. He left any room she entered, using the constant presence of their sons and daughters to keep conversation trivial. Even at night, he stood by her as they put the children to bed, but as soon as they were outside, he ignored her. He slept in another room, and locked the door. She placed her hand on his arm, and he flung it away, as though she were unclean. On the third night, she gave in and, even though her pride loathed doing it where the servants could see her, she fell to her knees before him and begged his forgiveness.

'How could you keep something like that a secret?' he asked. 'How?'

She reached out and took his hands in hers. 'I'm so sorry,' she said. 'It was all so long ago.'

'It wasn't always long ago,' he replied.

'It was,' she protested. 'When I met you, it had been sixteen, no, seventeen years earlier. I had already spent half my life trying to forget what had happened. I wasn't trying to keep a secret. Everyone knew. Everyone here, I mean, and I so much wished they didn't. I think one of the things I liked most about you, when we met, was that I didn't have to live with you knowing something awful had happened to me. You weren't sorry for me, like everyone else had been.'

His face softened slightly, though it could just have been the twilight playing on his skin. He gripped her by the wrists and pulled her up onto her feet. There was something undignified about a middle-aged woman on her knees.

'You could have told me,' he chided her. 'Not then, but later.'

'I know,' she said. 'I wanted to, often. But then I fell pregnant so quickly, and we were having our first child. We were embarking on a family together. I didn't want you to think I'd been there before.'

'But you had,' he said, and turned away from her.

'I swear to you I had not. Nothing was the same as before. I was on my own then. I had no one to take care of me. Except Sophon, and I only met him because I nearly fainted in front of him. It was all so awful. Everything was awful.' She began to weep as the long-hidden memories flooded through her. 'And then the baby was dead anyway. So I went through it all for nothing. I never even saw him.'

'What?' He turned back to face her, and wiped her tears away with his thumbs, though they were instantly replaced. 'What do you mean?'

'She took him away,' Jocasta sobbed. 'The cord was

wrapped around his neck. She said it would be worse if I held him, so she took him away. And,' she gulped the words, 'I've spent the rest of my life thinking about him. I imagined him growing up, getting bigger, learning to say my name, walking, running. I used to sit in here, on my own, so I could think about him in peace. Do you know what I mean? I just sat here, imagining him.'

'Do you still think about him now?'

She nodded, guilty. 'Sometimes. But when I try to find him in my mind, now I see Polyn instead. Or sometimes Eteo.'

'Do they look like you imagined he would?' Oedipus asked.

'I don't know,' she whispered.

'I wish you had told me,' he said. 'You've been hiding part of yourself from me.'

'I never wanted to spoil things,' she said. 'I was always frightened you'd guess. That you'd see the stretch marks on my skin and work it out.'

He shook his head. 'I didn't have anyone to compare you to. You know that.' He sat down beside her. 'What are we going to do now?'

'About these horrible rumours? I don't know. I can't prove the baby died.'

'Wasn't Sophon here? He is a witness, he can confirm you're telling the truth.'

'No,' she said. 'He wasn't here on that day. He wanted to be, but something happened. He was dragged off to the other side of the city for some reason, I think. I can't remember why. There was just me and Teresa.'

'Who?'

'She was the housekeeper. When you first arrived here.'

'Oh, her. She's probably dead by now, isn't she?'

'I don't know,' Jocasta admitted. 'Yes, she must be. She would be ancient.'

Oedipus nodded, and squeezed her hand. 'It will all be alright,' he said. 'Even if we can't find her, I will send a message home. My father will explain to everyone that I was born in Corinth. He'll swear to it, and so will dozens of people who knew me when I was a boy. I promise.'

'Will you send a message to him today?' she asked.

'Of course,' he said. 'I'm not entirely sure how to begin such a letter, but I'm sure I'll think of something.' He smiled at her, and she tried to smile back, but another sob broke through instead.

23

On the day of Polyn's funeral, I awoke early. The ceremony had to be carried out before dawn. Using a torch, I hunted around for my clothes, catching a glimpse of myself in the polished obsidian mirror Ani had given me for my last birthday, which seemed to have been a thousand years ago. I only half-recognized the girl looking back at me. Without Eteo, I felt like some of me was missing; I expected to see a scar or a missing eye or ear. Something that hurt so badly should be visible. I couldn't help thinking that the mirror might as well show nothing, if it couldn't show the truth. So I dropped it, expecting it to smash into a thousand tiny pieces. But it split neatly in two, and I was left with two worthless mirrors, where before I had only one.

The funeral procession would begin from the main courtyard of the palace, where Polyn had lain in state for several days. We had washed his body and covered it in oil and wrapped him in a white linen shroud. With every action we performed, I thought of the terrible lack of these same rituals for Eteo, who still lay outside the palace, mourned in secret, unburied. My sister and I had performed the prothesis for Polyn: chanting at his bier, tearing our hair, rending our garments, pummelling our breasts and hollering our grief to the skies for all to hear. The ritual informed the dead – wherever they were – of how they were missed by the living. But as the hours passed, I had begun to think that the ritual was for us, the living, to give expression to every corner of our grief. I had wailed for my brothers equally, and somehow they both knew it.

Ani and I would be allowed to participate in the ekphora, accompanying our brother's body to his final resting place: the tomb which already held our parents. Somehow, I had to think of a way to persuade my uncle that Eteo should also be laid to rest, even if he was not buried with the rest of our family. As Sophon had said, Creon was a superstitious man: I thought perhaps I could persuade him that my mother's shade could not be at peace while her younger son was prevented from joining her in the Underworld. But Sophon would scowl if he heard me saying such things: he thought that religion was nothing more than superstition, and it was beneath those who had studied to believe in what he considered to be stories for children. Our gods are conveniently like us, he would say, and why should they be? No answer I offered to this question ever satisfied him, until I gave in and said it must be because we invented them. We create gods that resemble us because that is all we know. They are not like us, therefore, but rather of us. Sophon believed that if horses could speak to one another, they would create gods which looked like horses. And perhaps he was right. But none of that would help me to persuade my uncle that Eteo could not be left outside the palace to rot.

I dressed in a plain linen tunic which I had not previously worn. The tunic I had for the prothesis was too badly torn to wear for the funeral procession, which was the formal, public display of grief. I would rather grieve in private, like other people. But that was not permitted for members of a ruling household. Over the simple tunic, I wore a dark grey linen robe. The hem had a stark, angular pattern woven into it, up and down, like mountains and valleys. I would wear my hair loose, rather than in its usual plait. And my feet were bare, as was proper for the ekphora. When you place a body in the ground, you should be touching the ground yourself.

I crossed the courtyard to find my sister before it became any lighter outside. If Creon had noticed that she was sleeping on the other side of the square, he had said nothing. But we were both trying to be discreet about it, in the hopes that he wouldn't find out. The slaves were surely keeping quiet to protect her. She hurried back with me to my room, and finished her preparations there. When the maid opened the door and told us our uncle awaited us, we covered our heads with dark linen shawls and followed her outside.

The main courtyard was crowded with people, even though it was still early in the morning. Thebes last buried a king and queen more than ten years ago. People would not let such a solemn a day go past without sharing in our grief. Ani and I walked with our eyes on the ground, as was appropriate, escorted by the maid until we reached the palace guards, and then by them until we reached Polyn's bier. There was a rustling from the crowd, as they bowed their heads. A priest stepped forward, his head covered and his manner supercilious. He offered up his prayers to the gods with the certainty of one who believed that the gods were lucky to have him.

The procession would now carry Polyn from the court-yard to the cemetery. Ani should have been the chief mourner, because she was closest to Polyn, both in age and in blood. But as she moved to take her place at the front of the litter, my uncle raised a hand, and the guards moved closer together, holding her back. Creon turned to face the crowd, including us in his speech almost incidentally, because we happened to be nearby.

'I shall accompany my nephew, hero and defender of Thebes, to his tomb,' he said. 'It is appropriate that one king should be attended by another.' The word he used to describe himself was Basileus: a ruler over his people. Before today, I had always heard my uncle called Anax, lord: a respectful title and one that conveyed his superior status to virtually anyone who spoke to him. But it had not been enough for his vaunting ambition and desire for power. I wondered if other people were as shocked as I was, but all I could hear was the crowd murmuring in agreement. Creon was their king now.

Ani was so quick that I heard her voice before I felt her move to the side of the guards, who had been distracted by Creon's speech, and place herself in front of them.

'I wish to speak,' she said. Her voice rang out like harsh music, and people instinctively turned to look at her, as they always had.

My uncle remained impassive, but Haem's expression spoke for both of them. Whatever she said, Ani would be lucky to finish this speech with her life. The crowd muttered in surprise, but their approval was audible. Even my uncle would not interrupt his grieving niece before a crowd of citizens, who were shifting their positions, all trying to catch sight of her. Though she was wearing the same dreary grey as everyone else, she shone as she spoke.

'People of Thebes, I thank you for coming here to pay tribute to my dead brothers.' Shock rippled across the square. Was she going to defend a traitor? 'Your presence is a great comfort to me and my sister in this darkest time in our lives. You know that we were orphaned when we were just seven and five years old. Since then, we saw our brothers as both parents and siblings: the only family we had.' I tore my eyes away from her to look at Creon. His guards were doing the same thing, casting questioning looks at him, hoping to find out what they should do, as my sister casually disregarded our uncle, eliding him from our family as she spoke. 'We cherished them and loved them equally. It was a day of unbearable cruelty which robbed us of the two of them. Today, Polynices lies before you as a hero. My brother Eteocles does not. His corpse has been dumped on the hillside behind the palace.' There were shouts from the crowd, but I couldn't make out the words or the intent. Were they angry with Ani for defending Eteo? Or were they angry with Creon for his brutal treatment of the dead? I couldn't be sure. 'Yes,' she continued. 'His body lies outside the palace on the hill, and it has done so for three nights.' Someone near the front of the crowd yelled 'Shame!' and more shouts followed.

'So I say this,' she continued. 'As we take Polynices – my brother, our king – to the cemetery, to the tomb of my family, I beg you to collect the body of my brother Eteocles – equally a brother, equally our king – and bring him too. I know you have been told that he was a traitor. But he was my brother, and I loved him. My sister Ismene loved him better than anyone. And so,' she paused to be sure she had absolute silence, 'so did Polynices. They argued – what brothers would not? – but they loved one another, all the same. Neither of them will rest easily if they are separated in burial. They were together in life and together in death. Let them be together again now, and forever. Please, Thebes, I beg you: do not let my family's tomb be desecrated by withholding what we owe.'

There was no doubting the mood of the crowd. Whatever they had been told about Eteo, they now stood in agreement with Ani. The sins of the living should be punished in life, but not after death. The limits laid down by the gods were quite clear. My uncle acted with decisive swiftness. He barked at the guards and several of them surrounded my sister. Four of them shielded her from the view of the crowd, while one pinned her arms to her sides, and another clamped his huge hand over her nose and mouth. She struggled frantically, but with no effect. I stepped forward to help her, but my uncle had foreseen this, and as he walked past me waving his hands calmly to quell the discontented crowd, he leaned in to my ear and said, 'Try to help her and I will kill her.' I knew he wasn't lying, so I stood powerless, watching my sister fight for air, then fall unconscious. When her body fell limp against the guard who was holding her arms, he bent down and swung her up into his arms.

'As you see,' my uncle said, his voice loud enough to command silence, though he did not shout, 'as you see, my niece is not well. Her words are pretty enough. Aren't they?' He gazed out at a crowd who had suddenly become aware of the number of armed men around them. You could see men's eyes flicker, as they remembered that they had left their sticks or knives at home to attend a funeral. They were not equipped for an uprising on a dark, bereaved day. Creon nodded, agreeing with their imagined response, and continued. 'Who could argue with the notion that brothers should be united in death? What man could be so audacious? I tell you, Thebes, I will argue. I say that no niceties should be observed when we speak about a man who turns on his city and on his own brother. None at all. Not because I choose to disrespect the dead. Not because I believe the gods of the Underworld will be pleased, if I rob them of their prize. But because I am the king of this city, and these are the choices I must make. Eteocles was a traitor. A traitor and a murderer. If he had not been, we would still have Polynices on the throne. I would not have been required to undertake the responsibility of kingship, so late in my life. It was against my choice, but I would not – will not – see Thebes descend into civil war. I will not see her undermined from within or from without. This is a city which has suffered enough. More than enough.'

The mood of the square was palpably changing again. Men who had cheered Ani were now clinging to the words of my uncle, seemingly unconcerned that they were supporting a diametrically opposite position to the one they had held moments earlier.

'But I, I have not suffered enough,' Creon said. 'You remember how I lost my wife in the Reckoning eleven years ago. And when Thebes lost her queen and king the following summer, I also lost my sister, and my brother-in-law. And now, this year, I have lost two nephews. But still I stand here before you, ready to face your anger, when I tell you that we shall not allow those who turn on their city to be treated in the same way as those who defend it. Because if I allow it for my nephew, a boy I loved,' his voice cracked so convincingly I almost believed him myself, 'and who I watched grow up alongside my own son, then I allow it for anyone. For everyone. And I will not see our city – my home – destabilized like this. Hear me now, and do not mistake me: anyone who betrays his city, who betrays you,' he pointed at the crowd – first one group, then another – including them all in his promise, 'that traitor – even if he is my own blood – will rot outside the city walls, unmourned, unwept and unburied. Thebes will stand, and the traitors will fall. Do you hear me?'

The crowd roared their approval. My uncle continued in a whisper, forcing people to quieten one another and lean in to hear him. 'So although I wish I could bury my nephew – and I do, Thebans, wish that very much – I will not endanger our city and I will not endanger you by giving way to my baser instincts. My hot-headed niece will spend a few days in the caves beneath the palace while she considers her behaviour here today. Guards: take her away, and give her bread and water, enough for three days. She will make her formal apology to the city Elders before she leaves her cell, I promise you that.'

It was a masterclass in rhetoric. As my sister's insensate body was carried out of the square, I turned to my uncle and begged.

'Let me go with her. Let me reason with her.'

He smiled without showing his teeth. 'There never has

been any reasoning with your sister, Ismene. She may look like her mother, but she has always had the disposition of her father. And if she isn't more careful – a great deal more careful – she will end up exactly like him.'

With these words, he signalled to the men who attended Polyn's bier. I recognized none of them: the aristoi might be somewhere in the courtyard, but they were not carrying my brother to his grave, as would have been appropriate. And neither was I. 'Come with me,' said my cousin, who had appeared beside me as Ani was carried away. 'Come back inside, before he turns on you as well.'

'I should be with Polyn,' I said.

Haem leaned so close to me that I could feel his breath on my skin. 'This is your only chance to bury Eteo,' he said.

24

Jocasta had never been able to understand how time moved so much more quickly as the years progressed. Looking back at her earliest years in the palace, she remembered the leaden weight of time, crushing her beneath its crawling pace, the hours which stretched into days, the days which expanded to fill months. But once the children were born, whole seasons seemed to pass before she had even noticed they had begun. The apples fell from the small tree in the shady northern corner of the court-yard, and she would dimly wonder when the pink-edged white flowers had bloomed and how she had managed to miss them. As she tried to cling to days that slipped through her grasp, she sometimes wished for the terrible days of the past, which dragged themselves out in front of her like a waterless desert she was forced to cross before she might sleep and repeat the whole tortuous process again the next day.

And this year, she would have given a great deal to be able to postpone summer forever. If she could only stop time at the start of spring, when the days were beginning to grow warmer, but the real heat was still months away. Thebes had limped from a devastated autumn into an unusually cold winter, but no one complained as the sharp north wind whistled through the gaps around windows and doors. Instead, people wrapped up in layers of clothes and shared blankets during the long winter nights. They congratulated one another on tolerating the cold so hardily. Everyone knew the Reckoning thrived in the heat. It had only ever visited the city in the summer, like a malevolent migrating bird. In the winter, it curled up, disappeared, shed its power like an old skin. Everyone was brave when their predator was gone. And, people whispered excitedly as they huddled around stoves and tightened their woollen robes around their thickest tunics, if it was cold enough for long enough, perhaps the disease would be wiped out altogether.

The hope that the plague might be exterminated by the snow – which was still falling three months after the shortest day of the year – was one which even Jocasta fell prey to. But when she asked Sophon for his medical opinion, he shook his head. He did not believe the plague was gone; it was more likely that it was only biding its time, waiting to unfurl its wings in the warm summer days. So Jocasta watched the trees change, from black to white as the blossom covered their canopies; from white to crimson, as the new buds were revealed, tightly wrapped against the branches; and from crimson to green, as the leaves unfolded and the fruit began to grow. And with each arriving day, the weight of foreboding which she carried around with her increased.

Gradually, the rains eased off, and the days grew hotter, more cloudless. By the time the long grasses swaying on the hillside behind the palace had yellowed in the dry heat, the diagnosis was undeniable: the Reckoning had returned. Word spread through the city more quickly than the plague itself, and once again, people stood in the streets in the heat of the sun, and prayed to the gods that their children would be overlooked again this time. They hastened to the temples and begged Apollo, the Archer, to shoot his arrows elsewhere, at other cities, other districts, other families. They poured wine and sacrificed kid-goats and new-born calves in the hope that this bloodshed might be enough to sate the Archer's greed. And then some withdrew, locked their doors and hoped that the strategy which had saved them last year would work a second time. Others were more angry than afraid because they knew no preventative measures could save them, not while the city harboured a king and queen who lived in a lawless, god-less union. There was no point praying that the Reckoning would brush past your home and leave your family untouched. The city's only hope lay in purging itself of the pollution it contained. Only then would the god cease his punishment.

Jocasta did not want to shut the palace gates again this year, if there was any way she could avoid it. She placated Oedipus by closing off the family courtyard first, and keeping the children and their nurse safe behind locked doors. She and Oedipus moved around the palace as usual, but visitors were never permitted to approach too closely. They didn't approach each other too closely either. Eventually, though, Jocasta had no choice. A messenger from Sophon told her that the disease was more powerful this year: although he did not consider it to be more conta-gious, it was killing a larger proportion of those it infected. She wavered then about shutting the gates, but allowed herself a little more time to make the decision.

In the end, it wasn't because of the plague that they had to shut the palace gates. It was because of the crowd.

It must have begun to form at night, because the gates were always closed at dusk. But one morning, the guards went to open up the main courtyard, yawning as they went because everyone struggled to sleep when the nights were so short and so hot. They found a small crowd pressed up against the gates, who began jeering and booing as soon as they caught sight of the men inside. Irritated by this rudeness, the guards responded with obstinacy, and left the gates locked. By the time Jocasta awoke, the watch commander had sent a message with one of the slave boys to say he was waiting to speak to her in the royal courtyard.

'Highness,' said the watch commander, bowing low. 'There is a crowd of people outside, and they are angry. I have said that the gates must be left closed until I countermand the order.'

'Do you know why the crowd is so angry?' she asked. His expression told her too much. 'Why today, in particular?' she clarified. He thought for a moment.

'No,' he said. 'But if you want my advice?' He paused to check that she did, and she nodded. 'Don't open the gates,' he said. 'They're troublemakers.'

'Is that your professional opinion?' she asked him, trying to smile.

'Yes,' he replied.

'And what do you think they'll do if they can't come in and petition their queen?' she asked.

'Give up,' he said. 'And go home. Some of them are drunk, madam, and that makes men behave in foolish ways. One idiot says they should march up to the palace and air their grievances, as though they couldn't do that during daylight hours. They arrive in the night like criminals, hammering on the gates as though they had any right to enter. They're nothing more than a noisy rabble, desperate to cause a nuisance. Give them the satisfaction and it'll only mean they resort to such behaviour more quickly next time.'

Jocasta nodded. 'Very well,' she said. 'I'll be guided by you. Leave the gates closed today and we'll open them again tomorrow.'

But when the guards looked out from their gatehouse the next morning, the crowd had doubled.

Jocasta did not want to disregard the advice of the watch commander. But, at the same time, she had lived for years feeling besieged in her own home. She refused to do so again. When she asked Oedipus for his opinion, he seemed unconcerned. Leave things till tomorrow, he yawned. We're all safe inside. So she took the advice of her guards, and left the palace closed for another day.

But on the third morning, the crowd had thickened again, and she decided she must speak to them, to find out what they wanted and why they wouldn't leave. She no longer agreed with the watch commander, that they would go home when they were bored. She found Oedipus idling in the courtyard, and asked him if he would come with her.

'Why? Do you think they want to see me?' he asked, his eyes half-closed against the sun.

'I don't know what they want,' she said, and the anxiety in her voice forced him to look up.

'You're afraid,' he said. She nodded. 'Afraid of people outside the gates?' he asked. She nodded again.

'The watch commander says there must be a hundred of them,' she said. 'More even.'

'You have the palace guards on your side,' he reminded her.

'Please,' she said, and reached out her hand to him.

Oedipus stood up and walked across the square hand-in-hand with his wife. 'I don't know what you think I'll be able to say that you can't,' he said, as they crossed into the second courtyard. Jocasta stopped when they reached the colonnade which connected it to the main square. She looked at Oedipus to be sure that he had heard it too: a buzzing sound from the front of the palace, indicative of far more than a hundred people. She nodded to the guards who walked out ahead of her. There was a slew of abusive shouts from outside the gates, but the guards did not react. They had always been so loyal to her, Jocasta thought, and she could feel tears prickling her eyes. She breathed through her mouth, hoping to control herself. She reached for her husband's hand, and he squeezed hers. But she didn't know if he was taking comfort or offering it. 'Wait for me here,' she said. 'I should talk to them alone, I think.'

'Are you sure?' he said. She nodded, and walked through the archway and into the public square.

The wall of sound was deafening. Jeering, baying, screaming at her. She couldn't even make out the words, almost any of them. She heard one high-pitched voice, screaming 'Whore', which carried over the melee. Jocasta walked slowly, calmly to a point in front of the locked gates, which people were thumping and kicking as they shouted. The gates barely moved in their sockets, and she took comfort in that. Her home was solid, even in the face of all these people. She did not speak, but simply stood waiting for them to stop. How had her city turned against her so entirely? Was this why Laius was so keen to travel? Did he know that Thebes turned on you, in the end? For the first time in her life, she wished she could ask her first husband a question. Gradually, the crowd subsided to a low malevolence.

'Thebans,' Jocasta said, refusing to shout. There was a sudden cacophony of hushing, as those who couldn't quite hear tried to silence those who were too far away to hear at all. 'You are gathered outside my gates and you are angry. I know the Reckoning has returned to our city. Perhaps you think I don't care. But I assure you, I am doing all I can.'

'Liar,' screamed someone, and it was repeated with approval. Jocasta felt the colour suffusing her cheeks.

'You may shout if you wish,' she said. 'But it will not change the facts. Doctors are working across the city: I have arranged it.'

'Lies,' shrieked another voice, but this one was quickly hushed.

'You may ask them,' Jocasta continued. 'They will tell you that I have paid them in advance to see any patient who needs their help. They will treat you and your loved ones, expecting no payment from you. Ask them. They have no reason to lie.' There was a shuffling among the crowd.

'Where has it come from then?' shouted one woman.

Jocasta looked across at her: a small, shabbily dressed girl with matted brown hair straggling to her shoulders and a baby balanced on one hip. The girl wore a brown tunic with its many holes patched in a pale grey fabric, clumsily made stitching holding each repair in place. The majority of this crowd wasn't vicious, Jocasta decided. Just scared. And she knew what it meant to be scared.

'I don't know,' she admitted, looking directly at the girl who had asked her the question. 'The doctors don't know either. But if you go back to your homes, and try to stay indoors for a few days, that will help to control the spread of it. Thebes will be rid of it more quickly if you heed my advice.'

'Is that why you've shut your gates?' sneered a man wearing a battered straw hat to protect him against the sun.

'Yes,' she said. 'It isn't safe for large numbers of people to congregate at the moment. That's why I'm asking you to go home. The disease thrives in conditions like this: hot weather, lots of people crowded together. I have closed the gates to try and keep us all safe.' The sneering man spat on the ground and Jocasta stiffened. 'The disease may well travel through bodily fluids,' she added, and had the spiteful satisfaction of seeing the people standing closest to him shudder away. 'I will order my gates to be reopened when it's safe again,' she said.

'It will never be safe,' a woman screamed. 'We're being punished.' The crowd surged forward and smashed into the gates again. Jocasta watched one man's head crack into an iron strut, and an angry red weal flowered on his forehead. Those at the front were in danger of being crushed.

'Punished?' she asked. 'For what?'

'For you,' someone yelled. 'For your relationship with him.'

Jocasta had almost forgotten Oedipus was listening in the shadows, though the crowd couldn't know he was there. 'Oedipus is my husband,' she said. 'Why would you think that deserves punishment?'

'He's your son,' came a voice from the middle of the crowd and across almost eleven years. Jocasta couldn't place it: was it her mother? It couldn't be: her mother had died years earlier. She looked hard at the direction the voice had come from, but she recognized no one in the sea of sun-browned faces and spittle-flecked teeth. 'My sons are in the palace,' she said. 'They are just ten and eight years old. Your accusation is a vicious slander.'

'Not those sons,' replied the voice. 'Your first son. You know the one I mean.'

'Who is that?' Jocasta said. 'I can't see you.'

The crowd separated to reveal an ancient woman whose spine had curved so completely that she was bent almost double. She leaned on a wooden stick disfigured by teeth-marks, as though she had been attacked many times by dogs. She wore ragged clothes so filthy that they could have been any colour before they were covered in grease and dirt. Her face was like a walnut, dark and wrinkled.

'Your first son,' the old woman repeated. Jocasta shook her head, trying to shake off the sensation that she was watching a conjuring trick. The voice of someone she knew, coming from a face she had never seen. The woman had almost no teeth, Jocasta noticed, just a few blackened stumps. A dirty stole covered the woman's head, and a few thin strands of white hair protruded from beneath it. 'You remember,' the woman said.

Jocasta felt the world shift, as though she had lost her footing and was falling sideways towards the ground. But she remained on her feet.

'You,' she said. 'My first child was stillborn. You would know that. You were there.'

Teresa's face split into a toxic smile. 'He wasn't stillborn,' she said. 'I just told you that, because I couldn't let you keep him. I couldn't keep my sons, so why should you be any different?'

'What?' Jocasta said. 'What are you saying to me?' The crowd was split between those who could hear her conversation with Teresa and those who had begun to peel away, persuaded by Jocasta's advice to go home. But a few people were moving closer, keen to hear what the old woman knew.

'King Laius revered the gods,' Teresa said. How she relished her audience, this once-powerful old woman who had become invisible. Her voice was growing louder, clearer with each syllable. 'He attended the Oracle, and consulted with the priests. They told him that he would one day be killed by his own son.'

'Oracles do not always speak the truth,' Jocasta said, her voice cracking on the final word. 'They're just words, interpreted by people like you, to say what you want them to say. They predict nothing, guarantee nothing. Laius died from a fall, after being injured by one of the Sphinx: he wasn't murdered by anyone.'

'You didn't always feel that way, my dear,' said Teresa, her blackened bottom tooth catching her top lip.

Jocasta felt the shame shroud her in heat. 'No,' she said. 'I used to believe every word that came to me from the Oracle, when I was lonely and afraid. Now I know better, because no poisonous old woman is trying to distort everything which happens for her own cruel purposes. Now I understand that Oracles give messages we aren't supposed to understand: the gods do not offer their wisdom in predictions, like soothsayers or magicians. I believed you to be long dead, but here you are, still trying to upset me by making up lies about my dead child. I would have thought that was beneath even you.'

She nodded to the guards, who had been standing by the main gates, in case Jocasta needed them.

The watch commander nodded back. They would arrest the old woman immediately. He murmured to his colleagues, and twenty men soon stood ready.

'They're not lies, not now,' Teresa said. 'Everything I'm saying is true.'

The crowd looked between the two women, the queen and the crone, unsure who to believe.

'You have always lied to me. But my son died,' Jocasta said. 'Arrest her.'

The crowd retreated from the gates, not wanting to miss what happened next, but not wanting to be caught up in the arrests either. Thebes had always been a martial city under the old king. They had little choice: the first visit from the Reckoning had made Hellas a lawless country for many years. But under the queen, the city had lost some of its hardness. She had kept the guards from exercising too much power. Nonetheless, when faced with a troop of heavily armed men, the citizens were nervous and they began to dissipate.

Teresa shrieked as the men carried her off, spears pointed outwards so no one could interfere with their progress.

'Horrible lying old witch,' Jocasta said, to no one. And she walked towards the gates to watch Teresa disappear from view. Only a few people remained outside now, including the shabby girl who had spoken before, whose baby was now crawling on the ground behind her.

The girl looked at her in disgust. 'So you say. But what's your explanation for the plague, then? You tell us the beggar-woman's lying, but why are the gods punishing our city, if it's not because we harbour criminals in you and your husband-son? Why?'

Jocasta looked at the girl who was sweating in the heat, blotches on her neck and shoulders. She felt only pity. The child was not yet twenty, and afraid for her baby.

'I can't answer that,' she said. 'No one knows where the plague came from all those years ago, and no one knows now. It is not unique to our city. It is happening across Hellas.'

'It's easy for you to say that,' the girl replied. 'Safe in your palace, knowing you'll live to see your children grow up.' And with that, she spat at Jocasta, the saliva landing thick and warm on the queen's cheek, dribbling down onto her upper lip. It was so unexpected that Jocasta flinched as if she had been slapped. She raised her hand to her mouth and wiped away the phlegm with her sleeve. The watch commander raised a hand, but she shook her head and walked away from the gates, back into the palace. What would it achieve, arresting a frightened girl?

25

Haem and I hurried through the corridors and colonnades of the palace, without anyone asking where we were going or why. The guards who seemed to have nothing better to do than stop me moving around the palace when I was alone were blinded by the presence of my cousin. We walked into the family courtyard, and Haem stopped dead. I looked at him, annoyed.

'I give you permission to enter the women's quarters,' I said. 'Come on. I need your help.'

'I can't,' he said. 'I'm risking enough bringing you back here while my father is busy elsewhere . . .'

'Busy taking the role that my sister and I should be playing in our brother's funeral?' I asked. He nodded, but did not speak.

'You know he is wrong about Eteo,' I said. He nodded again.

'He would never forgive me if he thought I had gone against his decision,' Haem said helplessly. 'I'm all he has.'

I could not reply. Creon would still have had two nephews, if he had been able to bear being the second or third most powerful man in our city. He would have a niece standing by him now, if he had not demanded that his men lock her in the cells beneath the palace. He would have me if I weren't sneaking around behind his back to try and ensure my brother received some sort of burial, to appease his shade and placate the gods. I could feel little sympathy for Creon's isolation. And my cousin was weak, I could see that now. His mouth had no strength, his soft jaw revealed no determination. I wondered how I could ever have thought I loved him.

I wished that Ani could help me, but whatever was happening to my sister, I could do nothing to change it. I would have to deal with my family one member at a time. Polyn was being carried to his tomb as I scurried off to my room to find what I needed. Ani would have to wait. At least I could overturn the most terrible injustice, and lay Eteo to rest. I swung open my door, and a sweet, rotten stench filled my nostrils. I knew it was him. I took off my formal dress and left it on the bed, so I was wearing only my charcoal-coloured tunic. I dug a thick scarf from my wardrobe and wrapped it around my face, to try and ward off the smell. I wondered how long I would have, before the funeral party returned to the palace. I needed to be quick. I opened the door of a small cupboard next to my bed, and groped around for the key which Eteo and I had found, all those years ago. My fingers closed round its cold edges and I exhaled. The key was the first thing.

I ran into the courtyard and towards the south corner. An old, battered door stood closed, but not locked. It contained only gardening tools: a small spade, a fork, some rope and a few other things. I took the spade and the rope and ran on towards the ice store. There was no sign of my cousin anywhere: he had ensured he could not be tainted by what I was about to do. The servants were nowhere in sight either. I rounded the corner of the deserted corridor and stopped by the door which led nowhere, to thin air. It was the only route out of the palace where I could be reasonably sure I wouldn't be seen. As I jiggled the key into the ancient lock, I wondered if Haem knew I could get out here, or if he thought I would be trying to leave via the main gate. The key stuck for a moment, and I thought the lock must have rusted over. But eventually there was a snapping sound and the door swung open into my waiting hand. I was worried that the hinges would rasp in protest, but they were quiet.

The rope was thick and dry, but still I forced it into six fat, ill-tied knots. I passed the rope around the bars which covered the tiny window at the top of the door, and fed it through until both ends hung loose in my hands. I pulled on them as hard as I could, but the bars didn't move. I would have to hope they would hold. I threw the spade out onto the ground beneath me, and looked around for a loose stone. I found a broken piece of flagstone just along the corridor against the wall, and pushed it into the space next to the doorpost.

I dropped the spade down onto the ground, then I took one length of rope in each hand, and jumped. I felt a quick burn on my palms as they slid down before my hands juddered into the knots. I was not so far from the ground now. I dropped down the rest of the way, bending my legs as I landed. I stumbled forward and pitched onto my knees. One of my ankles turned over on the uneven ground. But I had made it outside. And as the rope had pulled the door almost closed behind me, the stone I had wedged into the doorframe held it slightly ajar. I would be able to get back inside, when I had done what I needed to do.

I didn't have time to stop and think about the space that opened out before me. I had been enclosed behind the palace walls for so long, I had forgotten what it was like to see the whole of things, not just squares through the windows. But while I had been thinking about how I would get myself outside – and finding everything I needed – I had been able to avoid thinking about what I was coming out here to do. I could not stand here admiring the mountains and the trees, because I needed to walk around the edge of the palace and up the hill a little. I needed to look at my brother's broken body, not askance through a window, but standing beside him. And then I had to find a way to cover him with earth, as quickly as I could, to protect him from scavengers. I had nothing left to give him but this.

I picked up my spade, and began to walk up the hill. The palace was so forbidding from the outside, with its high stone walls and tiny windows: it faced inwards, mostly lit from within, from the open squares which poured light into the rooms along their sides. As I turned the corner of the building, I looked up the hill and there he was. I felt a horrible wave of revulsion: the gods force us to see our own death when we look upon the dead. Except it was scarcely him now, scarcely even a person. I could feel the tears running down my cheeks, as a burning sickness filled my throat. It wasn't my brother. It didn't even resemble him. Only by repeating this in my head could I persuade my legs to keep climbing the hill. It wasn't him. Not my brother. Not the man I loved.

The smell of death – I tried to think of the proper words, to distract myself from what they truly described

– the stench of putrefaction was much stronger out here. But at least I had prepared myself for that, covering my face once more with the scarf I had brought, breathing through my mouth, trying to set my mind on the physical task ahead of me. Still I could not prevent myself from collapsing to my knees and retching onto the ground. A body should be wrapped. My brother should have been kept in linen. He should be under the earth.

I hadn't anticipated the noise. There was a humming sound, like a distant buzzing, angry crowd. But the crowd wasn't distant at all: they were flying around him, crawling over him, defiling him further, as though the insults, the injuries he had sustained had not been enough. They swarmed around his neck, feeding off the blood which had coagulated around the fatal wound. I drove my nails into my palms as I forced myself to see that his eyes were gone: two blackened sockets were all that remained from the sharp beak which had enucleated him, my brother, my poor blinded brother. I could see the birds, sitting on the hillside above me, waiting for me to be gone so they could get back to their vicious work. I wanted so much to run away, to turn and shoot back down the hill, the way I had come. But I knew I had to dig next to where he lay: I wouldn't be able to carry him on my own. I could look at him no longer. So I turned my back on the brother I loved, and I began to dig.

For a while, I thought it was hopeless. It was hard to guess how much time I had before Creon and the funeral party returned to the palace. And even harder to guess how long it would be before any of them noticed that I was missing. Creon had planned the celebrations of Polyn's life in the main square this afternoon; he would expect me to be there, certainly. But it was possible that his argument with Ani this morning had put him off the idea of a full wake. My shadow was shortening all the time, but I had scarcely shifted enough earth to cover my own hands. I didn't know what Creon would do if he caught me out here. But it scarcely mattered now. What worse could he do to me than this? I kept digging.

The ground was dry, and so hard I was worried it would break the edge of the shovel I was using. But gradually, I found myself standing next to a pile of earth, though every muscle in my arms was screaming for me to stop, and my back ached from bending over. The sun was almost directly overhead now, it must be close to midday. I knew I should run back to the palace, as Creon would be back shortly. But I could not. I had done too much to give up now. If he slammed me into prison with my sister, so be it. Part of my mind would not be quiet, reminding me that it wasn't my own safety I should worry about: it was Ani's. What if Creon decided to punish her, as a way of punishing me? But I silenced the question: this is what Ani wanted, as much as I did. She was in no position to perform the task herself, but she would never forgive me if I valued her comfort over that of my brother. And I would never forgive myself. My parents were dead: I could never have another sibling. I would see Eteo into his grave, into Hades, where he belonged.

I dug more soil, more and more, and finally I had made a hole which looked like it could contain him. I turned to face the boulder against which my brother was resting. No, not resting: that was what a man would do. And this was not a man, not my brother, not any more. It was just a thing, a thing I needed to place in the ground to appease the gods. I crushed every instinct which told me not to touch the dead, to shy away from the insects and the ruination. I walked around to his flank – not his, its – and knelt down. I begged my brother's forgiveness, closed my eyes, and pushed. His body slid away from me, and lurched towards the grave. I opened my eyes a little, to see how far he had moved. Then closed them again as I shoved him once more across the small patch of ground. Finally, I heard the thudding sound of him dropping down into his grave. I opened my eyes, and realized I was crying so hard I couldn't see anyway. My brother was in the last home he would ever have.

It didn't take much longer to cover him over and pile the earth on top. I left a gold ring on his blackened hand to pay Charon for the ferry. I muttered a short prayer to the gods, asking them to be sure that the earth would lie light above my brother. Then I found five large stones, each the size of two fists, and used them to mark the head of the grave. It was a poor memorial, but it was the best I could do. And it was enough.

I had been gone for too long, I knew. I ran back around the palace wall, and hid the spade in the grass beneath the door: no one would see it from outside the palace, and I couldn't carry it back up the ropes. My arms were so tired from digging that I wondered if I could climb at all. But I needed to get back inside and this was easily the quickest, safest route. I reached up and pulled on the two ropes, making sure they would still take my weight. I twisted one below the other, once and then once more, and spread my arms wide to tug the loose knot as high as it would go, so that the cords were bound together. Otherwise, when I rested my weight on one of the knots, the ropes might easily slip from my hands and slither free of the bars at the top.

I reached above my head and pulled myself up until my feet found the first knot. I gripped the ropes tightly, and moved my foot until I found the next one, a few hands above the first. I reached my left arm up and then used my right to heave myself up another foot. My shoulders were burning less than my biceps, but I held on and kept climbing. Once my feet were on the final knot, I could grab the stone floor beneath the door to take my weight, lean forward and push the door open. It groaned quietly and slid away from me. With one last wrench, I dragged myself onto the flagstones and lay panting on the ground. I was trying to listen out for servants or guards who might find me, but I could only hear my own breath. After several moments, I raised myself to my knees and then my feet. I kicked the stone away from the door jamb and reached into my pocket for a small knife which had once belonged to Eteo. I hacked through the ropes and let them drop to the ground, pushed the door shut and locked it with my key. I hurried back down the corridor and saw that the courtyard was quiet. I scuttled across to my room just in time for Haem to step out of the north colonnade and call out.

'There you are, Isy. Are you awake at last? My father is waiting for us in the main square. I sent word that we would be there as soon as we had each had time to wash and refresh ourselves.' He was walking towards me as he spoke, so by the time he had finished his sentence, he was close enough to mutter, 'You have grass stains on your legs and you need to get all that soil off your hands. As fast as you can. We don't have long. He doesn't know you've been outside. Is it done?'

I nodded. 'I'll be quick.'

And as I changed my clothes and scrubbed my knees and elbows clean and tried to force a comb through my sweaty hair, I wondered how long it would be before Creon discovered that Eteo was safe, under the earth. And what he would do when he found out.

26

As Jocasta turned from the gate and walked alone across the main square towards the second courtyard, she could feel Oedipus's eyes upon her from the shadows. She wished she could break free of the protocol which expected her to be regal at all times, so she could hitch up her skirts and run. Instead, she walked as fast as she could and didn't pause when she crossed the colonnade where her husband was waiting. She heard him hurry to catch up with her. He said her name and – lifting her hand – she cut him off.

'I don't want to talk about it until no one else can overhear.' She kept moving and he strode along beside her. They crossed the second courtyard without seeing a soul: the slaves somehow knew to keep themselves scarce. She crossed into the family courtyard, and found herself short of breath.

'Where are the children?' she asked, looking around the deserted square.

'In lessons or in the nursery, the same as every morning,' he replied. 'Let's go to our room.' He took her hand, but she wrenched it away from him.

'We could be overheard by slaves in the next room,' she said. 'I will not have our conversation repeated. I want somewhere private.' Oedipus looked around the courtyard, feeling foolish. Another room was hardly likely to appear.

'Let's sit by the fountain,' he said. 'No one can overhear us there. We'd see them coming from any direction, long before they could hear us.' He reached out and took her hand.

'Hiding in the middle of the square,' she said, trying to smile.

He led her to the fountain. 'Sit here,' he said, and left her perched on the edge of the stone wall which surrounded it. He picked up two heavy chairs, and lugged them over to her. He placed them next to each other, but facing in opposite directions, so they could talk while keeping an eye on everything around them. He dug a piece of cloth from his belt, and dipped it in the fountain water. He reached over and wiped her hot, red face, like she did for the children on days such as these. She sat perfectly still and – when he had finished – he threw the rag on the ground.

'Was it really her? Teresa?' he asked.

'Yes.'

'I didn't recognize her.'

'I didn't either,' she said. 'Even when I knew it was her. She was unrecognizable. It was horrible, like hearing a familiar voice coming out from behind a mask.'

'You do know she was lying to you?' Oedipus asked.

Jocasta felt a shudder rack through her body. 'I don't,' she said. 'I don't know what to believe. I thought she was telling the truth then, but she could easily have been lying to me: then or now. She's a horrible woman.'

'And she has a grudge against us. She blamed me for

Laius's death, and then I threw her out of the palace. She looks like she's been living on the street ever since, waiting for the chance to get her revenge. She can't hurt me directly, so she's hurting you instead. You must be able to see that. She was a vicious old witch then, and she still is now. Her face finally reflects her true character.'

'But why would she make this up now? Isn't it just more likely that she's telling the truth at last? I told you, I have always felt that he was alive. Always.'

Oedipus reached over and took her hand in both of his. 'Jocasta, if something happened to one of the children —'

'Don't say that,' she hissed, making the sign to ward off the evil eye.

'I have to. If something happened to one of our children, I would do what you did. I know I would. I would imagine them continuing to grow up. I'd never stop. I thought about it last summer, when the plague came. I thought if anything happened to any of them, I wouldn't believe it. They're realer than you or me. They occupy space more than we ever could. And how could all of that just disappear? It couldn't. So they wouldn't disappear for me: I would carry them around, I'd imagine them. But that wouldn't make my imagination reality, would it?'

She ignored him, and he squeezed her hand again. 'Would it?' he repeated.

'It's not the same,' she said.

'No, it's much worse for you. You carried that child, Jocasta. He was inside you for nine months.'

'I didn't want him at first,' she said dully. 'I didn't want a baby. They made me have one. They wanted a girl to be

Laius's heir. So they made me get pregnant. I wished and wished not to be, and the death was my reward and my punishment from the gods.'

He squeezed her hand so hard that she yelped, and he apologized, rubbing the bones he had crushed a moment earlier. 'I wish I could have come sooner,' he said. 'I wish it every day.'

'You were just a child,' she said. 'That's precisely the problem.'

'There is no problem,' he said. 'She's locked up now, and she can die in prison, for all anyone cares. Spiteful old hag. No one can believe that I could be your son. No one. The idea is ridiculous. It was ridiculous a year ago, and it is even more ridiculous now.'

'How is it ridiculous?' she asked. 'You were adopted. Your father said so. You don't think he was lying as well, do you?'

Oedipus rolled his eyes, impatient at Jocasta's need to repeat an argument they had conducted several times before. 'No, I don't think he was lying. And I also don't think that he was lying when he said I was adopted from a family on the next street over, who couldn't afford to feed a fifth child. Why would he make that up?'

'I don't know.'

'Well, that's the question, isn't it? Do we believe my father, who has no reason to lie to us, or an old woman who has every incentive to do so?'

'Your father lied to you through your whole childhood,' she said. 'Why didn't he tell you you were adopted before?'

'Because he didn't think there was any need, until I

sent a messenger to him and asked,' he said. 'Some people do keep secrets even when there is no reason to.' The barb in his tone was pronounced. 'And why is my father suddenly the villain in this story?'

'Because . . .' She ran out of words. 'I don't know. He isn't.'

'Jocasta, please just think for a moment about what Teresa is suggesting. Do you really believe she could have stolen your baby, taking advantage of the fact that he – unlike all other babies – didn't make a sound when he was born? That she could have hidden him somewhere? Where? In the palace?'

'She wouldn't have hidden him here,' Jocasta snapped. 'Don't be an idiot.'

'Very well.' Oedipus raised his hands in mock surrender. 'So she hid him outside the palace. She happened to know someone so well that she could just give them a baby, no questions asked, and they would take it. Why had you never seen her with this friend? And where were they when she left the palace a few years later?'

Jocasta blanched to hear him describe her purgatory as a few years, when it had felt so very much like forever to live through.

'I don't know. Maybe they died.'

'Maybe they died,' he agreed. 'Before or after they went on an eighty-mile trek across mountains infested with bandits and brigands, carrying a baby? For no discernible reason except to give him away to a family who happened to live on the street next to my parents? And that family accepted this unwanted child, but then changed their minds and gave him away to their neighbours?'

'Of course it doesn't sound true if you say it like that,' she said. 'Stop trying to make me feel stupid.'

'Then stop being stupid,' he said. 'It sounds impossible because it is impossible. You had a baby which died. My parents adopted an unwanted child hundreds of stades away from here. These two stories didn't connect until I met you. You know it.'

'No,' she screamed, leaping up from the chair. 'You know it. You know it because you always have to be so incredibly clever. You know it because you would never be taken in by a malevolent old woman who probably wouldn't hate me so much if you hadn't thrown her out of her home. You know it because you would rather admit to anything than that I might be right about something and you might be wrong. Even when it's something as terrible as this. And instead of trying to make things better, you're just sitting there, correcting me and belittling me and telling me I'm stupid. How dare you?'

'I'm sorry,' he said.

'You aren't. If you were sorry, you wouldn't be doing it in the first place. I have tried to be calm about this. I tried last year, when we sent a messenger to your father. And I kept trying when he sent his reply and made everything worse, not better. And instead of acknowledging that, and trying to help me, you just pretended everything was perfect, and that all my fears were irrational and idiotic. And now look. Now, it's come back again, like I knew it would. Like I said it would. And it's what people out there believe. That's why they hate me. It's why they hate us. So why don't you go out there and tell all of them that they're stupid to believe something which is undeniably technically possible? Go on. Go and tell them. Go and tell them they're all idiots because you know best. Treat the rest of the city like you treat me.'

'I am sorry,' he said again.

'No,' she said. 'Not this time. I'm going to our room. To my room. I don't want you in there tonight. I don't want to share a bed with you. I don't want to see you.'

'Where do you want me to sleep?' he asked.

'I don't care. Sleep in the children's room, sleep in the garden, sleep wherever you like. But don't come near me. I can't bear it.'

That night, Oedipus slept on a too-hard couch covered in too-soft pillows in an unused bedroom, waking often and wondering for just how long his wife was going to be so angry. She hardly ever lost her temper, not even with the children. As he rolled over uncomfortably, he wasn't sure he could remember ever hearing her shout like that before. It was understandable, he supposed. The face of that rancid old beggar-woman would revolt anybody. And she of all people knew how to upset his wife. She had practised doing it for years. But surely Jocasta would calm down by tomorrow. She couldn't stay angry with him, when none of it – none of it – was his fault.

But when the morning sunlight poured in through the windows and he woke in a sleepy haze, his wife did not appear beside the bed, to kiss him and apologize for her harsh words. He watched, embarrassed, from across the courtyard, as two slave women knocked on Jocasta's door and received no reply. Was she really punishing him like this, for all to see? He wanted to hammer on the door and demand she stop being such a brat. But how would it look, a husband pleading with his wife to be allowed into her room?

By the afternoon, he was worried. She had been in there for nearly a whole day. She must be hungry. Although, now he thought about it, he couldn't be certain that she hadn't left the room during the night, could he? Perhaps she'd sent someone to the kitchens to collect some bread and fruit, so she could spend the day sulking, making him feel guilty and look stupid. He refused to rise to the bait. No one else seemed worried, after all. The children had asked their nurse where their mother was, but she just told them Jocasta had a bad headache, as was often true.

As dusk fell, Creon wandered awkwardly into the family courtyard.

'Sorry to intrude,' he mumbled. 'I was just looking for Jocasta.'

'She's got a headache, I think,' Oedipus replied. 'She's been in her bedroom all day.'

'Her bedroom?' asked Creon, and Oedipus felt a surge of resentment against his wife, as his awkwardness was clearly visible to all.

'Yes,' he said. 'She went to bed early last night and she hasn't come out again yet.'

'Has anyone been in to check on her?' Creon asked.

'No.'

'Should we . . . ?' Creon gestured at the door.

'Should we what?' Oedipus blinked at his brother-in-law.

'Make sure she doesn't need anything,' Creon said.

'I'm sure she would have asked if she needed something. But don't let me stop you,' Oedipus said.

And Creon went over and knocked on the door. 'It's your brother,' he called.

Oedipus held his breath for a moment, his ears straining to hear a reply. But Creon knocked a second and then a third time, before he gave up.

'She must be asleep,' he said.

'I think so,' Oedipus replied. 'She does sleep very heavily, when she has these headaches. You know.'

'Well, tell her I'll see her tomorrow and I hope she'll be feeling better,' Creon said, and he turned, his shoulders slumped, and walked back the way he had come.

The following morning, there was still no sign of Jocasta. Oedipus had spent the night in the courtyard itself, curled uncomfortably on one of her divans. He was certain he would have woken if she had opened the door. So perhaps she wasn't punishing him. Perhaps she did have a terrible headache. In which case, he wouldn't lose face if he went to her room, even when she hadn't apologized, would he? He took a deep breath, and knocked on her door. Their door. Palace etiquette had been thrown aside when they married and decided to share a bedroom instead of maintaining separate quarters. But Oedipus had never wanted to spend a single night away from his wife, and he never had, until now.

There was still no reply. He turned the handle and pushed at the door, but it didn't move. She had locked him out. Locked him out of their bedroom. He could feel the anger rising. What if she was sick and needed help? She hadn't thought about that when she locked the door in a fit of petulance, he was quite sure.

Oedipus could no longer leave things as they were. The children were becoming fractious, no matter how much the nurse placated them. Antigone wouldn't stop grizzling, and even Ismene, who was normally so placid if Eteocles was there to amuse her, was frowning and refusing every spoonful of food. Exasperated by their behaviour, he hurled a small wooden stool at the flagstones, and watched the splinters jump across the floor. All four children began to cry, but still his wife did not appear.

'Very well,' he shouted. 'You obviously want your mother. Go off to your lessons and I'll bring her to you.'

He beckoned a slave over, and told him they would need to break through Jocasta's door. The boy, who couldn't have broken through a sheet of papyrus, nodded sceptically.

'Fetch Creon,' Oedipus sighed. 'He'll help.'

While he waited for his brother-in-law to arrive, he examined the door. It was made of thick oak panels and had only one lock, in the centre of the left-hand side. There were two bright bronze hinges on the right, and it was difficult to say whether the lock or the hinges would be the easiest thing to break. Or would the panels of the door split through?

Creon came hurrying behind the boy, then shooed him away.

'The child says you want my help to break down the door?' he asked, frowning.

'She's locked it from the inside.'

'And there isn't another key?'

'I don't think so,' Oedipus said. 'I've never known her lock the door before. Shall we test it?' He backed up, eyeing the hard wooden surface.

'I don't think we could just smash through it with our shoulders,' Creon said. 'It's solid oak, isn't it?'

'Do you have a better suggestion?' Oedipus asked. 'She might be lying on the floor; she could be unconscious.'

Creon whistled the boy to come back over, and sent him to fetch the guards. A few moments later, the watch commander appeared with four men. Oedipus explained the problem and the commander nodded. Two of his guards fetched axes, which he instructed them to put to use.

The noise was astonishing. The metal blades rasped on the old wood, and even after several blows the door was barely scratched.

'Forgive me,' said the commander to Creon and Oedipus. 'It's awkward. Keep going,' he added, to the guards.

'Once they've gone through the wood panel in one place, it'll be quite quick,' Creon said. The two guards stepped back and handed their axes to their comrades, who swung the metal with fresh arms. Finally a small crack of light appeared on the upper left quarter.

'Concentrate your efforts there,' Oedipus said, pointing. The watch commander raised his eyebrow a tiny distance. He jerked his head up, and the guards did as Oedipus had asked. A few deafening moments later, and a chunk of wood had broken through.

'Force it,' said the commander, before Oedipus could offer any more advice. The four soldiers shoved their combined weight against the door, and felt the panel give a little.

'Come on,' said Oedipus. 'Surely that's enough.'

The men pulled back and shoved themselves against the door again. Finally, there was a splintering sound, and the panel closest to the lock gave way. One of the guards reached through and groped around for the key. If Jocasta had taken it away from the door, they would need to smash more of the door around the lock to break in. But his face relaxed. He had the key in his hand, and he turned it, first the wrong way, and then correctly. The lock clicked open and the men stepped back. Oedipus nodded his thanks, and opened the door.

'Where are you, my darling?' he said. 'Did you lock the door and then realize you didn't feel—?' He broke into a terrible howl.

Creon leapt forward. 'What is it?' he asked. And then, 'No.'

Jocasta was hanging from a hook in the ceiling. No one could remember what it had once been intended for. But now it held the queen, suspended by a rope. She wore a plain white gown which Oedipus couldn't recall ever seeing before. It looked like a child's nightgown, one she must have brought here all those years ago, and long since stopped wearing. Her face was puffed up and purple, her hair was matted to her skull. She must have tied the noose around her neck and then jumped from the bed.

'Get the doctor,' the watch commander said to his men. 'Go now.'

But it was much too late for that.

27

I followed my cousin out to the main square, where Polyn's wake was beginning. I had forgotten my five-stringed lyre, and had to run back to collect it. I hoped I would be able to play it well enough to mark the death of both of my brothers. The words I had composed were appropriately vague, but I would know – Eteo would know – they were for him as well as Polyn. I had not practised for several days; Thebans would consider it profoundly disrespectful for a sister to sit playing a phorminx while her brothers awaited burial. I knew what I wanted to sing, though: I had rehearsed it all in my mind. And the plangent tones of this instrument – which was old even when it was given to me – would be ideally suited to my song.

I wished Ani was there, hastening along beside me. Or rather, she would have been walking at her own pace, and Haem and I would have slowed down, to avoid leaving her behind.

'Have you seen my sister?' I asked him.

He shook his head. 'She's in the cells, in the caves beneath the main square,' he said. 'I'm sure of it. But I haven't spoken to my father about it. He issued the sentence this morning, he will not be in any mood to issue a reprieve this afternoon.'

It took me a moment to realize that he was speaking

literally. Ani had been taken to jail this morning, and then
there had been Eteo, and then it was now. I felt as though
Ani had been locked up a month ago. I wanted to step
back from the gathering crowd and spend some time with
my own thoughts, but of course I could do no such thing.
The sun was dropping fast, and the servants were beginning to light the torches, even though they were not
needed quite yet. Each one was placed in a bronze holder
around the walls of the main square, so that it never grew
fully dark. Creon was over by the altar, performing one
last set of ritual offerings to the gods he believes in so
devoutly. And yet, how could any priest pretend to him
that his gods would tolerate the burial of one man and
not another? It was nonsense. Either the dread lord of the
Underworld expected his dues to be paid for the dead, or
he did not. It could not be halfway between the two, and
any priest who said otherwise was no more respectful of
the gods than my uncle himself.

There was something not quite right in the courtyard. The servants were moving with their usual invisible
efficiency, the priests were intoning, the musicians were
playing, the crowd was gathering. But, something was
wrong, as if the incense which burned over the altars had
been tainted, or everyone in the courtyard had begun
speaking a different language. I felt eyes upon me, too
many of them. Of course people would stare – I have
grown up as the child of a polluted union, I am used to
the stares – but this was more than usual. Haem looked
across at me, frowning. He felt it too.

'What is it?' I asked. He shook his head. But we both
knew the answer, even before the watchman ran in through

the main gates, and prostrated himself before my uncle, pressing his forehead against the stones as though that would be enough to save him.

'Forgive me, Basileus,' he said.

My uncle looked irritated at being disturbed from his piety, but not as much as I would have expected. Perhaps he had prayed enough. Or perhaps he realized the gods would not hear him today.

'What do you want?' he snarled.

'Forgive me,' the man said again. 'I don't know how it happened. Or when.'

Creon pressed his lips together, as though he wished he could spit the man out, like a piece of rancid pork fat. 'Tell me,' he said. 'Be assured that I will not ask again.'

The man sat back on his heels, his grey tunic stretching taut across his belly. 'I was not the only man on watch, king,' he said. 'But my comrades and I drew lots, and it fell to me to bring this news to you. Your nephew, the traitor, has been buried.'

Creon's face was unreadable, even to me who had known him for my entire life. The anger was plain in the creases around his mouth. But I saw a trace of something else there too. Was it possible that he was relieved?

'Continue,' he said.

The man looked frantically around him, expecting guards to appear on all sides, their spears pointed down at his ribs. His chest was heaving with the effort of running into the palace and scraping himself down on the ground.

'It happened sometime today, Basileus. This afternoon, perhaps. The traitor lay open to the air this morning: I saw a dog feeding off him myself.' If he thought this would ingratiate him with my uncle, he was mistaken. Revulsion flickered across Creon's face. I felt my own chest tighten. Even the knowledge that Eteo was finally safe did not undo the damage done before I could bury him.

'He was buried today, on your watch?' Creon asked.

'There were six of us on patrol, majesty.' The man stumbled over his words, so quick was he to explain that it was not his fault alone. 'Whoever did it, they slipped past us.'

'For how long,' Creon asked, luxuriating now in the man's evident fear, 'would you estimate you were in dereliction of your duties?'

'Basileus, it was not for long. I promise, not long at all. Only enough time to return to the guardhouse and find my fellow watchmen to take over from me.'

Creon nodded. 'I should have you all executed,' he said mildly. Perhaps he was remembering how few guards the palace now had, after he had ordered so many to be killed on the day Polyn and Eteo died. 'You expect me to believe that a whole troop of men found their way out to the back of the palace and buried a full-grown man in the time it took you to return to the guardhouse? How long were you asleep for?'

The courtyard had grown very quiet when the watchman ran in, but you could hear the news spreading around the square. The traitor had been buried; someone had buried the boy; both of the dead kings were now beneath the ground; someone had heeded the words of the princess; Creon's law had been broken; the gods' law had been obeyed.

The tension was extraordinary, like the strings on a lyre

that has been allowed to grow too warm near a fire. As the wood expands, the strings snap, one after another. As each one gives way, the remaining strings are pulled tauter still, trying to do the work of themselves and their brothers. Even my uncle, people were muttering, could not order that his own nephew be disinterred. It was bad enough that he had sought to disobey the gods by leaving the boy unburied. But to dig him out of the ground was unthinkable. Was Creon really about to demand that the watchman commit such a terrible crime?

'I swear,' said the man, stretching himself out on the ground, his belly pushed into the flagstones, spilling down into the gaps between them, 'I was not asleep. They must have been lightning-quick.'

I felt useless nerves filling my belly. I had not even considered that Creon would have ordered guards to watch over Eteo. But I had not seen anyone when I was outside, not even a shepherd in the distance. Outside the walls, where the palace almost hangs over the hill beneath us, it is usually quiet. Goats graze on the other hills, and olives grow on the lower slopes. But no goatherds or farmers use the land around the palace. I suppose the men charged with keeping watch over Eteo had simply assumed it was unnecessary. I had been – though I could barely think the word – lucky. I corrected myself: in this one regard, I had been lucky.

'She was right,' I heard a man say. 'The girl was right.'

Crowds are curious things: made up of individuals, but with a character entirely their own. As people realized what the man was saying, they remembered what my sister had demanded this morning. She had asked for Eteo to be buried, as was proper, and now he had been. Yet the girl was in prison, wasn't she? Beneath the palace square? Was she beneath their very feet as they stood waiting for the music to begin and the wine to be poured to honour the shade of my brother, Polyn? But then how had the other king been buried?

It never occurred to any of them to wonder if I might have had anything to do with it. I was still the youngest child, the one they could overlook. I felt Haem next to me, breathing shallowly. He too had realized how close I must have come to getting caught. Or was he waiting for the watchman to admit that he had taken a bribe to look the other way, from the young prince, the heir to his father's throne?

I would never know the truth, because I realized at that moment that it was not important, and in the chaos which followed, I did not ask him. What mattered was that the people of Thebes were beginning to appreciate that my sister had been wrongfully imprisoned. And if she could arrange, from a subterranean cell, for her brother to be buried, she was powerful in a way that the all-powerful king was not. She must be a favourite of the gods, for who else could have assisted her? This morning, the king had seemed to be a stern but patriotic leader. Now, he seemed to them to be an arrogant fool, alienating the gods by persecuting their favourite. And what could be more pathetic than a grown man afraid of a girl?

Suddenly, anger was rippling through the courtyard, like wind across the wheat crops which grew in the lowlands outside the city. They were shouting, stamping, whistling and clapping their hollowed hands together.

The guards, to whom Creon looked, stood back, impassive. They were new recruits, and they had no experience in this kind of situation. My uncle sought out one he knew, but though there were a few older men who I recognized – standing with their spears by their sides, seemingly blind and deaf – he did not see them, or if he did, he realized they would not obey him.

The crowd called my sister's name, 'Ani, Ani', punctuated with the stamps of their feet. My sister must have felt the very walls of her cell shuddering from the noise and the dust which rose up as they smacked their sticks and boots into the ground.

'I'm going to fetch her,' I whispered to Haem, though no one could have heard me over the noise they were making. 'Before there's a riot.'

I was standing near to one of the older guards, and I grabbed his arm. 'Can you take me to Ani?' I said. 'Take me to my sister.'

The man looked around him as though he hadn't heard, or was uncertain what I might be asking. Then he dipped his head in a brisk nod, and walked away. I ran to keep up with him.

In the furthest corner of the square, behind the throne room and the temples, was a dingy forgotten corner with a battered ancient door – blackened over the years – in front of what I had always assumed (if I had ever given it any thought) was a storeroom, built into a recess in the outside walls. The white stone had turned grey with dirt and time. The guard reached to his belt and I thought he would produce a key, but instead he drew out a dagger by the hilt. It was this which he thumped against the door five times, before stowing it back at his waist. There was the sound of wood scraping on stone and something heavy shifting in its socket. The door swung open before us, and I could see that far from hiding a small cupboard, it opened onto a dimly lit flight of stairs. The guard who had opened the door from within raised his eyebrows at his comrade when he saw me, but he said nothing, and stepped aside.

The tunnels beneath the palace were dark and I was relieved when the guard pulled a torch from a wall-sconce and carried it ahead of us to light our path. The steps were smooth and worn beneath my feet, and the air was musty. Water dripped from the roof of the caves, and had left rust-brown deposits down the damp walls.

The sound of our feet – his boots, my sandals – echoed off the walls as we followed the twisting corridor through its many turns. I had no sense of which direction we were travelling in: without the sky to guide me, I was lost. But eventually, we came to a long straight stretch, where the man half-turned his head, and said, 'Not far, now.'

'Whereabouts are we?' I asked.

'You're going under the market square,' he said. 'The cells were built in the caves which open out onto the far side of the hill. Don't worry, Potnia, your sister isn't alone in the dark. Although the sun must be almost set by now.'

I was startled by the formal title: no one had called me 'Princess' in years. I was too young to warrant it until recently. But someone had used the honorific before, long ago. I couldn't remember who. My father, I supposed. I shivered, although I hadn't felt cold until just now.

As my companion had promised, the darkness grew slightly less complete when we reached the far end of this tunnel. Then he turned right, down a shorter corridor, and there were three small doors on the left-hand side, each one barred with a thick pine plank, and each one with a small grille in the top, through which the prisoner could be seen. But so little light was now spilling in from outside, it was virtually as dark as the tunnels we had come through.

'She's in the furthest one,' he said.

Even though I was desperate to see her, I hesitated before stepping forward. I had a sudden horrible vision of Ani lying dead in the cell, her tiny frame collapsed on the ground. I felt as though the walls and ceiling were rushing in to crush me, as though all the air had been taken from my lungs. I stumbled, and the guard put out his hand to support me. 'Steady,' he said.

'Forgive me.'

'Forgive you?' he laughed. 'You must be the only person in Thebes who would come down here voluntarily. And as it's getting dark, too. You're a brave girl. Now, give me a hand with the pine log, so your sister can get back where she belongs.'

He strode ahead, and I tried to shake the image of my dead sister from my mind, concentrating on following this stranger who thought I was brave.

'Here we go,' he said, as we slid the wooden bar from its housing. He allowed his end to drop to the ground and propped it against the door jamb. The door swung open of its own accord.

And there before my eyes my nightmare was made flesh. Next to a small, dirty cot, my sister swung from a rope she had fashioned from her own stole. I screamed, but the guard was quicker to act: he dropped his torch and ran forward and lifted her from the waist. Reaching into his belt, he pulled out the knife and slashed through the fabric noose. My sister slumped into his arms.

I reached down and picked up the torch from my feet. Its sputtering light flickered back into brightness. The guard turned and I saw Ani's face, reddish-purple next to the white rope around her neck. Then she coughed, and I almost dropped the torch again, in fear and relief.

'Ani!' I screamed. 'Are you alive?'

She did not reply, but the guard nodded. 'Her throat won't let her talk for a moment or two, Potnia. Lucky you came when you did.'

My sister opened her eyes and pointed upwards.

'I need to get her back to the main courtyard,' I said. 'Will you help me?'

The guard glanced at the ground. 'I'll carry her out of the caves for you. But I can't take her into the palace. I have three daughters. Your uncle—'

'I understand,' I said. There was no point arguing with him when we both knew the words he wasn't saying: my uncle didn't hesitate to punish guards with death. The man could not afford to take the risk.

I walked beside him, carrying the torch, while he carried my sister. When we finally found ourselves out on the hillside, he dipped Ani's feet to the ground and set her down. 'Can you stand?' he asked. She nodded uncertainly. But as he let go of her, she did not fall.

'Thank you,' I said to him. 'If it is ever within my power, you will receive a rich reward for the service you have done my family today.'

The guard smiled. 'Thank you, Potnia.' He took the torch from me, for it was still just light enough to see in the fading twilight. He retreated back into the caves, and I took my sister's arm, so she could lean on me. We began the darkening trudge up the hillside to the city walls.

'What were you thinking, sister?' I asked.

'I should have known it would be you who came,' she whispered. 'I was hoping it would be Haem.'

It took me a moment to understand her meaning.

'You wanted him to find you and cut you down?' My sister had always had a weakness for dramatic gestures, but this was excessive even for her. Her eyes glittered.

'I will be queen of Thebes, Isy. I am the rightful heir. The throne is mine. I knew Haem would have supported me if he'd rescued me from death by my own hand.'

I stopped dead. 'Are you serious?'

She pulled my arm, hurrying me along. 'Of course I am serious. Never more so. Our brothers are dead, I will be queen or I will be dead. I will not live like a child for the rest of my life.'

'But you nearly died. What if it had been Haem, and he hadn't been able to open the door in time? Or what if he hadn't had a knife to cut you down?'

'He's not an idiot,' she snapped. 'He would have done something when he saw me hanging there.' I shook my head. 'I have to separate him from his father,' she said. 'Or he is no use to me at all.'

'I thought you loved him,' I said, and she squeezed my arm.

'I do,' she replied. 'In a way.'

'Well, I'm sorry he didn't come,' I said. 'But he covered for me. I buried Eteo this afternoon.'

Ani nodded, though it made her wince. 'I knew you'd think of something,' she said.

We had reached the edge of the city and climbed a few steps into the deserted market square. I thought she would ask about Eteo, but she seemed happy to know no more than that he was properly interred.

'I thought our brothers were important to you,' I said.

'They were, Isy. But they're in the past and I am here now. They're both buried, you said?' I nodded. 'Then there's no more to discuss,' she continued, as we scurried across to the palace gates. She paused, then said, 'Isy, I overheard the oddest thing this afternoon, as I was waiting for you to come and get me.'

'What did you hear?'

'The guards walked past my cell to check on me several times,' she said. 'Two of them, making sure I was safely locked up. I don't know how they imagined I could escape.' Her thoughts had already returned to herself.

'And one of them said something . . . ?' I prompted her.

'They had both helped to carry Polyn to the tomb, to our family tomb,' she said. I nodded, as we continued to walk across the slippery cobbled stones. 'And they said when the tomb was opened for him to be placed inside . . .' She paused and looked up, to check I was hanging on her words.

'Yes,' I said.

'They said the tomb was empty. Don't you think that's strange?'

'I'm not sure strange is quite the right word for what I think,' I said. 'Empty?'

'Mother and Father must be buried somewhere else,' she said. 'But I can't think why, and I have been trying, all day.' I felt a sudden rush of love for her, the last of my family.

'I'll think about it, too,' I said. 'We'll make sense of it.'

'Well, that will have to be your responsibility now,' she said. 'I won't have time.' Annoyance rose up in my chest where the love had just been.

'Why not?' Sometimes, you cannot avoid giving Ani the pleasure of making you ask.

'Because when we walk into the palace,' my sister said, 'the people of Thebes will make me ruler of the city. I know they will. So that will be my life now.'

And as she spoke, we had arrived at the palace gates. We walked into the main courtyard and the crowd fell silent. But only for a moment, before they began shouting her name, and calling her Basileia, Anassa, queen.

28

When he saw Jocasta suspended from the ceiling, Oedipus snapped in two. One of the guards reached above him to cut through the rope which had taken her life, and her body fell into her husband's arms, as though he were carrying her across a threshold at the start of their life together. He held her for a moment, then laid her down on the bed, because she was heavier now than when she was alive. Creon stood back and allowed Oedipus to cling to his wife's body and weep.

By the time Sophon arrived, it was clear to everyone that there was nothing he could do. But the guards who had gone to fetch him hadn't delivered their message with any care for the fact that the man they sought was sitting in a room with the queen's four children. Come quickly, they had said. The queen needs you. Sophon had hurried out behind them, and the children followed him because their mother was the queen and if she needed their tutor, she might well need them. Besides, they hadn't seen her for two days, and if she wanted the doctor, she would want to see them and admire their songs and handwriting and stories. So they ran behind Sophon all the way to their mother's room. They could hear a man crying, which sounded terribly wrong, as men never cried. Especially not their father, though they had never known another man to be in their mother's rooms. But why would their father ever cry?

The grizzled watch commander had stepped outside the room to breathe some air untainted by the faint stench of death, and he noticed the children hurrying their way along the colonnade to see their mother. He muttered, 'Stop them', to the guard standing next to him, and pulled the bedroom door closed behind him. The guard stood for a moment, uncertain what he should do. His training had been in hand-to-hand combat: he had no idea what protocol required of him in this situation. But he had a son and a daughter the same age as Eteo and Ani, although his girl was the older one: tall with a grave expression that occasionally cracked into mirth when she found her little brother beguilingly funny.

'Come on,' he said, reaching out to Eteo, the child who had run most quickly through the courtyard. 'You're it.' He tapped Eteo's arm, and ran across the courtyard laughing like an imbecile. The watch commander was about to bellow at him, before noticing that his words had had the required effect: Eteo jabbed his brother and ran after the guard, squawking with delight at the unexpected game. Polyn patted Isy on the head and declared her it, and she raced after her siblings on her small, spindly legs. Picking on the youngest should have provided an easy victory, but Isy was nearly as tall as Ani already, and soon caught up with her sister.

The watch commander eased the door open a crack and peered inside.

'The children are outside,' he said. 'Just so you know.'

Oedipus was impervious to words. He knelt by the side

of the bed, his head resting on his wife's belly. Sophon leaned over the top of the bed, but there was no need to check for a pulse. Jocasta had been dead for many hours already. Creon stood apart from the others, his expression one of confusion rather than grief. He caught the watch commander's words, and frowned.

'Take the children to the kitchens,' he said. 'Tell the servants to look after them. Keep them out of the way until I come and get them myself. Do you understand?'

'Of course, sir,' said the watch commander. His hair and beard were grey: he was too old not to know that today would reveal who was in charge of Thebes now the queen was dead.

Sophon stood up, the bones in his back cracking as he straightened. He looked at Oedipus's shaking body and walked across the room to Creon.

'How did this happen?' he asked.

Creon shook his head. 'I don't know. She found those rumours very upsetting, about the missing baby. You know.'

Sophon looked puzzled. 'The baby was born dead. She knew that.'

'She didn't know it well enough, perhaps,' Creon replied.

'I am sure she did. There must have been something else, to force her to commit such violence against herself.'

'I don't think so.' Creon watched the old man realize he would not find his answers here.

'Oedipus.' Sophon spoke quietly, and Oedipus did not reply. The doctor shuffled over to the bed, and put his hand on Oedipus's shoulder.

'Oedipus, I need you to talk to me for a moment. Forgive me, but it cannot wait.'

Oedipus gulped himself quiet. He turned around, so he was sitting on the floor, facing the two men. 'What is it?' he asked.

'I need you to tell me what happened,' Sophon said.

Oedipus stumbled his way through a description of Jocasta's final act as queen: calming the crowds at the gate and sending them home. His voice cracked when he told Sophon about Teresa and her taunts. But Sophon merely nodded and encouraged him wordlessly, as though he were trying to calm a frightened dog. He listened right through to the end, when Oedipus described the young woman who spat at his wife, and surely pushed her over the edge into madness, and then argued with him once they were back inside.

'How else could she have done this to herself? To the children? To me?' he asked. 'Unless she was mad?'

Sophon didn't reply, but asked instead if Jocasta had felt unwell after the unpleasant exchange with the young woman.

'Unwell? I don't know what you mean,' Oedipus said. 'She was upset, so she came back here and locked herself in her room. She might have had a headache. You know how often she was prey to them, especially after an experience like that.'

'She didn't talk to anyone else before she came in here? Stop to play with the children, or anything?'

'No, of course not. If she'd taken time to play with them, she'd still be alive. I'm sure of it.'

'I doubt it,' said Sophon.

'I don't know what you mean.' Oedipus was becoming angry.

'You think she had plague.' Creon realized the point of the old man's questions. 'You think the woman who spat on her gave her the plague.'

Sophon nodded. 'I do,' he said. 'I have known Jocasta for almost thirty years. She didn't kill herself because she thought she was involved in an incestuous relationship with her own child. The very idea is preposterous. She hated that people were suggesting it, and I'm sure she was angry and upset. But that wouldn't be enough to make her take her own life. People kill themselves when they believe it's the best option they have. They're rarely correct, of course. But if they're suffering terrible pain, or they know – without any doubt – that they will soon be suffering, it isn't an incomprehensible choice.'

'People survive the plague,' Oedipus said. 'She would have given herself that chance.'

'I think she believed she would die,' Sophon replied.

'It's that old hag's fault,' said Oedipus. 'She will be executed before the end of the day. I'll do it myself with my bare hands.'

'Will that help matters?' asked Creon.

'Why would you say that?' Oedipus asked, dragging himself to his feet. 'Was this your idea? Were you in it together, you and Teresa?'

'I understand that you have lost your wife,' Creon replied. 'I ask you to remember that I have lost my sister.'

'Lost her? You couldn't wait to be rid of her, could you?

You've spent years weaselling your way into this palace. She never did anything without you in the end. Except this.' He gestured at his wife's body.

'I had no choice,' Creon said. 'She needed someone to help. All the things you weren't interested in. She needed someone to support her.'

'So you're accusing me of failing to take care of my wife?' Oedipus demanded.

'Gentlemen, please,' Sophon said. 'We have all lost someone we loved dearly. Now is not the time for attributing blame. It cannot help, and none of us can pretend that it is what Jocasta would have wanted. Please let's all pause for a moment before we say things we might regret.'

'I have nothing to regret,' Oedipus said. 'Throw him out of the palace and don't let him back in here again. Not while I'm here. Not while I'm alive.'

The old watch commander, who had been standing by the wall in silence, stepped forward uncertainly.

'You aren't in charge of the guard,' Creon said calmly. 'They obeyed your wife, and now they obey me.'

'Don't be ridiculous,' Oedipus said.

'It's not ridiculous,' Creon replied. 'You are not king of Thebes and nor will you ever be. Your wife was the queen, and her son will be the king. Until then, you or I will be the regent. It's perfectly clear in the laws of our city.'

Oedipus sprang at his brother-in-law, panting from the exertion, fingers curling into claws. The guard stepped forward between them, and echoed Sophon's plea for calm. He looked over to the old man for guidance.

'Gentlemen, I'm sorry to interrupt this argument, which you seem desperate to have over the body of a woman who would have loathed it,' Sophon said. 'But if she did have the plague, her body is still contagious.'

Creon and Oedipus faced each other, the guard's hands on their respective chests as he switched his gaze from one man to the other.

'We must bury her,' Sophon said. Oedipus opened his mouth to argue and Sophon raised a finger. 'I know you are sceptical so let me give you my diagnosis. But don't get any closer than you have been.' Oedipus looked over at his wife, whose bloated face told him nothing.

'She had a fever, undoubtedly,' Sophon said. 'You can see her hair was damp around the temples. It's still clumped together now.'

'Is that it?' Oedipus asked. 'You're saying she had plague because her hair isn't neat enough?'

'No,' Sophon replied. 'I'm saying she had plague because I believe she did. I saw the woman you described on my way to the palace. She had a child with her, a girl, I think. They were both dead by the side of the road. I recognized her when you described her hair and her clothing. I'd already noticed the signs of fever in your wife, so your account merely confirmed my diagnosis. Also, and this may be the most crucial point . . .'

Oedipus ran his hand across his forehead. He was burning from the shock and the grief and the anger.

'I think you have a fever,' said Sophon. 'You may be in the early stages of the plague, having caught it from Jocasta before she died. You need to be quarantined, and we need to cool you down as soon as we can. I'm going to send for some ice, as soon as you agree to let me treat you. I don't want you to be frightened. The effects of the disease vary and you may survive it perfectly well. I did, after all. But please believe me when I tell you I hope very much that you will heed my advice and stay away from your children.'

Oedipus slumped forward, unable to argue further. He staggered across the room to a couch and sank onto it, leaning his head back against the wall. Sophon took this as consent, and asked the watch commander to help wrap Jocasta's body. They peeled the sheets off the bed and wrapped them around the queen. Sophon sent another guard to the ice store, and asked him to bring as much ice as he could carry, and place it in the bath. Creon stood back, watching the men in silence. He could not help wrap his sister, but he could attend to the burial of her body.

'There is a grave for plague victims just outside the city wall,' he murmured to Sophon, who nodded. 'We'll take her straight there.' He turned to the watch commander. 'Thank you, sir, for your loyal service in this matter. Will you help me to carry the queen away?'

The watch commander was a widower and childless. He preferred to help Creon than ask one of his men to take the risk.

'Yes, sir,' he replied. 'Now?'

'Now.'

'I'll send word ahead that we'll need to exit the city shortly,' he said, and disappeared through the door. The ice had now arrived, and Sophon wrapped a large piece in a muslin cloth, and persuaded Oedipus to lie down on the couch, before resting the cold block on Oedipus's brow. 'Lie still,' he said. 'The cooler you are, the better you'll feel.'

Oedipus did not reply. Once he knew his diagnosis, he could no longer pretend he felt well enough to stand and fight. But still, he could not tolerate what was happening around him.

'She should be buried properly,' he said, his eyes closed. 'Not like this.'

'There's no other way,' Creon replied. 'The sooner she's buried, the safer everyone else will be. I'm sorry. You know as well as I do that she would never want to put her children at risk.'

Oedipus groaned, but did not speak.

'We need a stretcher to carry her,' said Sophon.

'The men can build a litter,' said Creon, and he left to give the order.

'You can't let them do this to her,' Oedipus said.

'There's nothing else to be done,' replied the doctor.

'What about the children? They'll want a tomb they can visit, for God's sake. They've lost their mother.'

'We'll think of something,' Sophon said. 'Don't worry about it now.'

After a time which seemed far longer to Sophon than to Oedipus, Creon and the watch commander returned with a makeshift stretcher. They laid it down on the bed next to Jocasta, and moved her onto it. They looked at one another and nodded, then lifted her. Sophon held open the door as they made their slow progress. The three men walked together, past the guards who hailed their queen as she left the palace for the final time. There was a scurrying sound from across the courtyard by the kitchens, but Sophon peered at the shadows and could see nothing.

The men continued through the second courtyard, Creon wondering how he would announce to the city that the queen was dead. They were concentrating so hard on carrying her that no one heard the bedroom door, banging shut a second time.

The slaves all knew what had happened. The palace had never contained news or even gossip for a moment. Perhaps he would be too late to make any announcement, Creon thought. This scandal would spread more quickly than any disease. But they came out of their kitchens, their guardhouses and their posts, all saluting the dead queen. Creon's jaw was set hard, but Sophon – who had seen so many die, and so many younger than Jocasta – could conceal his grief no longer. The tears ran down his cheeks, gathering in his damp beard. And still they carried her.

They entered the public courtyard, although the gates were still closed, and it was empty, except for the guardsmen who watched their commander struggling to keep his grip on the wood, and wished they could help. The sky was overcast, but it would not rain today. As the men reached the main gate into the marketplace, the guards opened it and waved them through.

Without speaking, the three of them turned to the left and continued their journey. The market was closed, so no one stood by to see them. They walked until they reached the small gate in the city walls, which led them to the Outlying. The stench of the plague pit was undeniable. Creon wished he could raise his sleeve to his face, to cover his nose. But it was impossible: he couldn't take the weight of the stretcher with just one hand.

No one watched over the plague pit: there was no need.

People brought their dead if they had to. Journeys here were always brief and brutal. The men put their burden down on the ground for a moment, while they decided where they should go. Creon glanced at the contents of the pit and shuddered. Most people didn't have sheets to spare for their loved ones' dignity, so the corpses were covered in the clothes they had died in, or nothing at all. He and the watch commander massaged their shoulders and arms, trying to revive them for one last exertion.

'Over there.' Sophon pointed to the far side of the pit. 'There's a jar of quicklime at the side of the pit there. We lower her in and then sprinkle that over her.'

Creon and the watch commander nodded. Neither had the energy to speak. They bent down, and lifted Jocasta one last time.

'No,' said a voice. 'You can't.'

*

They turned to see Oedipus, raving with anger, or the plague, or both. 'You can't leave her here. You can't.'

Sophon walked back towards him and looked at his fevered eyes. 'We must, my friend,' he said. 'There's no choice.'

Creon and the commander had not stopped walking, and Oedipus screamed when he looked past Sophon and saw they had gone further away. 'No.'

He pushed Sophon in the chest. The old man almost lost his balance, but recovered before he fell, and watched as Oedipus staggered after his wife.

There was no hope of catching them. Two healthy men, even carrying a corpse, could move more quickly than a man running a vicious fever. So by the time he reached them, sweat dripping down his face, they had already thrown the queen into the pit. For a terrible moment, Sophon thought Oedipus was going to hurl himself in after her. But he did not. Instead, he collapsed to his knees and wept as Creon and the watch commander stood catching their breath. Creon patted the commander's shoulder, thanking him for his work. The commander raised his eyebrows in a question, and Creon nodded. He would prefer to do the final task alone. The commander saluted and withdrew, back towards the city and the palace. Creon reached over for a shovel which had been left beside the pit, and began to scatter lime across his sister's body.

Oedipus could not tolerate anything that was happening in front of him. He wrenched himself back onto his feet, and grabbed for the shovel in Creon's hand. The two men teetered for an infinite moment by the side of the mass grave. Creon had to let go of the shovel to steady himself, and Oedipus grabbed it from him and swung it towards Creon's head. Creon dodged the blow, but Oedipus was readying himself to swing again. Creon looked around him for something he could use to defend himself. As Sophon watched him make a decision, he cried out, trying to stop it. But he was too far away, and the wind carried his voice towards the mountains.

Oedipus swung the shovel a second time, like an axe. And Creon ducked, scooping the powdered quicklime into his hardened hands. When Oedipus tried to hit him a third time, Creon flung the lime in his face.

Sophon had treated men in every stage of illness and injury, and he knew he would never again hear a sound like Oedipus made, as the caustic powder ate through his eyes. Creon could not have known what would happen when the lime met damp human tissue. His expression, even from a distance, was one of total horror. He ran from Oedipus, who had finally dropped the shovel so he could ball his hands into his eyes. But the pain was too great, and he could only stand and howl.

The horror was replaced on Creon's face by something else. 'Now you scream,' he said quietly. 'Now you know what pain is. I made that sound too, last summer. Not when I found the message from Eury saying she had the fever and had left. I didn't want to upset my son, you see, so I kept quiet.' He walked back towards his brother-in-law, safe in the knowledge that Oedipus could not see him. 'But when it was time to open up our house again, eight days later, do you know what I saw? I saw my dead wife, lying beside the walls of her own house, mourned but unburied. She must have sat beneath the windows, listening out for our boy, hoping she wouldn't hear him falling ill. Hoping she would live long enough to hear that she hadn't infected him. And she died where she had collapsed, alone, a few feet away from her husband and her son, unable to touch them or speak to them. And when I saw her ruined body, waiting for us outside, then – you can believe it – I screamed as you have screamed. But for another, not myself.'

And then Sophon could hear nothing, but Oedipus's anguished breaths, and Creon's trudging steps.

'Come on,' said Creon, as he reached the old man. 'We must go back to the city.'

Sophon looked at him. 'We can't leave him here.'

'I can,' said Creon grimly. 'I am regent now. Thebes will never accept a blind man, an incomer, as her king. And he will be better dying here than giving the plague to his children. My sister would say the same thing if she were alive.'

'She loved him very dearly,' Sophon said.

'She loved them more,' Creon replied. 'I am ordering you to accompany me to the palace. You will stay in quarantine and tell the slaves how to protect the children. He may have infected them already. In which case, you must tend to them and save their lives. If you prefer to stay here, trying to treat a dead man, I cannot stop you. But you will be throwing your life away. Come back with me. The gates will be closed once I return. They will never be reopened.'

Sophon looked away to the man demolished by every kind of agony, and he looked back at the man who had turned into a king.

29

I put my shoes back on. I didn't think I would ever tire of feeling the grass under my feet again, but I was mistaken. Delightful as it was to feel each individual strand forcing its way between my toes, the pain of treading on the stones which hid themselves beneath the grasses more than balanced it out. Besides, it was easier to wear shoes than carry them, although the leather was so tough at first that it blistered my feet. It has softened now, or my feet have hardened, as we have crossed the stades from the city. This is my first time outside Thebes, up on the mountain roads. We have a donkey to carry our packs. He's young and only occasionally bad-tempered. He limits the distance we can travel each day. After so many stades (the number varies, depending on the hilliness of the terrain), he stops for the night, and no persuasion from me or Sophon has any effect.

I look back to see the lower stretches of the mountains beneath me, and catch sight of Sophon's bald head through the waving grasses, like a large egg in a nest. I am still angry with him, though I feel the rage ebbing away with each step we take. I don't know whether it is the movement which cures my anger, or the distance I have put between myself and Thebes. Once we round the peak of the mountain – later this afternoon sometime – I will be out of sight of my city for the first time in my life. I could not stay there when my sister became queen, and used her first day as ruler to order that Creon be executed in the main square. I understood her reasons – he had turned against her and against our family, he had plotted against our brothers – but she could have banished him instead. Haem may never recover from it, I told her. She said he would learn to, or he would leave. I am not sure she cares which of these things happens. She wants people to know she is unafraid of her power. I'm sure they understand that now.

I plan to return to Thebes one day, but the roads are treacherous, and my plans may count for nothing. We will sleep outside for one or perhaps two more nights. I don't mind waking up covered in dew, my muscles stiffened from the hard ground. But I am decades younger than Sophon, and he struggles to raise himself in the mornings when we have slept on the ground, even if I have wrapped him in all the blankets we have with us. Still, he never complains.

He's coming up behind me, climbing towards me without noticing that I've perched on this boulder to wait for him. He's concentrating hard on the uneven ground; he doesn't want to lose his balance. He has a stick to help him negotiate his way over the rocks, and so do I. I found a branch by a dead pine tree, and I used a small knife to slice off the twigs which covered it. Because the tree is long dead, there is no sap bleeding out of it, gumming up my hands. It's more brittle, but I have been careful with it and it holds my weight when the path is uncertain.

I wave down to him, but he isn't looking up at me. I

want him to know there's a stream right by my feet, which means we can refill our bottles. He worries about water. He says it's from years of living in Thebes, where water was once in short supply. But he doesn't ever tell me I wouldn't understand because it wasn't like that when I was born. He just worries in silence. So I try to reassure him: we won't run out. Travellers used to take this path between the two cities all the time. If dying of thirst was a frequent occurrence, we would have seen the consequences somewhere by now: bodies by the side of the road. But still he worries. So now I just try to go ahead and find water, then wave back to him so he knows. But that only works if he remembers to look up.

He is filled with guilt and I am filled with blame. I don't know if the space between us can be crossed. Why had he never told me that my mother had not killed herself from shame, but that she had been infected with the plague? He says Creon forbade any mention of her, and told him – on the day she died – that if he ever raised the subject with any of her children, he would be banished from the palace immediately. Anyway, we never asked about it because we thought we knew everything already. She hanged herself, and everyone said it was from shame. They spoke about her so quietly and cruelly that we knew it must be so. And yet it was not. I grew up believing that my mother did not love us enough to stay alive. But the opposite was true. She loved us so much, she died to protect us. Sophon used to tell me in lessons that it is possible to change the past. When I expressed disbelief he gave the example of a wound, which might only be revealed as fatal many days after it has been sustained. I never understood it until now.

His head has disappeared from view, as the path curves away beneath me. I cannot hear him yet, but he must be closing in on my vantage point. I lift myself from the boulder, and sit on a smaller rock a little further up the path. He will need the high flat surface of the boulder, to rest his weary bones. The donkey trudges ahead of him, having decided that he keeps a more appropriate pace than I do. There are shoots of new green grass by the side of the stream, which the donkey will appreciate, as much as Sophon enjoys the cool mountain-water.

I have no idea what Corinth will be like. Thebes never did reopen her gates, after the two summers of the Reckoning. Ani has finally opened the city up again and most people are glad of it. But that wasn't so long ago, and word has not yet spread far enough afield for us to see anyone coming towards Thebes. The habit must have been broken years ago: there would have been no point crossing these mountains when you couldn't get into the city.

Or perhaps, as Sophon fears, the plague killed more people outside the city than inside. That happened before, with the first Reckoning, back when he was a boy. The whole world changed, he said, because so many people died. Things which had seemed permanent became temporary. So perhaps we will reach the city and find it inhabited only by bandits or skeletons or wild dogs or nothing at all. Perhaps we'll reach the outskirts and see that it is too late, and that there is nothing there for us, not even information. But I prefer to imagine that it will have survived, just as my city survived, in its own way. I think that people will be carving out their lives, in whatever circumstances remain for them. And I believe that one of them will be able to help me.

One of them will remember a time ten years ago when a blinded man wandered into their city, the place where he grew up. His eyes were gone, but you could see he had been handsome before that. He would have had a beard, I think, and he would have been accompanied by travellers he met near Thebes, who were heading to the city because they didn't yet know the gates had been closed. He would have told them that he had survived a brush with the Reckoning and that he could tell them how to protect themselves. My father was clever, and resourceful. They would have turned on their heels, weary and disappointed that their journey had been in vain. And he would have accompanied them back to his home. He might still be there now. He would be about forty years old.

He won't be able to see me, but that won't matter, because I was a child when he left Thebes. If anything, being able to see me would just confuse matters. It is the sound and the smell of people that doesn't change, even as they grow up or grow old. I know I will recognize him though, and Sophon will, of course. Sophon has survived so much, and for so long, he says appearances are all like masks for him. He can see through them to the true person within.

I know it would be better for him if we spent just one more night sleeping out in the open, but I hope it's two.

Because that gives me two more days of imagining what it will be like to find my father again.

And even though he hasn't heard my voice in all these years, when I say his name, he will know me straightaway.

Afterword

I can't remember when I first read the story of Oedipus (in a book of Greek myths when I was a child? In Greek lessons when I was a teenager, rolling my eyes at the discovery of yet another past tense?), but I certainly read the Sophocles play many years before I saw it performed. Perhaps this was a consequence of growing up in Birmingham, where there wasn't much call for Greek tragedies in the early nineties. Or perhaps they were being staged and I just wasn't paying attention: too busy with homework, or a Saturday job, or an unsuitable guitar-playing boy, no doubt.

I remember being startled to find out there were other versions of the myth: Books 9–12 of *The Odyssey* were a set text in my first term at college, so I was nineteen when I found out that Oedipus' story wasn't (and had never been) immutable. In Book 11, Homer describes the moment when Odysseus catches sight of 'beautiful Epicaste, mother of Oedipus' in the Underworld. Homer's version of the Oedipus myth is sketched out in just ten lines of verse, but it's subtly different from that of Sophocles: there's no mention of the auto-enucleation which forms a crucial climax in *Oedipus The King* (or *Oedipus Tyrannos*, to give it its Greek name. I can't stop you from calling it *Oedipus Rex*, obviously, but since he isn't Roman or a dinosaur, I can't bring myself to do it). And when did Epicaste become Jocasta?

So the Oedipus story was – to me – a book before it was a performance. It is such a relentless piece of storytelling (Aristotle thought it the most perfect Greek tragedy, and you don't want to make a habit of disagreeing with Aristotle. Well, maybe on medicine and anatomy) that it is almost impossible to stop before the story reaches its horrific conclusion. I tell it myself onstage nowadays, and there is something thrilling about being able to deliver the crucial pieces of story in the order they're revealed during the play. If you happen to find an audience who doesn't know what happens already, they invariably gasp at the key moment. It owes nothing to the person telling the story, and everything to the sheer weight of inevitable plot.

But most people don't read play-scripts, and although Greek tragedies are performed with pleasing frequency, *Oedipus Tyrannos* isn't performed as often as, say, *Hamlet*. It's not a school text for many of us. So I have long thought it would be fun to rewrite it as a novel. And if you're going to do that, you might as well retell the bit of the story that you're most closely drawn to, especially if you have always vaguely felt it's part of the narrative which has traditionally been overlooked. For me, that was the character of Jocasta.

Oedipus is famously clever; that's how he solves the Sphinx's virtually-impossible riddle, and earns his right to become King of Thebes. But his cleverness is also his tragic flaw: his quick-wittedness shades into quick-temperedness. This is a man who can solve a puzzle that has baffled all who came before him. But that same quickness explains how a man (who had been warned by an oracle that he would kill his father and was trying desperately to avoid his fate) could be reduced to a murderous frenzy at a crossroads by what amounts to a minor road-rage incident.

Jocasta has about 120 lines in *Oedipus Tyrannos*. People rarely remember that it is she who works out the terrible truth about her marriage, some time before her super-smart husband catches up. That's why she is already dead by the time he has pieced things together. So he is clever, in other words. But she is cleverer. And the earliest version of this myth, those ten lines of Homer I mentioned at the beginning? They're about her, the mother of Oedipus; his story is appended to hers, after Odysseus catches sight of 'beautiful Epicaste'. So I wanted to tell the story from her perspective, and have Oedipus be the more minor character. The myth – as so often – stands up no matter which way you look at it.

Jocasta is intriguingly blasphemous in Sophocles' play; she tells Oedipus that gods and oracles can't be trusted. But when she realizes that something truly terrible is happening, she turns to the shrine of Apollo and begs him for lusis – a release. That interplay between religious scepticism and sudden panicked faith was the key to part of her character. For me, she is and always will be the most courageous, complex character in the Theban story.

As for *Antigone*, it is the earliest of Sophocles' three Theban plays (they're often presented as a trilogy, alongside *Oedipus at Colonus*, but each play is in fact the sole survivor of its own trilogy, written decades apart. Which is why the timeline doesn't quite follow through from one to the next). I have always loved the tension within the play: Antigone is both law-abiding and anarchic, obedient and disruptive, freedom fighter and terrorist. She obeys the laws of the gods and disobeys the laws of men. She is the epitome (to put it in Greek philosophical terms) of phusis over nomos; a follower of natural law over man-made law. Arguing with her is like arguing with gravity. So, obeying the gods, burying her brother: these things simply matter more to Antigone than life itself. It's interesting that when Anouilh wrote his version of *Antigone*, in the early 1940s, he made her the younger sister of Ismene (Sophocles has Antigone as the elder). To Sophocles, Antigone is a dutiful, if excessive, sibling. To Anouilh, she is a rebel.

To me, she shines so brightly that Ismene gets lost in the glare. Sophocles can spare this younger sister just sixty lines. And even Antigone gets overshadowed by her uncle: Creon is the lead role in the play, if you count the number of lines each character has (believe me when I tell you that actors do this. And that the vast majority of them would rather have more lines than share their character name with the play's title). Creon has half as many lines again as his titular niece.

The battle between Creon and Antigone burns up all the oxygen in the room, or on the stage: it's what makes the play so compellingly claustrophobic. But I thought it would make a novel lopsided, so I decided to look hard at the Greek and see where I could find some space. Antigone is wedded to death, we're told, by the (biased, old, male i.e. allies of her uncle) chorus. Their bias aside, she has long seemed to me to be more attached to the glory of her own sacrifice, rather than the rightness of her cause. So I decided to focus on that side of her character, and give Ismene the lead role instead.

Antigone doesn't appear to exist before the fifth century BCE: she isn't mentioned in versions of the Oedipus story before then. Ismene is a good Theban name (there was a

River Ismenos by Thebes, as well as a hill and a village with the same name) but, sometimes in her earlier mythic outings, she isn't part of Oedipus' family. Meanwhile, the two brothers – Polynices and Eteocles – shift lives and deaths: sometimes one kills the other, sometimes they kill each other, sometimes one lives and one dies. The *Seven Against Thebes* by Aeschylus offers a much bigger vision of this fraternal conflict. I scaled things down to two men, boys really, who cannot tolerate each other, and let that stand in for a larger civil war. In other words, I have played extremely fast and loose with their story. But at least they both end up under the earth, which is what their sisters wanted for them.

The version of Thebes which appears in this novel bears some relation to the place you would see now, if you visited Greece. The lake and the mountains are real, as is the distance from Corinth (and indeed the sea – Thebes is a surprisingly long way from it, compared with other Greek city-states in the ancient world). The palace and its courtyards are imagined, and owe at least as much to Mycenae and Knossos as to historical Thebes. If you're a major nerd, you will see Isy and Jocasta using some items which appear in Greek museums. I did tell you I had played fast and loose with the myth, and I have been equally cavalier with the archaeology. But I figured that Sophocles' mythic Thebes owes something to fifth-century Athens, so I'm continuing a noble tradition of reworking the city (and the story) for my own purpose.

If you're wondering about some of the minor characters, Teresa of course owes something to Teiresias, not least her capacity to infuriate Oedipus by speaking what she says is the truth, and what he believes to be a vicious lie. And imagining the character as a woman is not me being ana-chronistically gender-blind, although I might have done it anyway (who doesn't long to write a female villain?). Part of the myth of Teiresias is that he changed from male to female, and then back again. He reported that women had much better sex. Hey, don't shoot the messenger.

Laius is largely offstage in this novel, as he is in the Homeric sketch, the Sophoclean plays and most versions of the story. He exists only to throw things into chaos with his death (although I did once see a production of *Oedipus* where our titular hero meets his father at the place where three roads meet, and instead of killing him, they have a fascinating chat and then go their separate ways. It was terrific). Laius's lack of interest in women and predatory interest in young men appear in some versions of his story, where he rapes the son of his guest-host (disregarding the bonds of guest-friendship was, to the Ancient Greeks, at least as dreadful a crime as rape). It was a small step from there to the character in this book.

And Sophon, the man with medical knowledge? He is an addition to the story, a modern creation. Though he shares more than just a couple of syllables with Sophocles, who once paid for a shrine on behalf of the cash-strapped Athenians for the god of medicine, Asclepius. Sophocles was an immensely popular and prolific playwright, as well as a skilled military general. So there was a touch of the polymath to him which I was happy to steal.

Sophocles was born in Colonus, not far from Athens, which gives him the setting for the least-performed of the Theban plays, *Oedipus at Colonus*. Because it is performed so infrequently, compared to *Oedipus Tyrannos*, people often forget that Oedipus' story ends much less miserably than it began. A blind exile, he wanders Greece with his daughter for a guide, and eventually settles on Colonus as the place where he will die, and be interred. The gods – so often his enemies – have told him that his bones will bring good fortune to the land which holds them. That is to be Colonus, ruled (at this point in its mythic history) by the Athenian king Theseus, of minotaur fame. After thwarting a last-ditch attempt by Creon – trying to claim the good fortune for himself – to take him back to Thebes, Oedipus dies as he wished: giving a last, enduring gift to the people of Athens. Even tragedies can have a happy ending.

Acknowledgements

A huge thank you to the guys at RCW, especially the quietly magnificent Peter Straus; and to everyone at Mantle, especially Maria Rejt, Lara Borlenghi, and Josie Humber.

Thanks to the crazy-generous writers who read early drafts of this, even though they were busy reading and writing for their own work: Sarah Churchwell and Lionel Shriver. You are my heroes. As is Edith Hall. If you want to know more about Greek tragedy, incidentally, anything she's ever written would be a great place to start.

Thanks to everyone at the BBC who has kept me in gainful employment over the years. Double points to Tanya Hudson and to all those who have worked on *Natalie Haynes Stands Up for the Classics*. You're tremendous.

Thanks to my brilliant friends who have offered unstinting moral support, almost always near cake or gin or both: Helen Bagnall, Damian Barr, Michelle Flower, Kara Manley, Joss Whedon. I am so lucky to have you. And special thanks to Julian Barnes for going to about 900 Greek tragedies with me (one day, I swear, we'll go to something with a death toll lower than, say, four).

A zillion thanks, as usual, to Christian Hill, who still runs the website even though he has a proper job, a family, and impenetrable books about programming to write.

Acknowledgements

Thanks to my mum, Sandra; my dad, Andre; and to Chris and Gemima. If you see Chris, tell him there are spaceships in this one.

And of course, thanks to Dan, for literally everything.

If you enjoyed *The Children of Jocasta*, discover Natalie Haynes's latest novel, *A Thousand Ships* . . .

Shortlisted for the Women's Prize for Fiction 2020

One of the *Guardian*'s and *TLS*'s 'Best Books of 2019'

In *A Thousand Ships*, broadcaster and classicist Natalie Haynes retells the story of the Trojan War from an all-female perspective, for fans of Madeline Miller and Pat Barker.

This was never the story of one woman, or two.
It was the story of them all . . .

In the middle of the night, a woman wakes to find her beloved city engulfed in flames. Ten seemingly endless years of conflict between the Greeks and the Trojans are over. Troy has fallen.

From the Trojan women whose fates now lie in the hands of the Greeks, to the Amazon princess who fought Achilles on their behalf, to Penelope awaiting the return of Odysseus, to the three goddesses whose feud started it all, these are the stories of the women embroiled in the legendary war.

Powerfully told from an all-female perspective, in *A Thousand Ships* Natalie Haynes puts the women, girls and goddesses at the centre of the story.

'With her trademark passion, wit, and fierce feminism, Natalie Haynes gives much-needed voice to the silenced women of the Trojan War' – MADELINE MILLER, author of *Circe*

'A gripping feminist masterpiece'
DEBORAH FRANCES-WHITE, *The Guilty Feminist*